Adolescent Needs and the Transition from School to Work

by

JOAN MAIZELS

UNIVERSITY OF LONDON
THE ATHLONE PRESS

Published by
THE ATHLONE PRESS
UNIVERSITY OF LONDON
at 2 Gower Street London WCI

Distributed by Tiptree Book Services Ltd
Tiptree, Essex

U.S.A.
Oxford University Press Inc
New York

© *E. J. Maizels* 1970

First Impression 1970
Reprinted 1971

ISBN 0 485 11113 6

Set by
GLOUCESTER TYPESETTING CO LTD
Printed by photo-lithography in Great Britain at
THE PITMAN PRESS
Bath

NOTE

In order to keep down the cost of this publication, many tables have had to be omitted. Anyone wishing for further information should write to the author c/o the National Institute of Economic and Social Research, 2 Dean Trench Street, London SW1.

ACKNOWLEDGMENTS

THIS BOOK attempts to consider the needs and opportunities of 15–18 year-olds during the transition from school to work. The study was made possible by a generous grant from the Joseph Rowntree Memorial Trust. It was sponsored by the National Institute of Economic and Social Research. An Advisory Committee consisting of Miss Jean Rowntree and Mr Ford Longman of the Rowntree Trust, Mrs Jean Floud of Nuffield College, Mr H. E. Edwards of the Ministry of Labour,[1] a representative of the Department of Education and Science, and the Director and Executive Secretary of the Institute, met from time to time during the early stages of the inquiry. The ideas expressed and the conclusions reached in this study are, however, entirely the responsibility of the author.

The success of the inquiry depended, in the first instance, on the willingness of employers to provide facilities for the interviewing of under-eighteens in their employment, and to supply information about the work on which young people were engaged. I am indeed grateful to all those firms which participated in the inquiry. I am also deeply indebted to the young workers who responded so seriously and thoughtfully to the many questions put to them about their experiences during the transitional years.

I must also acknowledge my debt to Mrs Winifred Moss, my partner in the pilot study which preceded the main inquiry, and to the discussions we had together at that time; to Mr G. A. Randall of Bradford University, for his advice in preparing the questionnaire for school leavers; and to Miss C. Creighton, now the Chief Youth Employment Officer for the Borough of Brent, for her whole-hearted support and co-operation. The Brent Education Committee kindly allowed me to consult the Youth Employment Bureau records and the staff of the bureau gave me every assistance during my visits. Special thanks are also due to the staff of the Tabulating Research Centre who dealt speedily with the coding and analysis. I was also very fortunate to have the help of Mrs B. Douglas of the National Institute, who organized the typing and duplicating of the original drafts.

I must express my appreciation to Mr C. T. Saunders and Mr G. D. N. Worswick, the past and present Directors, respectively, of the National Institute, for their interest in the work, and to Mrs A. K. Jackson, the

---

[1] Now the Department of Employment and Productivity.

Executive Secretary, for her constructive help throughout. I am also grateful to Dr M. E. M. Herford, the Appointed Factory Doctor at Slough, to Mr Barrie Hopson of Leeds University, and to Mr Randall, for their critical comments on certain of the draft chapters; and to Miss Jean Rowntree, Mrs Jean Floud and Mr Ford Longman for their consistent support and encouragement. I am particularly indebted to Professor O. R. McGregor, of Bedford College, London, who encouraged the publication of the study; and to Professor B. Bernstein of the Institute of Education, London University, who made a number of invaluable suggestions for improving the text and tables.

Finally, I wish to thank my husband, who was a constant source of advice and criticism which influenced the argument and presentation at many points of the book.

July 1968   J.M.

CONTENTS

PART IV
PRESENT EMPLOYMENT

PART V
OTHER ASPECTS OF THE TRANSITIONAL YEARS

PART VI
SUMMARY AND CONCLUSIONS

LIST OF TABLES

PART I

PART II

PART III

PART IV

PART V

APPENDIX I

PART I

AIM AND METHOD

CHAPTER I

THE BACKGROUND TO THE INQUIRY

The transition from school to work

Though increasing numbers of children since the end of the war have remained at school beyond the minimum age, this has not altered the fact that the majority of boys and girls, now, as in the past, leave school at the first opportunity to do so and start out to work.

Their break with school and their entry into employment has, however, come to be regarded, in recent years, as part of a longer phase in their lives which begins while they are still at school—with the development of expectations and aspirations about school and work—and extends well into their first years at work, including their adjustment to a working life. It is this phase which represents the 'transitional' years, so described because the young individuals proceed, through a series of stages and decisions, each entailing implications for the next, from full-time education to full-time employment.

A complex of factors, the most important of which are the informal influences of the home environment and the selective processes of educational procedures, help to shape the events which culminate in the decision to start work, and to produce occupational choices which, by and large, ensure continuity in the supply of the required categories of labour. The transitional years, viewed externally, represent a process in which successive generations of school leavers are differentiated into a multiplicity of occupations corresponding, approximately, to the demand for their labour. For the majority, this means entry into unskilled and semi-skilled work and the virtual end to any formal education.

From the point of view of the individual, it means that large numbers of fifteen- to eighteen-year-olds spend their formative years in an environment which is rarely conducive to the development of their potential; nevertheless, work is felt by many of them to be preferable to the boredom and pointlessness associated with their school days. Once at work they have only the most cursory contact with any of the relevant youth services. Since the change from school to work also coincides, in time, with adolescent growth, when the degree of success obtained in achieving their hopes and aspirations is crucial to their development, the transitional years are widely held to be, a period of stress, in some degree, for most young people.

Previous studies

Though the subject has become a popular research topic and one on which much has been written, there have been relatively few studies in Great Britain which have attempted to consider the transitional process as a whole.[1] On the contrary, there has been a tendency for research either to concentrate on the study of the development of vocational aspirations, preferences and choice,[2] or to select particular aspects of the transition for special inquiry.[3] Relatively little is known, moreover, about the nature, content or conditions of their employment, particularly as far as the majority of young workers are concerned.

Much of the literature, as has been pointed out by Keil *et al.*, consists of 'the impressions of teachers, personnel managers, youth employment officers, etc., which although invaluable in themselves, give only a partial insight into the problems of young people during this period of their lives and are loaded with moral judgments and evaluations'.[4]

There are no studies, as yet, which have examined the transition within a theoretical framework. Keil *et al.* and Chester have discussed a methodological approach which would allow for existing and future data to be

[1] These include:

M. Carter, *Home, School and Work*, Pergamon Press, 1962.
—, *Into Work*, Penguin Books, 1966.
15–18: Report of the Central Advisory Council for Education, H.M.S.O., 1959. (Hereafter referred to as *15–18*.)
T. Ferguson and J. Cunnison, *The Young Wage Earner*, O.U.P., 1951.
M. E. M. Herford, *Youth at Work*, Max Parrish, 1957.

[2] These include:

S. M. Chown, 'The Formation of Occupational Choices in Grammar School Children', *Occ. Psychol.*, **32**, No. 4, October 1958.
P. M. Freeston, 'Vocational Interests of Elementary School Children', *Occ. Psychol.*, **13**, No. 3, July 1939.
G. Jahoda, 'Job Attitudes and Job Choice among Secondary Modern School Leavers', *Occ. Psychol.*, **26**, Nos. 3 and 4, 1952.
—, 'Social Class Attitudes and Levels of Occupational Aspiration in Secondary Modern School Leavers', *Br. J. Psy.*, **44**, 1953.
T. Veness, *School Leavers: Their Aspirations and Expectations*, Methuen, 1962.
M. D. Wilson, 'Vocational Preferences of Secondary Modern Children', *Br. J. Ed. Psy.*, **23**, 1953.

[3] These include:

E. Eppel and M. Eppel, 'Young Workers at a County College', *Br. J. Ed. Psy.*, **23**, 1963.
G. Jahoda and A. Chalmers, 'The Youth Employment Service: A Consumer Perspective', *Occ. Psychol.*, **37**, No. 1, 1964.
E. T. Keil, D. S. Riddell, and C. Tipton, 'A Research Note: The Entry of School Leavers into Employment', *Br. J. Ind. Rel.*, **1**, 1963.
J. Maizels, 'The Entry of School Leavers into Employment', *Br. J. Ind. Rel.*, **3**, No. 1, 1965.
—, 'Changes in Employment among School Leavers: A Sample Study of One Cohort of Secondary Modern Boys', *Br. J. Ind. Rel.*, **5**, No. 2, 1967.
E. Venables, *The Young Worker at College*, Faber, 1967.
G. Williams, *Recruitment and the Skilled Trades*, Routledge and Kegan Paul, 1957.

[4] E. T. Keil, D. S. Riddell, and B. S. R. Green, 'Youth and Work: Problems and Perspectives', *Sociol. Review*, **14**, 1966.

coherently organized, analysed and interpreted.[5,6] Musgrove has suggested that the theory of socialization might be the conceptual focus for the development of a theory of occupational choice;[7] Roberts has argued that occupational choices have little to do with satisfactions and aspirations, as such, but are the product of a differential opportunity structure, school leavers standing in varying degrees of 'social proximity' to different types of occupations, according to their position in a highly stratified system of education.[8]

Although there is no agreed theory of the transition, existing evidence, nevertheless, strongly suggests that the decisions, situations, events and experiences which arise during this phase are largely socially conditioned; and that the ultimate choice of occupation, though perhaps regarded by school leavers and others as frequently self-determined, seems to be, directly or indirectly, the outcome of a collaborative process of social interaction between school leavers and others, whose course is largely set by the requirements of the economic and social system. Valid explanations for the characteristic behaviour patterns of the main actors during the transition have still, however, to be found.

Official comment

Official comment, as expressed in a number of government Reports issued over the years, has tended to regard the industrial environment as a harmful one as far as young workers are concerned, and to believe that the most effective antidote is continued exposure to an educational influence. The idea of part-time education persisted long after the early Factory Act provisions for day-time classes proved ineffective in practice. By the turn of the century, even when most children were in school until the age of twelve, powerful arguments were heard for making part-time classes compulsory and for raising the school leaving age.

Evidence submitted to the 1909 Royal Commission on the Poor Laws, for example, shows that the advocates of such measures considered that for the majority of boys, if not girls, 'their occupations were destructive to healthy development and morally, wholly demoralising'.[9] One of the witnesses was Sydney Webb, who referred to the 'four-fold evil of recruiting an army of casually employed, merely brute labour; of cheap substitutes for adult labour; of the failure to provide for healthy growth; of the

[5] Ibid.

[6] R. L. C. Chester, 'Youth, Education and Work: A Revised Perspective', *Soc. and Ec. Admin.*, 2, January 1968.

[7] P. W. Musgrove, 'Towards a Sociological Theory of Occupational Choice', *Sociol. Review*, 15, 1967.

[8] B. K. Roberts, 'The Entry Into Employment: An Approach Towards a General Theory', *Sociol. Review*, 16, No. 2, 1968.

[9] *Report of the Royal Commission on the Poor Laws and the Relief of Distress*, 1909.

creation of hooliganism in the undisciplined, precocious in evil', youth of the day.[10]

By 1917, a Board of Education Departmental Committee, inspired by the 'great work of reconstruction' that lay ahead of the country after the First World War and appalled by the 'noticeable deterioration in the behaviour and morality of young workers', both boys and girls, urged that an 'educational purpose should be the dominating influence without and within the school doors during the formative years between twelve and eighteen'.[11]

The primary aim of continued education was, evidently, so to strengthen and develop the character and industrial efficiency of the adolescent wage earner as to offset the adverse influences of unsuitable occupations and unfavourable working conditions. Since the 'moral and disciplinary influence' of the elementary school was soon undermined when young people entered industry, compulsory part-time classes were regarded as the means by which effective contact could be maintained with the 'forces of civilisation'.[12]

The arguments of the 1917 Departmental Committee were reinforced in 1926 by the Hadow Committee (whose proposals for the development of secondary education foreshadowed the 1944 Education Act) which saw the extension of secondary education to working-class youth as a 'corrective to industrialism and its grave effects on national life'.[13]

Any fundamental re-appraisal, however, of the conditions of young workers was effectively postponed by the economic and political events of the inter-war years. Only under the impetus of the Second World War did the welfare of adolescents at work and the question of their training and development become, once again, matters of serious concern.

There was, firstly, a shortage of skilled manpower and, secondly, the realization that population trends indicated a reduction in the future supply of young workers. The registration of boys and girls, which began in 1941, also brought to light so much wastage in terms of abilities that, in the words of Lady Williams, 'much shame was felt that the community had for so long ignored the most precious of its resources—the young generation'.[14]

An attempt to improve the methods by which industries recruited and trained their workers,[15] a survey of existing machinery for guiding and placing young workers in search of jobs,[16] and the provision in the

[10] Ibid.
[11] *Report of the Departmental Committee on Juvenile Education in Relation to Employment after the War*, Board of Education, 1917.
[12] Ibid.
[13] *The Education of the Adolescent*, Report of the Consultative Committee, H.M.S.O., 1926.
[14] G. Williams, op. cit.
[15] *The Recruitment and Training of Juveniles in Industry*, H.M.S.O., 1945.
[16] *Report of the Committee on the Juvenile Employment Service*, H.M.S.O., 1945.

Education Act of 1944 for compulsory further education at County Colleges for all workers between the ages of fifteen to eighteen, were the chief consequences of official recognition of the need for a more constructive educational policy towards young workers.

But the provisions under the Education Act were never put into effect. The recommendations for the recruitment and training of young workers which included, among others, agreed standards of employment in each industry, the appointment of qualified persons in industry for the recruitment and well-being of young workers, and the establishment of National Joint Apprenticeship and Training Councils, had a patchy response from industry. Further attempts to enlist industry's support by the establishment of the Industrial Training Council in 1958, were not much more successful and the outcome was disappointing. Only in 1962, with the publication of the White Paper on Industrial Training, was it recognized that, if training was to be improved, it could no longer be left entirely to industry. Under the Industrial Training Act,[17] Training Boards have been set up, each responsible for the training of workers (including young workers) in particular industries and empowered to place a levy on all firms in their industry to finance the cost of such training.[18] A Central Training Council has also been established to co-ordinate policy. Doubts have been expressed,[19] however, as to whether the composition of the Boards allows sufficiently for the influence of professional educators, since it is felt that employers and trade unions may, to a greater extent than is desirable, influence the character and coverage of industrial training, using the narrow criteria of the immediate needs of particular industries. Nor is there any guarantee that the Boards will insist on day release provisions.

The revision of the machinery for guiding and placing young workers in employment led to the setting up of a new body in 1948—the Central Youth Employment Executive—under what was then the Ministry of Labour, and to local educational authorities undertaking, many for the first time, a more comprehensive youth employment service than hitherto.[20] The service is, however, subject to much criticism, chiefly in regard to its evident failure to offer effective advice to more than a minority of school leavers. This criticism is not entirely answered by the most recent recommendations for an expansion in staff and services.[21]

Though a successively higher school leaving age has delayed entry into employment until the age of fifteen, and industrial training has been given a new priority, part-time education remains now, as in 1917, a privilege

[17] The Industrial Training Act, 1964.
[18] In mid-1969 there were twenty-six Training Boards.
[19] M. Carter, op. cit.
[20] The Employment and Training Act, 1948.
[21] *The Future Development of the Youth Employment Service*, H.M.S.O., 1965.

granted by employers to their employees, chiefly to boys in skilled occupations, and rarely to less skilled workers or to girls.[22] The majority of
boys and girls under eighteen enter employment for which no systematic
training exists, and where no day release is provided. Furthermore, there
seems to have been little follow-up of the questions which in the 1940s
were the subject of serious inquiry by the then Ministries of Education
and Labour, with the object of devising ways and means of preventing
the waste of youthful ability and of ensuring that the fullest possible
attention was given to technical and cultural education during adolescence.

At that time, the possibility of establishing agreed standards of employment for young workers was explored, as were, according to Lady
Williams,[23] questions as to whether employers whose conditions of employment did not comply with agreed standards should be allowed to
employ young people; whether adolescents should be restricted in their
choice of jobs to employers complying with agreed conditions; whether
extensive experience over a range of processes could be arranged so that
young workers could qualify for promotion; and whether the State should
continue some measure of supervision after the completion of full-time
education. These and other questions relating to apprenticeship training
were discussed by the Joint Consultative Committee prior to the publication of its report on the 'Recruitment and Training of Juveniles in
Industry'.[24]

That these questions subsequently fell into relative obscurity may be
partly due to the fact that the schemes envisaged for improving training
and welfare amenities for young workers were intended to link up with
the re-organization of the educational system, and the compulsory attendance of young workers at county colleges. The non-implementation of
these provisions of the 1944 Education Act would appear, in retrospect,
to have held back what might have become far-reaching changes in the
working lives of young people.

Not until the Crowther Report[25] were the social and personal needs of
fifteen- to eighteen-year-olds again brought under serious review, the relative immaturity of those who enter employment at fifteen or soon afterwards re-emphasized, and the need for an environment which allowed
for development again stressed. The arguments of the 1917 Board of
Education Departmental Committee[26] were repeated more forcefully by
the Crowther Committee, which regarded the 'difficult and important'
period of adolescence as requiring a dominant educational influence and

---

[22] *Day Release: The Report of a Committee set up by the Minister of Education*, H.M.S.O., 1964.
[23] G. Williams, op. cit.
[24] Op. cit.
[25] *15–18.*
[26] Op. cit.

recommended, therefore, the raising of the school leaving age to sixteen and compulsory day-time further education up to eighteen.

The Crowther Committee's findings were followed in 1960 by the Albemarle Report, which referred to the gap between the provision for social and recreational life for young people still at school and what was provided thereafter.[27] The Newsom Report, published three years later, emphasized the problems of initiating school leavers into the world of work, of preparing them for adulthood and of providing for their continued education.[28] Each committee stressed the need for greater help and provision during the transitional years.[29]

Recent reports, naturally enough, speak less harshly than do earlier ones of industrial conditions and their ill effects on the development of young workers. Nevertheless, there is a consistency between past and present. Each conveys an underlying anxiety about the attitudes of adolescent workers; each emphasizes the importance, for society, for these to be modified, particularly in the direction of strengthening the character and broadening the mind; each assumes that educational influences can effect such changes while leaving relatively constant the comparatively low status and level of skill, interest and responsibility, of most of the occupations available to under-eighteens; and each evades the fundamental question of the use made of the younger generation and the continued wastage of its talents, energies, and abilities.

This question, and those raised in the 1940s, await an answer; they would seem as relevant today as then and their serious consideration is long overdue.

The present inquiry

It is in this context that the present inquiry was conceived and planned, its aim being to attempt a comprehensive assessment of the needs and opportunities of fifteen- to eighteen-year-olds during the transition from school to work against the background of their working environment and of the existing community services.

It was believed that information collected from young people about their experiences during these years, about the kind of help they had received and required, and about certain aspects of their work, would provide a 'consumer perspective' of the experiences associated with leaving school and being at work, and thus indicate how present conditions and services might be improved. It was also believed that information collected from

27 *The Youth Services of England and Wales*, Ministry of Education, Cmnd. 920, 1960.

28 *Half our Future, Report of the Central Advisory Council for Education*, 1963. (Hereafter referred to as *Half our Future*.)

29 Though the Seebohm Committee could not give adequate consideration to the organization of services to young people, they, nevertheless, considered them to be in need of urgent development, and failing to meet the needs of more than a minority. (See *Report of the Committee on Local Authority and Allied Personal Services*, H.M.S.O., 1968.)

their employers about the nature of their employment, training, and prospects, would enable some analysis to be made of the work environment of different types of employment, together with some preliminary assessments of its suitability for school leavers.

The inquiry was essentially an exploratory one and was limited to 330 boys and girls in the fifteen to eighteen age group[30] and to the seventy-five firms in which they were employed. It was carried out during the first six months of 1965 in the area of Willesden, now part of the London Borough of Brent, Middlesex. Since it did not prove possible to obtain a fully representative sample of young workers and firms, the results of the study and its conclusions do not necessarily apply elsewhere, though on many questions their generality is strongly implied.

The information obtained from school leavers covers the main stages of the transition from school to work. The last years of school, the school-leaving decision, vocational choice, present and past employment, further education and training, social interests, important events and future plans and priorities, are each considered here. In particular, the opinions of young people and their employers about their employment, though by no means objective evidence, represents new material not hitherto available. This provides a basis for reconsidering the types of employment entered by school leavers, and the conditions and opportunities offered to them. The inquiry has also shown the kind of problems that might be encountered in providing similar evidence on a large scale, and has suggested some of the main lines on which further progress in this subject might be made.

Many of the findings and conclusions would appear to be directly relevant to those currently engaged or interested in possible policy and administrative changes in secondary school education, the youth employment service, industrial training, further education, and young people's welfare in general. It is also hoped that the evidence obtained will stimulate discussion of many of the outstanding questions concerning young people at work and provide a framework within which a new approach to the transitional years can be evolved.

---

[30] This represents one in seven of the total number of under-eighteens estimated to be employed in the locality of study.

CHAPTER II

THE METHOD OF INQUIRY

CHOICE OF LOCALITY

The limited size of the project, and the need to assess some of the services available to school leavers, meant that the study had to be confined to a single locality. It was necessary, however, that the locality chosen should fulfil certain conditions. An area, part industrial and part residential, was required, containing a substantial proportion of school leavers employed within it, and therefore using the education, youth employment and youth services. It was also important that the area contained a variety of employment as well as an adequate representation of large, medium, and small firms.

Many parts of London and the south could be so described, and the then borough of Willesden[1] seemed an appropriate choice. It is virtually a suburb of London and yet only five miles from the centre. One-half of its population lives and works in the borough. It is a major industrial centre employing 44 000 people in industry and 30 000 in shops, commerce, transport, and administration. It offers a variety of employment and, though engineering of all kinds dominates in manufacturing, other industries are well represented.[2] Its four main industrial areas contain a number of large firms employing 1000 persons or more, and a substantial number of medium firms with between 100 and 500 person employed in each. Nearly one-half of the manufacturing firms, however, are very small, employing 10 or fewer persons, and many of these are found within the residential areas.

RESEARCH PROBLEMS

In the course of organizing the study, two main research problems had to be faced. These were to identify the population of firms and young people

---

[1] In April 1965, under the London Government Act, 1963, Willesden merged with Wembley to form the new London Borough of Brent.

[2] 'From a list of 673 factories and workshops a man could choose from engineering on virtually any scale, woodworking, printing, instrument making, coach and vehicle building, sheet metal work, foodmaking, toolmaking, and textiles. Or he might wish to specialize—perhaps in billiard cue production, coffin making, fancy feathers, bookbinding or button carding. If a craftsman, he may wish to work in any of several hundred small businesses; or if unskilled and gregarious, he could join the thousands at Smiths, Guinness, Park Royal Vehicles, Heinz, A.E.I., or a number of other big companies . . . Willesden, close to the heart of London, is as much geared to oil, sweat, and iron as any northern community.'—Regional Report—Industrial South—*Times Review of Industry and Technology*, March 1965.

to be studied, and to select a sample from these populations for detailed questioning.

In order to select a sample of firms and young people, it was necessary to know in which firms under-eighteens were employed, their size and industry group and the numbers in each type of occupation. This information was not available from any official source; neither the Youth Employment Bureau, the local Employment Exchange, the Factory Inspectorate, nor the local office of the Ministry of Pensions and National Insurance had the required information. Information was available about the names, addresses, and size of firms in the area but this did not include details relating to the under-eighteens employed. The only exception was the Shops Inspectorate of the local Borough Council which recorded the number of under-eighteens employed in each shop and bank and in some offices. This information was based on visits to retailers and offices and therefore its accuracy depended on the frequency of such visits.

The use of school-leaving lists was considered but was not adopted. This approach would have required young people to provide the names and addresses of their employers; even if this information were easily obtainable, almost as many firms as young people would have had to be interviewed, since it was unlikely that in a random sample, many would have been employed by the same firm. Moreover, there was no certainty that an employer, whose name had been given by an employee, would have been willing to co-operate in the study. There was also the likelihood that a substantial proportion of addresses would have been outside the borough. The selection of a sample of school leavers and firms from school-leaving lists seemed, therefore, impractical although, if adopted, it would have resulted in a representative sample of school leavers, though not necessarily in a representative sample of those working in the borough.

The Youth Employment Bureau records were a source of some information, insofar as they indicated the type of occupation entered by those placed in employment by the bureau; but the names and addresses of the firms entered by school leavers were held to be confidential and could not therefore be used for the purpose of selecting a sample of firms.

The only way to obtain the necessary data was therefore to carry out a direct inquiry of the firms in the borough. Some 720 firms including factories, offices, hospitals, transport services, and other employing units, were circulated with a questionnaire which asked whether or not young persons under eighteen were employed and, if so, their number and occupation. After allowing for firms which had closed down, had left the area or were merely trading names, it was found that the total number of separate firms was 650. Of these, returns were received from 416, representing a response rate of 64 per cent, though this proportion was later raised to 95 per cent for firms employing over 100 persons as a result of telephone calls to non-responding firms. Firms which gave no information were mainly small ones employing fewer than 25 persons.

The direct enquiry of firms revealed that 44 per cent of the respondents —nearly 300 firms—did not employ under-eighteens (though these represented, in the main, the very small firm). Discounting these, and the non-respondents, just under 250 firms were left of the original number, from which a sample could be selected.

SELECTING A SAMPLE

Having identified the firms employing under-eighteens, the next problem was to consider whether it was possible to select a representative sample from the total. The problem was complicated, insofar as it was desirable to select not only a representative group of employers but also a representative group of young people at work. It was evident that a random sample of firms would not produce a random sample of young people, mainly because of the concentration of their employment in the larger firms, but also because of the very uneven employment distribution of girls and boys in different industries and services.

These difficulties could be met, in principle, by the use of stratified sampling, using industry—and size—groups as the different strata. Differential sampling fractions for five size-groups of firms were estimated on the assumption, which seemed reasonable, that the variance of the many characteristics to be investigated was smallest among small firms and highest among the large ones. Since there were relatively few large firms in the borough it appeared to be necessary to include them all in a stratified sampling scheme, the sampling fractions being progressively reduced as the size of the firm diminished.

This type of scheme would, however, have yielded an over-representation of under-eighteens employed in large firms, though this could have been corrected by the use of another sampling fraction indicating the proportion of young people at work in each firm who would, in fact, be interviewed. Thus, in the large firms, a random selection of, say, one in ten young people could have been interviewed as against one in three in the medium sized firms, and all young people in the small firms. Even with this correction, however, the sample would not necessarily have yielded fully representative sub-samples for boys and girls separately, or for the various occupational groups. There were many firms which did not employ girls at all, and others which did not employ boys; some employed only boy apprentices and others only girls in clerical work.

The pre-selection of a sample from a given list of firms assumes, of course, that the selected firms will, in the event, co-operate in the inquiry or, at least, that the degree of non-co-operation will be small enough as not to invalidate the results. Such a general degree of co-operation by firms could not, however, be taken for granted and it was decided, therefore, to test out the degree of co-operation likely to be encountered in the borough.

This was done by writing an explanatory letter to every firm in the borough engaged in manufacturing and construction industries and the transport, communication, and hospital services, outlining the objectives of the inquiry and asking them to return a (prepaid postage) postcard indicating whether or not they were willing to discuss their possible participation in the inquiry. Each letter also enclosed a copy of the analysis of the questionnaires relating to the numbers of young people employed in the borough.

Of the 240 firms to which letters were sent, replies were received from 100, of which 56 indicated their willingness to discuss the inquiry. The remainder definitely declined.[3] All 56 firms were visited and the purpose of the inquiry was explained and discussed in some detail; of these firms, 50 decided to participate by completing questionnaires and/or allowing some or all of their young employees to be interviewed during working hours. Six of these, however, eventually withdrew from the survey for a variety of reasons. Thus, of the 100 firms replying to the letter, 44 (or only 18 per cent of the number of firms to which letters had been sent) agreed to participate in the inquiry.

A random sample of one in four firms not replying to the letter was then selected (from a list of firms classified by alphabetical street order) and all 35 firms selected were telephoned. Of these, 13 (under two-fifths) finally agreed to co-operate, most of the remainder refusing to do so. Had the remaining 105 non-respondent firms been telephoned, and assuming the two-fifths ratio being maintained, a further 40 participating firms would have been obtained. Even so, the total number of firms which could have been included in the inquiry would then have been 100, or only two-

---

[3] *Employers' refusals.* It was not possible to follow up the reasons for the refusal of firms replying to the original request, since they were only required to return a pre-paid postcard indicating whether or not they were willing to discuss the survey. But when telephoning the random selection of non-respondents, the reason for refusing was usually given. In the majority of cases, it was because managements considered that their employees could not be spared for interview owing to the nature of their work or because the work of others would be affected. This was particularly so where young workers were on piece-work or certain continuous processes, and more so for girls than for boys. Shortage of labour and pressure of work were among other reasons advanced. Two firms felt that the survey itself was not particularly useful to them and could not see the point of their co-operation. Some of the smaller firms felt that their size alone should preclude them from any survey. One firm was worried that interviewing might disturb what was felt to be an unstable labour situation.

This evidence, so far as it goes, would seem to indicate that firms unwilling to participate in the inquiry were more likely than others to have processes or types of work from which employees could not be spared for the time required for the interview; and to be apprehensive about retaining their employees. It is also possible that they had, in general, less favourable conditions of work and opportunities for training than those who took part in the inquiry. Size of firm would also appear to have been an important factor, a higher proportion of small firms than of medium or large firms being both non-respondents and non-participators.

fifths of the total number of firms employing young people. This low proportion of participation would have made use of any pre-selected sample of firms impossible (Table 1).

Since the 57 firms which had agreed to participate in the inquiry together employed substantially more young people than the number which it had been intended to interview, these firms were, in fact, taken as the sample. Since they were almost entirely self-selected, rather than chosen on the basis of a sampling scheme, they cannot be regarded as representative of all firms in the borough employing young people. It would seem difficult, however, to carry out on a local basis any valid sampling of firms involving the interviewing of employees without some form of statutory obligation on the part of employers.

TABLE 1. Response of firms to inquiry.

| | Number of firms | | |
	Manufacturing industries[a]	Retail trades[b]	Total
Participating	57	18	75
Refusals	60	10	70
Withdrawals	12	—	12
No under-eighteens employed	6	12	18
Other non-respondents	105	—	105
Total	240	40	280

a Including construction, communications, transport, and hospitals.
b Including hairdressing, department stores, banks, and public administration.

THE TOTAL SAMPLE

In addition to covering firms engaged in manufacturing, construction, transport, communication, and hospital services, the inquiry was also extended to cover other employers. A random sample of 34 small retailers were approached, of whom 11[4] agreed to co-operate in the inquiry, while 3 out of 5 variety and department stores, 2 out of 4 banks and 2 out of 4 public administration offices also participated. This brought the total number of employing units wholly or partially taking part in the inquiry to 75 (somewhat fewer than the round 100 originally intended). The total number of young people interviewed was 330 (somewhat larger than had been anticipated), while information collected from employers related to

___

[4] A substantial proportion (one-third) of the small retailers approached were found to be no longer employing under-eighteens though shown as such in the records of the Shops Inspectorate. While useful in providing a general statistical picture of employment of under-eighteens in retail distribution these records were not sufficiently up to date to be reliable enough for selecting a sample.

nearly 650 young people, or about one-quarter of the total employed in the borough.[5]

THE INFORMATION COLLECTED

From young people

A pilot study was carried out in the locality between October 1962 and April 1963[6] in order to explore how information relating to school leavers' experiences might be collected. The results showed that young people could readily recall their past experiences during their final school years and when choosing and finding employment, could give some assessment of these and/or their present situations, and could respond with serious interest to the questions put to them. It was also evident that to assess the needs of young people in the years between leaving school and starting work, it was necessary to know something about each phase of the transition, including their school background, their experience in finding their first and subsequent jobs, their view of their present employment and its prospects, their opinion about the training received and the opportunities for further education, as well as information about their social interests, their future plans and on what issues they felt more help and support were needed.

Some of the questions used in the inquiry had been tested during the pilot study and were known to produce the information required. Further exploration was necessary, however, for questions designed to discover how young people viewed their jobs and what kind of information about their employment could be obtained. It was also necessary to test out the whole range of questioning in order to estimate the time required for each interview.

Because of the smallness of the intended sample it was felt advisable to use, for comparative purposes, a number of questions which had been used successfully in other, larger scale, inquiries. Because of the complexity

[5] As will be seen in Appendix I, the self-selected sample of firms in manufacturing industries and other services was biased in favour of the large firms, and these sometimes employed substantial numbers of young persons. In order to correct, to some extent, the balance of the sample as between size-groups, it was decided to interview all young people where fewer than twenty were employed in any firm, but only a proportion where twenty or more were employed. However, even this correction could not be rigidly adhered to in all cases, since some managements felt that it was not possible for all their young employees to be seen even when the total numbers were less than twenty. In the majority of firms, however, no difficulties of this kind arose, and all the under-eighteens were interviewed when their number was under twenty. In nine firms, each employing over twenty young people, a proportion selected at random was interviewed, averaging about one in four of the total number of under-eighteens employed.

[6] The pilot study (carried out jointly by Mrs Winifred Moss and the present author) was based on individual and group discussions with almost eighty school leavers, chiefly at work but also at home, at technical college and youth clubs. Small numbers of young workers and children in their last year of school also completed questionnaires, in which they described their previous day and assessed its best and worst features.

of devising questions to elicit attitudes to work, it was also decided to adopt, in modified form, some of the questions originally developed by Robert Hoppock[7] and used by J. D. Handyside when directing the National Institute of Industrial Psychology study of job satisfaction relating to a sample of 1000 employees from five firms.[8] In addition to Hoppock's 11-point scale for rating job satisfaction, the N.I.I.P. questionnaire contained check-list items relating to the job, the supervision and the firm. Subjects in the inquiry were required to decide which of the items seemed most closely to fit the job and to apply most closely to their employer and to their firm.

This technique seemed particularly appropriate to use in the interviewing of young workers. It seemed to offer a solution to the anticipated difficulties of interviewing the inarticulate and the shy; it was applicable to a variety of occupations; and it provided young people with a choice of response. This seemed important in so far as they were being interviewed at their place of work. The use of check-lists made it unnecessary for them to answer verbally a host of questions about their work, their supervision, and their firm; moreover, it allowed them to make their own selection of items, choosing as few or as many as they wished.

The same technique was used to discover how young people felt about their teachers and their schools; and how those who were not involved in any scheme of training or further education felt about continuing their education after leaving school. Using the same check-list for teachers as for supervision, young people were asked to tick those items which most closely applied to what they remembered about their teachers. New check-lists were devised, based on previous discussions with young people, relating to school and to attending classes after leaving school.

The questionnaire, after much pruning, finally contained 122 questions of fact and opinion.[9] It combined both verbal and self-completed questions, and was timed for an interview of about 30–40 minutes.

From employers

In order to assess the degree to which industry and commerce offered young people conditions which allowed them to develop and to use their abilities, information was required about the types of work available to them, the qualifications required of them and the opportunities provided for training, further education and promotion.

Apart from some specialized studies, very little published material was

---

[7] Robert Hoppock, *Job Satisfaction*, Harper, New York, 1935.

[8] The N.I.I.P. Study was essentially a methodological one carried out to explore the advantages and disadvantages of self-completing questionnaire techniques and interview methods. The study is described in 'Satisfactions and Aspirations' J. D. Handyside, *Occ. Psychol.*, **35**, No. 4, October 1961.

[9] See Appendix II.

available on which to draw for a framework of questioning suitable for obtaining data, both of fact and opinion, from employers about the occupations and employment of under-eighteens. Job description and job study techniques were considered but not adopted, since they are frequently designed for some specific purpose such as recruitment, selection, training, or promotion, and involve, to some degree, the direct observation of work processes.

The two questionnaires which were finally prepared combined some of the questions found useful in the pilot study with some of those used by the Industrial Training Council[10] in the preparation of training programmes. They were tried out in some preliminary interviews in large and small firms, and they seemed to yield satisfactory responses.

The first questionnaire was a general one. It asked for some statistical information relating to the total numbers employed in each skill and status category, the names of the occupations in which under-eighteens were employed, and the number of young people in each occupation. It asked some opinion questions about the recruitment, education, training, and future trends in the employment of young people; and gave a check-list for facilities like a canteen, rest-room, social club, etc.

The second questionnaire was designed to obtain information about specific jobs and covered hours of work, source of recruitment, qualifications, and experience required, how and where training given, the length of the basic and subsequent training and an assessment of the job experience and promotion prospects. While a brief job description was asked for, employers were also asked to select from a check-list, identical to that given to young people, those items which mostly closely applied to the job being described.[11]

Since both employers and young people were asked to select from the same check-list relating to jobs, and were questioned about the length of training and the prospects of promotion, it was possible to compare the replies and to see to what extent their respective views corresponded.

It was necessary that all interviews should be conducted in absolute privacy to ensure confidentiality. This was emphasized with all employers and almost all the interviewing was, in fact, carried out in very satisfactory conditions. Difficulties arose only in interviewing in small shops, and some of these interviews were subsequently abandoned.

DEGREE OF CO-OPERATION OF RESPONDING FIRMS

Of the 75 firms covered by the inquiry, 60 gave full co-operation in the sense of arranging for the interviewing of their young employees and of completing both the employers' questionnaires. In 6 firms, no interviews

[10] Now the Central Industrial Training Council.
[11] See Appendix II.

with young people were allowed, though the employers' questionnaires were completed, while in another 9 firms, interviews were held with young employees but the employers' forms were not returned. In all, 66 forms were returned relating to the numbers employed and policy questions; and 100 forms returned relating to specific occupations of young people, covering the employment of 647 under-eighteens (see Table 2).

TABLE 2. Degree of co-operation by firms and number of questionnaires completed

	Number of firms		Number of completed questionnaires
1. Full co-operation	60	1. Employees' questionnaires	330
2. Partial co-operation		2. Employers' questionnaires	
(a) Employers' forms only completed	6	(a) Job descriptions	100[a]
(b) Employees only interviewed	9	(b) General	66
Total	75	Total	496

a Covering the employment of 647 under-eighteens.

CHARACTERISTICS OF THE SAMPLE OF FIRMS AND SCHOOL LEAVERS[12]

In analysing the characteristics of the sample of firms in relation to what is known about the total of all firms in Willesden employing under-eighteens, it would seem that it is generally representative of the borough's industries and services, with the exception of retail distribution, clothing and textile factories, and small offices. The sample is biased, however, in two important respects. First, large firms (employing more than 500 persons) are over-represented in relation to the borough as a whole;[13] second, firms employing boy apprentices are relatively heavily over-represented, while those employing girl apprentices and boy sales assistants (both mainly in retail distribution) are under-represented.

Over-representation of larger firms might indicate that self-selection was strongest for firms with opportunities for training, facilities for apprenticeship schemes, and higher than average numbers of under-eighteens in their employment. If so, the results would reflect not the employment conditions for young people in general but only the most favourable of these in the area of study.

The sample of young people interviewed can be described as predominantly secondary modern school leavers in the sixteen to seventeen age

[12] See Appendix I for a more detailed analysis of the characteristics of the sample.

[13] However, the sample includes more small firms (employing fewer than 100 persons) than medium-sized firms (employing 100–500 persons).

group, the majority of whom left school at fifteen. Most had been at work for over one year and were still in their first jobs. Half of them lived in the borough and the majority came from the homes of skilled workers. The boys were predominantly manual workers including apprentices, and the girls predominantly non-manual.

Comparisons made between the characteristics of the sample of young people living in Willesden and such information as was available relating to the borough as a whole, did not allow for any precise assessment of the degree of sample bias. There was no comprehensive statistical information relating to age of leaving patterns, type of school attended, social class, and job changes of the under-eighteens at work in the borough. It is possible to assume, however, since the under-eighteens at work almost certainly consist predominantly of secondary modern school leavers, the majority of whom left school at fifteen, that the sample is reasonably representative in these two respects of the juvenile labour force in the borough. The sample is also fairly well representative of boys in apprenticeships and clerical work, and of girls in manual, clerical, and sales occupations.

The main biases in the sample were reflections of those resulting from the self-selection process of the participating firms. This meant, for the boys, an over-representation in employment in the large firms, in unskilled and semi-skilled manual employment, and as regards industries, in transport and communications; the most serious under-representation was in sales assistants as a result of the difficulties in interviewing in small shops. For the girls there was much less bias in the sample as regards size distribution of employing firms or as regards occupational distribution; the under-representation of apprentices was the most notable.

The total number of young people interviewed represents one in seven of the total estimated number employed in Willesden and just under one-half of the total under-eighteens employed in the participating firms.

Methods of analysis

The weakness of the sample design resulted in a selection of school leavers who did not constitute a fully random sample. This means that although their replies have, to a large extent, been quantified, the calculation of sampling errors could not be applied.[14] The results cannot, therefore, be interpreted as relating to any other population of school leavers, though on some questions their generality is strongly implied.

The size of the sample allowed for a relatively intensive study, in some respects, but restricted the analysis in others. It was found necessary, for instance, because of the size of certain groups, to combine or to exclude those whose attributes and responses in larger scale studies would have

---

[14] Where it seemed useful and appropriate, however, the chi-squared test of statistical significance has been used.

merited separate attention. It was not possible, for example, to examine social class except in very broad categories of fathers' occupations. The results of considering some questions in detail for quite small numbers indicate, however, that further exploration on the basis of larger numbers might yield interesting new material.

In spite of the relatively small size of the sample, the results were tabulated wherever the magnitude in the differences in the proportions of school leavers responding to different questions, and in the relationships between two relevant variables, seemed sociologically interesting. These must be interpreted with caution, however, particularly where numbers are relatively small.

PART II

LEAVING SCHOOL

CHAPTER III

THE DECISION TO LEAVE SCHOOL

INTRODUCTION

Since 1944, not only have boys and girls been kept at school until fifteen who would not otherwise have stayed if left to themselves, but there has been the possibility for increasing numbers to remain at school beyond that age. The majority of school leavers, however, are still fifteen-year-olds and it is these children who, in the eyes of the Crowther Committee, are considered to be at some disadvantage, compared with the leavers at sixteen.[1]

The Crowther Committee posed the question as to whether it was lack of opportunity or lack of desire which decided that more than four-fifths of the boys and girls in England should have left school before they were sixteen. The evidence, at that time, appeared to the Committee to establish that it was insufficient opportunity, at least for a very large number of children, and not a lack of desire for more education, that made them leave at fifteen.

Since 1958, when local authorities were asked to plan extended courses so as to provide for the education of those who wished to remain until the age of sixteen,[2] the percentage of pupils who voluntarily remain at school beyond the minimum age of fifteen has more than doubled in secondary modern schools. Yet the discussions with young people in the pilot stage of the present inquiry about their school leaving decision suggested that, among school leavers of under sixteen from secondary modern schools, there might be substantial numbers who were eager to leave school and start work at the earliest opportunity because they felt school had nothing more to offer them, although they had attended schools where extended courses were available.

The questions asked

Since the purpose of the present inquiry was to obtain a comprehensive picture of the needs of school leavers in the transitional years between school and work, information relating to their educational experiences and the factors which appeared to be associated with their school-leaving

---

[1] *15–18.*
[2] *Secondary Education For All: A New Drive*, H.M.S.O., Cmnd. 604, December 1958.

decision, was felt to be essential in the questioning of young people. Moreover, with the prospect of a higher school-leaving age being introduced within the next few years, and the content of the school programme for this extra year now being seriously prepared, it seemed relevant to include questions relating to the last year of school and to the raising of the school-leaving age.

The replies relating to the educational experiences of young people have been summarized in this and the following three chapters. The present chapter relates to their school-leaving decision, how they felt about leaving school, whether they had considered remaining longer and how their parents and teachers felt about their leaving. Chapter IV presents their impressions of teachers and schools; Chapter V describes how they felt about their last year at school and the extent to which this offered them a new experience; Chapter VI relates to their retrospective view of their school-leaving decision, to their regrets or otherwise, about leaving when they did; and to their approval or otherwise, of a higher school-leaving age.

Characteristics of the sample

The majority of boys (over three-quarters) and of girls (four-fifths) had attended secondary modern schools; but since the sample was small it has not been possible to distinguish between different types of secondary school; nor has it been possible to distinguish between secondary modern school leavers and the rest, except for boys and then only when differences in response justified separate analysis. The results reflect, predominantly but not exclusively, the attitudes and experiences of secondary modern school leavers. Moreover, though it has been possible to distinguish, for the sample of boys, two age-of-leaving groups and to present the results accordingly, so few girls left at sixteen that they could not be included in any separate analysis though reference is made to them in the text. The results for girls reflect, therefore, predominantly the views of fifteen-year-old leavers.

Furthermore, it would seem that only a minority took and passed any school-leaving examination; and that, judging from their assessment of their position in stream and class during their last year at school,[3] only a minority might be considered to have been in the highest 'ability' group. Probably the majority of the sample might, in fact, be assumed to

---

[3] The majority of the school leavers seen (nearly three-quarters of the boys and four-fifths of the girls) had been 'streamed' and by far the greatest number of these stated that they had been in the top stream; less than one in four had been in the middle stream, and only about one in seven had been in the lowest stream. However, only two-fifths of the boys, and one-third of the girls, had been both in the top stream and 'average' or 'above average' in class; these can reasonably be assumed to represent children of above-average ability. The remainder, representing the majority, would correspond approximately with children of average, or below-average ability with whose education the Newsom Committee was primarily concerned.

represent the boys and girls of average 'ability' with whom the Newsom Report[4] was mainly concerned.

EAGER, NON-COMMITTAL, AND RELUCTANT SCHOOL LEAVERS

Boredom with everything school stands for, or enthusiasm?' The opening words of the Newsom Report[5] seem particularly relevant in considering the replies of young people to the questions of how they had felt about leaving school and why they had felt the way they did. Though substantial minorities had not minded about leaving and one in five had been reluctant to do so, just over one-half of the young people seen had been eager to leave and over one in four, very much so (Table 3). Moreover, there were

TABLE 3. Willing, indifferent, and reluctant
school leavers.

How much wanted to leave school	Boys	Girls
	(Per cent of total)	
Very much	22	29
Quite a lot	27	27
Total willing	49	56
Didn't mind	32	20
Not very much	15	17
Not at all	4	7
Total reluctant	19	24
Total	100	100
(No. of 15–18s)	(183)	(147)

only very small differences according to the age of leaving. A somewhat higher proportion of leavers at fifteen had been very eager to leave compared with the older leavers but this difference was entirely due to the views of the secondary modern school leavers in the sample. Differences in feelings about leaving school were, in fact, greater between the sixteen-year-old leavers from different types of secondary schools than between the fifteen- and sixteen-year-old leavers from secondary modern schools.[6]

[4] *Half our Future.*
[5] Ibid.
[6] The small number of sixteen-year-old leavers in the sample of girls precluded any comparison between age of leaving groups.

THE REASONS FOR FEELINGS ABOUT LEAVING SCHOOL

There were a variety of considerations in the minds of young people when they came to leave school; and for each main group of leavers, the eager, the non-committal, and the reluctant, certain considerations played a more important part than did others. It is clear that a dislike of school and a dissatisfaction with certain aspects of it were paramount in the feelings of those who had been most eager to leave while, in contrast, a liking for school and a wish to study further were the most important considerations for those who had been most reluctant to end their school days (Table 4).

TABLE 4. Reasons for feelings about leaving school.

	Boys	Girls
	(Per cent of total)	
Disliked school or some aspect of it	19	33
Felt not learning anything	18	6
Felt lacked ability	14	9
Wanted to be independent	11	10
Wanted to earn money	8	11
Had job to go to or in mind	8	5
Course completed	6	5
Friends leaving	4	5
Family circumstances	4	7
Liked school or some aspect of it	15	22
Wanted further study	9	8
Other	6	7
Don't know	1	5
Total (Multiple replies)	100	100
(No. of 15–18s)	(183)	(147)

A dislike of school

The most frequently stated reason for wanting to leave school, was logically enough, a dislike of it, or of some feature of it. Over one-third of the boys and three-fifths of the girls who had been eager to leave school referred to their disliking school, associated, particularly for girls, with their teachers, their school work, or school atmosphere.

Comments about teachers were, more often than not, about their treatment of the children than about their professional demerits. 'I couldn't stand school,' said one girl who had left at fifteen. 'I didn't like the attitude of the teachers; they wanted to get rid of us. They even told us we could leave two weeks before the end of term.'

Another leaver at fifteen said that she disliked school because the teachers 'treated her like a child', a point of view which was also expressed by some boys. Another leaver felt that 'the teachers took no interest in you if you didn't grasp the subject right away—they left you to get on with it'.

The boys, too, had complaints. 'It's the attitude of the teachers. They make you feel small over petty things.' 'I didn't like school. The teachers caned you and told you off for homework.' 'The teachers picked on us because we went out at night, and we were never the teachers' pets.'

Secondly, there were references to school work either from those who had not got on well at school or from those who had found study and homework a strain. The latter applied particularly to sixteen-year-old leavers: 'The work got me down in the last year. It was too much. We were doing subjects we were not interested in and we had no choice' was the statement of a girl who had ten G.C.E. 'O' levels. A boy, also a leaver at sixteen, complained that 'school was just a lot of study and a lot of homework. I never had much time to spare'.

Then there were references, particularly by girls, to what was evidently felt to be the restrictive atmosphere of school. 'I did not find school all that happy. There was not enough freedom. I wanted to be independent.' 'I did not like conforming, especially at the grammar school.'

One boy referred to the change in atmosphere with the coming of a new headmaster. 'I liked school at first but it changed with the headmaster. All seemed changed. The atmosphere was like a concentration camp. I just lost interest.'

Not learning anything

The next most frequently stated reason for wanting to leave school, particularly for boys, was the feeling that they were not learning anything and were bored and fed up with school. This was sometimes combined with a reference to disliking school but more frequently the lack of anything new and interesting in the school curriculum or in school life was the sole reason offered. Over one in four of the boys wanting to leave school were in this category, compared with only one in twelve of those less eager to leave school. Girls were not nearly so inclined to refer to this aspect of school.

Typical comments of these boys and girls were:

'I was sick and tired of school. It was all right until I was fifteen but the last year was just repetition.'

'I was fed up with the same old thing. The type of things we did wouldn't help with a job and I used to get bored stiff.'

'I just got completely fed up. I couldn't see the purpose of it all.'

'I was bored at school most of the time. All the time we were not doing anything very much. It seemed a waste of time staying on.'

Feeling they lacked academic ability

The next important reason, in order of frequency for boys, was the feeling that they lacked academic ability. One in six of the boys gave this explanation for wanting to leave school compared with just over one in ten of those who had not minded or who had not wanted to leave school. Among the girls, however, this reason was again not so frequently offered.

Doubts about their academic ability were typified by comments such as these:

'I didn't get on well. I got left behind.'

'We were told we hadn't got a chance of getting G.C.E. so I thought I'd try to get a decent job.'

'I hadn't much of a brain. I didn't think that I could have learnt any more.'

'I didn't like school. I wasn't one of the brainy ones. It was all beyond me a bit.'

The question of how far such assessments of ability were valid could not be explored objectively in this study. The only corroborative information available was that given by the young people themselves about their position in class and stream;[7] for the boys, higher proportions of those who felt that they lacked ability were in fact to be found in the middle and bottom 'streams' and, though to a lesser extent, among those who assessed their position in class as 'average' or 'below average'. There would seem to be some basis, therefore, for feelings of doubts about ability in so far as the position in the 'streaming' system and in class were accepted as evidence.

Wanting to be independent

Another important reason, equal in order of frequency with the feeling they lacked ability, was that of wanting to be independent and to start work. In some cases, this was combined with 'wanting to earn money', and in others the financial aspects may have been implied though not mentioned. About one in six of the boys wanting to leave gave this explanation, but not more than one in twenty of the less-willing leavers expressed this need. The differences between girl leavers were not quite so great.

Wanting to be independent and to get out to work was expressed in terms like these:

'I just wanted to get out. It was the feeling of getting out to work, earning and being independent.'

'I wanted to see what work was like and to get out, earn my living and be independent.'

'I wanted to get out in the world. I felt a child at school, and at weekends I was a woman.'

'I was eager to get out to work. You had to do things at school. At work you're independent.'

[7] See footnote 3 on page 26.

To earn money

Second in order of frequency for the girls, but fifth for the boys wanting to leave school, was their wish to earn money. This was sometimes combined with other reasons, particularly with the wish to be independent, but more frequently it was the only reason offered and expressed quite directly. Nearly one in five of the girls and one in eight of the boys gave it as their explanation for wanting to leave school; only a very small proportion of other leavers offered this explanation and the reluctant leavers made no reference to it whatsoever.

A job planned or in mind

Small proportions of boys and girls, reluctant as well as eager to leave school, made their decision because of jobs arranged or planned for them. Apprenticeships were frequently mentioned in this connection. Some leavers would have preferred to have stayed on at school but left either because they felt they would lose the chance of securing the job in mind or entry to a skilled trade, or because they preferred the certainty of prospective employment to what they felt was the uncertain outcome of a longer school life.

Family circumstances

Some young people referred to their having wanted to help their parents by leaving school and earning money. Sometimes a parent had died or was unable to work; 'I wanted to earn my way; my father is not well and I wanted to help.' In some families there were other dependent children. The eldest of six children wanted 'to help my mother out. We're a lot in our family'. Though such references were a minority among the leavers in both groups, family circumstances would seem to have pressed more hardly on those who were reluctant to leave school and particularly on the girls among them.[8] The reluctant leavers were thus more likely to have experienced some degree of conflict between their wish to remain at school and what they felt to be their responsibilities towards their families.

Friends leaving

The fact that friends were also leaving school influenced the decisions of relatively few school leavers, apparently, and then relatively more of the less willing leavers than of others. This is mainly because some young people were apprehensive about feeling lonely or being on their own at school. 'My friends were leaving. I didn't have anyone to go to school with or to talk to.'

[8] It could be that one reason for this factor being somewhat more frequently stated by girls than by boys is that the girls tended to come from larger families than did the boys.

Completion of course

The completion of a five-year course as a reason for wanting to leave school came exclusively from the sixteen-year-old leavers. Some of these were eager to leave; some would have liked to have remained longer at school if there had been opportunity to do so; some could have extended their education if they had transferred to another school, but this they did not want to do.

Liking school

Though only a very small proportion of the leavers wanting to leave school mentioned that they had liked school, their feelings were not inconsistent with wanting to leave. Liking school, in their case, was combined with other reasons for wanting to leave which made leaving school more attractive than staying on.

Liking school was, however, by far the most frequently stated reason for not wanting to leave school, and for not minding about leaving, accounting for over one-third of the boys and nearly one-half of the girls among the less-willing leavers. Curiously enough, liking school was not associated with as much comment about school as was disliking it. Relatively few young people extended their explanations to include references to specific aspects of school which were liked, though some referred to their teachers as being nice, or to their liking their friends or the work. The enthusiastic leavers, evidently, felt it necessary to justify their feelings, and were more likely to criticise school than were reluctant leavers to commend it.

Wanting to study more

Those who had wanted to study more represented one-sixth of the boys and one-eighth of the girls, and were almost exclusively those who had not wanted to leave, or those who had not minded about leaving school. Their comments reflected different needs. There were, firstly, those who wanted 'more education', typified by such comments as 'I wanted to go further with my education', and 'I wanted to stay until I was at least seventeen. I didn't know what I wanted to do but I wanted more education.'

Then there were those who had just begun to enjoy their school work and were reluctant to give it up:

'I just got interested in school before I left and then it was too late.'
'I enjoyed studying. I got better at it in the 3rd and 4th years.'
'I was just beginning to educate myself and train my mind to take the work.'

A third group consisted of those who had wanted to study but either felt they would not have managed the examinations or that they did not want to take all the subjects involved:

'Some lessons I didn't like; some I did and these I would have liked to stay on for, but that would have meant doing subjects I didn't like.'

'I didn't feel that I had the brain, otherwise I would have liked to stay on and take G.C.E.'

'I would have liked to stay on and take just one G.C.E. but this wasn't possible. I would have had to take several, some of which I was no good at.'

Other reasons

Other miscellaneous reasons associated with feelings about leaving school came mainly from boys and girls who, not having strong feelings one way or another, had accepted with apparent good will what appeared at the time to have been a necessary, and even an inevitable, decision. 'I quite liked school but I did not mind leaving. I felt the time had come not to go on relying on my parents. I would not have minded staying.' Feelings were fairly evenly balanced between leaving and staying though some young people had felt apprehensive about what leaving school might mean.

'It was half and half. I wanted to get out to work and see what it was like but I was frightened as well—I felt it might be better to stay on.'

'I wanted to get out in the world. I felt I'd had enough of school, but I didn't want to leave the sheltered life of school.'

'Leaving school meant leaving your childhood and I had a happy childhood.'

CONSIDERATION OF REMAINING LONGER AT SCHOOL

Since the possibility of continuing education beyond the minimum leaving age existed, in principle if not in practice, for most of the young people interviewed, it is of some interest to note the extent to which they had considered, at any time, a longer school life for themselves and the reasons they gave for their decision to end their school days.

TABLE 5.   Whether considered staying
on at school.

	Boys	Girls
	(Per cent of total)	
Yes	63	52
No	36	48
Don't know	1	—
Total	100	100
(No. of 15–18s)	(183)	(147)

In spite of the fact that over one-half of the boys and girls seen had been eager to leave school, the majority had, nevertheless, considered staying longer, though the proportion doing so was higher for boys than for girls

4

(Table 5). Moreover, the proportions of boys who had considered a longer school life for themselves were identical for both leavers at fifteen and sixteen, and were closely similar for secondary modern school leavers and for others. As seems logical, those who had not considered continuing their education tended more frequently than others to have wanted to leave school, though this was more marked for the boys than for the girls. The enthusiastic leavers were, therefore, in a minority, albeit a substantial one, among the boys who had considered further education, but they accounted for the majority of the boys and girls who had not.

In replying to the question of why they had, or had not, considered staying on at school, young people often repeated or supplemented the comments made when discussing why they had felt the way they did about leaving school. In comparing the frequency distribution of the replies to the two questions, it would seem, however, that certain factors played a more important part in their attitudes towards staying on at school than in their feelings towards leaving it.[9]

Thus, for instance, higher proportions of boys and girls referred to job prospects and lower proportions to disliking school; relatively more girls referred to doubts as to their academic ability and relatively fewer boys to their wish to be independent and start work, when discussing their attitudes towards staying longer at school than when discussing their feelings about leaving school.

Similar differences were apparent when the frequency distributions for leavers at fifteen and at sixteen were compared, except that, among the boys, higher proportions of fifteen-year-old leavers referred to doubts as to their academic ability, and their job prospects, when commenting on the question of staying on at school, than when commenting on how they felt about leaving. Relatively more of both girls and boys, in both age-of-leaving groups, also referred to family circumstances.[10]

[9] Some reasons are not comparable, being classified differently for those not having thought of staying on. The comparison excludes 'not learning anything'; 'friends leaving'; 'course completed'.

[10] It is perhaps, of some interest, to compare the replies of school leavers interviewed by the Social Survey Division of the Central Office of Information in 1957 for the Crowther Committee (see *15–18*), and asked about their reasons for having left school, with the replies of those interviewed in Willesden in 1964–5, to a similar question. The two studies are not, of course, strictly comparable owing to differences in the selection and educational composition of the two samples. Nevertheless, roughly similar proportions in both inquiries referred to the completion of their school courses, to their wanting to start work and to be independent, and to their friends leaving school, as reasons for their decision; among those who had not wanted to remain longer at school or who had not considered the possibility, similar proportions in both samples also referred to their dislike of school.

On the other hand, much lower proportions in the Willesden inquiry gave as their reason for not staying on at school (although they had considered doing so) their wish or need to earn money; while relatively higher proportions of Willesden boys felt that they lacked academic ability. Among the girls who had not wanted to stay on at school, the proportion who doubted their academic ability was as high as one in four for the Willesden sample compared with only one in twenty-five of the national sample.

Those who had not considered staying on at school

Many of the references to academic ability revealed that an extra year of full-time education beyond the age of fifteen was regarded mainly as being appropriate only for the 'brainy' ones, who were 'good' at school. Over one-half of the boys and girls who had left school at fifteen without considering remaining longer at school were of this view. The extent to which doubts about academic ability seem validated by school performance can be judged by the replies given by young people concerning their position in class and in the 'streaming' system. These suggest, as might have been expected, that there was a tendency for those less highly placed in their class or streaming system to reject, more frequently than did others, any consideration of continued education; this tendency was much more marked for girls than for boys.

As regards the sixteen-year-old leavers, completion of their five year secondary school course emerged as the chief factor influencing their decision, and only relatively small proportions of these young people referred to their dislike of school or to being uncertain as to their academic ability. Over two-fifths felt that having completed five years secondary school education they had fulfilled their educational plans and were ready to leave. For some young people, further education would have meant transferring to another secondary school and this was not an attractive idea for them; in many cases, however, leaving at sixteen was part of an accepted sequence of events and the fulfilment of a thought-out plan for themselves. 'I stayed on an extra year, so I did what I planned to do. I never planned to stay on after sixteen' was the comment of one of the boys in this category.

Job prospects were referred to by one in seven of sixteen-year-old leavers (only one in twelve of the leavers at fifteen), having had either a specific job to go to, or plans to take up a particular type of employment. Boys were particularly affected by the fact that they felt that to remain longer at school would limit their chances of obtaining an apprenticeship. Some young people had obtained employment while still at school, and knew that they would receive some further education and training in their new employment. There was also the feeling that starting early in employment improved their chances of getting on in their work, an idea expressed in the words, 'I thought I'd stayed long enough. I thought it was better to take the job, get started early and I could start studying for the job'.

Those who had considered staying longer at school

The fifteen-year-old leavers among the boys who, having thought about a longer school life eventually decided against it, included one in four who doubted their academic ability; but in contrast to the generalized self-assessments of their contemporaries who did not think about staying longer at school (e.g. 'I was not the brainy type'), their comments were more frequently based on a specific reference to what they considered to be their inability to pass the G.C.E. or other relevant examinations (e.g. 'I knew I would not get G.C.E. so I did not think it worth while staying on.').

The sixteen-year-old boy leavers were more frequently influenced, than were leavers at fifteen, by job prospects and over two-fifths, a proportion twice as high as for the younger leavers, gave the fact that they had a job to go to or one in mind as the reason for their final decision to leave school. They were, moreover, judging from their comments, more likely than were leavers at fifteen to have felt anxious about the uncertain outcome, for them, of education beyond sixteen, compared with what appeared to be the more certain future offered by the type of employment they wanted.

One boy, for instance, expressed what had been in his mind by saying: 'I heard that promotion was more likely the longer the service in the firm. I thought of what would happen if I stayed on at school and did not do well.' Another comment of this kind was: 'I was not sure that staying on would help all that much. Perhaps my results would not be good enough and by then I would have missed the chance of training in my job.'

Another consideration was the opportunities for further education and training offered by certain employers which, for some boys, was evidently a preferable alternative to remaining at school.

Doubts about ability were also expressed by sixteen-year-old leavers and one in five gave up the idea of a longer school life because they felt or were told, that they might not be successful in passing 'A' levels; but there were several boys who, having decided to leave on these grounds, subsequently found that their examination results disproved these doubts. One boy, for instance, on the assumption that he would fail most of the seven subjects taken in G.C.E., decided to leave school. He subsequently obtained all seven 'O' levels. If he had anticipated this degree of success, he would have continued his education for a further two years. He had already started work, however, when he heard of the results and felt that he could not reverse his previous decision. He commented 'I wish I had known what others thought I could do in the exams.'

Just under one in five of the sixteen-year-old leavers, a much higher proportion than among the younger leavers, felt that there was little point in their remaining longer at school. In some cases this was associated with doubts about their possible academic achievements, but in others it was related to what they felt was a more sensible arrangement by which they continued their studies in some form of further education while in employment. In this way they felt they would get the best of both worlds. Sixteen-year-old leavers were also affected somewhat more frequently than younger leavers by the fact that there were no opportunities at their schools for continuing their education beyond sixteen. One in ten of the boys who had considered staying on would have had to transfer to another school (sometimes from a secondary modern to a grammar school), and this idea was not an attractive one for them.

The decision to leave school was evidently, for those who had given some thought to staying longer, more likely to have been affected by parental views than was eagerness or reluctance to leave school. About one in ten of the leavers, both at fifteen and at sixteen, referred to family circumstances. In many cases this seemed to arise because their parents had felt that the time had come for them to leave school; but in others it was because the children themselves thought they should leave school and help their families.

Small minorities of both fifteen- and sixteen-year-old leavers attributed their ultimate decision to leave school to some unsatisfactory situation at school. A change of headmaster; a feeling that they had had enough of school routine; a fear of not getting on with the teachers in the higher classes: 'a lowering of morale when the teachers said we would not get G.C.E.'; a clash with teachers over disciplinary matters, were factors which played a part, evidently, in the decision of some boys to leave rather than to stay on at school. Even age itself would seem to have influenced the boy who said: 'Age was creeping up. I had a fear of becoming eighteen and never getting a job.'

The girls' reasons

Among the girls who had left at fifteen, having finally decided against another year at school, there were two main reasons offered for their decision. Firstly, the dislike of school or some aspect of it. Over one in four felt this way; they corresponded closely, therefore, with their contemporaries who had not thought about staying longer at school, but differed substantially from the boys who had. Their dislike of school was both general and specific, relating either to the school as a whole (e.g. 'I just could not face the teachers for another year') or to the work (e.g. 'I did not like the idea of working so much on my own').

Secondly, there were family circumstances which accounted for one-sixth of the girls and which, as for the boys, arose out of a combination of parental pressures for them to leave, and of their own wish to start work and help the family income.

Doubts as to their academic ability, the feeling that there was no point in staying on, and the attraction of job prospects were offered as reasons for deciding to leave school at fifteen, in each case, by one in seven. Girls, like the boys, referred to the difficulties they thought they would have in passing G.C.E., or to the feeling that another year would not be particularly useful to them in terms of what they would learn. They were not affected to the same degree as boys by apprenticeships, except for those planning to take up hairdressing and dressmaking; nevertheless, they too, weighed up the relative advantages to them of another year at school and of starting work.

'I thought it would be better for me to get the experience and I would have longer at work. The interview for this job decided it for me.'
'I wanted to do window dressing but I had to wait until sixteen. I thought I'd try to go on to a college but I could not get in. I then thought it would be better to start work in a shop.'

Girls rather less frequently than boys expressed the wish to earn money, but a little more frequently than boys referred to school disciplinary events. These sometimes had serious consequences, as in the case of one girl who was planning to continue her education to eighteen, but who was not allowed to return to school after she was said to have broken certain school rules.

Some school leavers revised their decision to stay on at school, having tried another term or so. They found that they did not like or get on with the work. One girl, however, had a different reason: 'I had planned another year but found I was so much more grown up in the holidays that going back to school was just like being a child again.'

SOCIAL FACTORS INFLUENCING SCHOOL LEAVING

An attempt was made to trace the extent to which such factors as social class and family size were associated with the age of leaving, with eagerness to leave school, and with any consideration of a longer school life. Since the sample was small, it was first divided into only three socioeconomic groups, based on combining all managerial, professional, and intermediate occupations; then all skilled occupations (including foremen); and finally, all semi-skilled and unskilled occupations. The analysis of age of leaving according to these groupings showed that nearly three-fifths of the boys whose fathers were in the intermediate and higher status occupations left school at sixteen, compared with two-fifths of those whose fathers were in skilled occupations, and just over one-quarter of those whose fathers were in semi-skilled or unskilled work. Conversely, the proportion of boys leaving school at fifteen fell from over three-quarters of those with fathers in semi-skilled or unskilled work to two-fifths of those in the highest socio-economic group.

The differences between the occupational groups for the girls were not so marked, partly because in all occupational groups the fifteen-year-old leaver predominated. Nevertheless, when the sample was divided into two groups—manual and non-manual—the differences in the proportions leaving at fifteen was as marked for the girls as for boys. Two-thirds of the boys and four-fifths of the girls with fathers in manual occupations left school at fifteen compared with two-fifths of the boys and three-fifths of the girls with fathers in non-manual work (Table 6).

TABLE 6. Age of leaving and father's occupation.

| | Father's occupation | | | |
| | Boys | | Girls | |
Age of leaving	Manual	Non-manual	Manual	Non-manual
	(*Per cent of total*)			
15	64	41	85	(22)
16	36	59	15	(16)
Total	100	100	100	
(No. of 15–18s)[a]	(93)	(68)	(94)	(38)

a Excluding those for whom father's occupation not known.

The age of leaving is, in part, associated with the type of secondary school attended and whether or not children are expected to follow a five-year secondary school course; moreover, several studies[11] have demonstrated the bias in selective schools in favour of children from middle-class homes. The secondary modern school leavers in the present inquiry also contained a lower proportion of boys with fathers in the intermediate and higher social class groups than was the case for the fathers of boys from selective schools. Nevertheless, the age of leaving of secondary modern boys was also associated to some degree with the father's occupation; the decline in the proportions leaving at fifteen and the rise in the proportions leaving at sixteen was as much associated with the rise in the socio-economic status of the father of boys from secondary modern schools as for the sample as a whole.

The social class factors also appeared to be associated with feelings about leaving school (though not so markedly for girls as for boys). A relatively smaller proportion of the most, and a relatively higher proportion of the less, eager to leave, for example, were from the homes of professional or intermediate groups, while, conversely, relatively more of those wanting to leave and relatively fewer of those reluctant to do so were from the homes of semi- or unskilled workers. For girls, a rather different pattern was evident since it was the daughters of manual workers who were less inclined than others to want to leave school. Among the boys, two-thirds of those with fathers in non-manual occupations had considered a longer school life compared with just over one-half of boys from the homes of manual workers. Closer examination showed that this difference lay

[11] H. T. Himmelweit, 'Social Status and Secondary Education since the 1944 Act: some data for London', *Social Mobility in Britain*, ed. D. Glass, Routledge and Kegan Paul, 1954; J. W. B. Douglas, *The Home and the School*, MacGibbon and Kee, 1962.

mainly between the boys with fathers in semi-skilled or unskilled occupations on the one hand, who were the least inclined and the boys with fathers in skilled non-manual work, who were the most inclined, to have considered the possibility of continuing their education. No such differences applied to the girls.

Family size

The distribution of family size in the sample of young people seen in the present inquiry showed that the majority were from families with not more than three children. There was, however, a tendency for a higher proportion of the sample of girls to come from larger families than was the case for the sample of boys.

When the age of leaving school in the sample was analysed according to family size, the proportions of girls leaving at fifteen rose steeply from two-thirds among those from families with up to two children, to nine-tenths among those from families with more than two children. The differences in the sample of boys were relatively slight, but the rise in the proportions leaving at fifteen was much sharper in the sample of secondary modern school boys, the proportion leaving at fifteen rising to seven-tenths in families of three or more children. The results suggest that family size played some part in the decision when to leave school but that it operated in relatively smaller families for girls than for boys.

A similar pattern in the proportions leaving school at fifteen emerged in the analysis of the sample according to the position occupied by each in birth order. The only and eldest children contained somewhat lower proportions of fifteen-year-old leavers, for instance, than did children who came second, third, or later in birth order. Again, this was more marked for the girls than for the boys, the rise in the proportion of fifteen-year-old leavers occurring among the fourth and subsequent-born children for girls. This was, no doubt, a reflection of the differences in family size.[12]

Since children from larger families tend, on average, to perform less well at school, than do children from smaller families,[13] it might have been assumed, therefore, that they would be more eager to leave school. In the present inquiry, however, school leavers from families with three or more

[12] The association of age of leaving with both family size and father's occupation raises the question as to whether the two latter characteristics were themselves related. An analysis of the distribution of family size according to the occupation of the fathers showed, however, that the differences between the two major occupational groups in terms of the smaller family of two or fewer children and the larger family of three or more children, were not substantial. This suggests that, for the sample of young people seen, social class and family size operated, to a large extent, independently of each other.

[13] J. W. B. Douglas, op. cit. J. D. Nisbet, *Family Environment*, London, Cassell, 1953. A. H. Halsey and L. Gardner, 'Selection for Secondary Education and Achievement in Four Grammar Schools', *British Journal of Sociology*, 4, No. 1, 1953.

children tended to be far less eager to end their school days than were leavers from families with two or fewer children. It was not possible, within the limits of the present study, to explore this finding in more detail; nor to assess the relationships between family size, educational performance, and attitudes towards leaving, since the information relating to attainments was incomplete and non-objective. The fact that as far as boys were concerned, children from larger families also tended to have a more favourable impression of their teachers in certain respects, than did boys from smaller families, suggests that family size may influence the adaptations of children to school and teachers. Further study would seem to be required of the responses of children to their educational setting in relation to family size.

In the present inquiry, the majority of boys and girls from the smaller families were enthusiastic leavers; but in the larger families, by contrast, less than two-fifths of the boys and one-half of the girls were of this view. The proportions were even lower for those from families with more than four children. Conversely, those not minding about leaving school rose with the larger family (though not to the same degree), as did the proportion of those not wanting to leave school. As indicated by the chi-squared test, these differences are statistically significant at the 1 per cent level for boys and the 2 per cent level for girls.

TABLE 7. How much wanted to leave school and family size.

How much wanted to leave school	Size of family (number of children)			
	Boys		Girls	
	Up to 2	3 or more	Up to 2	3 or more
	(Per cent of total)			
Very much Quite a lot }	63	38	71	47
Didn't mind	23	43	14·5	24
Not very much Not at all }	14	19	14·5	29
Total	100	100	100	100
(No. of 15–18s)[a]	(92)	(84)	(55)	(87)
	$\chi^2=11\cdot65$; d.f. $=2$; $p<0\cdot01$		$\chi^2=7\cdot85$; d.f. $=2$; $p=0\cdot02$	

a Excluding those not answering.

Higher proportions of boys from the smaller families (those with not more than two children) had, nevertheless, considered staying longer at school compared with those from the larger families but the differences were not great. Among the girls, however, it was those from families with three or four children who had, more frequently than others, considered continuing their education.[14]

When asked how their parents had felt about their leaving, the replies indicated that the majority of boys and girls had had the active or passive support of their parents in their decision to leave school. The majority of both fifteen- and sixteen-year-old leavers (three-fifths of the boys and three-quarters of the girls) said that their parents had not minded about their leaving school at the time; but among the boys, the sixteen-year old leavers contained a slightly higher proportion of children whose parents were said to have wanted them to leave (one-fifth), and a somewhat lower proportion (one-seventh) whose parents were said to have wanted them to stay, than was the case with the younger school leavers.[15]

TABLE 8. Age of leaving and parents' and teachers' views of leaving

| | Age of leaving | | |
| | Boys | | Girls |
	15 years	16 years	15 years
Parents	(Per cent of total)		
Wanted child to leave	15	20	13
Didn't mind	62	61	74
Wanted child to stay	23	19	13
Total	100	100	100
Teachers			
Thought child should leave	5	18	4
Child not sure what teacher thought	41	28	43
Didn't mind	21	28	23
Thought child should stay	33	26	30
Total	100	100	100
(No. of 15–18s)	(97)	(86)	(119)

[14] With a larger sample it might have been possible also to trace the possible association of family size and birth order with attitudes towards leaving school. Among boys, intermediate children tended to be more frequently eager to leave school than did eldest and only children but among girls no such differences were apparent. Further examination showed that there was, in fact, considerable variation according to birth order but the figures were too small for any general tendency to emerge.

[15] This similarity in parental wishes between the two age-of-leaving groups was not so evident in the sample of secondary modern school boys. Nearly one-third of the parents of leavers at fifteen, for instance, were said to have wanted them to stay on compared with one-fifth of the parents of boys who had left at sixteen.

The two age-of-leaving groups also differed in what they said about their teachers' views of their leaving school. The majority of fifteen-year-old leavers (just over two-fifths), had not been sure what their teachers had felt about their leaving compared with one-quarter of the older leavers with this impression. About one-third of the younger leavers replied that their teachers had thought they ought to stay longer at school, but only a quarter of the boys who left at sixteen had felt their teachers were of this view. Only a very small proportion—one in twenty—of the boys leaving at fifteen said that they felt their teachers thought they ought to leave; but nearly one-fifth of the boys at sixteen had had this impression[16] (Table 8).

When the replies of young people concerning their own feelings about leaving school were compared with those relating to their parents' and teachers' views, the first impression gained is that of relative discord between them. Relatively more children, for instance, wanted to leave than of parents or teachers who were said to have wanted the child to leave, or to have thought he ought to leave; a much higher proportion of parents were non-committal about their child's leaving, than were either the children or the teachers; the proportion of teachers who felt the children ought to stay on was higher than both the proportion of parents who were of this view and of the children who had wanted to stay; moreover, fewer of the parents of girls had wanted them to stay than was the case among the girls themselves (Table 9).

In fact, however, the discord would seem to be essentially between the parents and the children on the one side, and the teachers on the other. For though fewer parents wanted their children to leave than the number of children who actually wanted to do so, so many parents gave their passive support to the children by not minding what the child decided, that the only parents and children in effective discord would appear to be those in disagreement because the children wanted to remain at school. This discord, however, applied only to the girls.

A different pattern emerged when the replies were analysed according to the father's occupation. The discord between the parents' views, on the one hand, and those of the girls and their teachers on the other, was much more pronounced for girls with fathers in manual, than in non-manual, occupations. Moreover, the difference between the proportions of boys who wanted to leave school and of parents who had wanted their sons to

[16] The differences for boys were very much sharper for the secondary modern school leavers mainly because relatively more of the leavers at sixteen (nearly one-third) had had the impression that the teachers felt they ought to leave, and fewer (one-sixth) that their teachers wanted them to stay on, than was the case for the sample as a whole. This was because there were no leavers from other types of secondary school whose teachers had felt they ought to leave and a relatively high proportion—two-fifths—who had felt that their teachers had wanted them to stay. This result is presumably due to the fact that grammar and technical schools offer courses beyond the age of sixteen which are not always provided by the secondary modern school

leave, was very much greater in the case of those with fathers in manual, than in non-manual, work.

TABLE 9. The school leavers', parents', and teachers' views of leaving school

	Boys	Parents	Teachers
	(Per cent of total)		
Wanted to leave	49	—	—
Wanted child to leave	—	21	—
Thought child should leave	—	—	11
Didn't mind	32	61	25
Child not sure what teacher thought	—	—	35
Didn't want to leave	19	—	—
Wanted child to stay	—	18	—
Thought child should stay	—	—	29
Total	100	100	100
(No. of 15–18s)	(183)	(183)	(183)

	Girls	Parents	Teachers
	(Per cent of total)		
Wanted to leave	56	—	—
Wanted child to leave	—	11	—
Thought child should leave	—	—	5
Didn't mind	20	75	21
Child not sure what teacher thought	—	—	40
Didn't want to leave	24	—	—
Wanted child to stay	—	14	—
Thought child should stay	—	—	34
Total	100	100	100
(No. of 15–18s)	(147)	(147)	(147)

A slightly higher proportion of teachers, moreover, of boys with fathers in non-manual occupations were felt to have wanted the children to stay longer at school, than applied to boys with fathers in manual work. A much higher proportion of boys from manual workers' homes, however, had not been sure of the teachers' views about their leaving than was the case for boys from the homes of non-manual workers.

It is not easy to explain why so many children should have not known what their teachers felt about their leaving though it could be related to the tendency for the enthusiastic leavers to be more alienated from their teachers than others (as is shown in the frequency with which they selected certain favourable and unfavourable references to their teachers[17]). It

---

[17] See Chapter IV.

would be open to the interpretation that for many children their leaving was not a matter for discussion with the teachers, and there was, therefore, little opportunity for the children to get to know the teacher's viewpoint. ˙This could have arisen if the child's leaving had become a long-accepted matter and was not a matter on which the teachers were expected to pass an opinion; it could also mean that the children felt their teachers were indifferent. Whatever the explanation, it is clear that the teachers emerge as having more frequently wanted the children to remain at school than was the case for either the parents or the children, even though a substantial group of boys and girls did not know, apparently, what their teachers' views were.

The same picture applies, more or less, when the replies relating to the parents' and teachers' views were analysed according to how the children felt about leaving. The views of parents were not substantially different whether or not their children wanted to leave school, except that a higher proportion of girls who were less willing to leave school felt that their parents had not minded about their leaving, than was the case among the more eager school leavers. It was evident, however, that among the reluctant leavers, higher proportions of boys and girls felt that their teachers had wanted them to stay compared with the rest of the sample; this was very marked for the girls; in other words, it seems, that where children, particularly girls, wanted to stay, or would not have minded staying, their views coincided more closely with that of their teachers than with that of their parents.

SUMMARY

When asked how much they had wanted to leave school at the time of leaving, the replies showed that over one-half of the girls and almost one-half of the boys had been eager to leave school; nearly one in four had wanted to very much. Girls tended more than boys to have strong feelings, one way or the other, and relatively fewer of them had not minded about leaving school. A dislike of school, particularly among the girls (which centred mainly on aspects of teachers, school work and school discipline); and among the boys, the feeling of not learning anything and doubts as to their academic ability, were the most important reasons for wanting to leave school; in contrast, a liking for school and a wish for further education were the most important considerations for those who had been less anxious to leave school.

The majority of boys and girls had considered, at one time or another, staying on at school though rather more boys had done so than had girls. A dislike of school and the feeling that they lacked ability were the chief reasons offered by those who had not thought of staying longer at school. Moreover, these boys and girls tended to refer to the extra school year as being only appropriate for the academically able pupils. Job prospects and the completion of courses were important reasons for sixteen-year-old leavers to have rejected any idea of remaining at school. For those who had considered staying on at school, doubt as to their academic ability was the chief reason for boys and a dislike of school for girls. Boys more frequently than girls referred to job prospects and the wish to earn money, while girls more frequently than boys referred to family circumstances and to the fact that there seemed no point in their remaining longer at school. Doubts about their academic ability were expressed less frequently by sixteen-year-old boy leavers for whom job prospects were very much more important than they were for the younger leavers. This was particularly so for boys entering apprenticeships.

Social class factors, as defined in very broad categories, though, in the case of boys, associated with higher proportions of enthusiastic leavers from the homes of manual workers, were not apparently as important as was family size. Much higher proportions of boys and girls from smaller families had wanted to leave school than had leavers from larger families. There was also a tendency for boys and girls less well placed in class or stream to reject more frequently than others any question of a longer school life for themselves. The proportions of boys considering staying on also varied with social class and relatively fewer of the sons of semi- and unskilled workers had thought of staying longer at school than had boys with fathers in skilled and intermediate occupations.

A surprisingly high proportion of children did not know what their teachers felt about their leaving; nevertheless, teachers emerge as having more frequently wanted children to remain at school than was the case for either parents or children. Where children wanted to stay, their views coincided more closely with that of their teachers than with that of their parents; boys and girls who had been reluctant to leave were less likely, moreover, to have had the support of their parents if they came from homes of manual workers.

It would thus seem that it was the nature of their experience of education or certain aspects of it, which led many school leavers to reject the idea of further education and to conclude that it was an unattractive or unrealistic proposition for them. To trace how this alienation arose was beyond the scope of the present inquiry. Since, however, the environment of school constitutes the major part of formal educational experience, it is of some interest now to consider how school leavers perceived their teachers and schools when asked to recall their chief impressions of them.

CHAPTER IV

IMPRESSIONS OF TEACHERS AND SCHOOLS

INTRODUCTION

There have been relatively few studies undertaken to discover the attitudes of children towards their teachers and schools. This is, perhaps, surprising since the attitudes of children and their motivation for learning might be assumed to be influenced in large degree by the professional competence and personal qualities of the teachers, on the one hand, and by the organizational and administrative characteristics of the school, on the other. As Floud and Halsey have said[1]:

> The child may come to school ill-equipped for and hostile to, learning under any educational regime, but for the most part his educability depends as much on the assumptions, values and aims personified in the teacher and embodied in the school organization into which he is supposed to assimilate himself, as on those he brings from his home.

Several studies which have been carried out have been based largely on eliciting from children at school their evaluation of what constitutes a good or bad teacher; how they rank in order of importance certain qualities of teachers and what they like and dislike about their teachers. These studies are important since they suggest that children may evaluate the teachers' ability to teach more highly than their personal qualities, though the ability to keep order with fairness about punishment, particularly in having no favourites, has also been shown to rank highly.[2,3] They were also particularly useful in the present inquiry since their findings suggested a basis for assessing the references of young people to their teachers and schools as 'favourable' or 'unfavourable' comment.

For the purpose of the present inquiry, it was necessary to devise questions to put to young people at work which would reveal something of their impressions of their teachers and schools, as they now recalled them. A check list of items, from which young people were asked to select those which most closely applied to what they remembered about their teachers and schools, was considered the most appropriate method for obtaining

---

[1] J. Floud and A. H. Halsey, 'The Sociology of Education', *Current Sociology*, VII, No. 3, 1958.

[2] Phillip H. Taylor, 'Children's Evaluation of the Characteristics of a Good Teacher', *British Journal of Educational Psychology* **32**, 1962.

[3] Eric A. Allen, 'The Attitudes to School and Teachers in a Secondary Modern School', *British Journal of Educational Psychology*, **31**, February 1961.

the information in the time allowed for interviewing. It was decided to use, however, the same check list for teachers as used elsewhere in the questionnaire for eliciting the opinions of school leavers about their supervisors at work (the latter having been adopted from a N.I.I.P. study[4]). Not only did this check list contain items which corresponded closely to the references made by children to teachers both in the pilot stage of the present inquiry and in other studies; but its use for obtaining comment about teachers and supervision allowed a comparison to be made of the relative differences with which school leavers regarded their teachers of the past and their supervisors of the present.[5]

FAVOURABLE AND UNFAVOURABLE REFERENCES

References relating to teachers and schools were divided into favourable and unfavourable comment and classified according to the professional aspects of teaching (i.e. those most closely related to the task of teaching); to the personal attributes of teachers; to the efficiency of the school and to its general atmosphere.

Teachers

Both boys and girls rather more frequently referred to the professional merits and demerits of their teachers than to their personal qualities; moreover, this greater frequency was apparent in both favourable and unfavourable items (see Table 10).

The net balance of favourable and unfavourable comment, on these two aspects of teachers' qualities, can conveniently be indicated by the ratio of favourable to unfavourable comments made (expressed as percentages of the total number of possible comments in each category).[6] This calculation shows that both boys and girls viewed their teachers' personal qualities more favourably, on balance, than they did the purely professional aspects of the way they were taught. The difference between the two aspects was rather small for the boys, but was substantial for the girls who made, on average, a notably smaller number of favourable comments about the professional qualities of their teachers than did the boys.

[4] J. D. Handyside, op. cit.
[5] See Chapter XVI, pages 244–6, 248-9.
[6] The sub-division of the items included in the check list was as follows:

| | Comment about teachers | | Comment about schools | |
	Professional	Personal	Efficiency	Atmosphere
	(No. of items)			
Favourable items	9	9	5	3
Unfavourable items	6	7	5	5
Total	15	16	10	8

TABLE 10. Proportion of favourable and unfavourable references to teachers, distinguishing professional from personal qualities.

	Favourable	Unfavourable	Total	Ratio of favourable to unfavourable
Boys		(Per cent)		
Professional qualities	36	22	30	1·6
Personal qualities	29	16	23	1·9
Total	32	18	26	1·8
Girls				
Professional qualities	29	22	26	1·3
Personal qualities	28	14	22	2·0
Total	28	18	24	1·6
Boys	Total number of possible references[a]			
Professional qualities	1647	1098	2745	..
Personal qualities	1647	1281	2928	..
Total	3294	2379	5673	..
Girls				
Professional qualities	1323	882	2205	..
Personal qualities	1323	1029	2352	..
Total	2646	1911	4557	..

a Number of items on the check list multiplied by number of boys or girls interviewed.

This finding is perhaps of some significance in the light of Allen's study,[7] in which he found that boys and girls placed professional competence as first in order of importance of favourable comment on teachers; and Taylor's study,[8] in which he found that children placed greatest emphasis on good teaching and least on personal qualities of the teachers. The fact that in the present inquiry school leavers, particularly the girls, were more favourably impressed with the personal, rather than with the professional, attributes of their teachers may mean that they had a less satisfactory experience of what was the most important aspect of school for them, to be taught and to learn, since to satisfy this need requires, above all, professional ability.

Schools

There was some difference between boys and girls in the emphasis they placed on efficiency and 'atmosphere' in the schools they had attended.

[7] Eric A. Allen, op. cit.
[8] Phillip H. Taylor, op. cit.

The proportion of references made by boys to items relating to school efficiency (30 per cent) was somewhat greater than those for school 'atmosphere' (26 per cent), while for girls the reverse patterns held (24 as against 29 per cent) (Table 11).

TABLE 11. Proportion of favourable and unfavourable references to schools, distinguishing efficiency from atmosphere.

	Favourable	Unfavourable	Total	Ratio of favourable to unfavourable
Boys		(Per cent)		
Efficiency	40	20	30	2·0
Atmosphere	30	24	26	1·2
Total	36	22	28	1·6
Girls				
Efficiency	30	18	24	1·7
Atmosphere	23	32	29	0·7
Total	27	25	26	1·1
Boys	Total number of possible references[a]			
Efficiency	915	915	1830	..
Atmosphere	549	915	1464	..
Total	1464	1830	3294	..
Girls				
Efficiency	735	735	1470	..
Atmosphere	441	735	1176	..
Total	1176	1470	2646	..

a Number of items in the check list multiplied by number of boys or girls interviewed.

Both boys and girls, however, took a much more favourable view, on average, of their schools' efficiency than of the general atmosphere within them. Among the boys, the proportion of favourable references to various aspects of school efficiency was double that for unfavourable ones; for the girls, a generally similar picture emerged, though the ratio of favourable to unfavourable references was somewhat smaller for them than for boys. As regards references to school 'atmosphere', there was a slight net balance of favourable comments among the boys but for girls the net balance was distinctly unfavourable.

This particular response of girls is of interest in the light of Morris's study of the development of value-judgments in adolescents, in which he suggests that formal staff pressures on girls at school are greater than on boys, since girls are expected to be better behaved; but girls themselves do not place such weight upon behaving 'better' than boys[9]. This may be one of the factors underlying the apparent greater critical sensitivity of girls to the atmosphere rather than to the efficiency of their schools.

Frequency distribution of the ratio of favourable to unfavourable references

The distribution of the ratio of favourable to unfavourable comment is of some interest (Table 12). It shows, for instance, that while about one in five of the boys and girls had more unfavourable than favourable comment to make of their teachers (and many of them made no favourable comment at all), the majority selected more favourable than unfavourable references and nearly one-quarter no, or hardly any, unfavourable references. Quite a different picture applied to the ratio of comment on schools. Over two-fifths of the sample selected mainly, or wholly, unfavourable items and only very small minorities wholly or mainly favourable ones; there was also a fair degree of consistency in the pattern of replies for boys and for girls. Even allowing for the fact that the check list of items relating to schools contained a higher ratio of unfavourable to favourable comment than did that relating to teachers, it nonetheless evoked relatively more critical comment. This may be due, in part, to the inhibitions of children in criticizing people rather than institutions; on the other hand, teachers may have redeemed schools whose aims and values, as manifested through types of organization and administration, did not correspond with those of their pupils.

TABLE 12. Frequency distribution of ratio of favourable to unfavourable references to teachers and schools.

Ratio	References to teachers		References to schools	
	Boys	Girls	Boys	Girls
	(Per cent of sample)			
Under 0·5[a]	11	7	23	25
0·5–0·9	11	12	20	23
1·0–1·9	17	23	20	22
2·0–2·9	11	15	12	5
3·0–4·9	14	12	11	8
5·0–9·9	11	8	6	5
10·0 and over[b]	25	23	8	12
Total	100	100	100	100

a Many in this group made no favourable comments.
b Most in this group made no unfavourable comments.

[9] J. F. Morris, 'The Development of Adolescent Value Judgments', *British Journal of Educational Psychology*, **28**, 1958.

THE FREQUENCY OF FAVOURABLE AND UNFAVOURABLE REFERENCES

Though favourable outnumbered unfavourable comment in general, there is, nevertheless, a relatively low 'score' given to the favourable items as measured by the frequency with which these items were selected. If the school leavers are regarded as 'consumers' of an educational service then the relatively low frequencies with which they selected what might be considered as some of the more positive aspects of this 'service' suggests that they were not wholly satisfied with what they had experienced. Moreover, the order of frequency with which favourable and unfavourable references were selected indicates the extent to which particular aspects of teaching and school organization made impressions on children which they retained after leaving school.

Teachers

The most favourable impression that young people seemed to have received of their teachers was that they were helpful. More boys and girls referred to this personal quality than to any other characteristic of their teachers. Only three other favourable items—that their teachers were

TABLE 13. Favourable references to teachers.

	Boys	Girls
Professional	*(Per cent of total)*	
Knew their job	50	46
Explained things clearly	50	38
Encouraged me	41	40
Efficient	31	13
Listened to what I wanted to say	31	32
Praised me when I did well	31	31
Good to work for	30	18
Clever	20	11
Full of ideas	13	15
Personal		
Helpful	58	58
Fair	51	34
Treated me like a human being	34	34
Pleasant	30	33
Reliable	20	15
Sincere	16	9
Kind	13	22
Confident	11	9
Always kept promises	10	12
Total (Multiple replies)	100	100
(No. of 15–18s)	(183)	(147)

fair, knew their job, and explained things clearly—were selected by as many as one-half of the boys, the majority of the remaining items being selected by minorities of school leavers (Table 13). Only two in five of the sample felt that their teachers had encouraged them; less than one in three that their teachers had listened to what they wanted to say, praised them when they did well, or had been pleasant; fewer, particularly among the girls, referred to their teachers as good to work for, clever, reliable, or sincere; and only just over one in eight of the boys and one in five of the girls remembered their teachers as having been kind.

The most unfavourable impression retained was, evidently, that teachers had been strict and had had favourites (one-third to two-fifths were of this view); between one-quarter and one-fifth of the sample remembered their teachers as sarcastic and moody; more than one in seven had never known where they were with them, felt too much was expected of the pupils, referred to their teachers as having nagged them and as having been either too old or too young; nearly one-quarter of the girls, but fewer of the boys, also felt that their teachers had been muddled (Table 14).

TABLE 14. Unfavourable references to teachers.

	Boys	Girls
Professional	(*Per cent of total*)	
Strict	39	31
Had favourites	33	41
Never knew where you were with them	20	16
Expected too much	15	14
Didn't seem interested	11	6
Muddled	10	23
Personal		
Sarcastic	22	23
Moody	21	19
Too old	17	15
Too young	15	14
Nagging	14	18
Frightening	9	9
Interfering	3	3
Total (Multiple replies)	100	100
(No. of 15–18s)	(183)	(147)

These results are open to several interpretations. First, the fact that most items were selected only by minorities of the young people seen, suggests that perhaps the check list of items did not correspond with the kind of comment that school leavers wanted, or were most likely, to make about their teachers.

Second, the check list did not provide for any qualified comment, so that while there were school leavers who had no hesitation about selecting relevant items, there were others who were unwilling to commit themselves without some qualification. The results may reflect, therefore, more frequently the opinions of school leavers who saw their teachers predominantly in the terms listed, but not so frequently the opinions of school leavers who felt that these terms applied only sometimes or in certain circumstances.

Third, it is possible to assume that the school leavers in the sample did not rate their teachers very highly, and though only minorities selected unfavourable items as such, the majority—by default as it were—would seem to have made their opinions clear. If, moreover, the frequency of reference to favourable aspects of teachers is regarded as a test of either the professional or personal qualities of the teachers concerned, a 'pass' mark was obtained on relatively few of the total number of items on which school leavers were invited to comment.

Schools

By far the most favourable impression of school for the boys was that they had been offered a good standard of education; over one-half of the boys referred to their school in this way and they contrasted sharply with the girls of whom only just over one-quarter shared this view. Only minorities selected any other favourable item. The next in order of frequency for the boys was that their schools had been up to date (two-fifths) and then, in very similar proportions (between one-third and one-quarter), that it had had a good reputation, and helped everyone to do their best, had been efficient and the right size (Table 15).

TABLE 15. Favourable references to schools.

	Boys	Girls
Efficiency	*(Per cent of total)*	
Offered a good standard of education	54	28
Up to date	40	31
Helped everyone to do their best	32	27
Had a good reputation	31	24
Efficient	30	14
Atmosphere		
Friendly	34	31
Just the right size	28	17
Easy going	17	11
Total (Multiple replies)	100	100
(No. of 15–18s)	(183)	(147)

The girls were more evenly distributed than were the boys in their favourable impressions of school and though more felt that their school had been friendly and up to date (nearly one-third) almost as many also felt that they had been offered a good standard of education, had been helped to do their best and that their schools had had a good reputation (about one-quarter). Less frequently selected than other items were those relating to the school as easy going and efficient.

The most unfavourable impression of school, for both boys and girls, was strictness about timekeeping, over two in five selecting this particular item. No other unfavourable aspect of school was referred to as frequently, and were it not for the relatively high proportions of boys who felt that they had been offered a good standard of education, strictness about time-keeping would have been more frequently selected than would any other aspect of school, favourable or unfavourable. The emphasis on punctuality would therefore seem to have made a greater impact on school leavers than did the helpfulness, friendliness, efficiency, and reputation of their schools (Table 16).

TABLE 16. Unfavourable references to schools.

	Boys	Girls
Efficiency	(*Per cent of total*)	
A lot of lessons seemed a waste of time	25	26
Not enough practical training	21	13
Only seemed interested in the brainy ones	16	19
Too set in its ideas	13	9
Needed fresh people at the top	9	3
Atmosphere		
Strict about time keeping	45	46
Too many rules and regulations	21	21
Too strict about our behaviour	17	23
Not enough discipline	17	17
Too big	6	17
Total (Multiple replies)	100	100
(No. of 15–18s)	(183)	(147)

The next most unfavourable impression was that a lot of lessons had been a waste of time, one-quarter of the boys and the girls being of this view; in fact, almost as many girls felt this way about their lessons, as felt they had been offered a good standard of education, and nearly twice as many as felt that their schools had been efficient. One-quarter of the girls also felt that their schools had been too strict about their behaviour, while one-fifth of both boys and girls felt that there had been too many rules and regulations. Rather more boys than girls, proportionately, felt that

not enough practical training had been provided, though similar proportions of each sex (one in five or six) felt that their schools had only been
interested in the brainy ones and that there had not been enough discipline.
About one in eight of the boys referred to their school as having been too
set in its ideas, and one in ten felt that there had been need for fresh
people at the top. Rather smaller proportions of girls were of these views.
Hardly any of the boys, however, felt that their schools had been too big, yet
as many as one in six of the girls had been affected by this aspect of school.

A similar inference might be drawn from these results as for those relating to teachers—namely, that the majority of school leavers did not rate
their schools very highly, if the absence of favourable comment, and the
frequency of unfavourable comment, are used as the criteria for measuring
the general consensus of opinion.

IMPRESSIONS OF TEACHERS AND SCHOOLS AND
ATTITUDES TOWARDS LEAVING SCHOOL

Though it was not possible to trace the precise influence of teachers and
school organization on the ultimate decisions of school leavers, further
analysis showed, nevertheless, that unfavourable comment was more frequent among boys and girls who had been eager to leave school, among
leavers at fifteen and among those who had not considered the possibility
of remaining longer at school. Moreover, the enthusiastic leavers had,
generally, a much lower proportion of favourable to unfavourable comments about their teachers and schools than had the non-committal or the
reluctant leavers (Table 17).

Teachers

It was the boys who had been eager to leave school who less frequently
referred to their teachers as having encouraged them, as being confident
and full of ideas. In taking the views of the most reluctant leavers into
account, the differences were even more pronounced; for it was these boys
who most frequently described their teachers as having listened to what
they wanted to say and as clever, fair, and helpful. Girls' references to
teachers did not reveal such marked differences; enthusiastic leavers appeared to have a less favourable view only in so far as fewer, proportionately, felt their teachers had been encouraging and confident.

There were pronounced differences between age of leaving groups in the
proportions who felt that their teachers had kept their promises and had
been kind and confident. It would appear that, generally speaking, the
younger leavers tended more frequently to select items relating to the
teachers' personal qualities (pleasant, kind, fair, etc.), while the sixteen-
year-old leavers tended to choose references to professional qualities
(efficiency, knowledge of their job, ability to explain things clearly, etc.).

TABLE 17. Favourable and unfavourable references to teachers and schools in relation to attitudes to leaving school.

	Favourable	Unfavourable	Total	Ratio of favourable to unfavourable
A. REFERENCES TO TEACHERS[a]				
Boys		*(Per cent)*		
15-year-old leavers:				
Wanted to leave school	29	23	26	1·3
Others[b]	35	18	28	1·9
16-year-old leavers:				
Wanted to leave school	28	16	23	1·7
Others[b]	38	15	29	2·5
Girls				
15-year-old leavers:				
Wanted to leave school	24	19	22	1·3
Others[b]	31	15	24	2·1
B. REFERENCES TO SCHOOLS[c]				
Boys				
15-year-old leavers:				
Wanted to leave school	29	31	30	0·9
Others[b]	36	23	29	1·6
16-year-old leavers:				
Wanted to leave school	37	20	28	1·9
Others[b]	42	13	26	3·2
Girls				
15-year-old leavers:				
Wanted to leave school	20	29	25	0·7
Others[b]	32	22	27	1·5

a For number of possible references to teachers (= 100 per cent), see Table 10.
b Didn't mind leaving school or did not want to leave school.
c For number of possible references to schools (= 100 per cent), see Table 11.

Logically enough, it was those who had most wanted to leave school who referred more frequently to certain unfavourable aspects of their teachers and higher proportions of the boys among them felt their teachers did not seem interested in them and had been moody, too young, too old, and had expected too much of them. The enthusiastic leavers among the girls, like the boys, not only more frequently than others had the impression that their teachers demanded too much of them but that they had nagged them. Proportionately more of them also described their teachers as having favourites, and as sarcastic as well as having made the children feel that they never knew where they were with them (Table 18).

The fifteen-year-old leavers were also more critical of their teachers in certain respects, than were the older leavers. The biggest difference was in the proportions who felt that their teachers had been frightening; one-sixth of the younger leavers had this impression compared with only a negligible proportion of older leavers. Relatively more of the younger leavers also described their teachers as nagging, as having favourites, as too old, or as strict. On the other hand, a higher proportion of the older leavers referred to their teachers as sarcastic or as muddled.

TABLE 18. Attitudes to leaving school and unfavourable references to teachers.[a]

	Wanted to leave school (1)	Didn't mind or did not want to leave (2)	Ratio of (1) to (2)
Boys	(Per cent of total)		
Didn't seem interested	16	7	2·3
Moody	28	15	1·9
Too young	20	11	1·8
Expected too much	21	13	1·6
Too old	21	14	1·5
Girls			
Expected too much	20	8	2·5
Nagging	20	8	2·5
Never knew where you were with them	20	12	1·7
Sarcastic	27	19	1·4
Had favourites	46	35	1·3
Too young	9	20	0·4
Total in sample (=100 per cent)			
Boys	90	93	
Girls	82	65	

a Since the inquiry was not based on a random sample, standard errors of the percentages making particular comments cannot validly be used. Instead, the comments in this and subsequent tables of the same kind are listed in order of the ratio of the percentages calculated for the two age groups making any given comment, as a guide to the probable relative importance of the differences in views of these two groups. For this purpose, only those comments are listed for which the percentage for one group (a) was at least 1·2 times that for the other, and (b) differed by at least 6 percentage points from that for the other group. It is, however, of interest to note—when interpreting the results—that had the sample been a random one, the standard error for the group of fifteen-year-olds would have been ±10 per cent of the percentages shown; for the sixteen-year-olds, the standard error would be ±11 per cent of the percentages shown. In other words, for the former group, frequencies of 20 and 50 per cent would read 20±4, and 50±10 per cent, respectively, using 2 standard errors in each case; while for the latter group, the corresponding frequencies would have read 20±4½ and 50±11 per cent, respectively.

Schools

The views of the willing and the less willing leavers contrasted sharply with each other as regards favourable comment about schools; the boys, particularly, were most at variance with each other as to whether their respective schools had offered them a good standard of education. Only one-fifth of the boys who had been eager to leave school had this particular impression of their schools compared with one-half of the less eager leavers and three-fifths of the really reluctant. The more willing leavers also tended to have, though not to such a marked degree, a less favourable view of their schools' efficiency and friendliness; though they were also more inclined to describe their schools as easy going, as having a good reputation and helping everyone to do their best. The balance of opinion among the girls was quite different from that of the boys, and it was the willing leavers who tended to feel that their schools had been friendly and the reluctant that their schools had been easy going or helpful.

Opinions differed sharply between fifteen- and sixteen-year-old leavers only in respect of certain favourable aspects of school. Older leavers were much more inclined to feel that their schools had offered them a good standard of education, had had a good reputation and had been efficient, and, to a lesser extent, that their schools had been friendly and helpful.

Unfavourable references to schools evoked a greater contrast in viewpoint between the willing and the less willing leavers both for boys and for girls, than did any reference to teachers (favourable or otherwise) or favourable reference to schools; and, though the frequency and subject of comment differed as between boys and girls, the girls were more sharply at variance with each other than were the boys (Table 19).

TABLE 19. Attitudes to leaving school and unfavourable references to school.

	Wanted to leave school (1)	Didn't mind or did not want to leave (2)	Ratio of (1) to (2)
Boys	(*Per cent of total*)		
Need fresh people at the top	15	5	3·0
Only seemed interested in the brainy ones	23	9	2·6
Too many rules and regulations	30	13	2·3
A lot of lessons seemed a waste of time	36	17	2·1
Not enough practical training	25	17	1·5
Girls			
Too many rules and regulations	28	6	4·7
Only interested in the brainy ones	28	8	3·5
Too strict about behaviour	27	9	3·0
A lot of lessons seemed a waste of time	31	20	1·6
Strict about time keeping	52	36	1·4
Total in sample (= 100 *per cent*)			
Boys	90	93	
Girls	82	65	

For the boys the greatest relative differences were in the much higher proportions of enthusiastic leavers who felt that their schools needed fresh people at the top, only seemed interested in the brainy ones, that a lot of lessons had seemed a waste of time and that there had been too many rules and regulations. They also more frequently, though not to the same extent, felt that insufficient practical training had been given them.

Among the girls the sharpest contrast in view was in the respective proportions who felt that there had been too many rules and regulations at school. Over one-quarter of the girls most eager to leave had had this impression compared with only one in sixteen among the less willing leavers. A similar criterion applied to the reference that the schools had only been interested in the brainy ones. The more eager the leaver, the relatively more frequently they also felt that the schools had been strict about time keeping, strict about behaviour, and that a lot of lessons had been a waste of time.

Similar opinions were more frequently expressed by younger than older leavers and, among the boys, it was the leavers at fifteen who were more inclined to describe their schools as having been interested only in the brainy ones, that a lot of lessons had been a waste of time, and that not enough practical training had been given. It was the older rather than the younger leaver, however, who more frequently referred to schools as having too many rules and regulations, reflecting perhaps a less tolerant view of school discipline by older children.

NEEDS AND EXPERIENCES

Because of the different terms used to classify the comments of children about their teachers and schools in the present inquiry, compared with previous studies, it is not possible to make any precise comparative analysis of results. This is unfortunate, since if the opinions of the children covered in these studies as to what they felt were the important qualities of teachers are a reliable guide to educational needs, then it might have been possible to use their evaluations to assess how far the needs of school leavers (in the present inquiry) had been fulfilled in the light of the latter's references to what their teachers were like.

Hollis' definitions[10] approximate most closely to certain items in the check list relating to teachers used in the present inquiry, though there is no precise correspondence. Allowing for these differences, a rough comparison of needs and experiences can be made for five aspects of teaching.

Hollis asked 800 children of different ages to rank in order of importance, seven statements about a teacher's behaviour. He found that 'the

[10] A. V. Hollis, *The Personal Relationship in Teaching*, M.A. Thesis, University of Birmingham, 1935.

quality of explaining difficulties patiently' was conclusively the most popular. Assuming this quality, therefore, to represent the most important requirement of teachers, and assuming the reference to 'explained things clearly' in the present inquiry corresponds closely to the definition used by Hollis, then it would seem that not more than one-half of the boys, and less than two-fifths of the girls, felt that they had been taught by teachers with this vital quality (Table 20).

TABLE 20. Needs and experiences: a comparison.

Statement relating to teachers' behaviour[a]	Ranking order in Hollis'[b] inquiry	Frequency in present inquiry			
		Boys		Girls	
		%	Order	%	Order
Explaining difficulties patiently/explaining things clearly	1	50	3	38	4
Friendly and sympathetic/helpful	2	58	1	58	1
Just and fair/fair	3	51	2	34	5
Allowing pupils to ask plenty of questions/ listened to what I wanted to say	5	31	8	32	6
Discipline/strict	7	39	6	31	7
Number of children	800	183		147	

a The first statement is that used in the Hollis inquiry: the second is the nearest equivalent in the present inquiry.

b A. W. Hollis, 1938, op. cit.

In the Hollis study, being 'friendly and sympathetic' ranked second in importance; the check list of items does not contain an equivalent to this, but using the term 'helpful' as representing rather similar behaviour, then it would seem that the teachers came much nearer to meeting the needs of the children covered in the present inquiry in this respect, in so far as almost three-fifths of school leavers referred to them as having this particular quality.

Next in importance in the Hollis study was the quality of being 'just and fair'; the boys' teachers in the present inquiry would seem to have fulfilled this requirement rather more frequently than did those of the girls, for while one-half of the boys referred to their teachers as having been 'fair', only one-third of the girls were of this opinion; moreover, about one-third of both boys and girls referred to their teachers as having had favourites. Substantial proportions of school leavers, therefore, would not seem to have had their need for fair treatment satisfied by the teachers who taught them.

The next comparable quality 'allowing pupils to ask plenty of questions' was ranked fifth; the nearest equivalent term in the check list of items was that relating to teachers who 'listened to what I wanted to say'. Under one-third of the boys and girls interviewed in the present inquiry, felt that their teachers revealed this characteristic. Least important, according to the children in the Hollis study, were the disciplinary requirements of teaching and, interestingly enough, the majority of school leavers in the present inquiry did not refer to their teachers as having been strict, though substantial minorities did. Since the majority of young people did not appear to regard their teachers as 'strict', while smaller proportions felt that their teachers had 'explained things clearly', it would seem that the teachers in question came much nearer to meeting their pupils' needs in the least important requirement on the 'Hollis scale' than they achieved for the most important.

SUMMARY

School leavers were asked to select from a check list of items those which most closely applied to what they remembered about their teachers and schools. Though favourable outnumbered unfavourable comment in general, the relatively low score given to favourable items as measured by the frequency with which these items were selected, suggests that school leavers did not rate their teachers or their schools very highly. Only one favourable item relating to teachers (that they had been helpful) was referred to by a majority of school leavers and only four other favourable items out of a total of twenty-six relating to school and to teachers, were selected by one-half or more, and then only by boys. This, combined with the relatively substantial minorities who commented on unfavourable aspects of teachers and schools, suggests that school leavers were not highly satisfied consumers of the educational service.

Certain favourable qualities of the teachers—most of all their helpfulness and their knowledge of their job, their ability to explain things clearly and their encouragement of the children, and for boys their fairness, could be said to have made the greatest impact on the young people seen, though only between two-fifths and three-fifths of the sample recalled their teachers in these particular respects. Rather fewer children remembered their teachers as, among other things, pleasant, efficient, and good to work for, and only small minorities recalled their teachers as having been, among other things, kind or clever. Strictness, having favourites, being sarcastic and moody, were essentially the substance of many of the unfavourable impressions left with children of their teachers and made a stronger impression than did certain favourable aspects of teachers; but teachers who nagged, who were too young or too old, who expected too much or who did not seem interested, also contributed to the unfavourable impressions that some school leavers had of the people who had taught them at school.

Schools which seemed to offer a good standard of education would seem to have made the greatest impact on boys since this was the only aspect of school selected which represented majority opinion. Strictness in time-keeping however made the next greatest impact on boys and the strongest impression on girls, exceeding in frequency all other references to school and accounting for nearly one-half of the total sample. Relatively fewer boys and girls remembered their schools as being friendly, up to date, helping everyone to do their best, with a good reputation and efficient.

Apart from an emphasis on punctuality, schools where the lessons were felt to have been a waste of time and the rules and regulations too many; where, particularly for girls, it was felt that behaviour was too strictly supervised and, particularly for boys, their practical training inadequate, would seem to have contributed most to the unfavourable impressions that substantial minorities of school leavers had of school after they had left their school days behind them.

A comparison between educational needs, as suggested by children's evaluations in a previous study, and the experiences of school leavers in the present inquiry, in regard to five characteristics of teachers, suggests that teachers came nearer to meeting children's requirements on what was felt to be of least importance—namely strictness—than on what had been ranked as of chief importance—the ability to explain things clearly.

CHAPTER V

THE LAST YEAR AT SCHOOL

ATTITUDES TO THE LAST YEAR AT SCHOOL

Attitudes to school could be assumed to vary as each school year brings its changes in teachers and activities, and as the time for leaving school and starting work approaches. It was thought of interest, therefore, to try to discover how school leavers regarded their last year of school and the extent to which this particular year was felt to have been more or less satisfactory than previous ones.

Their replies showed that in spite of the fact that substantial proportions of boys and girls had wanted to leave school, not more than one in five had actually disliked their last year at school, while more than one-half felt quite positively towards it (Table 21).

TABLE 21. Attitudes to the last year at school.

How liked the last year	Boys	Girls
	(Per cent of total)	
Very much	17	20
Quite a lot	37	30
Sub-total	54	50
Didn't mind	29	29
Disliked it	14	20
Disliked it very much	3	1
Sub-total	17	21
Total	100	100
(No. of 15–18s)	(183)	(147)

There is, logically enough, an association between the degree to which school was liked in the last year and the extent to which young people were eager to leave school; a much higher proportion of those who did not care for their last year at school were enthusiastic leavers compared with those who had liked their last year; similarly, a much higher proportion of those least eager to leave had liked their last year at school.

Even allowing for this, however, as many as two-fifths of the boys and girls who had liked their last year had also been among those most eager to leave school; and for them, a liking for their school-leaving year was not inconsistent with a wish to end their school days. Nor, in some cases, was a liking for school in the last year inconsistent with a dislike of school in general, since what was disliked was coming to an end. For such children, the last year was therefore liked because it was the last to be endured. The comments of some leavers make this attitude clear: 'I knew I had not long to go' and 'I had my mind on leaving, so it was the best year'.

Favourable experiences

But for nearly two-fifths of the sample of young people, the last year had been regarded favourably because it had offered them, to some degree, a more positive and satisfying experience than that of previous years. The last year at school for this group of school leavers was different for them in two important respects. Firstly, it had offered them a greater degree of freedom and responsibility than before. One in five commented on the friendlier relationships with teachers, on the relaxation of discipline, on the choice given to them in subjects, on their being allowed to work on their own and on their being treated by the teachers as adults and more grown-up. Relatively few of those who had disliked their last school year, however, referred to any such experience.

Some of many of the comments referring to these new freedoms were:

'It was a much better year. There was more freedom. We were not bullied and we could do what we liked.'

'The fourth to fifth year was such a contrast. We were treated as adults and there were several privileges. We could wear suits and nail varnish.'

'It was the best year of school. Up to the third year everyone is pushing you around. But in the last year you're older and you have certain privileges.'

'We were prefects and we were treated as complete adults. Everything seemed better. We could pick our subjects and we had time for private study. I thoroughly enjoyed it.'

Secondly, the last year offered to one in five of the boys and one in eight of the girls a more interesting year and one that had been, academically, more satisfying than others. References were made to having done better in their school work in this particular year and to having enjoyed the work and found it more worthwhile than at other times.

This experience, however, was confined exclusively to boys and girls who had liked their last school year and to girls who had actively disliked their last school year; and nearly two in five of the boys and one in seven of the girls who had liked their last year referred to what had been definite improvements in their academic work and/or interests (Table 22).

Typical comments were:

'It was the best year. We had better teachers and I got on better.'

'It took me five years to get up to where I was. I was told I was a late developer. I was just getting into the way of learning and using my brain.'

'I started to enjoy school in that last year. I seemed to hate it in the beginning, but I changed as I got older. It seemed to click.'

'I enjoyed it more than any other year. There was a broader outlook. I felt I was getting somewhere at last.'

TABLE 22. Reasons for attitudes to the last year at school.

| | How liked the last year at school | | | |
| | Boys | | Girls | |
	Very much Quite a lot	Didn't mind Disliked it Disliked it very much	Very much Quite a lot	Didn't mind Disliked it Disliked it very much
	(Per cent of total)			
More freedom, better relationships, etc.	39	14	42	8[b]
Got on better with work, work more interesting, etc.	38	—	15	9[c]
Always liked school	22	16	23	11
Not learning anything, nothing new	2	28[a]	5	16[d]
Disliked school or some aspect of it	—	14	—	31[e]
Best year	12	—	10	4
Worst year	—	9	—	5
Other	4	13	15	8.5
Don't know	2	2	1	—
No answer	3	1	—	—
Total (Multiple replies)	100	100	100	100
(No. of 15–18s)	(99)	(84)	(73)	(74)

a Two-thirds of those who disliked the last year felt this.
b and c None of those who disliked their last year referred to either of these.
d Over one-third who disliked their last year felt this.
e Nearly three-fifths of those who disliked their last year disliked school or some aspect of it.

Unfavourable experiences

The chief reason for boys' dislike of their last school year was the feeling that they had learnt nothing new and that school activities had been boring and repetitive. Moreover, twice as many leavers at fifteen than at sixteen complained of being bored:[1]

'It was the same old stuff. We did not really learn anything new although we got some privileges.'

'It was alright at first but then it dragged on. We did not do anything new. I regret now having stayed on.'

'It was most boring. We did not learn anything. We learnt the same in the fourth year as in the third.'

Quite a substantial group of leavers—approximately one in six—while feeling that the last school year had not offered them anything new or different from other years, had liked it, nevertheless, because they had always liked school. Their attitude was consistent, therefore, with their generally favourable view of their school years.

Equally consistent were those who disliked their last year because they had always disliked school; some, however, disliked school more in their last year either because they found it hard to endure ('It just seemed to drag on'), or because it seemed to be worse than other years ('It was worse; it was stricter than ever'; 'Being older the teachers got you down more'), or because some aspects of school previously liked or tolerated became more difficult. This was particularly so among the girls, many of whom in this category had, evidently, difficulties with their school work.

'There was too much homework. It spoilt things.'

'There was too much working on your own.'

'The subjects got harder and I got more and more fed up with the work.'

'The exams worried me. I would not have minded but for the exams.'

The proportion of girls who referred to some specific aspect of school disliked in their last year was more than twice as high as that for boys, and it would seem that this is partly due to relatively more girls having had difficulties with their school work. Proportionately more boys, on the other hand, referred to their having found their last school year more profitable from the work point of view. This contrast is the most important one between boys and girls in their attitudes towards the last year. It might be related to different levels of ability.[2] It might be that the girls tended to be more anxious about their work and more critical of their

[1] One major difference between the fifteen- and sixteen-year-old leavers was, of course, that only a small minority of the younger leavers had taken any G.C.E., R.S.A., or similar qualifying or school-leaving examination in their last year, whereas the majority of the leavers at sixteen had done so. Fifteen-year-old leavers also tended to have been 'streamed' to a greater degree than had leavers at sixteen, but this would appear to be partly due to the fact that 'streaming' was not so prevalent in secondary modern schools in the fifth year. Fifteen-year-old leavers also tended to contain higher proportions of boys in the middle and bottom streams than leavers at sixteen.

[2] Slightly higher proportions in the sample of boys were in the top stream than in the sample of girls.

failures[3]; but rather more of the boys, proportionately to girls, had taken courses which had prepared them for school-leaving examinations, and this may have added to their sense of achievement in their last year at school.

Streaming, class position, and examinations

Since the feeling of not learning anything seemed to be one of the chief reasons for not liking the last school year, it was thought of interest to trace the extent to which the position occupied by school leavers in the streaming system, and in class, appeared to have influenced attitudes towards the last school year.

The analysis showed that, in fact, higher proportions of those in the top stream and, irrespective of stream, those above-average in class, were to be found among those who had liked their last school year than among those who had not been so enthusiastic. Though the differences for boys were not very substantial, those for girls were, the proportions in the top stream and class position being almost twice as high among those who had liked their last year at school (nearly one-half) than among those who had either disliked this particular year or had not minded it (about one-quarter). The contrast was even greater when those who had not been streamed were excluded from the analysis. Well over two-thirds of the 'streamed' girls who had liked school had been in the top streams, compared with little more than one-third among those with negative or non-committal views of their last school year.

Taking examinations in the last year, however, would not seem to have influenced attitudes at all, the proportions liking or not liking their last school year being almost identical, irrespective of whether school-leaving examinations had been taken or not.

For girls particularly, and to a lesser extent for boys, it was a position in class lower than 'above average', which would seem to be associated, at best, with a non-committal attitude towards, and at worst, a definite dislike of, the last school year. This would not be inconsistent, however, with other findings in this study, since higher proportions of those who were least enthusiastic about their last year at school complained that they were not learning anything, as also did higher proportions of those who most wanted to leave school, compared with the rest of the sample.

Those who benefited from a new experience

Since liking the last year at school was associated not only with a liking for school in general but, to a greater degree, with whether this particular

---

[3] This is suggested by a study of 290 adolescent girls of whom 57 per cent had problems connected with school work, particularly examinations. See M. Hall, 'A Study of the Attitudes of Adolescent Girls to their own Physical, Intellectual, and Social Development', *Education Research*, **6**, No. 1, November 1963.

year had offered a different experience in work and relationships from other years, it was thought of interest to trace who had benefited from this experience. To what extent, for instance, had those with some sort of difficulty or dissatisfaction with school been exposed to a new and more satisfactory school experience; or to what extent had those with a generally more favourable regard for school experienced yet more favourable conditions in their last year?

The analysis,[4] though based on relatively small numbers nevertheless showed that there was a tendency for those who had liked school and who had, apparently, fewer difficulties and doubts than had others, to feel more positively about their last year. Boys and girls who had disliked school, who had encountered difficulties with their school work or with their teachers, or who were uncertain about their academic ability, did not, to the same extent as did others, feel that their last school year had brought any change for the better for them. Thus there was a tendency for school life to improve more frequently for those whose school experiences were already more favourable than for others. The fact that there were some school leavers whose dissatisfactions with school were, evidently, offset in their last school year by some definite improvement either in their school work, in their treatment by the teachers, or in the atmosphere within the school, suggests the need for careful study of those factors, environmental and personal, which may underly such changes.

SUMMARY

Just about one-half of the young people interviewed had liked their last year at school and relatively few—not more than one in five—had disliked it. Though a much higher proportion of those who did not care for their last year were also those most eager to leave school, as many as two in five of those who had liked their last year had been enthusiastic leavers.

The last year was regarded favourably because it had offered a more satisfying experience than had other years—either because school work itself had been more interesting or more fruitful—but more often because school leavers had found relationships easier with teachers, discipline more relaxed, responsibilities more frequently given and they themselves treated by teachers as more adult. The chief reasons for disliking the last year was for boys that they had learnt nothing new and that it had been boring and repetitive; and, for girls, a dislike of school or some aspect of it.

The age of leaving only slightly affected the proportions who had liked their last year but relatively more of the boys leaving at fifteen than at

---

[4] Using comments given when discussing attitudes towards leaving school as an indication of difficulty or dissatisfaction with school, three main groups were distinguished. Those who felt they were not learning anything; those who had doubts as to their ability; and those who had disliked school (or some aspect of it). Their replies regarding their last year at school were then analysed.

sixteen felt that the last year had offered them nothing new. It would seem that those with special difficulties dislikes or doubts—e.g. those who had disliked school, those who felt that they were not learning anything and those who doubted their academic ability, were less likely than were others to feel that the last school year had improved things for them; school life would seem to have got better for those who were already more favourably disposed towards it.

CHAPTER VI

A RETROSPECTIVE VIEW

REGRETS ABOUT LEAVING SCHOOL

Looking back on their decision to leave school the majority of young people seen (just under three-quarters of the boys and over three-quarters of the girls) had, at the time of interview, no regrets. On the contrary, many, judging from their comments, felt that they were deriving more pleasure from being at work than when they were at school, and that their decision to leave had, in retrospect, been justified by their experiences of being at work. In direct contrast were the views of those who looked back on their school-leaving decision with regret or uncertainty. Not only did smaller proportions of these refer to the satisfactions of being at work; but higher proportions were dissatisfied with their status and type of employment (having hoped for something better), or with some other aspect of their working life (Table 23).

TABLE 23. Reasons for regrets about leaving school.

| | Whether regrets about leaving school | | | |
| | Boys | | Girls | |
	No	Yes/Uncertain	No	Yes/Uncertain
	(Per cent of total)			
Likes being at work/ present job	51	25	45	..
Learning something new/ useful	10	2	3·5	..
Did **not** like school	10	—	9	..
More freedom/ independence, etc.	8	—	22	..
Likes earning money	5	2	3·5	..
Would like more education	6	53	1	..
Would like better job	1	22	—	..
Some aspect of working conditions or being at work	2	11	1	..
Misses friends	—	11	2	..
Other	13	20	9	..
Don't know	5	4	19	..
No answer	5	4	3	..
Total (Multiple replies)	100	100	100	100
(No. of 15–18s)	(128)	(55)	(112)	(35)

Regrets about leaving school were much more often expressed by leavers at fifteen than by those who had left school at the age of sixteen or over. Over one-quarter, for instance, of the boys and one-seventh of the girls who had left school at fifteen now regretted their decision or were uncertain of it, compared with only one in twelve of the boys and hardly any of the girls who had left at sixteen. Similarly, proportionately more of those with doubts or regrets had left at fifteen than had those without regrets.

The reasons for not having regrets

The boys and girls who had no regrets about having left school were distinguished from the rest of the sample by the frequency of reference made to their being happy in their work, and to the advantages of a working life, compared with being at school. About one-half of the boys and over two-fifths of the girls whose decision to leave had been, in their view, fully vindicated by events, spoke enthusiastically of being at work:

'I am very glad to be at work. The happiest days are not at school but at work.'

'Work is much better than school. There's not so much discipline. You're treated as an older person. It's not like school.'

'I'm happy where I am. I enjoy what I am doing and what I am learning. I've made more friends. I have more free time. And the money is useful.'

Some felt that they had got on better at work than they did at school:

'I've got on so much better at work. I've grown up more at work than if I'd stayed on at school.'

Other boys and girls had compared notes with their contemporaries at school and concluded that being at work was still preferable. Boys, particularly, commented on this because they felt leaving school had given them an earlier start in their working careers, and had made it easier for them to know what they wanted to do:

'It would have taken another year to find out what I wanted to do. Being at work helped me find out what I wanted. If I'd stayed on at school I would still be wondering, like some of my friends are. I feel more confident.'

'There's a feeling of uselessness at school, but work means you've started on the road somewhere, whatever you want to do. Boys who are still at school will still have to start at the bottom.'

Then there was the feeling of being treated differently, of meeting more people, and gaining more experience of life in general:

'Being at work broadens your interests. School life is so confined.'

'People treat you better because you have opinions of your own. They listen. At school you have to do what the teachers say.'

'I have found people I never met before. We all share the same interests and I'm doing work that I like.'

Girls, rather more frequently than boys, referred to the fact that going to work had given them more freedom and independence and had helped them grow up more quickly than had school. Over one in five commented on this aspect of working compared with less than one in ten of the boys:

'I'm much more independent now. I could not have what I have now if I was still at school. I have money to buy clothes and I can wear what I like. I can do what my friends do.'

'Everything has been a change. Life has been more exciting. I seemed childish at first but I grew up quickly.'

Both boys and girls, however, referred to being free of school worries:

'I feel freer at work. I used to worry about my homework.'

'There's not nearly so much worry as I had about school work. I used to think about school every day and worry about the work. Now I don't have to worry.'

The chance to train and to attend day or evening school provided by some types of employment, particularly apprenticeships, was referred to by one in ten of the boys, but by relatively few of the girls. Attendance at classes and learning a skilled trade was seen to have definite advantages over what might have been an uncertain academic future at school:

'I am doing the same exams as I would have done at school and it only involves extra work in the evening. Meanwhile I am getting experience and earning money.'

Almost one in ten of the boys and girls who had no second thoughts about their school-leaving decision, had disliked school and had found, therefore, additional pleasure in being at work:

'I wanted to leave so badly. I am so pleased to be out of it.'

'I could not have stuck another year of it. I had enough of school.'

Relatively few boys and girls (under 5 per cent), however, referred to the satisfaction of earning money as such, and it was more frequently mentioned in connection with some other aspect of work than on its own merits.

Reasons for regrets and uncertainties

Since the numbers were small, it was necessary to exclude the replies of the girls, and to combine the replies of boys who had either regrets or doubts about their school-leaving decision.[1] In the combined analysis,

[1] There are, however, two important differences between these two latter groups. Firstly, hardly any of those with regrets referred to their being happy in their present employment, compared with about one in five of those with doubts who made such references; secondly, a much higher proportion of those with regrets had wanted (or now wanted) more education and a better type of job, than was the case among those who had doubts. These two groups had much in common with each other, however, seldom referring to any other advantage of being at work; the 'doubters' were, therefore, in most respects, much more similar to those with regrets than to those without.

only one in four of the boys referred to the satisfactions of being at work and of their present type of employment (compared with one-half of the boys who had no regrets); over one-half expressed a wish for more education, and one in five for a better type of job (though these two were frequently combined in the same reply); just over one in ten felt dissatisfied with some specific aspect of going to work or of their job; and a further one in ten referred to missing the friends and companions of their school days[2] (Table 23).

The references to the wish for further education were of several kinds, though they frequently contained specific mention of examinations, such as the G.C.E., and to the improved job prospects for those with academic qualifications. There were, for instance, references which contained undertones of self-recrimination, expressing regret at not having worked harder at school, or to having been too easily discouraged from trying to achieve academic success:

'I could have done a lot better at school. I could have got better results and got my "O" levels. Then I could have done better in the job line.'

'I wished I had taken more notice of the teacher. I could have passed with more effort. But now it's harder to take G.C.E. once you've left.'

There were also comments from boys who felt that they needed more education than they had received and wished their standards were higher:

'I wish I'd got a better education. I didn't get on well at school and I wanted to leave.'

'You need a good education to get on in this world. I wish I could have stayed on, but I didn't think I was brainy enough. My friends were leaving too.'

'I thought I could learn to spell and to read better, but I did not learn as much as I should have. If I'd stayed on I would have learnt more. But I didn't think I was learning anything.'

Other references came from reluctant leavers who had never really relinquished a wish to stay on at school:

'I just would have rather stayed on at school. I wanted to take G.C.E., I liked school and I would have been better off at school. We did better things and had more free time.'

'I'm glad I started work, but I would like to go back to school. I wish there was a system by which you could go back and broaden your education, and then try for a different kind of job.'

'I'm having second thoughts now. Perhaps I should have gone on to grammar school and taken my "A" levels. I did want to be a teacher once.'

[2] In the reasons given for their present feelings, the main feature which distinguished the fifteen-year-old leaver among the boys was the wish for more education and, to a lesser extent, for a better type of job; among the girls, fifteen-year-old leavers would seem less frequently than girl leavers at sixteen, to have been satisfied with being at work.

Over one in five of the boys referred to their wanting a better type of job. Sometimes plans for particular types of job, particularly apprenticeships, had not materialized after leaving school and some boys found themselves either in a different trade or in less skilled work than they had originally intended.[3] This either made them regret having left school, since by staying on they felt they might have improved their job prospects or, as in the case of the reluctant leavers, made them feel particularly aggrieved that their present job opportunities were limited because of the age at which they had left school. Rather more, proportionately, of the boys who would have liked a job with higher status or skill were, in fact, leavers at fifteen.

Boys who referred to some aspect of work, or being at work, as unsatisfactory, most frequently mentioned the hours of work and the absence of long holidays. Some, however, referred to the special difficulties they encountered in studying at evening classes and preparing for examinations, when they were no longer in full-time education.

Relationship between present regrets and attitudes to leaving school

Were the enthusiastic leavers more likely to express regret at leaving school than were those who had been less eager to finish their schooling? Evidently not. Those who were now without regrets tended more frequently to be those who had wanted to leave school, while those who now had regrets or uncertainties, were more frequently those who had not wanted to leave school.

There was, however, a complex pattern of relationships revealed in the analysis of present views about the school-leaving decision and past attitudes towards leaving school; and while there was a general tendency for those who had been happy to leave school to remain satisfied with their decision, there were several minority groups who had changed their opinions since leaving school.

Firstly, the proportions of the now regretful and uncertain leavers among the boys was higher (nearly one-third), than was the proportion of the one-time reluctant leavers (one-fifth). Opinions had changed, in fact, to the extent that two in five of those with present regrets or uncertainties had formerly been enthusiastic leavers, one in three had not minded leaving school very much, and only the remainder (about one-quarter) had felt reluctant to leave school. But views had also changed the other way, and there was thus a minority, one in ten, who now had no regrets about having left school, though at the time they had been unwilling to do so.

A similar pattern was evident for girls, except that identical proportions now had regrets or doubts as formerly had not wanted to leave school.

---

[3] See Chapter IX for the differences in the proportions wanting and obtaining certain types of employment.

Nevertheless, over one-half of those now looking back with some regret or doubt had been eager to leave school, one in six had not minded about leaving and the remainder, one in three, had been reluctant to do so. Again, there was a small minority (one in six) who, though they had not wanted to leave school at the time, had now no regrets about having done so.

Present employment and vocational aims

Since satisfaction with being at work seemed to be associated with retrospective views about leaving school, further analyses were made in order to trace the extent to which the type of employment entered, the degree of satisfaction with present job, and original vocational aims seemed also to have influenced attitudes to school leaving. The results suggest that all these factors seem to be associated in some degree with regrets or otherwise about leaving school, particularly for boys.[4]

Firstly, it seems evident that regrets and doubts about having left school were more likely to occur among boys in semi-skilled or unskilled manual work, than among boys in apprenticeships or non-manual work (Table 24). Among boys expressing some degree of regret, for instance, two-fifths were in relatively unskilled manual work, compared with just over one-quarter of those in this type of work who had no regrets. In contrast, only one in seven of those with regrets or doubts were in apprenticeships, compared with over one-third of those who had no such uncertainties about their school-leaving decision.

Similarly, whereas only one in seven of the boys in apprenticeships had any regrets or doubts, two-fifths of those in semi-skilled or unskilled manual work looked back on their school-leaving decision with some degree of regret. Girls, however, would not seem to have been as affected by the type of employment entered in their attitudes towards leaving school. Secondly, there was a tendency for those with regrets and doubts to be more likely to be dissatisfied, to some degree, with their present jobs than were those without regrets.[5] Thirdly, it would seem that those with regrets and doubts were more likely to have failed to realize their original vocational ambitions than were those who had no regrets, the gap between first hopes and ultimate achievements being much larger for those who looked back on their school-leaving decision with some degree of regret, than for those who did not.[6]

Among the boys who had no regrets, for instance, the proportion in semi-skilled or unskilled manual work (one-quarter) was little more than the proportion (one-fifth) who had originally planned to enter this type

[4] The replies of girls could not always be included in the completed analysis because of the small numbers, but reference is made to their replies where relevant.

[5] See Chapter XVI for the discussion of job satisfaction.

[6] See Chapter IX for the discussion of aims and attainments.

of employment; but among those with regrets or doubts, twice as many had entered such work as had originally planned to do so. In contrast, while one-third of the boys who now had regrets or doubts had wanted apprenticeships, less than one in seven had obtained them; among those without regrets, however, the difference between those who had wanted skilled trades (about one-half) and those who had actually obtained them (just under two-fifths) was very much smaller. The same pattern was evident for girls, relatively more of the girls without regrets having realized their original vocational aims than was the case for those with regrets or doubts.

TABLE 24. Regrets about leaving school and type of employment originally wanted and subsequently obtained: boys.

	No regrets		Regret or uncertainty	
	Employment		Employment	
	Wanted	Obtained	Wanted	Obtained
Unskilled and semi-skilled	(*Per cent of total*)			
manual work	19	26	18	40
Trainee	18	22	18	26
Apprentice	47	37	36	14
Clerical	9	12	12	16
Sales	—	2	—	2
Other non-manual	7	1	16	2
Total	100	100	100	100
(No. of 15–18s)	(121)[a]	(128)	(51)[a]	(55)

a Excluding not answering.

The tendency for boys with second thoughts about their school-leaving decision to be those with frustrated vocational ambitions, was confirmed in the replies they gave to the question of whether taking up their present employment had meant giving up something that they particularly wanted to do. Less than one-third of those without regrets had had this experience, compared with over one-half of those who had some degree of regret about leaving school.

Thus, young people who looked back at their school-leaving decision with some degree of regret, or doubt, were more likely than were others, not to have realized their vocational aims, and were less likely to have had a satisfactory experience of being at work. It would seem, therefore, that one factor to be considered in the working lives of some young people, is the feeling that things might have been better for them if they had, or could have, remained longer at school; there is the possibility that, in these cases, such doubts may have accentuated the difficulties associated with the transitional years between school and work.

OPINIONS ON RAISING THE SCHOOL-LEAVING AGE

When asked whether or not they approved of the proposal to raise the school-leaving age to sixteen, the majority of the boys (three-fifths) supported the idea; girls, however, did not favour the proposal nearly to the same extent, only just over two-fifths approving, while almost the same proportion disapproved. Roughly equal proportions of boys and girls—one in seven—were uncertain just what they thought of the idea.

The boys' support of a higher minimum school-leaving age did not vary with the age at which they had left school, even though nearly one-half of the boys who had left school at fifteen had been eager to do so, and over three in five had had no regrets about leaving school. Opinions differed substantially, however, among the girls and over nine-tenths of those disapproving or in doubt about the idea of raising the school-leaving age had left school at fifteen, compared with only two-thirds of those who supported the idea.

The reasons for their approval

The chief reason for approving a higher school-leaving age offered by both boys and girls (but more frequently by girls than by boys) was that the extra year would enable school leavers to be better educated. This was

TABLE 25. Reasons for approving or disapproving a higher school-leaving age.

| | Whether approve of raising school-leaving age | | | |
| | Boys | | Girls | |
	Yes	No/Uncertain	Yes	No/Uncertain
Better for individual and/or country to have more education	*(Per cent of total)*			
	39	1	46	5
Improve employment prospects/chances in life	35	1	26	4
Too young for work at 15	26	1	37	1
Should be left to individual choice	1	48	1	61
Waste of time if child lacks ability	—	14	—	5
Waste of time unless required for job	—	17	—	5
Better to start work early	—	6	—	8
Parents can't afford	—	4	—	12
Other (including conditional approval)	9	13	—	8
Total (Multiple replies)	100	100	100	100
(No. of 15–18s)[a]	(111)	(71)	(66)	(80)

a Excluding those not answering.

considered a good thing, not only for the individual but for the country as a whole (Table 25).

'It is best for everyone to have the best education they can get; and some people develop later. It would be best for the country.'

'People should go in for more knowledge. It sets the standard of education higher.'

'Everyone would benefit. It would be bound to increase the educational level of the nation.'

Some school leavers argued for compulsion on the grounds that, however unpopular it seemed, the individual would benefit in the long run.[7]

'It is best to be compelled. Most don't want to stay on, but it is for their own good.'

'It's a good idea. You hate it when you're there, but when you leave you realize you would have learnt more. It is better to be forced to stay on.'

'Most people leave school too early. If they are made to stay on they would do better. They would accept it better. People become interested when they are about fourteen, but with only one year to go a lot of people don't bother to try.'

The next most frequently offered argument in support of a higher school-leaving age, among the boys, was that more education would improve employment prospects for school leavers and give them a better chance in life. Over one-third of the boys felt that better jobs were likely for those with a better education, but only just over one-quarter of the girls were of this view. Frequent references were made to the extra year providing more people with the opportunity to take G.C.E.; it would seem from these references that many school leavers saw the G.C.E. as the main qualification for opening doors to wider choice in employment; the absence of this qualification limited opportunities:

'It is a good thing. Give some people a chance to develop later. Everyone might be able to take G.C.E. You have a better chance with more education.'

'Jobs that are going will be for people with more knowledge and qualifications.'

'It is a good idea. People would not get stuck in dead-end jobs, and it would stop people going into unskilled jobs.'

Girls rather more frequently than boys, however (one-third compared with just over one-quarter), referred to the relative immaturity of the fifteen-year-old leaver, who would be helped by an extra year at school to acquire self-confidence and understanding.[8] References were also made

---

[7] The Crowther Committee felt that voluntary persuasion would not be effective in raising the proportions staying on at school until sixteen. (See *15–18*, Chapter 12, paragraph 181, 'The limits of voluntary staying on'.)

[8] This was rather more frequently the view of boys from non-secondary modern schools.

to the need for children to have time to think and to consider their future plans and decisions:

'Fifteen to sixteen is a very in-between age; you don't know quite what to do. You need the influence of the teachers up to sixteen.'

'I was not ready to leave at fifteen. Another year makes all the difference. You realize you mature a lot in that last year.'

'Fifteen is too young to leave school. No chance to learn anything. You go into a firm and do any kind of work and the firm underpays you.'

'You'd be a bit older at sixteen. Just a bit more manly. They could teach you more in that last year of what you have to face afterwards.'

These reasons: the advantages to the individual and/or to the country of a better educated population; the improved employment prospects for those with a longer school life; the relative immaturity of those entering employment, represent the substance of the arguments of the supporters of the idea of a higher school-leaving age. They correspond more or less identically, though in much simplified form, with those used by the Crowther Committee in its advocacy of a school-leaving age of sixteen.[9] The Crowther Committee were of the view that educational advance was a form of capital investment that served the national interest and that the demand for more educated workers was growing at all levels of industry; and that a boy or girl at fifteen was not sufficiently mature to be exposed to the pressures of the world of industry or commerce.

The reasons for disapproval

The reasons for disapproving or for being uncertain[10] about a higher minimum school-leaving age naturally follow a different course. The majority of boys and girls who were against any change took this view because they felt that school leavers should continue to choose for them-selves when to leave school, and that since the possibility of a longer school life existed for those who wanted it, it was unfair to change the situation and thus to deprive children now at school of a choice available to former pupils. What was the point in changing when those who wanted more education could have it? And was it not unfair that future generations of children who, it was assumed, were as likely to get bored with school as had their predecessors, would have to endure the ordeal for another year? Over one-half of the girls, and nearly one-half of the boys, who disapproved of any change in the school-leaving age put forward these arguments in support of their point of view:

'People can stay on now; there is nothing that compels you to leave. I think you should leave it to people themselves to choose what they want to do.'

---

[9] *15–18* (see Part III, Chapters 11 and 12, 'Why the School Leaving Age should be Raised').

[10] These two groups were combined for the purpose of analysis, though reference is made in the text where either differed considerably from the other.

'It would not be really fair to make people stay at school if they're not happy. People who decide it are not having to stay themselves. If they felt as I did they would let people leave if they want to. Keep it as a choice as now.'

'It would make children resentful. Some people hate school so much that it would lead to more of them staying away. Leave it so that they can stay if they want to.'

A less frequently stated argument was that an extra year at school was a waste of time for those who did not do well at school or who were not seeking particular types of employment. Though relatively few girls were of this opinion, over one in five of the boys held this view:

'I was not much good at school. I was keen but not brainy. For people like me it is best to get out to work.'

'It's all right for those who want to take G.C.E. but what is the good for the others? Quite a few are practically illiterate.'

'Not everybody is suited to it. They haven't got the brains. It would be a waste of time for them. I have seen people in the C stream who can't read or write after four years. Another year would just be a waste of time.'

Girls, on the other hand, more frequently than boys, argued against a change in the age of leaving because they felt there were many parents who could not afford to keep their children longer at school. One in seven made references to this type of difficulty, compared with less than one in twenty of the boys:

'Some mothers have got big families. They can't afford it. If the child can't learn any more, it is better they start to earn.'

'Depends on the person. Some children have to leave if their families are poor. They need to help their families, so it would be unfair on them.'

There was also the argument that a longer school life would postpone the entry to employment, and therefore delay the individual's advancement in employment. This point of view was sometimes associated with the argument that if children were not academically 'bright', then an early start to work would set them well on their way.

The comments of those with doubts about the idea of a higher school-leaving age are of interest, since they suggest that some of the uncertainties arose because school leavers were divided between what they felt was a sound idea in principle, and what they felt, on the basis of their own experience or knowledge, might not work out in practice. Their approval was, therefore, frequently conditional:

'It's alright if they change the schools. Mine was overcrowded. We had forty to fifty in a class. We were all cramped together and the teachers could not cope. It would be alright if the numbers were not more than twenty.'

'I would not approve if people are all in different classes. People develop differently. There's a need for all to take the G.C.E. Everybody should take the

7

same exam; and then you wouldn't have some just waiting for the school-leaving age to come.'

'If anybody wants to leave it's because they're not enjoying school. They should enjoy it and then they would get the advantage of learning.'

Regrets about leaving school

Opinions about raising the school-leaving age were associated with regrets about leaving school in some respects. Boys who had regrets or doubts about their own school-leaving decision appear to have been much more likely to be in favour of a higher school-leaving age than were those without regrets; girls, however did not show this tendency at all. It is, however, of some interest to note that all the boys and girls who expressed regret at leaving school were either for or against a higher school-leaving age; none of them expressed doubt on this matter.

The approval or disapproval of raising the school-leaving age to sixteen was, however, associated to a marked degree with the boys' (but not the girls') own wishes at the time, to leave school. The majority of boys who were against, or uncertain about, the idea of a longer school life were also those who had most wanted to leave school, though this was largely accounted for by those who definitely disapproved of a higher school-leaving age, rather than by those who had doubts. Among the supporters of more education, however, only two-fifths had wanted to leave school, and nearly one-quarter had been reluctant to leave.

Moreover, the boys who disapproved of a longer school life not only tended more frequently than others to dislike school, but more frequently to have felt that they wanted to get out to work, that they wanted to be independent and that they were not learning anything at school; but boys who approved of a higher leaving age tended more frequently than others to have wanted to learn more and to have left school because they had completed their course. No such tendencies applied to the girls suggesting that boys' attitudes towards a higher school-leaving age were, to a greater extent than were those of girls, associated with their own reasons for wanting, or for not wanting, to leave school.

Present employment

When views on a higher school-leaving age were considered in the light of their present employment, boys in apprenticeships were, generally, more likely, and girls in office work less likely, than others, to disapprove. It is possible that the opinions of apprentices, a high proportion of whom came from the homes of skilled tradesmen, were influenced by very special considerations which apply particularly to skilled trades. Firstly, apprenticeships require an age-of-entry qualification; some of the boys in the sample referred to this when commenting on the idea of a higher leaving age, and on their own decision to leave school; secondly, skilled trades required a three-, four-, or five-year term of apprenticeship during which time boys are learning the trade and are not eligible for the fully-skilled rate of pay. Another year at school for boys in skilled trades might seem to them only to postpone the entry to, and completion of, apprenticeships and to delay the final stage of qualifying as a skilled adult. Thirdly, apprenticeships appear to offer some boys a realistic alternative to full-time education since they are based on a programme of training and provide some earnings during the period of training; are frequently associated with recognized courses of part-time study; are one source of recruitment to higher technical grades.

The fact that boys in semi-skilled and unskilled manual work were more likely than were boys in apprenticeships to have regrets about leaving school, to have been frustrated to a greater degree than others in the non-realization of their original vocational aims, and to have wondered whether they might not have done better in employment by staying on longer at school, might explain why they were more likely than other boys to favour a higher school-leaving age.

SUMMARY

The majority of boys and girls had no regrets about having left school when they did. The most important reason for this was evidently that they were happy being at work and found that being at work was better for them than being at school. In direct contrast were the views of those who looked back on their school-leaving decision with regret or some uncertainty. A much smaller proportion of these than others referred to the satisfactions of being at work, rather higher proportions were dissatisfied with some aspect of their work and referred to their past or present wish for more education.

Leavers at fifteen tended to regret leaving school more frequently than did leavers at sixteen and more frequently than older leavers, tended to have wanted a better type of job than they had actually obtained and/or more education than they had received. Though those who had no regrets about leaving tended to be those who had been most eager to leave school and vice-versa, some school leavers had had second thoughts since leaving school so that some enthusiastic leavers regretted having left while some reluctant leavers no longer minded having left school. Those who looked back on their school leaving were more likely than were others to have been frustrated in their vocational ambitions and not to have realized their original vocational aims. This was particularly marked for the boys who were more likely than others to be in semi-skilled or unskilled manual work and to have had at least one job change.

The majority of boys (three-fifths) also supported the idea of raising the school-leaving age to sixteen, but only two-fifths of the girls were in favour and almost the same proportion were against, the idea. About one in seven of boys and of girls were uncertain as to their approval or otherwise.

The boys support for a higher compulsory leaving age did not vary with the age of leaving school but almost as many as two in three of the girls leaving at fifteen disapproved of the proposals. The chief reasons for approving a higher school-leaving age were the advantages for the individual and/or the country of a better educated population; the improved employment prospects for those with a longer school life and/or qualifications; and the relative immaturity of the fifteen-year-old leaver for entering employment. The chief reason for disapproving of, or for being uncertain about, a higher compulsory leaving age was the view that school leavers should continue to have freedom to choose the age at which they wished to leave school, and that it would be unfair to future generations of school leavers to deprive them of a choice that their predecessors had enjoyed.

A relatively higher proportion of boys who disapproved or who were uncertain of a longer school life for all, came from the homes of skilled workers and were themselves in skilled trades: those who approved tended to have fathers in intermediate occupations or less skilled work and were themselves either in non-manual work or in relatively unskilled jobs. Approval among girls tended to come more often from those with fathers in non-manual occupations and from those in clerical work.

PART III

CHOOSING AND FINDING EMPLOYMENT

CHAPTER VII

VOCATIONAL PREFERENCES

INTRODUCTION

It is evident, so far, that many young people recalled the first phase of the transition—namely the school-leaving year—as having ended for them with unfavourable impressions of their educational experience and with doubts and uncertainties about themselves and their futures. In the present and subsequent chapters included in Part III, their experiences during the next phase of the transition when choosing and finding employment are considered.

In the pilot stage of the inquiry, many of the young people seen gave the impression that this situation had been one in which they had found it difficult to decide what to do, and to learn about employment possibilities; and also one in which they would have liked more help than they had received. Though a statutory service—the Youth Employment Service— exists to provide school leavers with information, to give vocational guidance and to help them find suitable employment, it has a number of evident weaknesses. In particular, its vocational guidance efforts have been shown to be 'frustrated by too few staff, with too little time, offering advice too late in school life'[1] to influence the decisions of more than a comparatively few; moreover, its job placing service is used by a minority of school leavers, and less intensively by some than by others.[2]

The present inquiry was begun before the Working Party on the Future Development of the Youth Employment Service published its report.[3] Though the proposals of the Working Party chiefly related to the need for more staff and to their training, for earlier and closer liaison with schools, and to the strengthening of links with education and industry, the importance of more research was also emphasized.[4] Reference was made to the need for more investigations into the work of the service itself, and into the techniques and procedures used; to studies relating to the occupational choice of young people, to their conceptions of jobs and to their job changing; and to the attitudes of parents, teachers, employers, and the 'non-users' of the service.

---

[1] G. Jahoda and A. D. Chalmers, op. cit.
[2] *The Work of the Youth Employment Service*, 1959–62, 1962–5, and 1965–8, H.M.S.O.
[3] *The Future Development of the Youth Employment Service*, op. cit.
[4] Ibid., Chapter VII.

The information obtained in the present inquiry is particularly relevant, therefore, to certain of these areas of inquiry, since it relates to the occupational histories of young people who have already made and implemented their vocational decisions. Since the aim of the questioning was to obtain a 'consumer-perspective' of this particular phase in the lives of school leavers, it has been possible to show the extent to which original aspirations were realized, and some of the factors which may have influenced success or failure; the chief sources of help and information used, their adequacy and some of the factors which may have influenced their use; the incidence and pattern of job change; the school leavers' own assessment of the adequacy or otherwise of the help received; their criticisms of the official service and their suggestions for its improvement. It has also been possible, in the analysis of the material, to examine certain aspects of their social and educational background, and to suggest where these may appear relevant to their subsequent experiences.

The presentation of the material

The presentation of the results follows, more or less, the order of questioning. In the present chapter, the vocational preferences of young people are described and examined in the light of the reasons offered for their choice, so that it is possible to see the different emphasis placed on certain aspects of their intended or hoped-for employment. Then follows, in Chapter VIII, an analysis of the sources of help and information used when choosing and finding their first jobs; in Chapter IX, a comparison is made between their original aims and their subsequent attainments; and in Chapter X, their assessment of the help sought and received is described. Information relating to changes in their employment has been summarized in Chapter XI.

Classification of occupations

A relatively simple classification of occupations was used in the analysis, partly to avoid excessive atomization of the sample but also because of the difficulties which arose in classifying, in comparable terms, the jobs named as first preferences and those subsequently obtained. There was a tendency for some school leavers to be vaguer when describing the jobs originally intended, particularly in regard to manual work whose skill and status was not always specified, than when referring to their past or present employment. This applied also to boys who had obtained work designated as 'trainee'; this term was not used at all when first preferences were named, though nearly one-half of all boys in manual work outside apprenticeships found employment so described. The term itself was an ambiguous one, since it sometimes referred to status and conditions approximating to apprenticeships, but at other times to jobs which were hardly distinguishable from manual work where no specific training course was provided. The classification framework used was, therefore, based on 'levels' of employment which distinguishes for boys, apprenticeships, other manual and non-manual occupations; and for girls, clerical, manual, and other non-manual occupations, the latter referring chiefly to jobs as sales assistants.

ORIGINAL PREFERENCES

Most studies[5] of the vocational preferences of school leavers have concentrated on the job choices nominated by children before they have left school and, since the object was frequently to examine the factors influencing the formation of choice, such inquiries were carried out during the last year or months of school life at the time when children were preparing for work and making their vocational decisions.

In the present inquiry, young people already at work were asked to recall their original preferences in order to trace the extent to which these were realized and the nature of the vocational help sought and obtained in relation to their original aims and subsequent attainments. It is not possible to assess the modifying influence of being at work on the replies, nor on the extent to which alternatives, once considered, were neither mentioned nor remembered in response to this question. The fact that relatively few boys and girls referred to more than one choice of occupation, while only a small minority referred to types of work outside the most popular choices (apprenticeships, other manual work, and clerical work), suggests that, perhaps, early aspirations were now regarded by some as unrealistic and were, therefore, revised in the light of experience at work.

Carter[6] found, for instance, that one-third of boys and girls interviewed before leaving school referred to what he describes as 'ideal' jobs, which they would have preferred but which they did not intend, for a variety of reasons, to seek immediately, if at all. Only about one in ten of the young people seen in the present inquiry referred to original preferences which might, perhaps, be considered 'ideal' in Carter's sense. For girls, such preferences[7] included work in the medical and social service field,[8] while for boys, professional and semi-professional work,[9] the Police and Armed Services were in this category. As will be seen,[10] some of these 'ideal'

---

[5] See studies listed in footnote 2, Chapter I, page 4.

[6] M. Carter, op. cit.

[7] These preferences were: nurse (children's, general, midwife), teacher, medical social worker, work with animals, veterinary surgeon, librarian, singer, air hostess, commercial artist.

[8] Wilson (op. cit.) found that preference for nursing was sometimes associated with an interest in domestic subjects and that girls with strong interests in home-making frequently specified childrens' nursing, ignoring the intellectual requirements.

[9] These preferences were: chemist, teacher, film producer, journalist, artist, opinion poll interviewer.

[10] See pages 130-2 for the job preferences given up.

choices were, in fact, acted upon and abandoned only because of subsequent failure to qualify, or of unexpected events or uncertainties about
the future; other 'ideal' choices apparently represented serious intentions,
present employment being regarded as a temporary measure while age
and academic qualifications and/or job experience were obtained.

It was to be assumed that the replies of most young people concerning
the type of work they had wished to enter on leaving school would reflect,
in some degree, the type of work actually obtained; since the majority of
boys seen were in manual work of varying skills and the majority of girls
in clerical work, it is hardly surprising therefore, that the pattern of their
original vocational preferences was similar, though not identical, to that
of their present employment. The replies of boys were, in fact, dominated
by references to apprenticeships or other types of manual work, while
those of girls referred mainly to clerical or other types of non-manual
work[11] (Table 26).

TABLE 26. Original vocational preferences.

Type of employment wanted	Boys	Girls
	(Per cent of total)	
Apprenticeship	41	7
Other manual:		
Factory	13	6
Other	4	4
Trainee	17	1
Sub-tota	34	11
Clerical	9	48
Sales	—	17
Other non-manual	9	11
Armed Services	2	—
Don't know	1	1
No answer	4	5
Total	100	100
(No. of 15–18s)	(183)	(147)

Most young people were fairly specific about the type of work they had
originally wanted and, depending on their preferences, mentioned the
exact trade or profession they had wished to enter, the type of office work

[11] Other studies, including those of Carter and Veness, have shown that among secondary
modern school leavers, manual work, including apprenticeships, accounted for the majority of
boys' preferences, and non-manual work including clerical and shop work, for the majority of
girls'. Boys have been found to be inclined to want to make something, but girls tend to refer to
office work as cleaner than manual work. (See Carter, 1962, op. cit. and Veness, op. cit.).

desired, or the type of shop and merchandise in mind. Boys and girls who had thought of relatively unskilled manual work, however, were more frequently vague as to the actual job they had wanted to do; boys in this category tended to refer, for example, to 'engineering work' or to 'something in the electrical line' and girls, simply to 'factory work'.

Though some young people evidently decided on certain jobs because they did not know what else to do, hardly any, apparently, left school without some idea, however vague, of the type of work, industry or service they might enter. Moreover, the majority of boys and girls seen (about four-fifths) had decided on the type of work they wanted before leaving school. This result is consistent with the findings of previous studies[12] which have shown that vocational plans are not only made early on in secondary school life, but that these become fairly specific during the last year of school, to the extent that many young people look for employment before leaving school so as to have work ready for themselves when they leave. In the present inquiry, nearly one-half of the boys and two-fifths of the girls had obtained employment before leaving school. The relatively few who made their choice at the time of, or after, leaving school were those who had been uncertain about what to do, or who had anticipated a longer school life for themselves.

Social class and educational background

The limits set to vocational choice and opportunity are known to be broadly set by socio-economic and educational factors. These could not be explored in any detail in the present inquiry but such evidence as was obtained is consistent with the findings of other studies.[13]

First, a much higher proportion of the sons of manual workers planned to take up semi-skilled or unskilled manual work and a lower proportion had non-manual employment in mind, than was the case for boys with fathers in non-manual work. Similarly, while the majority of boys seeking manual work, skilled or otherwise, came from the homes of manual workers, only a minority of those wanting non-manual employment were themselves sons of manual workers. The differences in social class were not so marked in the preferences of girls though girls wanting clerical work were a little more likely to come from the homes of non-manual workers much higher proportions, however, of the daughters of manual workers, wanted work in shops than was the case for girls with fathers in non-manual occupations.

Second, boys from secondary modern schools were much more likely than were others to have stated a preference for manual work, both

---

[12] See studies listed in footnote 1, page 4 and G. Jahoda and D. Chalmers, op. cit.

[13] Particularly J. Floud, 'Social Class Factors in Educational Achievement', in *Ability and Educational Opportunity*. O.E.C.D., Paris, 1961, and J. Floud and A. Halsey, 'English Secondary Schools and the Supply of Labour', *Year Book of Education*, 1956.

skilled and unskilled, and less likely to have intended to take up clerical or non-manual work. Moreover, while four-fifths of boys whose preferences were for apprenticeships or other types of manual work had attended non-selective schools, only a little more than one-half of those intending to take up non-manual work had done so.

Third, the age of leaving was associated in some degree with the vocational preferences of school leavers, in that the kind of work anticipated by leavers at fifteen was relatively much more concentrated in unskilled or semi-skilled manual work, while proportionately more of the older leavers wanted employment as apprentices or clerks. Relatively more of the boys who had considered apprenticeships, had also considered remaining longer at school, as had fifteen-year-old leavers who had intended to take up clerical employment.[14]

In examining the reasons for reluctance or eagerness to leave school, rather more of the boys intending to take up manual work (other than in the skilled trades) wanted to leave school because they felt they lacked academic ability. In analysing vocational preferences according to the position in class and stream at school, as assessed by the young people themselves, there are certain striking contrasts between the different 'ability' groups, suggesting that educational performance, as defined in these rather crude terms, would seem to have been associated with employment intentions. Thus, a rather higher proportion of boys wanting non-manual employment or apprenticeships were in the top stream, than were boys planning to enter other types of manual work; moreover, among boys wanting unskilled or semi-skilled manual work, the proportion in the bottom stream at school was twice as high as among boys wanting apprenticeships or non-manual work. If the non-streamed boys are excluded from the analysis, the proportion coming from the middle and bottom streams was still appreciably higher for boys planning to take up unskilled or semi-skilled manual work than for boys with other aspirations. Similarly, while each stream contained all types of vocational preferences, it was the top stream which produced a majority of choices for apprenticeships and the middle and bottom streams a majority for semi-skilled or unskilled manual work. A similar tendency was evident for girls, higher proportions of would-be clerical workers coming from the top streams, and a substantially higher proportion of girls wanting manual work or work in shops coming from the bottom streams.

Position in class at school would also seem to have been associated with ideas about future work, particularly for boys. A higher proportion of boys who assessed their class position as 'above average' had opted for skilled trades than had others, while relatively more of the 'average' or 'below-average' in class intended to take up less-skilled manual work than did

[14] There is, of course, an inter-relationship between father's occupation, type of school attended, and age of leaving.

above-average boys. Moreover, while preferences for apprenticeships were made almost in equal proportions by boys above-average or average in class (and by remarkably few boys below-average, only one in twelve), boys seeking manual or clerical work came predominantly from 'average' class positions. Among the girls, however, the differences were relatively small, though there was a tendency for proportionately more of the 'above-average' girls to want clerical work, and of girls from 'average' or 'below-average' class positions to nominate other types of work.

Differences in vocational preferences, as defined in broad occupational categories would, therefore, appear to have been sharper in relation to educational performance (particularly the position in class for boys), than in regard to other aspects of educational background or to social class. Though social class itself is associated with educational performance,[15] Wilson's study[16] of the preferences of secondary modern school children showed that ambitions were modified in the light of what appeared to be academic limitations, and that the tendency for less intelligent children to choose lower grades of occupation was not solely due to the influence of home environment. Freeston's study[17] showed that children tend to aim at the highest levels available to the group to which they belong, and that any segregation of children into different types of secondary school had a profound effect on their attitudes to vocational choice; children of average ability, if separated from the highly gifted, were less likely to adopt inappropriate ambitions. The evidence of the present inquiry, so far as it goes, suggests that separation into different streams of ability and even class positions, may have had a similar effect on some children and on the level of their aspirations.

THE REASONS FOR THESE PREFERENCES

A study of the underlying motives involved in deciding on jobs or careers fell outside the scope of the present inquiry. The replies of young people to the question of why they had wanted particular types of work were, therefore, accepted at their face value. It seemed useful, however, in showing the different emphasis placed by children on certain aspects, to apply the classifications used by Veness in her study of school leavers.[18] She applied the terms—'tradition-directed', 'inner-directed', and 'other-directed' (used originally by David Riesman[19] to describe societies and the character

[15] J. Floud, op. cit.; H. T. Himmelweit, op. cit., J. W. B. Douglas, op. cit., and J. D. Nisbet, op. cit.

[16] M. D. Wilson, op. cit.

[17] P. M. Freeston, op. cit.

[18] T. Veness, op. cit.

[19] D. Riesman, 'The Lonely Crowd', *Yale University Studies in National Policy*, No. 3, Yale University Press and Oxford University Press, 1950; D. Riesman and N. Glazer, 'Faces in the Crowd', *Yale University Studies in National Policy*, No. 4, Yale University Press and Oxford University Press, 1952.

types they engender), because these seemed relevant to the discussion of vocational guidance problems and to the possible improvement of diagnostic tools in job-placement.

'Tradition-directed' choice refers to situations in which family or neighbourhood traditions are such that no other choice is seriously considered; an 'inner-directed' choice is made with reference mainly to the individual's own talents and interest; an 'other-directed choice' is one made with primary reference to outside sources of information or advice or to considerations of prospects, security, and position. These categories are not, of course, mutually exclusive when applied to the reasons for job preferences, since any process of choice involves more than one consideration. They indicate, however, the chief factor considered.

TABLE 27. Reasons for original job preferences.

	Boys	Girls
Inner-directed	(*Per cent of total*)	
Good at subjects required or associated with intended work	23	23
Always wanted this type of work	22	17
Like some special feature of the job	13	31
Other-directed		
Job prospects	19	16
Others suggested and advised	8	8
Tradition-directed		
Parents, relatives, etc., in same or similar work	11	1
Other		
Alternatives not attractive or suitable	6	16
Did not know what else to do	3	2
Don't know	1	4
No answer	4	1
Total (Multiple replies)	100	100
(No. of 15–18s)	(183)	(147)

In the present inquiry, the replies of most young people could be grouped into these three broad categories, though, for the purpose of more detailed analysis, replies associated with 'inner-' and 'other-directed' choices were further sub-divided. Moreover, there were minorities whose choice did not fit any of these terms since it had been made either because the alternatives considered were not suitable or attractive, or because there was uncertainty about what to do (Table 27).

Inner-directed choice

This choice represented by far the most frequently offered reason when young people recalled their original job preferences; the replies of almost three-fifths of the boys and over two-thirds of the girls were of this order. There were, however, three categories of reply within this broad definition. First in order of frequency for boys, and second for girls, were references to their academic and/or practical suitability, an assessment derived chiefly from their school achievements or experiences.[20]

Thus a boy who had planned to take up sheet metal work, for example, commented on the fact that metal work was one of the subjects that 'he was really good at'; a girl who thought of becoming a typist/secretary had wanted to do something with writing because she liked English and it had been her best subject. 'I started a commercial course at school; I got on alright and I liked it.' 'I liked maths and was good with figures, so I wanted office work with figures,' was the comment of a girl who planned to become a ledger clerk; a boy who had always been good at technical drawing had hoped to become a draughtsman.

Far more references were made to commercial and craft, than to academic, subjects. This suggests that it was the vocational training received at school which played some part in determining the choice of certain school leavers. Nearly one in four, in fact, seem to have been attracted to certain kinds of work because of their personal interest and achievement in subjects directly related to possible careers; but, as further analysis shows, this factor was less likely to apply to boys attending secondary modern schools,[21] and more likely to apply to boys and girls seeking skilled manual or clerical work.

Next in order of frequency for boys, particularly for the sons of manual workers, but third for girls, were references to long-felt attraction or interest in the job considered. About one-fifth of the boys and one-sixth of the girls made such comments as:

'Ever since I can remember I've wanted to do drawing.'
'I've had it in mind since I was thirteen.'
'It's appealed to me since I was a child.'

But for girls the most frequently offered explanation for their job preferences was the attraction of some special aspect of the job itself. Nearly

[20] M. D. Wilson (op. cit.) concluded that school subjects were likely to pre-date and influence vocational choice in the case of those most closely associated with school subjects. The disproportionate popularity of certain choices, e.g. woodwork and needlework, were in her view, due to the comparative success which children experienced in these subjects at school, not because they were particularly gifted but because the educational demands in these subjects were better adapted to the needs and abilities of the children. In the present inquiry, interest and achievement in school subjects was the chief reason offered for the preferences of the sons and daughters of manual workers.

[21] Wilson also found that school subjects were mentioned more frequently by grammar school than by secondary modern children.

one in three of the girls referred to the special appeal certain jobs had for them. A prospective telephonist commented:

'I would be with people all the time and in touch with the outside world but I'd also be working on my own. I thought I would like that.'

'I liked the idea of meeting people; perhaps window-dressing and working with different materials.'

was the comment of a girl hoping to work in a shop. A would-be typist said:

'I wanted a career in an office but it appealed to me to sit at a desk and answer the phone and to keep papers tidy.'

Boys were also attracted to jobs for similar reasons though not in the same degree. Only about one in twelve made such comments as:

'I liked the idea of travelling about and meeting lots of people. You get to know things as you travel.'

'I liked the idea of using my hands and making things. I thought it would be interesting and varied and I wanted to be out of doors.'

Other-directed choice

Two categories of reply were distinguished here, namely, the prospective rewards of a job and the interest aroused by other persons, pamphlets, films, etc. More than one in four of the boys and girls attributed their original job preferences to these other-directed motives. The advice of parents, relatives, friends, teachers, youth employment officers, and others, or the interest gained by learning about a job or seeing others do it, was, evidently, less frequently the chief factor in determining choice than was the belief that the job itself offered security, good prospects and pay, useful skills for the future, or represented a step towards the achievement of ultimate goals.

One in five or six of the young people seen, and more frequently the daughters of non-manual workers, were attracted by the material and other advantages of certain types of employment.

'I wanted a secure job and the Civil Service offers security.'

'It's a good job. In the years to come they will always need toolmakers. They can't do without us. And the money is good once you're an adult.'

Not more than one in twelve, however, felt they had made their choice in response to advice and information.

'My father and the youth employment officer told me about it and made me interested in it.'

'I was walking round the shop with my mother and I thought it looked interesting work.'

'The neighbours thought it would be a good idea and as there was a vacancy I thought I would try it.'

Tradition-directed choice

In the sample of young people seen, it was boys rather than girls who were likely to have been influenced in their original choice of employment by tradition direction; and it was family rather than neighbourhood traditions which would seem to have been the chief determinant in these cases. About one in ten of the boys (and a negligible proportion of the girls) referred to the trades and professions in which one or several of their family were employed. Typical of these references were:

'I wanted to follow my brother.'
'I've inherited it from the family—they're all in engineering drawing.'
'All my relatives are in the Civil Service.'
'My mother and father—and others in the family—are in the catering trade.'

Uncertain choice

Not all young people, however, had inner convictions, strong impulses, regard for prospects, or family traditions to help them in making their decisions. Some school leavers, particularly from the homes of manual workers had been uncertain as to their abilities and interests and apprehensive as to whether they would like, or be suitable for, certain types of employment. Sometimes this was because first preferences had to be abandoned and this made other jobs seem less attractive; in other cases it was because they did not know what to do. Job choice for one in six of the girls and one in twenty of the boys, had been largely a process of eliminating alternatives until an acceptable one could be found. A girl who finally decided to take up cookery, commented:

'I was not interested in maths; I thought about window dressing but there were no openings there. The youth employment officer suggested catering. We used to have a shop but I did not like that. If you're not trained it's either a shop or an office, and I did not want either.'

Other comments of this kind were:

'I had no strong ideas. I was no good at maths; I did not fancy an office. I thought about carpentry or something like that.'
'I wanted a job where you wear a suit every day, a reliable sort of job. But I did not learn much at school so I thought I would be a labourer. I like using my body.'

Then there were a few boys and girls—less than one in twenty—who left school without any firm ideas at all. Their decision arose out of not knowing what else to do.

'I had no idea. I just wanted some sort of training but I did not know in what.'
'I did not know what to do. I had this idea on the spur of the moment. I did

8

not fancy factory work but did not know what else to do. I could not think of anything else.'

'I had no idea. I did not fit into any pattern. Dad had it all worked out but I did not have any ambitions. Driving, painting, decorating . . . I did not know what to do.'

Vocational aims

As seems logical, the reasons for job preferences were associated in some respects with the type of work which school leavers had wanted to do. Boys who had planned to enter skilled trades, for instance, were, proportionately, twice as likely as were boys seeking less-skilled manual work, and three times as likely as boys seeking non-manual employment, to have considered job prospects; moreover, the material and other advantages of their intended jobs was first in order of frequency for would-be apprentices, but only fourth for boys planning to take up other types of work. For these latter boys, the most frequently mentioned reason for their job preferences was their long-felt wish, the proportion referring to this being twice as high among boys seeking non-manual work (two-fifths) as among boys planning to enter skilled trades (one-fifth).

On the other hand, almost as many boys seeking apprenticeships referred to their liking for and interest in certain subjects at school, and only slightly fewer to their always having wanted this type of work. Their reasons for wanting skilled work were much more evenly distributed between three categories—i.e. job prospects, liking a particular subject at school, and always having wanted a skilled trade—than was the case for other school leavers.

The two chief reasons for girls seeking clerical work were firstly, their interest in and liking for certain subjects at school (perhaps the influence of commercial courses) and secondly, job prospects. Moreover, three times as many would-be office workers, proportionately, referred to their academic or practical achievements in school subjects, and twice as many to job prospects, than was the case among girls seeking other types of work. Girls in this latter category, by contrast, were much more frequently influenced either by the particular appeal of certain jobs or by always having wanted to take up certain kinds of work. Over two-fifths, for instance, of girls wanting non-office work had responded to the attraction of particular features of their intended jobs; (the proportion was as high as two-thirds among girls seeking shop work, most of whom referred to the attraction of 'meeting people'), compared with only one-sixth of would-be office workers who had felt this way.

Similarly, whereas only about one in eight of the girls intending to take up clerical work referred to their always having wanted this work, the corresponding proportion among girls seeking non-clerical work was as high as one-third.

Office work was more likely than was other employment, however, to have been chosen because the alternatives did not seem attractive or suitable. One in eight of the girls seen in the present inquiry gave this as their reason, compared with less than one in twenty of other school leavers. Further analysis showed that this was largely due to girls choosing clerical work when they discovered or realized that their first preferences, often work requiring training or further education, could not be followed. Earlier studies have commented on the tendency of girls to accept clerical work after relinquishing more attractive hopes.[22]

JOB CHOICE—THE VENESS[23] STUDY AND THE PRESENT INQUIRY

The Veness study and the present inquiry are not, of course, strictly comparable. The former was intended to provide data about the aspirations of school leavers, in particular as they related to work, and to attempt to identify the ambitious child. There are, therefore, considerable differences in the age, educational composition, and representativeness of the two samples and in the methods of selection, questioning, and analysis used. Nevertheless, school leavers in both inquiries followed the same frequency order of reasons for their choice of employment; in both cases, the most frequently mentioned were 'inner-directed' choices, the least frequently being 'tradition-directed'. When, however, the results of the Veness study were related to all school leavers, irrespective of educational background, and the non-committal and non-responding were excluded from the Willesden analysis, the boys in the two samples corresponded with each other only in the similar proportions who were influenced by their academic or practical interest at school in the subjects associated with their job intentions, or by the attraction of some feature of the job itself; relatively fewer Willesden boys attributed their job choice to sources of advice and information or to family tradition, and substantially more, proportionately, to the prospective rewards and advantages of the job in mind (Table 28).

Girls, however, differed from each other in all respects and the girls covered by the present inquiry were much more likely, proportionately, than were girls in the Veness study, to have been influenced by the appeal of some feature of the job considered and by job prospects, and were less likely to have been influenced by their interests or achievements at school subjects, by the advice of others, by sources of information or by family tradition. These differences arise, no doubt, from the differences in the

[22] M. B. Stott, 'A Preliminary Experiment in Occupational Analysis of Secretarial Work', *The Human Factor*, 9, Nos. 7 and 8, 1935.
[23] T. Veness, op. cit.

composition of the two samples and in the type of question used for collecting the data.[24]

TABLE 28. Motivation in job choice: a comparison of the results of the Veness[a] and present inquiries.

Motivation in job choice[b]	Boys		Girls	
	Veness inquiry	Present inquiry	Veness inquiry	Present inquiry
Inner-directed	*(Per cent of total)*			
Popular school subjects/good at subjects required	29	25	34	23
Some special interest/liked some special feature of job	11	13	18	32
Other-directed				
Others suggested or advised, etc.	20	9	29	8
Job prospects	10	20	9	16
Tradition-directed				
Runs in family/parents, relatives in same or similar work	15	9	9	1
Total[c]	100	100	100	100
(No. of 15–18s)	(513)[d]	(170)[e]	(388)[d]	(138)[e]

a T. Veness, op. cit.

b Excluding non-comparable categories: where there are two headings the first refers to the Veness inquiry, the second to the present inquiry.

c Multiple replies in the present inquiry.

d Excludes non-committal replies and the replies of those who could not name their preference.

e Excludes non-respondents and don't knows.

The fact that 'inner-directed' choice was the principal element in both inquiries is, however, of some interest. Moreover, though the frequency with which school leavers in the present inquiry offered reasons for their job preferences varied to a greater or less extent according to certain factors in their educational background, to broad categories of social class and to their vocational aspirations,[25] 'inner-directed' choice predominated for all groups. This suggests that the most important factors influencing their job choice was a desire to continue in their working lives, to use skills, talents, interests (some of which may have been developed or encouraged at school), and a liking for things and activities central to the job itself. Of lesser importance were the desire for the status or personal security the job might afford, the wish to follow family patterns or the response to the suggestions and advice of other people.

[24] The occupational preferences of the Willesden sample were particularly biased in favour of apprenticeships and clerical work.

[25] See pages 98–99.

The implications of 'inner-directed' choice for vocational advisers are discussed by Veness,[26] particularly when ability is assessed as not being equal to interest or when interest cannot find a suitable outlet. Veness suggests that the post-war employment situation may itself have allowed school leavers to give full consideration to their own demands and interests. Full employment and labour shortages would appear to extend rather than to restrict choice, though opportunities vary with local conditions. Technical change and innovation, however, as well as chronic labour shortages may reduce demand for school leavers in certain categories of employment[27] and a relatively wide choice of firm or enterprise is not necessarily coincident with a wide range of occupations.

There are also implications for educators if, as Wilson[28] suggests, a casual relationship may exist between vocational choice and attitudes to school subjects, and if the subjects provided and the demands they make on children result in an unrealistic appraisal of their abilities and disabilities and a narrowing of their interest. Quite apart from the limitations this relationship may place on the individual's freedom of vocational choice, it may also produce further rigidity in the supply of new recruits to the labour force by reducing the possibility for natural talent and interest to find its own level within the widest possible range of occupations.[29]

SUMMARY

School leavers were asked to recall their original job preferences. These followed a similar though not identical pattern to those in which they were at present employed, in terms of certain broad categories of types of employment. Thus the replies of boys were dominated by references to apprenticeships and to other types of manual work; those of girls referred mainly to clerical and other types of non-manual work. The majority of boys and girls had decided what they wanted to do before leaving school, the relatively few who made their choice at the time of or after leaving school being those who were uncertain as to what to do or who had anticipated a longer school life for themselves. In examining some of the factors which may have influenced their choice of employment it was evident, as in other studies, that father's occupation, the age of leaving school, the type of secondary school attended, and educational performance were associated with differences in the extent to which preferences were

---

[26] T. Veness, op. cit.

[27] The direct inquiry of firms in the Willesden area revealed that nearly 300 of 720 factories offices, hospitals, transport services, etc., did not employ under-eighteens. Though these represented in the main small firms, a follow up inquiry showed that a considerable number of them had replaced young people with older men or married women because of the difficulties in recruiting or retaining under-eighteens.

[28] M. D. Wilson, op. cit.

[29] J. Floud, op. cit.

concentrated in types of work of different skill and status. Differences in vocational preferences would appear to have been sharper in relation to educational performance, as measured by position in stream and in class, than in regard to other aspects of educational background or to social class.

In examining the reasons offered by school leavers for their original preferences, classifications used by Veness[30] were applied. The analysis showed that 'inner-directed' choice—one made with reference mainly to the individual's own talents and increases—was the chief motive for more than one-half of the boys and two-thirds of the girls. The desire to continue in their working lives to use skills, talents, and interests, and a liking for things and activities central to the job itself, would seem to have been more important factors influencing job choice than were the desire for the status or personal security the job might afford, the wish to follow family patterns or the response to the suggestions and advice of others.

'Inner-directed' choice was frequently associated with reference to their suitability for their intended jobs, an assessment chiefly derived from their school achievements or experiences. Since more references were made to commercial and craft than to academic subjects, it is suggested that vocational training at school would seem to have played an important part in influencing the choice of certain school leavers, particularly that of boys seeking to enter skilled trades and of girls intending to work in offices.

[30] op. cit.

CHAPTER VIII

SOURCES OF VOCATIONAL HELP

INTRODUCTION

A number of studies[1] have stressed the central and decisive influence of parents and the family circle on the formation of occupational choice. This influence works in various ways; indirectly, by the occupations of parents, relatives, and friends and directly, by their interests, opinions and experiences; negatively, by the advice to avoid certain kinds of jobs; positively, by the emphasis placed on others. The same informal circles have been shown to be the most important source of information about jobs and are used nearly as, or more, frequently in getting jobs than is the Youth Employment Service. By the time the service comes into operation, job attitudes have hardened and choice has narrowed, information imparted is selectively interpreted and the service itself perceived, at best, as an agency solely for finding work.

The discussions held with young people during the pilot study had shown that there were school leavers for whom the process of choosing and finding work had been associated with uncertainties and difficulties. Most of those seen wished they had known more, and had been able to get more help. The aim of the questioning in the present inquiry was, however, not to study the process of job-choice itself, nor the effectiveness of informal and formal vocational guidance (particularly as these have already been the subject of detailed and expert investigation[2]), but to discover from young people who had been at work for some time, their experiences in regard to the help and information sought and obtained by them when making, and implementing, their ultimate decisions as to what work to do. Three questions were prepared in this connection covering (a) the source of help in making the final decision, (b) the source and the amount of information obtained about the intended job, and (c) the method by which first employment was obtained.

---

[1] Notably those of: M. Carter, op. cit., C. M. Chown, op. cit., G. Jahoda, op. cit., and M. D. Wilson, op. cit.

[2] G. Jahoda and A. D. Chalmers, op. cit.

SOURCE OF HELP IN DECIDING ON
INTENDED EMPLOYMENT

In devising the question concerning the source of help when thinking about and deciding what work to do, emphasis was placed not so much on the process of choice, but on the ultimate decision. It was also assumed, largely on the basis of the comments of school leavers in discussions held during the pilot study, that there would be young people who, in retrospect, might feel that they had made up their own minds as to what to do, without the help of others. Allowance was made, therefore, for young people to nominate either particular persons (parents, relatives, friends, etc.), if they felt that any one of these had given most help, or to nominate themselves if they felt that they had been mainly responsible for the decision made.

The question differed considerably, therefore, from those used in other studies of job determinants which have rightly assumed that no child is immune from the influence of some external agent in their choice of employment. In the present inquiry, these influences were taken for granted since the intention was not the study of job determinants as such, but how young people at work viewed their past decisions and the help they felt had been given.

TABLE 29. Chief sources of help in making
vocational decision.

	Boys	Girls
	(Per cent of total)	
Self	60	59
Parents	23	26
Teachers	8	6
Relatives/friends	8	7
Y.E.O.	7	9
Other	—	1
Total (Multiple replies)	100	100
(No. of 15–18s)	(183)	(147)

In the event, the majority of young people, three in five, felt that they had made up their own minds as to what kind of work they wanted or intended to do, and only about one in four attributed help in their decisions to their parents. Relatively few mentioned others—teachers, other relatives, friends, or youth employment officers—as the chief source of help (Table 29). The fact that the latter group were infrequently referred to as a chief source of help would appear to confirm the view that vocational help from the Youth Employment Service is offered too late in life to affect the decisions of more than a minority of school leavers. But the replies are open to other possible interpretations. In view of the type of questions asked, the help of others may have been acknowledged only when it was felt to have been a direct and dominant influence on their decisions, in contrast to what may have been unobtrusive and indirect influences. It is also possible that help of this kind was now felt to have been ineffective or inadequate; or that, with the passing of time, it now seemed a less important factor in their decisions than it had previously.[3] Whatever the explanation, boys and girls showed a remarkable consistency in the pattern of their replies.

Further analysis showed that there was some variation in the relative importance of sources of help according to certain factors in their social and educational background and to their vocational preferences. The sons, but not the daughters, of non-manual workers, for instance, were more inclined than were others to refer to their having made up their own minds and less likely to have referred to the help of friends or relatives. Likewise, boys who had attended non-secondary modern schools were more likely than others to feel that they had made up their minds without help, and to refer less frequently to the help of their parents.

When educational performance was considered, the replies showed a curious contrast between boys and girls. For the boys, the proportions nominating particular sources of help were much the same for both top and lower streams, and for above-average and other positions in class. For the girls, on the other hand, relatively more from the top streams and above-average positions in class felt that their decisions had been made without the help of others. Girls from the higher 'ability' groups would, therefore, seem to have been more frequently independent-minded in regard to their decisions than were their equivalents among the boys, who in their turn, were more frequently dependent on the help of parents and relatives. (This 'independence' did not apply, however, when obtaining their first employment, relatively more of the higher 'ability' groups, both boys and girls, relying more frequently on the help of others than on their own efforts compared with school leavers from lower positions in stream and in class.)

Though less than one in ten of all school leavers referred to the help of the Youth Employment Service when deciding on their intended employment, the proportion was as high as nearly one in five among girls seeking non-clerical work (manual and non-manual), compared with a negligible proportion among girls intending to enter offices. In the case of girls wanting non-manual work, this meant that they referred as frequently to the help of parents, teachers, friends, and relatives as did would-be office workers; girls seeking manual work, however, relied less frequently on their parents and much more often on themselves. No such differences

---

[3] The result would appear consistent, however, with the fact that 'inner-directed' choice predominated over 'other' or 'tradition-directed'. (See Chapter VII.)

were apparent for the boys, whose sources of help were apparently not associated with their intended type of employment.[4]

INFORMATION ABOUT INTENDED EMPLOYMENT

How young people may be helped to learn about the kind of work which exists, and whether it is what they want, remains, as yet, one of the great unsolved problems of the educational and vocational guidance services. The lack of knowledge about local employment opportunities was demonstrated in Jahoda's study[5] of school leavers, as was the limited extent of their information about their intended employment, a finding which accords with other studies.[6]

In the present inquiry, the intention was not to discover their knowledge of opportunities as such, but how far young people felt they had learnt what they wanted to know about their intended jobs, and from what sources they had obtained the information. The replies showed, firstly, that only a minority (less than one-third) felt that they had obtained most of the information they required, while as many as one-third of the boys and over two-fifths of the girls felt that they had discovered little or no information; secondly, that schools and the Youth Employment Service played a more important part in disseminating information about specific jobs than they evidently had in helping young people come to a decision about the type of work to enter; thirdly, that the great majority of young people relied on information being given by word of mouth rather than through visual material.

Sources of information

In general, the three chief sources of information for boys were their parents[7] (as reported by one-quarter of the boys interviewed), their schools (one-fifth), and the youth employment officers (one-sixth); relatives and friends were infrequently used. For girls, however, schools were by far the most frequently used (over one-quarter); youth employment

---

[4] The source of help in deciding on employment was, logically enough, strongly associated with the reasons offered for preferring a particular type of employment. Where parents, for instance, had been the chief source of help, the chief reasons offered for job preferences were 'other-directed', namely that others (including parents) had advised certain kinds of employment, or that job prospects were considered promising. Where young people felt that they themselves had decided, or had been helped by those outside the family, the most frequent reasons offered were 'inner-directed', namely that they had been good at related subjects at school, or had been always attracted to certain types of work or by particular features of the work in mind. How far this was because children with strong inner impulses were more unlikely than others to seek or obtain the help of their parents, or because strong parental influence made it difficult for them to follow their inclinations, could not be ascertained.

[5] G. Jahoda and A. D. Chalmers, op. cit.

[6] S. M. Chown, op. cit. and G. Jahoda, op. cit.

[7] Where parents were the chief source of help in job decisions they were also, for boys, by far the most frequent source of information about their intended employment.

officers were next in importance (under one-fifth), and then their parents (one-eighth).[8] Relatively few school leavers had obtained information from other sources, though books, employment interviews, previous part-time employment while at school, and writing to firms for information, were among the references made. Some leavers felt that their information had been 'picked up' here and there, and specified no particular source (Table 30).

TABLE 30. Sources of information about intended employment.

	Boys	Girls
	(Per cent of total)	
Parents	24	13
School	22	27
Y.E.O.	17	18
Friends	8	5
Relatives	4	12
Books	7	5
Writing for information	4	2
Interviews	3	2
Previous employment	1	4
No particular source	7	3
No information obtained	6	16
Total (Multiple replies)	100	100
(No. of 15–18s)	(183)	(147)

The frequency with which various sources of information were used varied somewhat according to the type of employment wanted. Boys seeking apprenticeships, for instance, were a little more likely than were others to have obtained information from the Youth Employment Service, and less likely to have used friends or to have consulted books. Boys seeking non-manual work, on the other hand, more frequently than any other leavers referred to their use of books and less frequently to parents and schools; rather more of them, however, proportionately, had failed to discover what they had wanted to know. Boys who intended to take up less skilled manual work corresponded fairly closely with would-be apprentices in their reference to various sources, except that they were less likely to have used the Youth Employment Service, and more likely to have relied on friends, or to have gathered their information haphazardly.

[8] Parents, relatives, and friends were much more frequently cited as sources of information by school leavers in the Veness study, accounting for some two-thirds, about one-fifth and just under one-third, respectively. The proportions referring to schools and youth employment officers, however, corresponded closely with the results in the present inquiry (see Veness, op. cit.).

The fact that girls referred more frequently to schools as a source of information was, on analysis, largely accounted for by the very high proportion who nominated this source among would-be office workers. Over two in five of the girls intending to take up clerical work referred to their schools, and only small minorities to their families, friends or youth employment officers. It will be recalled that many more, relatively, of would-be office workers referred to their interest or achievements in school subjects when giving their reasons for their particular job preferences. It seems likely, therefore, that commercial courses at schools were an obvious source of information about clerical work, and it is for this reason that references to school predominate in the replies of girls seeking office work. By contrast, girls wanting other types of work were much less likely to have obtained information from school, and more likely to have referred to the Youth Employment Service; they were twice as likely, moreover, to have felt that they had obtained no information.[9]

THE AMOUNT OF INFORMATION OBTAINED

The fact that rather more girls, proportionately, than boys had failed to obtain information from any source, was confirmed when school leavers were asked to recall how much information they had been able to discover, before starting work, about their intended jobs. Making some allowance for the fact that young people must have gained some knowledge about various types of employment, including their own, since being at work, a higher proportion of girls than of boys still referred to their having discovered little or nothing about the work they intended to do. Rather fewer girls also referred to their having found out some of the information required, but slightly higher proportions of girls than of boys evidently discovered most of what they had wanted to know. As many as one in three of the boys and over two in five of the girls, however, would seem to have learnt little or nothing, in comparison with what they felt they had needed to know, about the work they intended to do, and less than one in three felt that most of the information required had been obtained (Table 31). These results compare unfavourably with those obtained by Wilkins[10] and Jahoda,[11] who found two in five and three in five, respectively, of school

---

[9] Opinions of 50 of the 66 firms participating in the inquiry were fairly evenly divided between those who felt that school leavers were sufficiently informed, both in general and about their particular firms, and those who felt that school leavers, teachers, and youth employment officers were relatively ill-informed about the types of employment available, and about training, prospects, and conditions offered. A number of the latter firms, however, made suggestions as to what might improve the situation, the main emphasis of which was the need for closer liaison between industry, schools, and the Youth Employment Service. Several firms also stressed the importance of visits to enterprises by school leavers and of allowing them direct contact with workers employed in the jobs or firms to which children were attracted or in which they were interested.

[10] L. T. Wilkins, *The Adolescent in Britain*, The Social Survey, July 1955.

[11] G. Jahoda, op. cit.

leavers more or less fully conversant with the kind of work they were planning to do. It seems possible that the rather lower proportions of well-informed school leavers in the present inquiry is the result of a retrospective view.

TABLE 31. Amount of information
obtained about intended employment.

How much information	Boys	Girls
	(Per cent of total)	
Most	25	31
Some	36	23
Little or none	33	44
No answer	6	2
Total	100	100
(No. of 15–18s)	(183)	(147)

Social class and educational background

Since the majority of school leavers, whatever the sources of information used, had found these to be inadequate in terms of what they had wanted to know, it seemed important to examine in some further detail certain features of their social and educational background, the sources of help and information used, and their vocational preferences in order to see which of these factors, if any, were associated with their success or failure in obtaining the information they required.

The occupations of the fathers of the school leavers seen would seem to have some association with the extent to which information was obtained, though it seemed to have applied differently for boys than for girls. Firstly, appreciably fewer of the sons of manual workers felt that they had discovered most of what they had wanted to know (one-fifth) compared with the sons of non-manual workers (one-third); equal proportions of both, however, had learnt something of what they had needed to know, but rather more of the boys from the homes of manual workers than of others felt that they had obtained little or no information (two-fifths as against one-quarter). The differences according to social class were more striking for boys, when further analysis showed that of those who had discovered most of what they required, over one-half were the sons of non-manual workers whereas among those who had discovered least, over two-thirds were the sons of manual workers. The contrast between the girls, however, was not so much in the proportions who had discovered most but in the relatively small proportions of manual workers' daughters who had obtained only some of the information wanted and the relatively higher proportions who had discovered little or nothing.

Size of family would seem to have played some part in the amount of information obtained by boys, but not by girls. Among the boys who had discovered most, for instance, a higher proportion than of others were 'only' children, while among those who had discovered least, a higher proportion than of others were from families with more than three children. Likewise, relatively more of the boys who were 'only' children had discovered most of what they had wanted to know, compared with boys with one or more siblings, while the highest proportion who discovered little or nothing were from families of four or more children. Perhaps the 'only' children had more intensive parental care at this stage than had the children with siblings.

Attitudes to leaving school

Girls who had been eager to leave school were more likely than were others to have discovered little or nothing about the work they intended to do. In fact, more than one-half of the enthusiastic leavers among the girls were relatively ill-informed about their future employment, compared with just over two-fifths of the girls who had been less willing to leave. This tendency was evident for the boys but was not nearly as marked. How far it was associated with an impatience to start work could not be ascertained, though it may have been associated with a dislike of school as such and a rejection of what information school and other educational services might have offered.

Educational performance, as assessed by school leavers themselves in terms of their position in stream and in class, was also associated, in some degree, with the amount of information that was felt to have been discovered. Thus, relatively more boys from the higher stream (three in ten) felt that they had discovered most of what they had wanted to know, compared with those in the lower streams (three in twenty), but the proportions who had discovered least were more or less identical in all streams. Girls who were streamed did not show this tendency but rather more of them who had been 'above average' in class, relatively to others, referred to their having learnt most of what they had required, while very much higher proportions of girls in 'average', or 'less-than-average', class positions evidently discovered little or nothing. Position in class would also seem to have been associated with the amount of knowledge gained by boys, in that relatively fewer of the boys in 'average', or 'below-average' class positions had succeeded in finding out what they had wanted to know, and relatively more had failed than applied to boys in higher class positions.

Vocational preferences

There was considerable variation in the amount of information obtained by school leavers according to the type of work they wanted to do. A higher proportion (one-third) of boys hoping to take up non-manual work, for example, referred to their having discovered most of what they had wanted to know, than did boys hoping for apprenticeships (one-quarter) or boys wanting other types of manual work (only one-sixth). Would-be apprentices and other manual workers were more likely than others to have discovered little or nothing.

Since, however, there was some association between vocational preference, on the one hand, and the sources of information and help used, on the other, the comparative success or failure of school leavers in their search for information about particular occupations would appear to have been influenced, in part, by the persons whose help or advice was sought or offered.

The chances of finding out what they wanted to know were evidently higher if young people had been helped in their vocational decisions by their parents and, for boys, if they had made up their own minds as to what they wanted to do. Much higher proportions of school leavers, particularly girls, had discovered little or nothing, if persons other than their parents had influenced their decision.

Effectiveness of different sources of information

In assessing the effectiveness of the sources of information used, a number of interesting features emerge from these results. First, boys and girls who had learnt most about their intended jobs were more inclined than were others to make more frequent use of most of the different sources of information available. Second, boys who had discovered most were more likely than others to have used parents, schools, and relatives and to have written for information to firms and services, but to have used the Youth Employment Service less frequently than others. In fact, it was the boys who had discovered only some, or little or no, information who—in addition to their parents and schools—used the Youth Employment Service most intensively.

Girls showed a different pattern in their replies, being much more likely, in general, to have relied on their schools for information. The contrast in the use of sources, moreover, was mainly between girls who had discovered least and the rest, since the former referred much less frequently to any source of information, and nearly one-third felt they had learnt nothing. How far this was due to their having special difficulties in obtaining information or to their not using the sources available could not be ascertained. Schools, however, emerge as a more satisfactory source of information than does the Youth Employment Service, particularly for boys, the most successful of whom tended not to use the service for information, in contrast to those who were least successful in their search for information.

Since some information was presumably gathered when applying for jobs, it was thought of interest to see whether the methods by which first employment was obtained were associated in any way with the amount of information discovered. In this connection, the Youth Employment Service would seem to have played a more effective part than hitherto in giving information, since rather higher proportions of boys obtaining their first employment through the service felt that they had learnt most of what they had wanted, compared with boys who had either obtained work through their own efforts, or who had relied on informal help. Among girls, the influence of the service would appear to have operated in reducing the proportions who had learnt little or nothing and in raising the proportions who had learnt something. Girls who had obtained work either themselves or with the help of private and informal sources, were more likely than the users of the official service to have learnt nothing though just as likely as others to have learnt most of what they required.

SOURCE OF HELP IN OBTAINING FIRST EMPLOYMENT

Parents, siblings, other relatives, friends, and neighbours have been shown all to play an important part in arranging jobs. A survey conducted by K. R. Allen[12] indicated that nearly two in five National Servicemen considered that they had been most helped by their families in seeking work. In the Sheffield[13] survey, over one in three of the first jobs were obtained through the help of family and friends; in the study of Jahoda and Chalmers,[14] the proportions were just over one in five. Carter refers to the unpublished work of Marsh and Willcocks[15] who, on the basis of interviews with 2000 girls aged between fifteen and twenty concluded that the 'informal and personal contacts of the girls, their relations and friends, functioned far more frequently in introducing girls to their future work than did formal channels'.

Official reports[16] show that the Youth Employment Service was responsible during the years 1962–5 for the placement of some two-fifths of school leavers each year, though the proportions were higher for secondary modern than for other leavers; however, for England the proportions were lower for each educational category of school leaver during 1962–5, than for the preceding three years, and though the actual numbers of leavers was higher, the numbers placed were rather fewer.

Since the majority of school leavers are from secondary modern schools, they are also the principal users of the Youth Employment Service, but the

12 K. R. Allen, *Some Environmental Factors Affecting the Progress of Students in Technical Colleges*, unpublished M.A. Thesis, July 1960, (summarized in *Technical Education*, May and June 1961).
13 M. Carter, 1962, op. cit.
14 G. Jahoda and A. D. Chalmers, op. cit.
15 M. Carter, 1966, op. cit.
16 *The Work of the Youth Employment Service*, op. cit.

analysis of official figures shows that they also use the service more intensively than do other school-leaving groups, representing a higher proportion as placements than as leavers.

Carter suggests that there is even some doubt about the precise proportions of leavers placed, because the criteria for classification vary from one
area to another and a not inconsiderable number of children who find
jobs by other means and then inform the youth employment officer, are
counted as having been placed by the service.[17] His own study in Sheffield
suggested that no more than just over one in four of the boys and girls
were placed in their first jobs by the official service; the proportions in a
Lanarkshire study[18] were just under one in three; in Willesden, London,[19]
for the years 1960–63, the placement rate was over two-fifths and as high
as three-fifths for secondary modern school children. The Willesden inquiry also showed that there were year-to-year differences in the
proportions of placements to leavers.[20]

The study of placement records of the Willesden Youth Employment
Bureau was carried out initially for the purpose of constructing a sample;
but it became evident that a rather more detailed examination might
reveal something of the characteristics of the school leavers using the
bureau, the type of employment available to them and the nature of their
first and subsequent employment.

In the event, the inquiry showed not only that a relatively high proportion of total placements related to children seeking a change of employment, but that there were striking contrasts in the occupational
distribution between selective and non-selective school leavers, the great
majority of secondary modern boys becoming manual workers in relatively
unskilled work, while the majority of technical and grammar school boys
were placed either as apprentices or in clerical or other non-manual work.
Moreover, the concentration in manual work was even greater for the
subsequent, than for the first, placements of secondary modern school
leavers.

The analysis also suggested that young people wishing to work within
the borough were more likely, than those seeking work outside, to use the
Youth Employment Service; that, if placed by the service, young people
were more likely than others to be placed in small rather than large firms,
and that the vacancies registered with the bureau were relatively
concentrated in unskilled or semi-skilled manual work.

Though the majority of young people covered by the present inquiry
felt that they had decided for themselves what work they wanted to do,
only a minority (about one-quarter) had obtained their first jobs without

[17] M. Carter, 1966, op. cit.
[18] G. Jahoda and A. D. Chalmers, op. cit.
[19] J. Maizels, 1965, op. cit.
[20] Ibid.

9

help. The Youth Employment Service, which would seem to have played a minor role in helping school leavers decide on what employment to follow, or in providing them with information, assumed much greater importance for them in finding them work.[21] One in three of the school leavers seen were placed in their first jobs by the official vocational guidance service, representing the largest single source of help. The combined influences of parents, teachers, friends, relatives, and other agencies, however, accounted for slightly more school leavers than had used the official service (Table 32).

TABLE 32. Sources of help in obtaining
first employment.

	Boys	Girls
	(Per cent of total)	
Y.E.O.	32	32
Self	24	29
Relatives/friends	19	25
Parents	13	7
Teachers	6	3
Writing to firms	20	13
Press ads.	4	10
Firms' notices	2	11
Other	6	5
No answer	1	—
Total (Multiple replies)	100	100
(No. 8s)	(183)	(147)

In comparing these results with those obtained in the Lanarkshire[22] and Sheffield[23] studies, Willesden's leavers tended to use the Youth Employment Service more frequently than did others; while Lanarkshire leavers, more frequently than others, referred to their having found their first job themselves. The differences between the findings of each study were not, however, substantial.

Relatively few school leavers in the Willesden, as in the other, inquiries, had used press advertisements or notices outside firms as a means of finding their first jobs; one in five of the boys, but only one in eight of the girls, had sent off written applications, the addresses of which had sometimes been

---

[21] The 1965–68 Report shows an increase since 1962–65, in the proportion of school leavers placed in employment by the Y.E.S. This increase is entirely accounted for by a rise in the proportions of placements relating to secondary modern school leavers; the proportions in each educational category placed in employment are still lower, however, for the years 1965–68 than for the years 1959–62.

[22] G. Jahoda and A. Chalmers, op. cit.

[23] M. Carter, 1962, op. cit.

given them by the youth employment officer. Girls, but not boys, had used private employment agencies, mainly for clerical work.

Factors associated with methods of finding first employment

In the present inquiry an attempt was made, not only to discover how young people had obtained their first (and subsequent) employment, and whether or not they had used the official service, but to trace the extent to which their use of the service or other means of finding work was associated with any special features in their social and educational background; or with the type of work originally wanted and subsequently obtained;[24] and with the number of jobs held.

There was little variation according to social class, however, in the frequency with which school leavers had relied on the various formal and informal sources of help when finding their first jobs: but attendance at secondary modern schools was, in the case of boys, associated with a much more frequent use of the service. One-third of the boys from non-selective schools referred to their having obtained their first jobs through the official service, compared with only one-fifth of those from other types of secondary school. Boys from secondary modern schools were also more inclined than others to have relied on their parents, but less inclined to have had the help of relatives or friends, or to have relied on their own efforts.

The fact that leavers at fifteen among the boys were less inclined, than were leavers at sixteen, to use the Youth Employment Service was, on further analysis, found to be largely due to the higher proportions of the latter having entered apprenticeships; successful apprentices were more likely than other boys to have had the help of the Youth Employment Service. When apprentices were excluded from the analysis, there were few differences between the two age-of-leaving groups, and virtually none in their respective use of the service.

When attitudes to leaving school were analysed according to the type of help received when finding first jobs, it was evident that enthusiastic leavers, particularly the girls, were less inclined than were others to use the Youth Employment Service. For boys, this meant that they were more likely to find work themselves and to write to firms; for girls, that they were more likely to rely on relatives or friends (Table 33).

Further analysis of the reasons offered for attitudes towards leaving school showed that it was those who disliked or who were dissatisfied with some aspect of school who were less likely than were others, to have used the Youth Employment Service. In fact, it would appear that a favourable view of school and a wish for further study (both associated with the reluctant leaver), pre-disposed leavers to a more frequent use of the Youth Employment Service; in contrast, unfavourable experiences of school

[24] Young people were also asked to comment on possible improvements to present arrangements for finding work, their references to the Youth Employment Service are described in Ch. X.

would seem to have been associated with less frequent use of the service and with more frequent reliance on the help of relatives, friends, or on their own initiative.

The frequency with which official and private sources of help were used, however, did vary according to job preferences and this particularly applied to the use of the Youth Employment Service. Its help, for instance, was much more frequently sought by would-be apprentices than by boys seeking less skilled manual work; and by girls planning to take up office or other non-manual work.

As is discussed more fully in Chapter IX, school leavers were, in the first instance, generally more likely to be successful in their vocational aims if they were helped in some way to find their first jobs than if they found

TABLE 33. Attitudes to leaving school and sources of help in obtaining first employment.

| | How much wanted to leave school | | | |
| | Boys | | Girls | |
	Very much Quite a lot	Didn't mind Not very much Not at all	Very much Quite a lot	Didn't mind Not very much Not at all
	(Per cent of total)			
Self	27	19	31	25
Y.E.O.	26	35	18	34
Relatives/friends	18	19	30	20
Parents	14	13	7	6
Teachers	6	8	3	3
Writing to firms	25	3	11	13
Press ads.	4	1	6	12
Firms' notices	3	15	13	10
Other	1	2	11	4
Total (Multiple replies)	100	100	100	100
(No. of 15–18s)[a]	(90)	(92)	(82)	(65)

a Excluding not answering.

employment entirely unaided. Moreover, the Youth Employment Service, in particular, would seem more frequently to have helped the would-be apprentice and, to a lesser degree, girls seeking non-manual work other than in offices, to achieve their aims than was the case when other official or private sources of help were involved.

The question arises as to what extent children who were dissatisfied in some respect with school, identified the Youth Employment Service as an integral part of an educational authority from whose influence they were anxious to escape; or, in their eagerness to leave school, rejected further officialdom, of whatever kind; or, arising from their school experiences, assumed that the service was unlikely to be of much help to them. The evidence of the present inquiry does not indicate which of these several considerations may have played a part in influencing the eager school leaver to find work other than through the official service. Any investigation of the use of the service, however, would need to look closely at school experiences and their possible connection with attitudes to other ancillary services.

Where parents were the chief source of help and advice in the job decisions of young people, they, together with relatives or friends, were also the chief source through which school leavers obtained their first jobs; moreover, school leavers who had relied on their parents for initial advice were much less likely than were others to have used the Youth Employment Service when it came to obtaining their first jobs. The use of the official service was, therefore, more likely either if young people had decided for themselves what to do or, if others—including the service—had helped in their decision. The weaker the parental influence, therefore, the more likely it was the help of the official service would be sought.

SECURING EMPLOYMENT

A relatively high proportion of school leavers (over one-half of the boys and just under two-thirds of the girls) had, evidently, obtained the first job for which they applied; most school leavers could, therefore, be assumed to have had little difficulty, in this sense, in finding their first employment. Less than one-third had tried for between two to three jobs and one-fifth for more than three, before finally obtaining work. Boys who had experienced the greatest difficulty were leavers from areas outside the south-east region who had come to the London area because of its employment opportunities.

The proportions of successful first applications are thus considerably higher in the present inquiry than in the Sheffield study,[25] where not only were boys more frequently successful than girls in their applications but where less than one in three of the school leavers seen obtained work on their first application.

Applying for more than one job was not, however, necessarily associated with difficulty or failure to obtain the work wanted. Most of the school leavers seen in the present inquiry had rejected alternative offers rather than experienced rejection themselves. In fact, none of the girls referred to their having failed to obtain any job for which they had applied, though among the boys nearly one in ten had failed in one or more of their applications for work.

The number of jobs tried for was, apparently, associated with the methods used to obtain employment only in so far as leavers who used their own initiative were more likely than others to have tried for more

[25] M. Carter, 1962, op. cit.

than one job while, in contrast, leavers who had relied on the help of
teachers and parents were rather more likely to have tried for and obtained
the one job.

Time taken to find first employment

The sample of school leavers was more or less evenly divided between
those who had obtained their first jobs while still at school, and those who
had waited until they had left school before trying to find work. For just
over one in five, first jobs were obtained within a few days of leaving
school; for rather more, just over one in four, there was a period of several
weeks before employment was found. Not all school leavers, however,
spent this amount of time looking for work, since if leaving school coincided
with the summer holiday season, many referred to their having taken a
holiday before starting work. In other cases, the time taken was associated
with the number of jobs that had to be applied for. Boys who entered
skilled trades were more likely than others to have found their jobs while
still at school, while boys who entered non-manual employment were
more likely to have taken longer to find their first jobs. Girls, however,
showed little variation according to the type of employment obtained.

The kind of help used when looking for work would not, however,
appear to have been associated with the time taken to find work. Those
who took longest to find work were more likely to have relied on their own
efforts, or on the help of the Youth Employment Service, and to have used
less frequently than others, the help of parents, teachers, friends, or
relatives. These tendencies however, mainly reflect the different frequencies with which boys seeking and obtaining different types of employment
used the various sources of help.

SOURCE OF HELP IN FINDING FIRST EMPLOYMENT AND CHANGES IN EMPLOYMENT[26]

It seemed of interest to discover whether there was any particular association between the source of help in obtaining first jobs, and the number of
job changes of the young people interviewed.[27] In a sense, such a relationship might indicate the relative effectiveness of the different sources of
help available. For this purpose, the young people seen were divided into
two broad groups: those who were still in their first jobs, and those who
had had at least one other job since starting work.

On this criterion of 'effectiveness', i.e. finding a first job in which the
school leaver remained for a number of years, it would seem that the

---

[26] Job changes are separately analysed and discussed in Chapter XI.

[27] The sources of help used by school leavers when seeking a change of employment are
discussed in more detail in Chapter XI.

Youth Employment Service was the least effective method as far as boys were concerned. A much higher proportion of job-changers (two-fifths) had originally been placed in their first jobs by the service, than had boys who were still in their first jobs (just over one-quarter).[28] Moreover, the more frequent use made of the Youth Employment Service by job-changers was, in their case, associated with a less frequent use of parents and teachers (Table 34). There was little difference, however, between

TABLE 34. Sources of help in obtaining first employment. Job-changers and others.

| | First employment | | | |
| | Boys | | Girls | |
	Only 1 job	More than 1	Only 1 job	More than 1
	(Per cent of total)			
Y.E.O.	28	42	36	26
Self	24	24	18	34
Relatives/friends	19	20	28	21
Parents	14	8	8	2
Teachers	9	—	2	9
Writing to firms	26	9	19	5
Press ads.	3	5	—	14
Firm's notices	—	7	—	12
Other	7	9	6	12
Total (Multiple replies)	100	100	100	100
(No. of 15–18s)[a]	(124)	(58)	(89)	(58)

a Excluding not answering.

job-changers and the rest in the proportions who had relied either on the help of friends or relatives or who had found their first jobs without help.

The least effective method for girls, however, was to have found their first jobs without help: one-third of girls with more than one job experience had relied on their own efforts compared with only one-fifth of those still in their first jobs. Moreover, the Youth Employment Service, and to a lesser extent friends, relatives, and parents had been used more frequently by those who had remained in their first employment, than by those who had had at least one change of job; job-changers, however, tended to have been helped more frequently by teachers and by private employment agencies.

There were other differences of interest between the two groups of leavers. Boys and girls still in their first jobs were much more likely than others to have sent written requests or applications to firms. This in itself

[28] An analysis of one cohort of secondary modern school leavers also showed a higher incidence of job-change among official first placements. (See J. Maizels, 1967, op. cit.)

implies the exercise of some discrimination or a pre-knowledge in choosing firms in which they wished to work, either on their own part or on that of others who advised or helped them. Girls who were in their second or subsequent jobs, on the other hand, had used press advertisements and notices outside firms to an appreciable extent; by contrast, these particular methods were not used at all by girls still in their first jobs.

The fact that the Youth Employment Service placements were associated, in the case of boys, with the highest proportions who had changed, and in the case of girls, with the highest proportions who had remained in their first jobs, could not be investigated more fully on the basis of the information available. It would seem, however, that part of the explanation lies in the different types of employment in which young people were placed.

Boys who obtained work in skilled trades or in other types of manual and non-manual work used the Youth Employment Service in almost equal proportions; but three-quarters of the boys with more than one job were less skilled manual workers and one in six were in non-manual employment; almost all the apprentices, however, were still in their first jobs. Since the job-changers contained more boys placed in their first jobs by the service than found work through other means, it follows that it was boys placed by the service in semi- or unskilled manual work who were most subject to job change. Though apprentices are, in any case, less frequently mobile than other boys, it would seem that they were also more suitably matched—in a vocational sense—i.e. in terms of their interests and abilities and the type of jobs and firms entered, than were other placements.

Carter,[29] who found that one-half of the boys, and nearly one-half of the girls, placed by the Youth Employment Bureau had left their jobs within the first year, suggests that many of the jobs notified to the local service (outside apprenticeships), had a high rate of turnover; and that it was the employer with unattractive work who tended to seek the help of the service. He also suggested that the children who used the Youth Employment Bureau for this type of work may have been more pre-disposed than others to the risk of job change.

The Willesden[30] analysis of youth employment bureau placements, and of the actual distribution of under-eighteens at work in the borough, showed that employers who used the bureau consisted predominantly of small firms,[31] that the vacancies registered were relatively concentrated in unskilled and semi-skilled manual work; and that there was a tendency for the placements of boys through the bureau to be considerably more concentrated in unskilled and semi-skilled manual work, and less concentrated in apprenticeships, than applied in the total at work.

[29] M. Carter, 1962, op. cit.   [30] J. Maizels, 1965, op. cit.
[31] The relationship between frequency of job change and size of firm is examined in Chapter XI.

The reason why boys who obtained manual work other than through the official services were less likely to change their jobs can only be speculated upon. It may be due to the kind of help that boys received from their parents, relatives, and friends who might themselves have been, or known others who were, employed in the same firms in which the boys found their first jobs. In such cases, this may have enhanced the chances of their remaining in their first employment. It may have been because they had a wider choice of possible jobs than if they had used the official service, since this has only a partial cover of outstanding vacancies.

Though the association between youth employment placements and job change operated in a different way for girls than for boys, the relatively high proportion of job-changers who found work entirely through their own efforts is also partly explained by the type of employment offered. Relatively more girls who had at least one other job were manual workers than was the case among girls still in their first jobs; and girls in manual work were rather more likely than others to have found their jobs by themselves. Nevertheless, it should be noted that one in four of the girl job-changers also obtained their first jobs through the Youth Employment Service, which represented the second most frequent source of help used. A possible explanation of this is that girls in non-manual work (relatively more of whom were among the job-changers than among those still in their first employment) were rather more likely than others to have sought the help of the Youth Employment Service, not only in getting jobs, but in deciding what to do and for relevant information. Moreover, these were girls who were more likely than others to have entered employment which differed from their original preferences.

Whatever the explanation for the particular role of the Youth Employment Service in connection with job change,[32] it is evident that school leavers were less inclined to use the official service when seeking their second, than when finding their first, jobs. Not more than one in four of the boys and one in eight of the girls were placed in their second jobs by the service, though over two-fifths and one-quarter of boys and girls, respectively, had sought the help of their local bureau when finding their first employment. Instead, school leavers turned more frequently to relatives and friends, and were much more inclined than previously, to rely on their own initiative.

SUMMARY

When deciding what work to do, most young people felt that they had made up their own minds; only about one in four attributed help chiefly to their parents and relatively few nominated any other person, including

---

[32] This is more fully discussed in Chapter IX in connection with original vocational aims and ultimate attainments.

the youth employment officer, as having helped them at this stage. Where parents were the chief source of help, school leavers were more likely to refer to external suggestions and advice or to job prospects as their reasons for their choice of employment; where young people felt that they had made up their own minds or had been helped by others than their parents, they were more likely to refer to 'inner-directed' choice. Parental help in boys' decisions were also associated with the family being the chief source of information about the intended jobs; boys who had relied on the help of others or on their own decisions, were more likely to have obtained information from schools or youth employment officers. These tendencies did not apply to the sample of girls. The three chief sources of information for boys were their parents, their schools, and youth employment officers; but for girls, schools were more frequently used, then youth employment officers and then their parents. But whatever the source of information, it would not appear to have been very effective, since only a minority—less than one-third—felt that they had discovered most of what they wanted to know about their intended jobs; as many as one in three of the boys and over two in five of the girls, moreover, felt that they had discovered little or nothing.

Boys and girls who had learned most, tended to have made more intensive use of a number of different sources, the most adequate, for boys, being their parents, schools, relatives, and written material obtained from firms; the least adequate had been the Youth Employment Service. For girls, schools were the most satisfactory source of information. The Youth Employment Service would seem to have played a more effective part in giving information when placing leavers in their first employment, since rather more of the boys who obtained their first jobs in this way felt that they had learnt most of what they required compared with boys who had obtained work through other means.

The Youth Employment Service also assumed greater importance in finding leavers their first jobs than in helping them decide what jobs to take up or in providing them with job information. One in three of the young people seen obtained their first jobs through the official service, which thus represented the largest single source of help at this stage.

The users of the service were more likely to be secondary modern school leavers, would-be apprentices, girls wanting non-manual work and leavers who attributed their vocational decisions to others than their parents. The weaker the parental influence at the stage of deciding on jobs, the more likely it seems that the help of the official service was sought in job finding. Attitudes to leaving school were also found to be markedly associated with the use of the service and the more enthusiastic leavers who disliked or who were dissatisfied with some aspect of school were much less inclined than were others to find work through the Youth Employment Service and much more inclined to find work themselves. A favourable view of school, on the other hand would seem to have been associated with a more frequent use of the official service.

The possible effectiveness of the different sources of help in finding jobs was assessed, using as a criteria of effectiveness the factor of job change. When young people were divided into those still in their first jobs and those in their second or subsequent employment, it was evident that the official service was the least and parents and teachers the most, effective of the methods used in finding their first jobs, as far as boys were concerned. A much higher proportion of job-changers had originally been placed in their first jobs by the service than had boys who were still in their first jobs; these latter boys had tended to make more frequent use of their parents and teachers. No differences however emerged between job-changers and the rest in the proportions who had relied either on their friends or relatives or who had found their first jobs themselves.

The least effective method for girls, however, was finding their first jobs without the help of any formal or informal agency; in contrast to the boys, the official service, and to a lesser extent friends, relatives, and parents were more frequently used by those who had remained in their first employment.

These contrasting tendencies may be partly explained by the type of employment obtained, which in the case of boys placed by the Youth Employment Bureau and in the case of girls who found their own jobs, were relatively concentrated in semi-skilled or unskilled manual work. School leavers were less inclined to use the official service when seeking their second than when finding their first jobs and turned more frequently to relatives or friends or increasingly relied on their own initiative.

CHAPTER IX

AIMS AND ATTAINMENTS

INTRODUCTION

Success or otherwise in realizing vocational aims is determined by a complex of factors, not the least important of which are the demand for particular kinds of labour on the one hand, and the abilities, interest, qualifications, and personal situation of the individual seeking employment on the other. Since the demand is broadly influenced by economic factors, frequently short-term, and the supply by demographic and educational factors, inevitably long-term, the adjustment between them is rarely, if ever, precise.

However, special circumstances apply to children starting work for the first time. They are less mobile, for instance, than are adult workers and are, therefore, more proscribed by local employment conditions. Carter describes how the industrial structure of Sheffield imposed certain limitations on the type of employment available to school leavers, particularly boys.[1] School leavers are also relatively inexperienced and unqualified; they are generally ill-informed about the range of employment available, and about the jobs of their particular choice; and, even disregarding all these considerations, some of their preferences may be unrealistic.

They are also keen to start work and, as is evident from the Sheffield study,[2] may take the first opportunity offered rather than wait for the job of their first choice that might not, in the event, materialize.

It was not possible, in the present inquiry, to study the demand situation which faced school leavers, since this would have required an investigation of the full range of jobs available to them at the time they left school. Their present employers were asked, however, to describe the qualifications and experience required for the jobs in which young people interviewed were employed. This information is more fully discussed in Chapter XIII; the analysis showed, interestingly enough, that the proportion of leavers with some academic qualifications was a little lower than that estimated to be required by the employers.[3] Personal characteristics,

---

[1] M. Carter, 1962, op. cit.

[2] Ibid.

[3] Just over one in four of the job specifications completed by employers, relating to the jobs of 647 young people under eighteen, referred to some 'O' levels as being a minimum requirement. About one in five of the 330 young people interviewed had one or more G.C.E. passes at 'O' level. Assuming the same frequency for the remainder of the 600 covered by the job descriptions, demand, in this sense, did not match supply.

however, such as personal appearance, alertness, reliability, etc., were much more frequently nominated as essential than were academic or practical aptitudes, though there was some variation according to the type of employment described.

In order to trace the relationship between the jobs nominated and obtained, two comparisons were made. The jobs entered were classified first according to whether they were identical with, similar to, or different from, those first hoped for; and second, according to the proportions originally wanting and subsequently obtaining certain types of employment. Naturally enough, rather fewer school leavers obtained particular jobs which corresponded more or less exactly to their first choice than entered the type or broad category of employment wanted. If, however, the proportions obtaining jobs which were identical or similar to first preferences are combined, there is a closer approximation between the proportion obtaining such jobs and the proportion entering the types of employment originally preferred.

School leavers were also asked whether, at any stage of the process of job choice, they had given up ideas about other types of work which they had particularly wanted to do. It was hoped that, in addition to tracing the extent to which aims were fulfilled, it would be possible also to assess how far young people, in giving up their original preferences, now felt that their present employment was, to some extent, only second-best.

Degree of similarity in jobs obtained

The first of the comparisons showed that over one in three of the young people seen were, at the time of inquiry, in work which in terms of the job, status, type of employment and enterprise, corresponded more or less exactly with what they had originally wanted. An almost equal proportion, however, were in jobs that were quite different from their original preferences; smaller proportions, about one in six, had found work that was similar in some respect with their intentions, having found either the job they had wanted but not the type of enterprise or industry planned, or the firm and industry they wished for but not the particular job for which they had hoped (Table 35).

Since rather different bases were used in other studies for comparing preferences with attainments, it is difficult to assess how consistent are the proportions achieving their objectives in the present inquiry with those in other samples of school leavers. Carter found that one-third of the boys, and just under one-half of the girls, took jobs which were precisely the same as, or closely related to, their choice of work;[4] similar proportions

[4] M. Carter, 1962, op. cit.

were found in the Veness study, when just under one-third of the boys and
over one-half of the girls entered the actual trades and training courses
they had named two years earlier.[5] Jahoda, on the other hand, found that
rather higher proportions of school leavers (over one-half of the boys and
nearly two-thirds of the girls) had realized their interview choices.[6]

In these three studies, however, girls were consistently more successful
than boys in obtaining the jobs of their choice, whereas, in the present
inquiry, they hardly differed from the boys in the degree to which they
managed to realize their preferences.

TABLE 35. Difference between jobs wanted and
obtained.

How different is present job from that wanted	Boys	Girls
	(Per cent of total)	
More or less identical	38	35
Similar in some respect	15	17
Quite different	36	38
Don't know	11	10
Total	100	100
(No. of 15–18s)	(183)	(147)

The types of employment obtained

There were, however, differences between occupational groups, in that
much higher proportions of apprentices among the boys, and office
workers among the girls, were in jobs more or less identical with their first
preferences (over one-half), than was the case among leavers in relatively
unskilled manual work. By contrast, over one-half of these boys and three-
fifths of the girls were in jobs which were quite different from what they
originally wanted.

The second comparison showed the gap between intention and realization according to the type of employment wanted. This also varied for
certain occupations. Thus, on leaving school rather smaller proportions
of boys actually obtained than had wanted apprenticeships.[7] On the other
hand, the proportions of boys and girls whose first jobs were in semi- or
unskilled manual work exceeded the proportions who had originally preferred this type of work; and none of the boys who entered work as sales-
men had planned this type of work for themselves. The proportion of girls

[5] T. Veness, op. cit.
[6] G. Jahoda, op. cit.
[7] Almost all the girls wanting apprenticeships found them; but they were very few in number.

who became sales assistants was rather smaller than that originally wanting such work. There was a very close relationship, however, between boys and girls wanting and obtaining clerical work, though girls rather than boys slightly exceeded in number those originally wanting to enter offices (Table 36).

The largest gap between the jobs originally preferred and actually obtained was for school leavers who had wanted non-manual work other than in offices. Though only small minorities expressed such preferences, boys seeking this type of employment were less 'successful' than were would-be apprentices; and only one girl in this category actually found work which corresponded in some degree, with her first choice. It will be recalled, however, that the job preferences of this particular group of school leavers, more frequently than others', required age, educational or other qualifications which, for a variety of reasons, they were not able to meet. Moreover, some of these preferences may have been much farther beyond the bounds of real possibility than were, for instance, the wishes of would-be though ultimately unsuccessful, apprentices.

In the event, therefore, rather more young people entered relatively unskilled manual work, rather fewer boys the skilled trades, and rather fewer boys and girls work requiring some degree of industrial training and further education than would have been the case had their original aims been realized. Thus, at the time of the inquiry, only forty-seven of the seventy-five boys who had originally wanted apprenticeships had actually found work in any skilled trade, the remainder taking up less-skilled occupations; eleven of the thirty-six boys who had sought non-manual work were in relatively unskilled manual jobs; and of the twenty-seven girls who had hoped to find non-manual work but not in offices, nine were in clerical and five in manual, jobs.

There was thus a reduction in the average level of skill, training, further education and status provided by the jobs actually entered compared with what would have been offered by those originally preferred. Moreover, as is more fully discussed in Chapter XI, as school leavers moved out of their first and into their second and subsequent jobs, there was a general tendency for the proportions in relatively skilled occupations to fall and in relatively unskilled work to rise.[8] Between first and subsequent jobs there was a shift from more to less skilled employment and the downward shift in skill and status was more marked after the second change of employment and applied more frequently to boys than to girls. Thus the gap between aims and fulfilment widened for school leavers over the course of time.

[8] This conclusion is supported by an analysis of the changes in employment of one cohort of secondary modern school boys in Willesden. The second or subsequent Y.E.S. placements of school leavers in Willesden during 1960–63 showed a higher concentration in less skilled manual work than was evident for first placements. (See J. Maizels, 1965, op. cit.)

TABLE 36. Type of employment wanted and obtained
according to present type of employment.

	Original preference	First employment	Present employment
	(Per cent of total)		
Boys			
Apprenticeships	41	37	30
Other manual	34	48	54
Non-manual	20	15	16
Don't know	1	—	—
No answer	4	—	—
Girls			
Clerical	48	52	52
Manual	11	21	26
Other non-manual	35	27	22
Don't know	1	—	—
No answer	5	—	—
Total	100	100	100
(No. of 15–18s) Boys	(183)	(183)	(183)
Girls	(147)	(147)	(147)

SUCCESS AND FAILURE IN ACHIEVING ORIGINAL JOB PREFERENCES

One indicator of the average degree of success of any group of school
leavers in achieving their original job preferences is the proportion of those
originally preferring a particular type of work who were in such work at
the time of the inquiry.[9] As Table 37 shows, this proportion varied considerably from one preferred occupational group to another. Among the
boys, the most successful, on this criterion, were those originally intending
to enter unskilled or semi-skilled manual work; not far short of nine-tenths
of this group were in such work at the time of the inquiry. The least successful were those preferring some type of non-manual work, only two-
fifths of whom eventually found such work. Apprentices, three-fifths of
whom were successful on this criterion, were in an intermediate position.
Among the girls, those originally preferring apprenticeships most frequently found jobs of their choice (four-fifths); those seeking unskilled and
semi-skilled manual work were also largely successful (nearly three-
quarters); but only one-half of those preferring sales or other non-manual
work were found in such work at the time of the inquiry.

For both boys and girls therefore, non-manual work appeared relatively
the most difficult to obtain, and unskilled or semi-skilled manual work, as

[9] The non-realization of original preferences would seem to be relevant to job changing. As is
shown in Chapter XI, twice as many boys with more than one job were in work which differed
from that originally preferred as were boys with only one job.

was to be expected, the easiest (excluding the relatively few girl apprenticeships).

TABLE 37. Degree of success in attaining original job preference and
average degree of preference for present job.

Type of present employment	Boys		Girls	
	Degree of success[a]	Average preference[b]	Degree of success[a]	Average preference[b]
	(Per cent)			
Apprenticeships	63	86	81	73
Other manual work	86	55	71	32
Non-manual (incl. sales)	44	55	49	78
Total	100	100	100	100
(No. of 15–18s)	(67)	(64)[c]	(68)	(64)[c]

a Proportion originally preferring specified type of work who obtained such employment.

b Proportion of those now in specified occupation who had originally wanted such employment.

c Including small numbers not expressing original job preferences.

Since, as already indicated, some proportion of girls experienced a
'downgrading' of occupations from their original preferences, the total of
young people now in each occupational group contained varying proportions of those who had originally preferred that particular type of
work. These proportions indicate the average degree of original preference
for the work expressed by young people in each occupational category at
the time of the inquiry. Of the boys now in unskilled or semi-skilled manual
work, for example, little more than one-half had originally wanted such
work; the same average degree of preference was found for boys in non-
manual work whereas, by contrast, the corresponding proportion for those
now in apprenticeships was nearly nine-tenths. For the girls, the main
contrast was between unskilled or semi-skilled manual work, with a degree
of original preference of only one-third, and the other occupational
groups, for which the proportions were in the region of three-quarters.

To some extent the excess of the degree of success over the average preference[10] for each occupation can be interpreted as an indication of the
extent of 'job frustration'. On this basis, the prevalence of job frustration
can be assumed to be greatest among boys and girls in unskilled and semi-
skilled work. However, frustration depends not only on the non-attain-
ments of original job preferences, but also on whether young people felt
that something worthwhile had to be given up. The relinquishment of a
job preference that had been particularly wanted must, therefore, also be
taken into account.

10 As defined in Table 37.

10

Relinquishment of original aims

In so far as the employment obtained proved acceptable and, in time, was regarded as perhaps a wiser choice than was the original job preference, modification of vocational aims was not necessarily associated with disappointment or regret. As Carter found, the fact of obtaining a job in accordance with the aim did not necessarily mean that children were satisfied with the job obtained;[11] some, as is shown in the job histories,[12] found their first jobs unsuitable or not up to their expectations, and changed to other jobs or to other types of employment. Nor did it follow that young people who obtained work other than that which they would have preferred, were necessarily dissatisfied. Some of these felt, in retrospect, that things had turned out better for them than, perhaps, would have been the case if they had followed up their first choice.

However, in order to discover how far school leavers still felt committed, in some degree, to their first preferences, they were asked whether they now felt they had had to give up any ideas about types of work which they had particularly wanted to do. Their replies could be interpreted as an indication of the extent to which young people still felt relatively strongly about their first aspirations, and regarded their present employment, however satisfactory, as second-best.

In replying to this question, it was evident that there were some school leavers who, even if their present employment differed in some way from their original aims, felt neither attached to their first preferences nor regretful that they had failed to achieve them. There were, in addition, a small number who, in response to this question, revealed that their job preferences on leaving school were, in fact, second choices, their prior aspirations having been abandoned before leaving school.

The appeal or attraction of their original preferences still remained for just over one in three of all the boys and girls interviewed (Table 38). The majority of boys who felt this way referred to their having had to abandon the idea of apprenticeships (though in some cases it was the idea of a particular trade that had had to be relinquished rather than a skilled trade itself); one in four of the boys referred to less skilled jobs in factory or other manual employment and a further one in three to non-manual occupations. Girls, rather more frequently than boys, referred to their having given up the idea of non-manual work (over two in five) and office work (nearly one in five).

The proportions are, of course, considerably reduced when related to the sample as a whole; nevertheless, even on this basis, as many as one in six of the boys felt that they had had to abandon the idea of entering skilled trades, and one in eight the idea of the Armed Services or profes-

[11] 1962, op. cit.
[12] See Chapter XI.

sional and intermediate occupations. For the sample of girls, one in six felt that they had had to give up a preference for non-manual work and one in seven, work in offices or shops.

TABLE 38. Original job preference
relinquished.

Whether employment particularly wanted given up	Boys	Girls
	(Per cent of total)	
Yes	37	34
No	60	63
Uncertain	3	3
Total	100	100
(No. of 15–18s)	(183)	(147)

In terms of their present employment, modification of aims meant that some occupational groups included higher proportions than did others of boys and girls who still felt that their present jobs were second best compared with their first preferences. This applied particularly to those now in manual work.

Reasons for giving up first preferences

The reasons offered by young people for having relinquished their original aims differed as between girls and boys. The chief reason offered by boys, for instance, was that they did not have the necessary qualifications, including that of age, for the work they wanted. Relatively few of the girls, however, had been affected by this factor. Both boys and girls had found, almost in the same degree, that there had been no vacancies in the trade or firm they had wished to enter. Far more boys than girls, proportionately, had rejected their first preference because of uncertainties about its future prospects, or had themselves been rejected at interviews or in tests for the work of their first choice. Equal proportions of both, however, had been persuaded by parents, friends, or others to give up their first ideas in favour of other types of employment or jobs. Girls, far more than boys, had taken up alternative employment because they had believed working conditions were better elsewhere—a factor which applied to relatively few of the boys (Table 39).

The reasons offered for giving up first preferences also differed according to the type of work originally wanted. Boys seeking skilled manual work were more likely than others to have been affected by there being no vacancies; boys seeking other types of work were more likely to have failed tests or interviews, to have been uncertain about future prospects and, if wanting non-manual work, to have found that they did not have the necessary qualifications. The latter were also a little more likely, evidently, than others to have been persuaded against their preferences by their parents or others. Girls seeking non-manual employment, particularly non-office work, were more likely to have been affected by the feeling that they lacked ability, a reluctance to take on lengthy training, or by there being no vacancies in the trade, enterprise, or training college. Girls who had originally been attracted to hairdressing or to certain types of outdoor or manual work, were more likely to have been influenced by the prospect of better conditions elsewhere.

TABLE 39. Reasons for relinquishing original job preference.

	Boys		Girls	
	a	b	a	b
	(Per cent of total)			
Did not have necessary qualifications	9	25	1	4
No vacancies in trade, firm, school, etc.	7	18	5	14
Uncertain about future	5	15	1	2
Persuaded or advised against	5	15	5	16
Failed test, interview, etc.	5	13	1	4
Felt lacked ability	4	12	6	18
Training took too long	2	6	5	7
Working conditions better elsewhere	2	4	7	20
Job or self felt to be unsuitable	1	3	3	4
Miscellaneous	2	6	4	10
Total (Multiple replies)	100	100	100	100
(No. of 15–18s)	(183)	(73)	(147)	(57)

a Proportion of total sample.
b Proportion of those who had relinquished original job preference.

Occupational interest

Using the Rothwell-Miller system of classifying jobs according to occupational interest,[13] the correspondence between job preferences and actual attainment was very close for boys. This is undoubtedly due to the fact that boys unable to obtain apprenticeships, for instance, tended to find work within the same category of occupational interest; the would-be tool maker, for example, became a capstan operator; the would-be carpenter and joiner went into coach building. Thus in every sphere of occupational interest, the preferences of boys corresponded fairly closely with attainments. This was not the case for the girls, rather more of whom obtained work in the mechanical, computational, practical, and personal spheres of interest than was indicated by their original preferences and

[13] K. M. Miller, 'The Measurement of Vocational Interests by a Stereotype Ranking Method', *Journal of Applied Psychology*, **44**, No. 3, 1960.

rather fewer in the clerical and aesthetic fields. This is partly due to girls entering offices and becoming calculating machine operators, ledger clerks, etc., and to rather more girls obtaining factory work as machine operators, assemblers, bench hands, etc., than had originally intended to do so. It was easier, evidently, for boys than for girls to find work which, in terms of occupational interest, was consistent with that of their original preference.

SOCIAL AND EDUCATIONAL BACKGROUND AND SOURCES OF VOCATIONAL HELP

It seemed important not only to trace the extent to which preferences and attainments corresponded but, in so far as some modification of original intentions had occurred, to consider who were the school leavers most likely to have succeeded in, or failed to realize, their aims, and the possible factors associated with their success or failure. An attempt was made therefore, to look at certain features in their social and educational background and at the sources of help and information when deciding on, and obtaining, their employment, in the light of their original aims and their subsequent attainments.

When aims and attainments were compared according to the occupations of their fathers, the sons of manual workers were consistently more successful in realizing their preferences than were the sons of non-manual workers. Though more or less equal proportions of boys, irrespective of their social class background, had originally wanted to enter skilled trades (just over two-fifths) almost this proportion of boys from the homes of manual workers did so on leaving school and one-third were still in apprenticeships at the time of inquiry. Less than one-third of the boys from the homes of non-manual workers, however, obtained apprenticeships on leaving school while only one-quarter were still in skilled trades at the time of interview.

A more striking contrast was evident for the other categories of job preferences. The proportion of boys with fathers in non-manual occupations who obtained semi-skilled or unskilled manual work on leaving school and subsequently (one-half), was almost twice as high as the proportion originally wanting this type of work; for boys with fathers in manual work the difference between intention and attainment was not nearly so great.

Less than one-seventh of the sons of non-manual workers actually obtained non-manual work themselves on leaving school and only one-fifth by the time they were interviewed, though nearly one-third of them had originally hoped for this type of employment. Again, the differences between original preferences, plans and their fulfilment was smaller for the sons of manual workers who had wanted non-manual employment, though the proportion actually obtaining such work (one-tenth) was much lower than for the sons of non-manual workers.

Differences between girls according to their social class background were very slight and seemed to have affected, if at all, girls wanting non-manual work other than in offices, who were a little less likely to find this type of employment if their fathers were manual than if they were non-manual workers.

Position in stream

In the Carter[14] and Veness[15] studies there was a tendency for school leavers in the high I.Q. or scholastic ability groups to enter non-manual work as well as, in the case of boys, apprenticeships. In the present inquiry, however, though ability (as measured by the information given by young people themselves as to their position in stream and in class) was associated with a similar outcome, the gap between aims and fulfilment was rather wider for the 'top ability' groups than for others.

Boys from the top stream, for instance, who had wanted apprenticeships, were less likely than were boys from middle and bottom streams, or non-streamed boys, to have obtained them, either on leaving school or subsequently. Over two-fifths of boys from the top and non-streamed groups, for instance, had wanted apprenticeships but whereas very nearly the same proportion of non-streamed boys obtained them, only one-quarter of boys from the top stream did so; middle and bottom stream boys, however, were relatively more successful since one-third of them had originally wanted, and just over one-quarter actually obtained, employment in skilled trades. Moreover, much higher proportions of top and non-streamed boys obtained less skilled manual work than had originally intended to do so, compared with boys from the lower streams even though the latter were much more concentrated, relatively, in aims and attainments in this type of work.

At first glance, this may seem as if the aspirations of top-stream boys were too heavily biased in the direction of skilled trades. On further analysis, however, it appears that streaming may not have been the only operative factor. Firstly, the middle and bottom streams contained slightly higher proportions of the sons of manual than of non-manual, workers and it was the would-be apprentices among the former who were more likely to have realized their ambitions to enter skilled trades; secondly, streaming was not so prevalent among sixteen-year-old leavers, and it was would-be apprentices leaving at sixteen who were more likely than others to have realized their aspirations by entering skilled trades according to their intentions.

When job preferences and attainments were related to position in class

[14] M. Carter, 1962, op. cit.
[15] T. Veness, op. cit.

at school, as assessed by the young people seen, it appeared that though the broad occupational distribution of original job preferences was significantly different as between boys in 'above-average' and 'below-average' positions (as shown by the chi-squared test), there was no significant difference in the occupational distribution for first and subsequent employment (Table 40). Fewer of the 'above-average' boys obtained apprenticeships proportionate to the number who had wanted them than was the case for boys from 'average' or 'below-average' class positions. Conversely, more than twice as many boys from 'above-average' class positions had obtained other kinds of manual work than was originally intended, whereas among their contemporaries from lower positions in class, the differences between inten ions and attainments was not nearly so great.[16] On the other hand, 'above-average' boys in apprenticeships tended to increase in number between first and subsequent employment, whereas the number of apprentices from lower class positions was somewhat reduced during subsequent changes of employment.

TABLE 40. Position in class and vocational aims and attainments: boys.

Type of employment	Above average in class			Average or below in class		
	Employment			Employment		
	Wanted	First obtained	Present	Wanted	First obtained	Present
	(i)	(ii)	(iii)	(iv)	(v)	(vi)
	(Per cent of total)					
Apprentice	59	36	40	33	30	25
Manual	19	50	47	40	55	55
Non-manual	18	14	13	24	15	18
Total	100[a]	100	100	100[b]	100	100
(No. of 15–18s)	(58)	(58)	(58)	(124)	(124)	(124)

	χ^2	d.f.	p
(i) and (iv)	13·55	2	< 0·002
(ii) and (v)	1·01	2	< 0·50
(iii) and (vi)	4·42	2	< 0·20 p < 0·10

a 4 per cent were uncertain.
b 3 per cent were uncertain.

In the sample of girls, the intentions of would-be office workers who had been 'above average' in class did not match attainments as closely as did their equivalents in lower class positions; but three times as many 'average'

[16] Social class would not, however, seem to have influenced this tendency since rather more of the 'average' or 'below average' boys were the sons of non-manual than of manual workers, and it was the former who were evidently less likely to have realized their ambitions to enter skilled trades.

or 'below average' in class, consisting of would-be shop assistants, went into manual work as had originally planned to do so. Most intending shop assistants, however, from 'above-average' class positions went into office work; but rather more of the manual workers who had been 'above average' in class were in manual work at the time of inquiry than when first leaving school and twice as many as had originally specified this type of work for themselves.

In terms of their present employment the tendency was, as shown in the Veness and Carter studies,[17] for relatively more school leavers from the higher 'ability' groups to be in apprenticeships, if boys and in non-manual work, if girls. Proportionately more of the boys from 'above-average' class positions were actually in skilled trades, for instance, while boys in skilled work also contained relatively more who had been 'above average' in class, and if streamed, in the top streams. The same tendency applied to girls, more of whom proportionately were in clerical work from the higher ability groups than were girls in manual work or, even more, girls employed as shop assistants.

Nevertheless the fact that the gap between aims and attainments was wider for the higher than for the lower 'ability' groups means that it was the former who, more frequently than the latter, were required to modify their aims and to find alternative employment which offered them less training, skill, or prospects than would have the work they originally preferred. The evidence suggests that in the case of unsuccessful apprentices, there were factors in their social background (e.g. the occupation of their fathers) and as is shown,[18] in their methods of obtaining help when seeking information, deciding on and finding employment, which may have contributed something to their failure to achieve their hopes.

Age at leaving School

Would-be apprentices who left school at sixteen were much more successful than were leavers at fifteen in achieving their objectives. Just over two in five of sixteen-year-old leavers had wanted to enter skilled trades on leaving school; exactly the same number had done so by the time of interview. Though nearly the same proportion of leavers at fifteen as at sixteen had originally wanted apprenticeships (two-fifths), only about half of these boys had actually obtained entrance to skilled trades either on leaving school or subsequently; moreover, though from both age of leaving groups rather more entered less skilled work than had intended to do so, proportionately more of the early leavers found themselves in work which did not correspond with their first preferences than was the experience of leavers at sixteen. The majority of boys who had obtained apprenticeships had, therefore, left school at sixteen (two-thirds); for manual and

[17] See M. Carter, 1962, op. cit. and T. Veness, op. cit.
[18] See pages 138-9.

non-manual work, however, only just over one-third and one-half respectively were late leavers (Table 41).

TABLE 41. Age of leaving and vocational aims and attainments: boys.

Type of employment	Leavers at 15			Leavers at 16		
		Employment First			Employment First	
	Wanted (i)	obtained (ii)	Present (iii)	Wanted (iv)	obtained (v)	Present (vi)
	(Per cent of total)					
Apprentice	38	18	18	44	42	44
Other manual	40	64	65	28	42	41
Non-manual	17	18	17	20	16	15
Total	100[a]	100	100	100[b]	100	100
(No. of 15–18s)	(97)	(97)	(97)	(86)	(86)	(86)

	χ^2	d.f.	p
(i) and (iv)	2·40	2	<0·30
(ii) and (v)	13·50	2	<0·002
(iii) and (vi)	15·03	2	<0·001

a 5 per cent were uncertain.
b 8 per cent were uncertain.

In view of the fact that sixteen-year-old leavers tended to represent more of the boys who had been in the top streams at school and sons of non-manual workers, their apparent success in obtaining apprenticeships would appear to contradict the tendency already shown for sons of non-manual workers and boys from higher streams to be less likely than others to realize their ambitions to enter skilled trades. The explanation seems to be that a substantial proportion of sixteen-year-old leavers (nearly one-third) were not streamed; and it was the non-streamed boys who were more likely than others to have fulfilled their wishes for apprenticeships.

Leavers at sixteen also tended, however, to have fewer fathers in manual occupations than did the early leavers. Their relative success in obtaining apprenticeships suggests that a longer school life outweighed the possible disadvantages of social class; among leavers at fifteen, it was possibly the influence of fathers who were themselves in skilled trades which facilitated the entry of their sons, even though they left school at fifteen.

Type of school attended

Boys from secondary modern schools were much more likely than were others to have stated preferences for manual work, either skilled or relatively unskilled, and were less likely than were others to have preferred non-manual work. Their subsequent experiences in finding work contrasts with boys from other types of secondary school in three respects. First, fewer, proportionately, achieved the apprenticeships they wanted compared with boys from non-secondary modern schools; second, while the relatively few secondary modern school leavers who had wanted non-manual work obtained it, only one-half from selective schools did so. Third, while both groups of leavers found other types of manual work in rather greater numbers than anticipated, the proportion of boys from selective schools who did so was twice as many as had originally specified such work (though this proportion dropped slightly between first and subsequent employment).

Secondary modern school leavers, however, were much more likely than others to feel, in retrospect, that their present employment had meant giving up something they had particularly wanted to do. Over two in five of the boys from such schools felt this way compared with less than one in four of other leavers.

When the reasons given for wanting or not wanting to leave school were analysed, it emerged that a very much higher proportion of girls who had disliked school, who felt they lacked ability or were not learning anything, obtained than had originally wanted, relatively unskilled manual work; this tendency was not, however, at all apparent in the sample of boys.

There were also some very striking contrasts in the sample of girls between the less and the more willing leavers in regard to the proportions who felt that their early preferences had had to be abandoned. Over three-quarters of those who felt this way, had also very much wanted to leave school compared with only about two-fifths of those who had no such feelings about their early aspirations. Similarly, over two in five of enthusiastic leavers now felt that their original preferences had had to be relinquished whereas only one in seven of the reluctant leavers felt this way. This suggests that girls tended to feel more strongly, both about leaving school and about the type of jobs they had wanted, than was the case for the boys.

Sources of help in deciding on and obtaining employment

There was a close relationship between the non-attainment of aims and the extent to which school leavers still felt committed, in some degree, to their first preferences. This was evident when the sources of help used when deciding on and finding employment were analysed according to the similarity of their present to their intended employment, and to their present feelings about their early aspirations.

Boys who had obtained jobs which corresponded closely with their intentions and who had no feelings about having had to relinquish their original ideas were both more likely to have relied on their parents' help

for decisions and for arranging their first jobs. It was only boys who had
not given up their early intentions who, more frequently than others, had
also used their parents for information about the work they wanted to do.
By contrast, boys who regarded their present jobs as second-best, as it
were, were more likely to have used the Youth Employment Service for
information and, like the boys in jobs which differed from their original
preferences, were more inclined than others to have found their first job
without help. This tendency was more marked for the latter than the
former who, more frequently than others, had turned to relatives and
friends for finding first jobs.

For boys who were successful in finding more or less the same jobs as
they had intended, parental help would seem to have been the particular
important factor which distinguishes them from boys who failed to find
exactly what they wanted and who now looked back with some regret
about the jobs they would have liked.

Girls did not show these same tendencies at all. Those who had obtained
work more or less identical with their first preferences were more likely
than others to have made up their own minds as to what to do; to have
relied less frequently on the help of their parents; to have used official
sources of information more frequently and to be a little more likely to
have found their own jobs without help. By contrast, girls whose jobs
differed from their first preferences were more inclined to have had the
help of their parents in deciding what to do, less likely to have used official
sources of information, particularly schools (as were the girls who felt they
had had to abandon their original choice), and much more frequently to
rely on the help of relatives and friends In finding their first job. The girls
who now felt that early preferences had had to be abandoned were, however, more likely than others to have been placed in their first jobs by the
Youth Employment Service.

Thus for girls, success in finding what they wanted would seem to have
been associated with a certain amount of independence in deciding what
to do, with reliance on official sources for information, and with no undue
bias in the help obtained from any one source in finding their first jobs.
Failure on the other hand (in contrast to that of the boys), was associated
with dependence on the help of parents in deciding what to do, less frequent use of official sources of information, less self-reliance and more
frequent recourse to the help of either relatives, friends, or youth employment officers, in finding their first jobs.

How far this reflects a situation in which fathers were able to give more
effective help to their sons than to their daughters because they may have
had more specialized knowledge about employment opportunities for boys
but not for girls, can only be speculated upon. It is also possible that the
help parents were able to give was, to some extent, dependent on the type
of employment wanted by their children.

The type of employment wanted and obtained

Success or otherwise in attaining original job objectives was, in some degree, associated with the extent to which the sources of information and help had been used by different groups of school leavers. Since the numbers were small the association could only be demonstrated in the case of the apprentices, though the evidence suggests that the same tendency applied to other groups.

Four groups of boys can conveniently be distinguished, for the purpose of analysis; those who had originally wanted apprenticeships; those who had succeeded in entering skilled trades; those who had failed to obtain skilled work; and those who had entered skilled trades though this was not their original intention.

The most striking feature of the differences between the unsuccessful would-be apprentices and others is that the former did not refer to their teachers at all as helping them in their decisions, their schools were much less frequently used as a source of information about the work they wanted to do; and neither parents, teachers, or youth employment officers were used to the same extent as by others, when they tried to find their first jobs. They, much more than other boys who were seeking and finding apprenticeships, relied on their own efforts, particularly using press advertisements.

Boys who were successful in entering skilled trades were, by contrast, more likely to have had the help of their teachers when deciding on what work to do; to have used their schools more frequently than any other source as a means of obtaining information about the work they wanted; and to have used the Youth Employment Service, predominantly, as a means of finding employment.

Since would-be apprentices who left school at sixteen were more successful than others in obtaining entry to skilled trades it would seem that their more frequent reference to the help of the schools may reflect their extra year at school and the type of vocational course taken during the last year.

The tendency for boys who were unsuccessful in obtaining apprenticeships to deviate in some degree from others in the frequency with which they had used various sources of help also applied, however, to other school leavers.

Girls who had not obtained office work as at first hoped were much more inclined than were successful office workers to have relied on the help of their parents in deciding what to do; they referred less frequently to their schools and more frequently to the Youth Employment Service as sources of information; they were more inclined to rely on the help of friends and relatives in obtaining their first employment. Successful office workers, on the other hand, were more likely to have been placed in their first jobs by the official service.

Girls and boys who had failed to realize their preferences for non-manual work (other than office work for girls) differed from those who had achieved these objectives in that they had relied much more frequently on their own resources both in deciding on and obtaining their first jobs; none of the boys had sought the help of the youth employment officers and both boys and girls were more likely to have failed in their search for information about their intended employment. The successful, leavers however, were those who had tended to secure help in the process of deciding and finding work than relying on themselves.

Though there was a general tendency for boys to be more successful than others in finding the exact job they wanted if they had had the help of their parents and girls if they had relied on their own efforts, this did not apply in terms of finding the type of employment preferred (which included jobs which differed slightly or considerably from those originally wanted). For success in this latter sense, the intervention of official sources, i.e. schools and particularly the Youth Employment Service, at various stages of the process of job choice was evidently an important contributory factor.

This suggests that leavers placed by the Youth Employment Service were required to modify their aims, either as a result of vocational advice or because of the type of vacancy registered with the bureau. This situation did not apply to boys who, helped by their parents, obtained the exact job they wanted; parents were likely, presumably, to have had only the particular job preferred by their sons, planned or arranged for them; it may have been the prospect of this job which influenced the boys' choice; or the choice itself was, in certain circumstances, acted upon by parents in such a way that their sons were able to achieve their objectives fairly precisely.

The modification of aims, which seems to have been required of leavers who were successful in obtaining the type of employment, if not the particular job, preferred, when placed by the bureau, was also required of leavers who accepted different types of employment. These were leavers whose original preferences were presumably inconsistent with official opinion or with the type of vacancy registered. There were, however, leavers who must have used the bureau in their search for employment but who found the advice given or the alternative employment offered, unacceptable. The comments of young people about the Youth Employment Service[19] indicate that rather more had contact with the service[20] than were actually placed in employment by it. The question, therefore,

[19] See Chapter X.

[20] This is supported by the analysis of job changes in one cohort of secondary modern school boys in Willesden, which showed that one in three job changers consulted the Youth Employment Bureau, over a change of employment but were not placed by the bureau at the time (see J. Maizels, 1967, op. cit.).

arises as to how far these leavers represented young people who did not wish to modify their aims at this stage or at the suggestion of officials, and, in so far as they were unsuccessful, only accepted alternative employment when they felt that they had discovered for themselves what the alternatives were.

This tendency, if it applies at all, would be consistent with an image of the service as exclusively concerned with getting young people jobs[21] and with the point of view of some young people in the present inquiry, who felt that the vocational advice they had been offered corresponded with neither their own inclinations nor their future interests.

The evidence of the present inquiry suggests, therefore, that there may be factors other than those of demand and supply, which influenced the subsequent attainment of vocational aims. If success or failure is associated in some degree with the methods adopted and the type of help sought and received during the process of job choice, then it would seem important to discover more precisely those factors which influence the behaviour of school leavers when choosing and finding their first jobs and particularly their use of official services. The relinquishment of original aims was still recalled by as many as one in three of the young people seen; moreover, the non-attainment of preference resulted in a reduction in the average level of skill and status of the jobs actually taken compared with those originally preferred. These facts prompt the question of whether with more effective help, official or other, there might not have been a more satisfactory outcome for the school leavers concerned.

SUMMARY

The work obtained on leaving school or subsequently, was for many young people in accordance with their intentions. As many as one in three, however, had not realized their first preferences and boys wanting apprenticeships and girls and boys wanting skilled non-manual or intermediate occupations, tended to be less successful than others in finding work which corresponded with their aims. Rather more young people entered relatively unskilled manual work, rather fewer boys the skilled trades and rather fewer boys and girls work requiring some degree of further education and training than would have been the case had their original aims been realized. Moreover, about one in three of the boys and girls seen felt that entering their present employment had meant the relinquishment of ideas of doing work which they had particularly wanted. There was, overall, a reduction in the average level of skill, training, and education required in jobs actually taken compared with those originally preferred.

Though more or less equal proportions of boys from the homes of manual

[21] G. Jahoda and A. D. Chalmers, op. cit.

and non-manual workers had originally wanted apprenticeships, the sons of manual workers, particularly skilled, were more likely than were others, to have entered the skilled trades; they were also more likely, if they had wanted to enter non-manual occupations, to have done so; moreover, relatively fewer of the boys with fathers in manual occupations entered manual occupations themselves, proportionate to those who had originally planned to do so, compared with boys from the homes of non-manual workers, much higher proportions of whom went into manual work than had originally so intended. The closer correspondence between the aims and attainments of the sons of manual workers is largely due to the fact that relatively fewer of them planned to take up non-manual work and relatively more of them had intended to enter manual work, than was the case among the sons of non-manual workers.

Though relatively more school leavers from the top streams and class positions than of others were employed if boys, in apprenticeships, and if girls, in offices, much higher proportions of them had wanted than had actually obtained these occupations. This meant that it was the leavers from the higher 'ability' groups who, more frequently than others, had had to modify their original aims and to take alternative employment which offered them, apparently, less training and prospects in acquiring skills than would have their preferred choice.

Attainments would, however, seem to have been associated, in some degree, with the sources of help and information used when deciding on and obtaining employment. These factors would seem to have operated differently, however, for boys and for girls. First, boys in jobs identical with their preferences were more likely than others to have been helped in their decision by their parents (though the majority of all leavers attributed their decision to themselves); to have felt that their schools were the chief source of information, and to have relied on their parents in obtaining their employment. Girls whose present jobs corresponded with their original aims, however, were more likely than others to have come to their decision without help; to have used their parents as the chief source of information, and to have relied on their own initiative in getting their jobs.

More detailed analysis in the case of apprentices revealed that boys who had successfully fulfilled their wish to enter skilled trades were more likely, than were others, to have had the help of their teachers in deciding on what to do, to have used their schools as the chief source of information, and to have used the Youth Employment Service in obtaining their employment. By contrast, boys who had not fulfilled their aims did not use their teachers or their schools, were much more likely to have received help and information from family or friends, and to have obtained employment on their own initiative. A tendency for the unsuccessful would-be apprentice to deviate from the successful in his use of sources of help and information, and to rely less on his school, and more on his family or on his own efforts, was evident for other groups of leavers who had not succeeded in realizing their original aims. The evidence therefore suggests that in addition to the factors of supply and demand, the methods adopted and the type of help sought and received in the process of job choice may also be associated with the attainment of vocational aims.

CHAPTER X

ASSESSMENT OF HELP

INTRODUCTION

The Report of the Working Party of the National Youth Employment Council on the future development of the Youth Employment Service was based mainly on the consideration of evidence submitted by individuals and organizations, professionally or otherwise concerned with the work of the service.[1] Since, however, the Working Party did not obtain views of school leavers themselves, the comments of the young people seen in the present inquiry are of considerable interest. Much of their comment relates directly to the type of question discussed in the report and to its specific recommendations;[2] and many of their comments are highly critical of the Youth Employment Service in particular.[3]

It was not the intention of the present inquiry to study the functioning of the Youth Employment Service. Young people were simply asked, as the last of a series of questions relating to their experiences when choosing and finding employment, whether they felt there was enough help for young people to find the work they wanted, and for suggestions as to what might improve the help available, including the Youth Employment Service.

ASSESSMENT OF HELP AVAILABLE

As many as two-fifths of the boys and one-half of the girls interviewed felt, when asked, that there was enough help available for young people at the present time to find the work they wanted. This relatively large proportion of favourable views is, perhaps, somewhat surprising in view of the fact that only a minority of school leavers had actually obtained the jobs originally wanted, or had managed to find out what they wanted to know about their intended employment, while as many as one in four had found their first jobs without outside help. However, there were substantial proportions who felt that there was insufficient help—about two in five of

[1] *The Future Development of the Youth Employment Service*, op. cit.

[2] In particular, the development of vocational guidance work in schools; earlier contact with children by the youth employment officers; vocational guidance interviews; the expansion of the official service; improved information about opportunities for employment and training for school leavers.

[3] A substantial proportion of comment on the Youth Employment Service came from school leavers living outside the borough of Willesden.

the boys and one in four of the girls—while more than one in five were in some doubt (Table 42).

TABLE 42. Adequacy of help
in obtaining employment.

Whether enough help	Boys	Girls
	(Per cent of total)	
Yes	39	52
No	38	24
Uncertain	20	24
No answer	3	—
Total	100	100
(No. of 15–18s)	(183)	(147)

The assessment made varied, naturally enough, with young peoples' own experiences of the help sought and received. Parents, as a source of help in deciding what work to do were associated, for boys, with relatively higher proportions who felt positively about the help available for young people; uncertainty was less frequently expressed among those who had relied on persons other than their parents. Relatively more of the boys with favourable opinions had obtained their information from youth employment officers; among girls, a positive assessment was more frequently expressed by those who had learnt about their future employment from their friends. There was also an expected association between opinions on the help available and the extent to which young people felt they had discovered what they wanted to know about their intended employment. Those who had failed to find out what they had wanted to know were more likely than others to have a negative view about the help received; conversely, rather more of those who had a positive view had been successful in obtaining the required information about their future work than was the case among those who felt dissatisfied with the help they had received.

School leavers who had obtained their first employment through the Youth Employment Service were much more inclined, evidently, to have a favourable opinion of the help generally available (Table 43), and to hold this view if the Youth Employment Service, rather than other agencies had been instrumental in finding them their employment, or if young people had used their own initiative. Likewise, relatively more school leavers were critical of what help had been available or were doubtful, if they had found their jobs themselves or had been helped by parents, teachers, relatives, or friends. Substantial minorities, however, who had used the service (nearly one-third of the boys and one-quarter of the girls), had unfavourable opinions of the help available, while as many as one in seven were uncertain.

TABLE 43. Adequacy of help and sources of help in obtaining employment.

| Source of help | Whether enough help | | | |
| | Boys | | Girls | |
	Yes	No/Uncertain	Yes	No/Uncertain
	(Per cent of total)			
Y.E.O.	39	24	30	20
Relatives/friends	21	16	34	26
Self	20	26	23	35
Parents	11	12	5	3
Teachers	3	9	6	4
Writing to firms	18	21	8	19
Press ads.	4	4	8	19
Firm's notices	—	3	8	3
Other	8	5	12	10
Total (Multiple replies)	100	100	100	100
(No. of 15–18s)[a]	(72)	(107)	(77)	(70)

a Excluding not answering.

SUGGESTIONS FOR IMPROVEMENTS IN THE HELP AVAILABLE

Suggestions for improving the help available were by no means directed only to the official Youth Employment Service. Comments relating to the service came mainly from the boys, over one-half of whom made such references, compared with less than one-quarter of the girls; the majority of boys' suggestions were, in fact, concerned with the service, but those of girls were more evenly distributed between the service and schools. Girls, however, were much more likely than boys, either to feel that no improvements were required, or that they did not know what to suggest, though girls used the service in getting their first jobs just as frequently as did the boys (Table 44).

Much of the critical comment relating to the Youth Employment Service was evidently derived from personal experience. The fact that rather more school leavers referred to contact with the service than actually used it when getting their first and subsequent employment, suggests that they tended to seek information, advice, and jobs from the service in the first instance but, finding it unsatisfactory in some way, turned to other sources of help or to their own devices.

What did young people have to say about the Youth Employment Service? Their references were divided into several categories, the most important of which related to the personal attention given to school leavers

TABLE 44. Suggestions for improving
help available.

	Boys	Girls
	(Per cent of total)	
Relating to Youth Employment Service		
More personal attention	22	12
Wider coverage of jobs and better information	21	10
Better type of job to be offered	11	1
More bureau and staff	7	5
Relating to others		
More films, lectures, written material, visits, etc.	11	5
More help from teachers and help to be given earlier	8	10
Better jobs, conditions, pay, prospects	5	3
Other	7	8
No improvements required	13	26
Don't know	19	27
Other		
Young people should help themselves	2	3
Y.E.O. helpful	4	3
Total (Multiple replies)	100	100
(No. of 15–18s)	(183)	(147)

by youth employment officers. One in five of the boys, and one in eight of the girls, expressed dissatisfaction with the service, either because they felt insufficient interest had been shown in them; or because there had not been enough time, in their view, for their needs to be discovered, information ascertained, or decisions made; or because they had the impression that officials had persuaded them to take up certain types of employment which, in their view, did not always correspond with their own inclinations or their future interests. Typical of the references made, many of them sharp and downright, were:

Insufficient interest

'The youth employment officer didn't seem to worry about me. There should be better ones. I had an interview but they never got in touch with me again. I did it all on my own.'

'No-one seemed much interested. No-one asked me what I wanted to do. I didn't know anything.'

'I had a chat with the youth employment officer and he gave me addresses but he could have told me more. He just seemed to leave it to me.'

'Doesn't seem to matter what the job is as long as you're employed. The Youth Employment Service just want to keep the unemployment figures down. You're just a number on a card. It's not personal enough.'

Insufficient time

'You need a personal interview with the youth employment officer—not just coming out of the class for five minutes. There should be a longer interview where they definitely get to know you.'

'The youth employment officer needs more time. She was very nice but there should be more centres and time to understand people. It takes a long time.'

'The youth employment officer is alright but they don't seem to get deep into what you want. Seem to palm you off with any old rubbish.'

'The youth employment office interview is too short. He only asked a few questions. They don't really find out about you.'

Unwelcome advice

'The youth employment officers have set ideas of what they want you to do and try to push you into it. She pushed me so much that I finally got a job on my own.'

'The youth employment officer tried to push me into something which would have been better for the firm than for me. Then he tried to get me to join the Army and then into a firm where my Dad had just been declared redundant.'

'There ought to be more Youth Employment Bureaux where you could go without obligation and where you could just go in and ask questions without being talked into anything. They tried to talk me into cabinet making.'

'The youth employment office want to push you into any old jobs. They offered my mates jobs without a future. They should take more care before they offer jobs.'

All these comments are of interest since they reflect an awareness of the vocational guidance function of the service on the part of its clientele.

Information and employment

Second in order of importance, accounting for one in five of the boys, but not more than one in ten of the girls, were criticisms that the Youth Employment Service offered too narrow a choice of employment, that many of the jobs offered or suggested were in low status occupations with poor prospects and that the information given about jobs, general and specific was inadequate.

Typical of the references in these categories were:

'The Youth Employment Bureau is not briefed well. They should send leaflets about the different jobs. We had to get the information ourselves. The Youth Employment Service should be able to provide the information on any job you're interested in. But we were only offered jobs without prospects.'

'Youth Employment Service scheme is peculiar. Seems only to think of the jobs for next week. It needs more planning. You need to know what jobs there will be in the future and then you can plan what to do. When I told them what I wanted they didn't seem to have much to offer. They never gave me what I wanted because they didn't know there were vacancies in this firm. It's always the same firms that ask the Youth Employment Service for people.'

'The Youth Employment Bureau is not always up to date with their information. I applied to a firm as soon as I was told but the firm had no vacancies. I went all over the place to find electrical work because the Youth Employment Bureau misled me. Jobs are entirely different from what the Youth Employment Bureau says and you find that out in the interviews. That's a waste of time. I got sent after an engineering job which turned out to be for a van boy.'

Third, a small minority of school leavers saw the inadequacies of the service as mostly due to staff shortages; their suggestions were mainly directed, therefore, to an expansion of the service to allow for more staff and more bureaux.

'There should be more people at the Youth Employment Bureau to go round the schools. You need to start at fourteen and more information is needed. We don't get enough. There is too much rush at the end.'
'We need twice the number of youth employment offices and you need them on the spot.'
'There should be more than one Youth Employment Service so that we could go to several. We could have more chance then.'

Though substantial minorities, particularly among the girls, had no suggestions to offer, specific praise for the Youth Employment Service was rarely expressed. Relatively few school leavers referred positively to any help received from youth employment officers or expressed confidence in the service. This did not mean that those who were evidently satisfied with the way things had worked out had not used the official service. Girls whose comments were favourable, or who had no suggestions to make, were almost evenly divided between those who had been placed in their first employment by the Youth Employment Service and those who had found work through other means. A much higher proportion of girls who used the official service for their first employment were also, apparently, satisfied that there was enough help available for young people, than was the case among those who had not used the service.

Other suggested improvements

Not all the suggestions made directly concerned the Youth Employment Service, however, and about one in four of the boys and a smaller proportion of the girls commented on other possible improvements. Some felt there was need to improve the methods by which school leavers learnt about different types of work and the training and qualifications required. Lectures, films, leaflets, visits to firms, talks by young people already at work and others from industry or commerce, and <u>trial periods at work</u> during the last year at school, were among some of the ideas offered.

'We should have a chance to see what work is like. Perhaps a week at work before you decide, otherwise you're in the dark.'
'More time off from school to go and see what jobs are like. I would have gone back to school if I'd known about work.'

Other school leavers felt that vocational help should come primarily from the schools and be offered much earlier on in school life, so that there was time not only to gain more information but to talk things over with the teacher.

'There should be more talk about work between the children and the teachers. Teachers should sit with the children and talk to them about what they would like to do.'
'Teachers should know the advantages and disadvantages of different jobs. If it's left to the youth employment officer, he only visits the schools once and then you have to go and see him. There should be one or two periods a week for questions and discussions in the last year. We should have someone on the school staff who knows all about jobs—a special member of the staff who is on the spot.'

In the eyes of some school leavers, improvements were needed not so much in vocational advice and information as in conditions of employment. Employers were felt by some to offer insufficient pay or opportunities for training; or to delay promotion or the giving of responsibility; other young people felt that while work, as such, was plentiful, jobs in firms where young people were encouraged and provided for, were relatively scarce. There were also a few references to school leavers being used as cheap labour, for running errands, or for the odd jobs.

Since many of the criticisms and suggestions made by young people in regard to possible improvements in the help available, derived from their own experience, it might have been assumed that there would be differences between them according to their sources of help in choosing and finding employment, the amount of information they discovered and the type of work wanted and eventually obtained. None of these factors, however, would appear to have been associated with any major differences in viewpoint; there was, indeed, generally speaking, a remarkable unanimity of opinions between young people—when divided according to these factors—as to what they felt should be done, and in the proportions who either offered criticisms or suggestions, or who felt there was no need for change or who were uncertain what to think.

It was evident that boys who had relied on the help of their parents when deciding what work to do were rather more inclined than were others to feel that there was need for the Youth Employment Service to have a wider coverage of jobs. Boys who had depended on the help of others, however, were rather more inclined to emphasize the need for efficient ways of providing information to school leavers about employment. Girls, on the other hand, who had relied on their own efforts in deciding, were more likely than were others to feel that teachers should be the main source of help.

There were, logically enough, rather more favourable comments from boys who had been placed in their jobs by the Youth Employment Service than among those who had found work through other means, while proportionately more of the girls who had used the service were evidently satisfied and offered no suggestions for improvements. Boys in non-manual occupations tended more frequently than others to feel that youth employment bureaux should offer better types of jobs, while boys from secondary modern schools were rather more frequently critical of present arrangements than were others. But all these differences were relatively slight compared with the striking contrasts in the frequencies with which certain criticisms and suggestions were offered according to whether young people felt that they had had enough help during the period in which they were choosing and finding their first employment.

TABLE 45. Adequacy of help and suggestions for improvement.

| | Whether enough help | | | |
| | Boys | | Girls | |
	Yes	No/Uncertain	Yes	No/Uncertain
	(Per cent of total)			
Relating to Youth Employment Service				
More personal attention	10	29	3	23
Wider coverage of jobs and better information	7	27	9	10
Better type of job to be offered	3	17	—	1
More bureaux and staff	6	7	—	10
Relating to other				
More films, lectures, written material, visits, etc.	11	10	4	6
More help from teachers and help to be given earlier	3	10	4	14
Better jobs, conditions, pay, prospects	3	7	3	4
Other	7	8	6	11
No improvement required	31	3	45	6
Don't know	20	8	22	31
Other				
Young people should help themselves	3	1	4	3
Y.E.O. helpful	10	1	3	3
Total (Multiple replies)	100	100	100	100
(No. of 15–18s)	(72)	(107)	(77)	(70)

Among those who felt they had had sufficient help, only a minority offered suggestions or criticisms, the majority giving the impression that they were apparently satisfied, or at least non-committal. The opposite was true for school leavers who felt that help had been insufficient, most of whom referred to there being need for improvement, and, particularly among the boys, had something to say, critical or otherwise (Table 45).

Moreover, not only did the comments of boys who had insufficient help apply overwhelmingly to the Youth Employment Service but their references to the need for more personal attention, wider coverage of jobs, and better information about them far exceeded, in proportion, those of boys who were satisfied with the amount of help they had received. Girls who had an unfavourable view of the help received tended, on the other hand, much more frequently than others to refer to the defects of the Youth Employment Service in respect of the individual attention experienced and required, and to suggest the need for an expanded service. They, rather more frequently than boys, or than girls who were satisfied with the help received, were inclined to suggest that vocational help should come from teachers.

The image of the Youth Employment Service and the degree to which it was felt to require modification and improvement was most closely associated, therefore, with the amount of help school leavers felt they had received when making their final decisions. While this is hardly surprising, there is an apparent inconsistency in the results, in that although school leavers were evidently more likely to feel that they had had enough help if they had used the service as a means of finding employment, their use of the service was not in itself, generally, associated with any substantial difference in the frequency of their criticisms or suggestions.

The explanation seems to lie partly in the type of evidence obtained. School leavers were asked for the chief source of help when finding employment. Many of those who referred to the official service in this connection, presumably found the help offered acceptable, and were therefore more inclined than were others to feel that they had received the help they wanted. But substantial proportions of boys and girls placed in employment by the service also had an unfavourable or an uncertain view of the help they had received. Moreover, no evidence was obtained which related to the nature of the help requested and offered, or the reason why it was rejected in favour of the help of others or the use of their own initiative. When asked for their opinions on how facilities might be improved, it became evident that many more young people must have expected, or requested, help from the Youth Employment Service, than ultimately accepted the employment that it offered. Some of these, however, were presumably satisfied with the help received from other sources.

It seems likely that those who felt that they had not received enough help included school leavers who were dissatisfied either with the official service which had placed them in employment; or with a service whose help had proved unacceptable to them; or with the help received from others; or with the results of their own efforts. Their dissatisfactions combined to produce criticisms and suggestions which centred on the Youth Employment Service. On this interpretation, the Youth Employment Service was, as it were, the centre of 'attack' by the dissatisfied, irrespective of whether they had used the service or not.

SUMMARY

Nearly two in five of the boys, and one in four of the girls, felt that there was not enough help available to young people to find the work they wanted, while one in five were uncertain. The assessment of help varied with school leavers' own experiences of the help sought and received, and those who had found their first jobs through the Youth Employment Service were more inclined than were others, to have a favourable view of the help available.

When asked how help to school leavers might be improved, three in five of the boys but less than one-half of the girls offered suggestions and criticisms which, in the case of boys, centred on the official service. The service was more likely to be the centre of criticism for leavers dissatisfied with the help they had received (from whatever source), than were informal sources, presumably because the help of the latter was regarded as a gesture of goodwill, and the help of the former as a professional matter. The most frequent criticism of the service related to the lack of individual attention on the one hand, and the type of advice or employment on the other. The latter is consistent with other evidence offered in the present inquiry, which suggests that the service may be more frequently associated with modification of vocational aims than with finding the sort of jobs people want. It is possible, since rather more leavers had some contact with the bureau than were actually placed by it, that dissatisfaction arose when the advice or alternative employment offered was felt to be unacceptable.

How far dissatisfaction with the service was also associated with an image of the service as exclusively concerned with getting young people jobs, as in the Jahoda and Chalmers study, could not be ascertained.[4] If this factor operated in the present inquiry, it could mean that school leavers expected the service to find them jobs which corresponded with their preferences and found alternative suggestions unwelcome since they did not look to the service for vocational guidance.

In so far as the service was identified with job finding, rather than vocational advice, the modifications required in finding school leavers employment, might have been associated in the minds of users and non-users alike with ineffectiveness and consequently with a lowering of its reputation.

[4] Op. cit.

CHAPTER XI

CHANGES OF EMPLOYMENT

INTRODUCTION

The precise extent of job changing amongst young workers is not known. Several studies suggest that there is considerable movement between jobs and occupations during the first year at work; substantial numbers evidently change their employers at least once during their first year of employment while only a minority of eighteen-year-olds are estimated to be still in their first employment by the time they have been at work for three years.[1] It is also evident that job change is higher among the unskilled and semi-skilled manual workers than among those in jobs of higher skill and status. Though some job changing arises out of changes in the local employment situation and some is presumably the result of deliberate planning or of the exploration of possible alternatives, it has been argued that much is the inevitable outcome of inadequate help and guidance during the process of job choice and of haphazard methods of finding first and subsequent jobs.[2] Other factors have also been suggested as relevant. Herford found that it was the more 'immature' youngsters who changed jobs frequently.[3] Carter found that there was a higher rate of job change among boys and girls in the Sheffield study who had been in the lower streams of academic ability at school, and suggests that more frequent job changes are likely if there is indifference by parents and children to the kind of work undertaken, or by employers to the use made of young labour.[4]

In the present inquiry young people themselves were asked about their previous employment, if any, the methods by which they found employment and the reasons for change; and for their assessment of their job experiences.

JOB CHANGERS AND OTHER SCHOOL LEAVERS

The majority (two-thirds), of the boys and girls interviewed in the present inquiry were still in their first jobs (Table 46). Naturally enough, the

---

[1] T. Ferguson and J. Cunnison, op. cit., *15–18*, M. E. M. Herford, op. cit., J. Maizels, 1967, op. cit., L. T. Wilkins, op. cit.

[2] M. Carter, 1966, op. cit.

[3] Op. cit.

[4] 1962, op. cit.

roportions varied according to the time young people had been at work. Thus, as many as four-fifths of those who had left school only a year or less ago were still in their first jobs and none of the boys at work for six months or less had made any change. This was not the case for the girls, however, and as many as one in four of the relatively recent entrants to work had shifted from their first employment within the first six months.

TABLE 46. Changes in employment.

Number of jobs	Boys	Girls
	(*Per cent of total*)	
1 only	66	60
2	18	26
3	7	6
4	5	4
5 or more	3	—
No answer	1	4
Total	100	100
(No. of 15–18s)	(183)	(147)

The proportions moving from their first jobs rose sharply among those who had been at work for between one and two years but less markedly so for those at work for over two years. Of the young people entering their third year of employment, as many as one-half of the boys and three-fifths of the girls had had at least one other job since leaving school. But the majority of job changers had moved only once since they started work; only three of the 183 boys seen had had more than five other jobs while none of the girls had had more than four. Boys also differed from the girls in that though rather fewer of them, proportionately, changed jobs, some of them did so more frequently. Thus the average number of jobs per job changer was slightly higher for boys than for girls (2·9 as against 2·4). For the sample as a whole the average number of jobs held was 1·6 for boys and 1·5 for girls. When related to the average time at work this meant a rate of job change for the sample as a whole of just over one job per year per school leaver.[5,6]

Though these results are not entirely inconsistent with those of other studies, they reflect a somewhat lower incidence of job change for the sample as a whole.[7] This is due, no doubt, to the fact that the sample of young people seen contained a substantial proportion of boy apprentices

[5] The average time at work for boys was 15·8 months and for girls 14·3 months. The rate of job change was therefore 1·3 for boys and 1·2 for girls.

[6] This is lower than the annual rate of 2·2 jobs per school leaver for one single cohort of secondary modern boys in the same area., (See J. Maizels, 1967, op. cit.)

[7] *15–18*, op. cit.

and girl office workers who tended to have changed their jobs far less frequently than did other workers. Only five of the fifty-five apprentices and three in ten of girls in offices had had more than one job since leaving school, compared with nearly one-half of the boys and girls employed in relatively unskilled manual work.

TABLE 47. Changes in employment, social class, and age of leaving school: boys.

	One job	More than one job	
	(Per cent of total)		
Father's occupation			
Manual	53	73	$\chi^2 = 5\cdot63$
Non-manual	47	27	d.f. = 1
Total[a]	100	100	$p < 0\cdot02$
(No. of 15–18s)	(112)	(47)	
Age of leaving			
15	42	80	$\chi^2 = 26\cdot1$
16 or more	58	20	d.f. = 1
Total[b]	100	100	$p < 0\cdot001$
(No. of 15–18s)	(120)	(61)	

a Excluding father's occupation not known, and those not answering.
b Excluding those not answering.

The amount of job changing has been shown to vary not only with the type of job and occupation followed but with the age of leaving school, the type of school attended and the level of educational performance.[8] In the present inquiry the only major differences between job changers and the other school leavers in these respects was in relation to age of leaving and social class. Higher proportions of the boys with more than one job experience had left school at fifteen and came from the homes of manual workers, than was the case for boys who left school at sixteen and with fathers in non-manual occupations; the differences were statistically significant in both cases (see Table 47). It seems likely, however, that since the age of leaving was associated in some degree with the type of employment obtained (as indeed was social class) the differences which emerged between job changers and the rest probably reflected, to a large extent, the relative instability of certain types of employment rather than the age of leaving (or social class) as such. There were no apparent differences, however, in the incidence of job change as far as the type of secondary school attended was concerned; nor were job changers any more likely than others to have

8 Ibid.

been eager or reluctant to leave school; there was only a very slight tendency, moreover, for boys and girls with more than one job experience to come, more frequently than others, from the lower positions in class or in stream at school.

Choosing and finding employment

There would seem to be, *a priori*, a higher risk of job change for children who lack sufficient help and information when deciding what work to do and when finding their first jobs; and who find it necessary to modify their original objectives. It was thought of interest, therefore, to trace the extent to which job changers differed, if at all, from other school leavers in the sources of help used when choosing and finding their first jobs and in the degree to which they had attained their original choices.

The analysis showed that the non-attainment of vocational aims was a far more important factor associated with job change than was the vocational help sought, the amount of information obtained or the type of assessment made of the help received though there were, nonetheless, quite distinct differences, in some respects, between job changers and other school leavers in their respective use of sources of advice and information.

It was evident, for instance, that among boys, job changers were more inclined than were others to feel that they had arrived at their own vocational decisions by themselves and were less inclined to refer to the help of relatives, friends, or youth employment officers; their equivalents among the girls, however, were less inclined to feel that they had made up their own minds and more inclined to refer to the help of their parents.

The only difference between job changers and others in regard to the sources of information used was that the boys with more than one job experience were less likely than were others to have obtained information from their schools, while the corresponding group among the girls were more likely to have referred to the Youth Employment Service, to friends, and to relatives. Boys but not girls, with experience of more than one kind of employment were also more likely than others to have been placed in their first jobs by the official service;[9] in other respects, they also differed from each other; job changers among the boys, for instance, were less inclined than were other boys to have the help of their parents in arranging their first jobs, and none of them referred to their teachers in this regard; they were also less inclined than others to have obtained their own jobs; job changers among the girls, on the other hand, were more likely to have used their teachers but were far less inclined than were other girls to have had the help of friends or relatives in finding their first jobs and were a little more inclined to have found work on their own initiative.

[9] See Chapter VIII, pages 118–21.

Only among boys was there any apparent difference between job changers and others in regard to the amount of information obtained about their intended employment and the adequacy of the help available to young people in finding the work they wanted. Boys with experience of more than one job were less likely than others to have discovered most of what they had wanted to know and more inclined to have learnt little or nothing. Equal proportions of both groups of leavers, however, felt that there was enough help; but rather more of the job changers made a negative assessment and fewer were uncertain than was the case among other boys.

Aims and attainments

A most striking contrast between young people with more than one job experience and those still in their first employment was revealed when the differences between their present jobs and their original preferences were examined. Twice as many, proportionately, of the boys with more than one job were in work which was quite different from that originally hoped for, as were boys with only one job; conversely, more than twice as many boys, proportionately, who were still in their first employment, were in work which corresponded more or less precisely with their original aims, than were boys who had moved out of their first jobs.

These differences were statistically significant at the 1 per cent level. Similar differences were apparent for the girls, though these were not statistically significant (Table 48).

TABLE 48. Changes in employment and difference between present and preferred job.

How different is present job and that originally preferred	Boys		Girls	
	One job	More than one job	One job	More than one job
	(Per cent of total)			
Identical	43	19	56	36
Quite different	31	68	30	46
Similar	16	6	14	16
Uncertain	10	7	—	2
Total	100	100	100	100
(No. of 15–18s)[a]	(120)	(61)	(90)	(52)

$\chi^2 = 23.27$; d.f. $= 3$; $p < 0.001$ $\chi^2 = 4.35$; d.f. $= 3$; $p > 0.20$

a Excluding those not answering.

When the types of employment entered were compared, by occupational groups, with those originally preferred, further differences between the two groups of school leavers were apparent. Among the boys still in their first jobs it was the apprentices whose attainments more or less matched their original intentions; by contrast, less than one-half of the would-be apprentices among the job changers had achieved their objectives. Curiously enough, however, the gap between aims and attainments was wider for boys still in their first jobs who had hoped for other types of manual work (many more of whom found such work than had originally wanted to do so), or who had intended to take up non-manual work (hardly any of whom did so), than was the case among job changers, many more of whom went into non-manual work on leaving school than had evidently planned to do so (Table 49).

TABLE 49. Changes in employment and aims and attainments.

	One job		More than one job		
	Employment		Employment		
				First	
Type of employment	Wanted (i)	Obtained (ii)	Wanted (iii)	Obtained (iv)	Present (v)
(Per cent of total)					
Boys					
Apprenticeship	45	44	33	14	6
Other manual	31	55	44	58	75
Non-manual	17	1	19	28	19
Don't know	7	—	4	—	—
Total	100	100	100	100	100
(No. of 15–18s)[a]	(120)	(120)	(61)	(61)	(61)
Girls					
Clerical	50	57	43	38	40
Manual	10	25	25	41	33
Non-manual	30	18	27	21	27
Don't know	10	—	5	—	—
Total	100	100	100	100	100
(No. of 15–18s)[a]	(90)	(90)	(52)	(52)	(52)

	Boys			Girls		
	χ^2	d.f.	p	χ^2	d.f.	p
(i) and (iii)	3.84	3	> 0.20	5.98	3	> 0.10
(ii) and (iv)	40.58	2	< 0.001	4.79	2	> 0.05
(ii) and (v)	38.67	2	< 0.001	3.22	2	0.20

a Excluding those not answering.

These results suggest that it was the boys who failed to find apprenticeships who were more likely than others to have moved out of their jobs, sometimes, though not always, in search of more skilled work; and that it was their presence among the less skilled manual workers which may have been one of the factors contributing to the incidence of job change in this particular occupational group.

The differences in the sample of girls in regard to the type of employment wanted and obtained did not appear to be associated with job change as such, although among the girls with only one job, rather more had taken up clerical work on leaving school than had originally intended to do so, while among girls with more than one job, slightly fewer girls had managed to find office work than had wanted to; girls wanting non-manual work, other than in offices, were rather more frequently successful among the job changers than among others. Girls were, however, irrespective of the number of jobs held, generally rather more frequently successful than were boys in finding the *type* of employment they wanted, irrespective of the number of jobs held.

Size of firm entered

When the size of firm first entered by job changers and others was compared, further contrasts between the two groups of leavers was evident. The great majority of boys and girls who had remained in their first jobs had started work in the larger firms of 500 or more employees; the reverse was true for leavers who had changed their jobs, the majority of whom had begun work in small firms of 100 or fewer employees (Table 50). Further

TABLE 50. Changes in employment and size of firm first entered.

Size of firm (number of employees)	Boys		Girls	
	One job only	More than one job	One job only	More than one job
(Per cent of total)				
100 or fewer	15	65	27	62
101–500	22	14	25	12
501 or more	62	12	47	14
Don't know	1	9	1	12
Total	100	100	100	100
(No. of 15–18s)[a]	(120)	(61)	(90)	(52)

$$\chi^2 = 55.27; \text{d.f.} = 2; p < 0.001 \qquad \chi^2 = 26.89; \text{d.f.} = 2; p < 0.001$$

a Excluding those not answering.

analysis showed, moreover, that none of the young people still in their first jobs had entered the very small firm of 25 or fewer employees, though among job changers, as many as one-half of the boys and one-third of the girls had evidently done so. Two studies[10] have shown the tendency for

[10] E. Teresa Keil, David S. Riddell, and Colin B. Tipton, op. cit., J. Maizels, 1965, op. cit.

12

school leavers to enter industry predominantly through the small firm. The size of firm distribution of the adult population implies that young workers must eventually move to larger firms. This tendency evidently applied to certain of the leavers in the present inquiry, though as is shown later,[11] not to all job changers.

THE PATTERNS OF JOB CHANGES

The next stage of the analysis was based on information collected from young people themselves who had changed their jobs. Here an attempt was made briefly to examine each job change and to trace the fluctuations, if any, in the jobs and types of employment obtained, the methods used to find employment, the size of firm entered, the length of time spent in each firm, the reason for changing, and the assessment of each job experience. Did young people improve or worsen their status and prospects as they moved from job to job? Did they alternate between large and small units? How rapidly did they change their employment? Did they change their employment in the hope of gaining more money or were they more frequently dissatisfied with some other aspect of the work? And, looking back, how did they feel about the jobs they had left? Had these been worthwhile in some respect or were they now seen as a waste of time?

The analysis is, of course, limited by the relatively small number of job changers in the sample of school leavers seen, by the even smaller numbers who had changed their jobs more than once and by the fact that it was not possible to examine the inter-relationships, if any, between some of the factors which are described below. Even so, the tendencies which emerge are of interest, particularly in so far as they may apply to greater numbers of the school-leaving population.

Types of employment

From a comparison of the present occupational distribution of the boys themselves and of the jobs they held between their first and subsequent employment, it is evident that there was a reduction in the proportions of skilled and non-manual jobs and a rise in the proportions of relatively unskilled manual jobs. Though there were some compensating movements of boys changing from unskilled to skilled work or from manual to non-manual work, the general tendency was a downward shift of skill and status. Moreover, this was more marked after the second change than after the first, though the most substantial 'drop out' of apprentices actually occurred after the first change of employment.

Thus, whereas about one in seven of boys in their first jobs held apprenticeships, the proportion dropped to less than one in twenty for second

[11] See pages 164-5.

jobs, remaining constant at this figure irrespective of subsequent job changes. Between first and second jobs there was a slight rise, both in the proportions of other types of manual work and in non-manual work; from the third job change onwards, however, there was a sharp increase in the proportions of less skilled manual occupations and a corresponding fall in the proportions of non-manual jobs.

Further scrutiny revealed this to be mainly due to the differences in occupational distribution between boys with only one job change, on the one hand, and that of boys with two or more changes, on the other. Boys with only one other job, for instance, tended at the outset to include proportionately more apprentices and non-manual workers and proportionately fewer other manual workers, and even among the boys who left apprenticeships, most went into shops or offices. Only one of the boys with more than two jobs began his working life as an apprentice; more frequent job changers were more likely to have begun in manual jobs and remained in them. It was, therefore, not so much the shift of apprentices as of non-manual workers to other manual occupations which accounted for the higher proportions of relatively unskilled jobs between first and subsequent job changes.

In the sample of girls, there was also a fall between first and second jobs in the proportion of apprentices—mainly due to girls leaving jobs in hairdressing and dressmaking. These went either into manual work or into shops, so that between first and second employment, there was a slight rise in the proportion of jobs in manual occupations and as sales assistants. Though there were relatively few girls who changed their jobs more than twice, there appears to have been a constancy in their subsequent job changes after the second job change had occurred, the main shift in employment being from apprenticeships to manual employment.

Type of job

In addition to changes in types of employment there were considerable changes in the type of job obtained both within and between occupational categories; this was particularly marked for the boys.[12] It was comparatively rare for boys to find the same kind of job at the second or subsequent change of employment whereas girls were more likely to find at least similar jobs. More than one-half of girls who had only one change of job, changed to other types of clerical work, apparently requiring additional skills or responsibilities (the junior clerk becoming a typist, or the typist becoming a shorthand typist). Girls, more frequently than boys, also tended to return after the second or third change, to the kind of work they had previously done—particularly to shops.

[12] The 61 boys who changed their jobs had 50 specifically named occupations among them; the 52 girls had 29.

It was more typical for boys, however, to change their jobs as they changed their employers, as the following examples show:

2 jobs
> Shop fitter—junior postman
> Apprentice compositor—sales clerk
> Park gardener—shop assistant

3 jobs
> Van boy—loader—assembler
> Butcher's improver—sales assistant—hospital porter
> Trainee butcher—storekeeper—drilling machinist

4 jobs
> Platter printer—fireman—wood machinist—ribbon cutter
> Carpenter's mate—tea boy—messenger—junior operative
> Filing clerk—sales assistant—delivery boy—trainee fitter

5 jobs
> Apprentice plumber—delivery boy—plumber's mate—trainee welder—warehouse labourer

6 jobs
> Trainee pastry cook—wood machinist—pattern operator—shop assistant—capstan operator—garage hand

Size of firm

As already indicated[13] there was a shift from the smaller to the larger firm between first and subsequent jobs. Further examination showed, however, that this tendency applied only to boys with one job change; the subsequent employment of other school leavers showed a movement, if anything, towards the smaller firm. There was a slight reduction in the proportions in small firms from first to second employment among the more frequent job changers, but no corresponding rise in the proportions in medium and large firms, mainly because a number of boys in this category were unable to remember the size of firm in which they obtained their second jobs; this may indicate that they were in small or medium sized firms.

The shift from small to large firms among boys with only one job change was a very substantial one, the proportion in firms of 100 employees or fewer falling sharply and that in firms of 500 or more rising steeply, between first and present employment. Moreover, it was the very small firm of under twenty-five employees which tended to lose and the very large firm of 1000 or more to gain, young workers between the two job changes.

This does not mean that there were not boys who changed from large to small firms or, that among the more frequent job changers, there were

---

[13] See page 161.

not boys who alternated between the large and small unit. However, the analysis showed that this occurred to a relatively minor extent. The movement to large firms was predominantly of boys who had started work in small firms, mainly (as has been shown)[14] as apprentices and then found, and remained in, other types of employment in the larger unit; though this meant that they joined an occupational group with a higher risk of job change than previously, the size of firm may itself have been conducive to their subsequent job stability.[15] None of the boys who had remained in their first employment, for instance, had started work in firms of under fifty employees and the majority were in larger units of 500 or more.

It was, therefore, the boys in other manual occupations who, when changing their jobs, tended to find work in firms whose size corresponded fairly closely to those in which they had first started to work.

Girls showed the same tendency to move from smaller to larger units between first and subsequent jobs, particularly between the first and second, though in their case the shift was mainly from the small (fifty employees or fewer) to the medium-sized firm (between 50 and 500 employees). There was no apparent relationship distinction between the size of firm entered by girls and the frequency of job change.

Methods of finding work

It has been previously shown that job changers tended to use the Youth Employment Service far less frequently for their second and subsequent jobs than for their first.[16] This tendency was, moreover, much more marked for boys with only one job change than for boys with several. The latter tended to use the service almost as frequently for their second job as for their first; they also referred less frequently to the help of their friends and more frequently to the help of their parents when making their second change than when obtaining their first employment. For subsequent jobs, however, there was a fall in the proportions using the Youth Employment Service and a rise in the proportions finding work themselves.[17]

Girls ceased entirely to use the official service after the second job change, and even between the first and the second the reduction was considerable (from one-third to one-seventh). The tendency was for them to rely more frequently on their own resources or on the help of relatives or friends after they had left their first jobs.

[14] See page 161.

[15] The length of time at work did not affect the tendency for boys with only one job change to move to larger firms, since it applied even when boys who had been at work for less than one year were excluded from the analysis.

[16] See Chapter VIII, page 121.

[17] In the analysis of Youth Employment Bureau records, it was also evident that the use of the official service fell after the first job change but rose again after the fourth or fifth change of employment. The numbers of frequent job changers interviewed in the present inquiry was too small however, for such a tendency to appear among them.

Length of time in jobs

It is sometimes assumed that job changers move quickly from job to job (though time, presumably, has a different significance for job changers themselves than for the outside observer). In the present inquiry the average time spent in each job was 5·5 months for boys and 6·5 months for girls. This average did not vary much though there was a tendency among the boys with only one job change to remain in their first jobs a little longer (8 months) than did other boys (5·3 months). If anything, boys with more than one job tended to stay in their second jobs rather longer, on average, than in their first and to move out of their third jobs rather more quickly. There was also a tendency for boys with more than three jobs to spend rather less time in each successive job, staying only 2·5 months, on average in their fourth or subsequent employment.

Though girls tended to spend, on average, a little longer than boys in each job, they too were inclined to move successively more quickly as they changed jobs, particularly after the first though the lowest average time was 3·2 months for girls in their third or subsequent employment.

REASONS FOR JOB CHANGES

There are two possible interpretations of the replies of young people to the question of why they changed employers. The first is that adopted by the Social Survey[18] which, assuming that the question was itself an invitation to rationalize, concluded that it was impossible to say what objective factors were of importance in influencing frequent job change.

The second interpretation is the approach of T. Ferguson and J. Cunnison[19] who, in regard to the replies of Glasgow boys, excluded those which proved impossible to classify, but found that the frankness of the remainder 'inspired belief in the reliability of the information given'. The difficulties of assessing the reliability of information obtained from young and adult workers alike need not be understated. Nevertheless, in the present inquiry the reasons offered for job changes were interpreted as valid explanations of events, and accepted as indications as to how young people themselves now saw their past experiences and decisions.

Their replies were analysed according to the number of jobs from which they were either dismissed or left voluntarily. This showed that the majority of jobs had been terminated by the young people themselves, while in just over one in five cases employment had ended because of dismissals (one in ten due to redundancy, about one in twelve because of unsuitability and one in twenty for disciplinary reasons).

A variety of reasons were offered for voluntary terminations. Most indicated that the young people concerned had found their jobs unsatis-

[18] *15–18.*
[19] Op. cit.

factory in some way. Criticism centred particularly on dislike of the job itself, dissatisfaction with pay and dislike of, or difficulties with, employers, supervisors or fellow workers (Table 51). The latter was particularly important for girls, nearly one-third of whom made references to difficulties of this kind. Girls were also more inclined, than were boys, to have been dissatisfied with the hours or physical conditions of work, but both commented with almost equal frequency on poor training facilities and prospects.

Of lesser importance than these dissatisfactions, were factors apparently beyond the control of young workers, such as questions of health or fatigue; travelling difficulties; or their families moving to other areas. Relatively few boys—one in ten—and even fewer girls had been motivated by the attraction of a better job or the hope of finding work which corresponded to their original preference.

TABLE 51. Reasons for changes in employment.

	Boys	Girls
	(Per cent of total)	
Dismissals		
Redundancy	10	9
Unsuitability	7	9
Disciplinary	5	5
Voluntary leaving		
Dislike of the job itself or some aspect of it	17	14
Dissatisfaction with pay	14	14
Did not like employer, fellow worker, supervisor	12	30
To try for better or preferred job	10	3
Dissatisfaction with training	7	6
Health or fatigue	7	6
Dissatisfaction with prospects	6	7
Dissatisfaction with hours, physical conditions	5	13
Travelling difficulties	4	6
Family circumstances	—	5
Other miscellaneous	9	10
Total (Multiple replies)	100	100
(Number of jobs)	(111)	(72)

It was comparatively rare for any reason to be offered more than once, though there were cases where jobs had been lost or given up because of certain repetitions of circumstances. Five boys, for instance, shared between them ten of the total number of dismissals; two of these had twice lost their jobs for disciplinary reasons and two others had twice been dismissed because they were considered too slow for the work. Some leavers tried more than once to find a better job or discovered that their second jobs were no improvement on their first as far as prospects or pay were concerned.

More typical, however, was a different reason for each job change though, logically enough, this frequently meant a succession of criticisms about different features of the jobs obtained. Thus, having left one job because of not getting on with fellow workers, the second job would be ended because of poor training; or having given up the first employment because of poor prospects, the money in the second job would not be good enough, while in the third the employer, fellow workers, or supervision turned out to be unsatisfactory; a job that was otherwise acceptable was ended because of travelling or health difficulties; a second job proved to be boring. Job changers, both boys and girls, tended, therefore, to offer different explanations for each change of job and, if these explanations are accepted, to have experienced, therefore, a variety of disappointments in one form or another. For some school leavers, moreover, and particularly girls, some jobs were the sources of more than one disappointment—since in their case two explanations were sometimes offered, as if to strengthen their case. 'There were too many changes in management and anyway there were no prospects'; or 'I never got on too well with the supervision and I was bored as well—there was not enough to do.'

Ferguson and Connison found that the predominant reasons given among the less frequent job changers were to obtain better prospects; among boys with average job experience it was the search for better pay and among boys who changed jobs most frequently, it was the dislike of the job or other reasons.[20]

In the present inquiry, the small numbers precluded analysis of this detail, though between boys with only one job and others certain differences were evident. Dissatisfaction with prospects, criticisms of training, the wish to find a better job and health reasons accounted for nearly one-half of the reasons offered by boys who had had only one job change, but for not more than one in five of the reasons given by more frequent job changers. The latter were more inclined to refer to dissatisfaction with pay, to difficulties with or dislike of their employers, supervisors or fellow workers and were the only boys to have experienced dismissal due to their unsuitability for certain jobs. The differences, however, were not substantial.

ASSESSMENT OF JOB EXPERIENCES

Though dissatisfaction with some aspect of the jobs undertaken was, more often than not, associated with changes in employment, as many as one-

20 Op. cit.

half of the total number of jobs experienced at one time or another were, nevertheless, now regarded as having had some positive value for the young people concerned. Asked to assess each job in terms of whether they now regretted the experience, the balance of retrospective opinion was not an unfavourable one. There was an expected tendency, of course, among the more frequent job changers, for them to be more likely to have had at least one job experience which they now regretted; first jobs were also more likely, though not always, to be regarded with favour than were third, fourth, or subsequent ones. Altogether, however, not more than one-third of the boys' jobs and one-quarter of the girls' were now felt as having been entirely unsatisfactory experiences.

The reasons for these assessments are of interest, for though many of the changes in employment were not anticipated at the outset, they were, nevertheless, felt by the young people themselves to have brought them certain advantages. Favourable views, for instance, were associated with the feeling, particularly among boys, that they had gained useful experience and versatility in several types of work, even though these were not neces-sarily highly-skilled tasks; one in five of the boys and girls referred to their having enjoyed the work itself; one in eight also felt that they had learnt something specially useful to their present employment and training. There were also references to having liked working with certain people; to being helped to adjust to a working life; and to having learnt that the original choice of employment was not, after all, one for which they were suitable or which they liked.

Unfavourable opinions were, on the other hand, associated with the feeling that the spell of employment had been a waste of time during which nothing had been learnt or gained; one in six of the boys and one in ten of the girls were of this viewpoint. A dislike of the work itself and difficulties encountered with employers, supervisors or fellow workers also accounted for some of the negative job experiences. There were, of course, some young people with mixed feelings about certain of their jobs.

SUMMARY

About one in three of the boys and girls seen in the present inquiry had changed their jobs since leaving school, though less than one in ten had had more than two changes of employment. The average number of jobs for those with more than one job experience was just under three; the average for the sample as a whole, related to the average time at work, was just over one job per year. A brief examination of some of the respective characteristics of job changers and other school leavers suggest that the job changers were predominantly fifteen-year-old leavers who failed, more frequently than others, to find the work of their first choice; who were more likely than others to be in work which differed considerably from that originally preferred, and to have started work in relatively unskilled manual occupations, chiefly in small firms. They were more likely than others to have obtained their first jobs through the Youth Employment Service, but were less inclined to use the official service for their subsequent, than for their first, jobs. The results also suggest that in the sample of boys seen, it was the would-be apprentice who had failed to find entry to skilled trades who was more likely than other boys to change his employment.

The analysis of patterns of job change showed that between first and subsequent employment there was a downward shift in the skill and status of occupations, mainly due to the movement of apprentices and non-manual workers leaving their first jobs and then remaining in other types of employment; the more frequent the job changer, the more likely it was that they had started in and then continued to find, less skilled manual work. There were considerable changes in the type of job undertaken and it was rare for boys, though not for girls, to find the same kind of work in their subsequent as in their first employment. Changes in employment also produced a shift from the small to the large firm but this was mainly due to the movement of leavers making only one change of employment, the more frequent job changers tending to continue to work in small firms.

The chief reasons for changing jobs were, among boys, a dislike of the job itself, dissatisfaction with pay, dislike of or difficulties with employers, supervisors, or fellow workers and the wish to try for a better job than that originally preferred. Girls were more frequently influenced by their reactions to people and to the atmosphere of the work environment, than by considerations of pay or the job itself. Surprisingly, one-half of the jobs were now assessed as having brought some positive benefit, either to work experience, to job satisfaction or to training. Where nothing had been learnt or where the jobs or the people had been disliked, then such employment was regretted and felt to have been a waste of time.

The fact that so many jobs were regarded by job changers as having some positive benefit for them suggests that if haphazard methods of trial and error could have been replaced by the kind of 'systematic exploration' advocated by Professor Rodger, by which young people discover for themselves the type of work suited to their capacities and inclinations, then the experience might have been more rewarding.[21] But the benefit derived was more a matter of luck than design. The young people concerned were not embarking on a process of self discovery; they were, after all, less likely than others to have had the opportunity of testing out their first preferences; they were more likely to have had to modify their original aims before they started work and were then more likely to have begun their working lives in jobs and firms where, apart from any personal predisposition, the risk of change of employment was higher than elsewhere.

[21] A. Rodger, 'Arranging Jobs for the Young', *New Society*, No. 10, 6 December 1962.

The analysis also shows that for school leavers with only one job change, particularly boys, first jobs were frequently a prelude to more stable employment in firms and in jobs where conditions, in some respect, were more favourable. The more frequent job changers, again particularly boys, did not, on the whole, better their position. As far as their status, specific skills or their jobs satisfaction were concerned they remained, in a sense, where they had started. On the other hand, they acquired some versatility and gained experience of a variety of jobs, people, and enterprises. These could, perhaps be regarded as positive assets both to the individual and to the community were it not that traditional attitudes to job changes tend to favour those which result in some tangible improvement in status or prospects and disapprove those which have no such rewards,[22] though the latter would seem to be the more typical outcome for job changers.

A more objective approach might be to recognize changes which stem directly from unsuitable jobs and firms. The evidence of the present inquiry suggests that there may be a residue of jobs, chiefly in small firms, where the standards of working conditions, training, prospects, and the treatment of young people are lower than elsewhere. Job changes in this context could be regarded as the inevitable response to such conditions of young people who have come from similar jobs or who are new entrants to industry. There would seem to be need at least for detailed investigation before jobs are offered as suitable employment by the Youth Employment Service.

Some changes in employment may also be necessary if natural inclinations for exploration, variety, and experience are to have an outlet or if uncertainties as to how and where interests and talents may best be used are to be resolved. But neither traditional attitudes nor present conditions of employment favour experiment. Adolescents are generally expected to choose one or other type of occupation and to remain in it; while the type of employment available to those who do not wish to specialize or who are uncertain about what to do is unlikely, generally, to offer realistic opportunities for self-discovery.[23]

[22] Ferguson and Cunnison refer to 'good' reasons for change when training, prospects, and higher wages are the result: and to 'frivolous' reasons when the job or the foreman is disliked. Op. cit.

[23] The characteristics of the actual employment of the school leavers seen are described in Chapters XII and XIII.

PART IV

PRESENT EMPLOYMENT

CHAPTER XII

PRESENT EMPLOYMENT, AS DESCRIBED BY EMPLOYERS

INTRODUCTION

In spite of recurring official interest in, and concern about, young workers, information about their employment is sadly lacking. Relatively little is known about the nature of the work they do, the processes on which they are engaged, the conditions of their employment, the training they receive or the prospects before them, particularly in regard to the boys and girls who enter the less skilled occupations or those to whom no formal schemes of training apply.[1]

In the present inquiry special emphasis was placed, therefore, on the work situation by including the collection of information from employers of under-eighteens as well as from the young people themselves. It was hoped that information relating to the characteristics of the work performed, the training given, and the prospects offered might enable some analysis to be made of the work environment in these respects, in different occupations, and so make possible some preliminary assessment of its suitability or otherwise.[2]

The wide scope of the present inquiry did not allow, however, for objective job studies to be undertaken in the detail suggested by the Central Youth Employment Executive[3] for the purpose of vocational advice, or as carried out by some organizations for the purpose of training and selection programmes. Information from employers[4] was obtained by their completing relatively simple job description questionnaires which covered such aspects as the characteristics of the jobs in question, the method and length of training, the promotion prospects, as well as the methods of recruiting young workers and the qualifications required.[5] Employers' opinions were

---

[1] See Gertrude Williams, *Recruitment and the Skilled Trades*, Routledge and Kegan Paul, 1957, *Apprenticeship in Europe*, Chapman and Hall, 1963, and Kate Liepmann, *Apprenticeship: An Enquiry into its Adequacy under Modern Conditions*, Routledge and Kegan Paul, 1960.

[2] The total work environment would include many other variables, particularly the social system represented by each type of organization. For a discussion of this and its measurement see K. Inkson, R. Payne, and D. Pugh, 'Extending the Occupational Environment: The Measurement of Organizations', *Occupational Psychology*, 41, No. 1, January 1967.

[3] C.Y.E.E., Memorandum No. 20.

[4] See Chapter II for the method of selecting the sample of employers.

[5] See Appendix II for questionnaire.

also sought on the question of day release and on future trends in the employment of under-eighteens.

The replies of employers could not be verified. In many instances, no qualifying comments could be included, while only certain aspects of the jobs in question could be covered by questionnaires and interviews. The information obtained from employers is, therefore, incomplete and imprecise in certain important respects. Moreover, the sample was not a random one; it is over-representative of the large firm, and of boy apprentices and girl office workers;[6] the very willingness of certain employers to participate in the inquiry also suggests that they may represent firms with higher-than-average conditions of employment, training provisions and interest in young people.

In spite of these limitations, however, it has been possible to obtain a rather more adequate picture of the work, training, and prospects associated with certain types of employment of young people than has hitherto been available, though necessarily on a small scale and in a local setting. Furthermore, the information offers a factual basis, though limited and not without bias,[7] for reviewing certain aspects of the work situation of young adolescents and for considering the criteria by which their employment might be assessed as suitable or otherwise for them.

Method of analysis

One hundred job descriptions were completed by sixty-six employers, and the replies weighted according to the number of under-eighteens actually employed in each job described. The descriptions covered the employment of just under 650 young workers. The information was then analysed according to the usual five main types of employment, namely, apprentices, trainees, other manual, clerical, and sales. Since almost all apprentices and trainees were boys, while clerical workers and sales assistants were girls, only other manual workers were distinguished by sex. Size of firm was also examined for certain questions, but because of the need to separate occupation by size of firm factors, the analysis here applies only to boy apprentices. Even then it was found necessary to combine the small firm of 100 employees or fewer with the medium-sized firm of between 100 and 500 workers. Nevertheless, certain differences are evident according to firms of under or over 500 employees, though these may reflect differences between skilled trades rather than between firms of different sizes.

---

[6] See Appendix I for characteristics of the sample of employers.

[7] As Chapter XVII shows, there was a tendency for employers to stress more frequently than their employees, some of the more favourable aspects of employment.

JOB CHARACTERISTICS

Employers were asked to select from a check list of twenty-six items those most closely applied to the jobs in question. The items used were adapted from a N.I.I.P. study[8] and were identical with those submitted to the sample of young people interviewed. Job characteristics have been divided into four main groups corresponding, approximately, to 'interest', 'demand', 'physical', and 'social factors' associated with each job.

Interest factors

Nine items were included to indicate characteristics likely to increase or diminish the interest of young workers in their jobs. Less than one-half of the jobs covered were, however, regarded by employers as being interesting for young workers. Most occupations would seem to have been regarded as varied (two-thirds); as offering a chance to use initiative and brains (about three-fifths), and just over one-third as skilled and associated with an interesting product or service. Almost one-third, however, were referred to by employers as having not much skill and about one in seven as routine or monotonous. Further analysis according to the type of employment described, showed that these proportions concealed the very high scores for positive interest factors associated with jobs as apprentices, trainees and, to a lesser exent, non-manual workers and the relatively high scores of negative interest factors associated with other types of manual work (Table 52).

TABLE 52. Interest characteristics of jobs, by type of employment, as described by employers.

| | Apprentices | Trainees | Other manual | | Clerical | Total[a] |
			Boys	Girls		
Positive		(*Per cent of total*)				
Varied	90	85	33	16	74	67
Chance to use initiative	96	84	21	8	46	60
Uses brains	90	75	21	—	51	57
Interesting	88	69	25	5	14	45
Skilled	94	80	10	—	22	37
Interesting product or service	71	66	11	15	5	35
Negative						
Not much skill	4	5	52	97	38	31
Routine	3	—	32	77	1	15
Monotonous	—	2	10	92	6	15
Total (Multiple replies)	100	100	100	100	100	100
(Number of jobs)	(218)	(61)	(88)	(83)	(164)	(647)

a Including sales assistants.

[8] J. D. Handyside, op. cit.

Apprenticeships, for instance, had a high score on almost all positive interest items: as did three-quarters or more of the jobs as trainees; but only one in three of other manual jobs for boys were described as varied, one in five as offering a chance to use initiative or brains, one in four as interesting and one in ten as skilled; over one-half were described as requiring little skill. Manual jobs for girls contrasted even with those of boys, in that almost all of them were said to require little skill and to be monotonous, and the majority routine. They were less likely than were the boys' jobs to be varied or interesting, to require the use of the brain or to offer a chance to use initiative; and were far less likely to be mentioned in these three respects than were clerical or sales jobs.

Demand factors

These items, six in all, were intended to indicate the physical and other demands on young workers of the jobs performed. The highest scores applied to keep the workers busy (over two-thirds), and responsible (three-fifths). Lower scores applied to, they can pause when they want to (just over two-fifths), requires nimble fingers (one-third), competitive (over one quarter), and difficult (one-fifth). There were, again, differences between the main types of employment though these were not so marked as in regard to the interest factors. Four-fifths of other manual jobs for boys and all the corresponding jobs for girls were associated with keeping the worker busy compared with just over two in three of the apprentices and trainees and one-half of clerical occupations. This would seem, in part, related to the speed and intensity of manual workers' jobs being, possibly, determined by production demands and methods of wage payment. On the other hand, almost all the relatively unskilled jobs for girls were said to allow them to pause when they wanted, whereas this facility was available

TABLE 53. Demand characteristics of jobs, by type of employment, as described by employers.

| | Apprentices | Trainees | Other manual | | Clerical | Total[a] |
			Boys	Girls		
		(Per cent of total)				
Keeps them busy	69	67	84	100	51	70
Responsible	83	87	31	55	34	61
Worker can pause when wants	33	23	6	92	69	44
Requires nimble fingers	18	5	—	97	60	36
Competitive	63	44	9	—	5	29
Difficult	49	48	1	—	5	22
Total (Multiple replies)	100	100	100	100	100	100
(Number of jobs)	(218)	(61)	(88)	(83)	(164)	(647)

a Including sales assistants.

for very few of the similar jobs for boys. This difference probably results from the different types of production processes involved, since a similar contrast between these two groups appeared in regard to the need for finger dexterity. Clerical jobs were also more likely than the skilled manual jobs to allow workers to pause, perhaps associated with differences in the respective pace of office and production work. It was apprenticeships and trainee jobs, however, which were more likely than office or other manual work to be regarded as responsible; four-fifths of these jobs were so described compared with much smaller proportions of other jobs. Apprenticeships were, interestingly enough, more likely than other jobs to be regarded as competitive, though this on further analysis was shown to be exclusively among boys employed in the large firms of over 500 persons. Skilled jobs, together with trainees, were also more likely than were others to be described as difficult (Table 53).

Social factors

In this category were five items associated with fellow workers, the steadiness of the job, the usefulness of what was being taught, prospects for promotion, and pay. About three-quarters of the sample of jobs were referred to as being steady, and offering prospects of promotion; three-fifths were also described as teaching young people something useful and over one-third as well paid. Two in three of the jobs were also said to be associated with working with a good crowd. The majority of jobs had,

TABLE 54. Social characteristics of jobs, by type of employment, as described by employers.

	Apprentices	Trainees	Other manual		Clerical	Total[a]
			Boys	Girls		
			(Per cent of total)			
Offers promotion prospects	76	89	25	55	74	74
A steady job	68	92	73	98	64	74
Work with a good crowd	50	58	34	99	82	65
Teaching something useful	91	85	39	13	37	57
Well paid	29	—	10	83	40	37
Total (Multiple replies)	100	100	100	100	100	100
(Number of jobs)	(218)	(61)	(88)	(83)	(164)	(647)

a Including sales assistants.

therefore, a fairly high score in regard to most items in this category. There were, however, considerable contrasts between occupations, particularly in regard to pay, prospects, and the usefulness of what was being taught. Almost all girls' manual jobs were regarded as well paid compared with only a minority of other jobs and only one in ten of the corresponding jobs for boys; boys' manual jobs were also the least likely of all to be associated with promotion prospects, only one in four being so described, compared with over one-half of the corresponding jobs for girls and over three in four of all other jobs. Most apprenticeships and traineeships were considered as teaching something useful, but not more than two in five of the boys and one in eight of the girls' manual jobs were so described (Table 54).

Physical factors

Five factors were distinguished as associated with the physical environment of the work. Most jobs, for instance, involved being indoors; nearly two-fifths were performed sitting down while one-third were associated with a lot of moving about. Very few were described as dirty or noisy. Clerical jobs and girls' manual work, however, were chiefly sedentary jobs, while apprentices, trainees, and, to a lesser extent, boys' other manual work, involved more frequent moving about. Only the less skilled work for boys was described as noisy and only manual work of all kinds as dirty (Table 55).

TABLE 55. Physical characteristics of jobs, by type of employment, as described by employers.

| | Apprentices | Trainees | Other manual | | Clerical | Total[a] |
			Boys	Girls		
	(Per cent of total)					
Mainly indoors	52	85	44	100	82	70
Mainly sitting	3	1	12	89	87	37
A lot of moving about	57	54	25	2	4	30
Noisy	6	5	68	2	—	12
Dirty	6	5	10	—	—	4
Total (Multiple replies)	100	100	100	100	100	100
(Number of jobs)	(218)	(61)	(88)	(83)	(164)	(647)

a Including sales assistants.

Size of firm

The tendency for jobs as apprentices to have higher interest factors as well as better promotion prospects and greater usefulness of the skills acquired, than other types of work, applied to a more marked degree for apprentices in large firms of over 500 persons than in smaller firms. In the large firms, all positive interest items applied to all apprentices, compared with less than four-fifths of those in smaller firms. Twice as many of the skilled jobs in large than in small and medium firms were considered responsible, most as difficult and one-half as competitive: in the smaller firms, few were felt to be difficult, responsible, or competitive. Large firms were also associated with higher scores relating to steady jobs, a good crowd to work with, good pay and promotion prospects, the latter applying to all apprentices employed in the large firm.

RESPONSIBILITY FOR VOLUME AND QUALITY OF OUTPUT

Employers were asked to assess the extent to which the amount and quality of the work performed in different types of employment were determined by the young workers themselves, by their supervisors or by the machines that they were required to operate. It was thought that the replies to this question might suggest how closely the work of young people was supervised and the degree of responsibility for their work that was expected or required of them. The results showed that in about one-half of jobs, young workers were said to play an equal or major part in determining both the amount of work done and its quality. In only one in seven of the jobs were they expected to take full responsibility. Supervisors played a relatively minor role in regard to most jobs and exercised full control in less than one in eight of the jobs described. Machines played an even less significant part in determining output or quality and in the majority of jobs, no part at all. There was a slight tendency for the responsibility of young workers to apply more frequently to the volume of output than to its quality, and for supervision to be more frequently fully involved in regard to the quality, rather than the amount, of work done but the differences were not substantial. There were, however, certain interesting differences in the degree of responsibility expected of workers according to the type of employment in which they were engaged.

Volume of output

In manual jobs, for instance, girls were more likely than others to be given minor, and boys full, responsibility in determining the volume of work they did; apprentices, on the other hand, were more likely to be expected to take an equal or a major part, trainees an equal part and clerical workers an equal or minor part, in determining work volume. Similarly, the degree to which supervisors influenced output also differed according to the type of work done. They exercised less frequent control over the output of manual workers than that of others, and in over two-fifths of the boys' jobs played no part in determining output. This tendency would appear to be partly due to the fact that machines, which hardly influenced the output of other workers, were said to play an equal part in determining the output in over one in four of the jobs of less skilled manual workers.

Supervisors were more likely to share equally in controlling the output of trainees and to have a partial or equal share in the output of apprentices. Clerical workers, however, were most likely of all workers to have their output determined predominantly by supervision.

Quality of output

These tendencies did not apply to the same extent in regard to responsibility for the quality of work done. The proportion of workers having no control in this regard was much higher for all types of manual than for non-manual jobs; full or major responsibility was much more frequently required of clerical workers and apprentices than of other manual workers.

Supervisors were much more likely, therefore, to have full responsibility for the quality of the work of trainees and manual workers than for apprentices and clerical workers; but since supervisors also played a major part in influencing the quality of clerical work, only apprentices emerged as the workers least likely to have the quality of their work influenced predominantly or wholly by their supervisors. Machines, which seem to have been of predominant importance in girls' manual work were said to have partially determined the quality of just over one in five manual jobs; an equal part for the quality of the work was attributed to machines in two in five jobs as trainees, however.

While the overall tendency was for a relatively high proportion of young workers to be equally or predominantly involved in determining the volume of their output and the quality of their work, this tendency was much more marked in the case of apprentices than of other workers. Clerical workers, while less likely to be fully supervised in regard to the quality of the work, were much more likely to be so in terms of the amount of work done. More precise studies of the jobs in question would be required, however, to assess how far there were other limits set on the work performed and on the 'discretionary' and 'prescribed' aspects. Relatively simple tasks, even if not closely supervised, may still offer the worker little discretion over decisions. It is the discretionary content of work which, according to Jacques,[9] determines the intensity and weight of responsibility.

PROMOTION PROSPECTS

It will be recalled that when employers were asked to select from a number of items those most closely applying to the jobs in question, nearly three-quarters of the jobs were referred to as offering promotion prospects, though a very much lower 'score' applied to the relatively unskilled manual jobs than to other types of employment.[10]

In order to discover more precisely what these prospects were, employers were asked to assess the likelihood of their young workers, if remaining in

[9] E. Jacques, *The Mental Processes in Work*, Glacier Project Papers, Heinemann, 1965.
[10] See pages 179-80.

the firm, continuing in the same job indefinitely or being upgraded to more skilled work, to supervisory grades or to management posts. The assessment was made leaving out of account any personal qualifications for promotion. Their replies showed, first, that upgrading to more skilled work was very much more probable than was upgrading to positions of authority; second, that apprentices were very much more likely than were other workers to reach supervisory grades; third, that the chances of promotion, of whatever kind, were very much less likely for the less skilled manual workers and shop assistants than for young people employed in other types of work (Table 56).

TABLE 56. Promotion prospects, by type of employment,
as assessed by employers.

Likelihood of promotion	Apprentice	Trainee	Other manual		Clerical	Total[a]
			Boys	Girls		
			(Per cent of total)			
Continuing in same job						
Very likely	7	13	65	52	25	30
Fairly likely	46	61	11	46	26	35
Not very likely	43	26	24	2	49	34
Upgrading to more skilled work						
Very likely	89	66	31	1	78	61
Fairly likely	6	33	21	53	16	23
Not very likely	5	1	48	46	6	16
Upgrading to supervisor						
Very likely	27	8	9	—	8	13
Fairly likely	72	85	30	55	60	63
Not very likely	1	7	61	45	30	23
Upgrading to management						
Very likely	4	3	7	—	1	2
Fairly likely	45	16	—	—	5	19
Not very likely	47	81	93	100	94	78
No answer	4	—	—	—	—	1
Total	100	100	100	100	100	100
(Number of jobs)	(218)	(61)	(88)	(83)	(164)	(647)

a Including sales assistants.

Though less than one in three of the total number of workers were said to be very likely to continue indefinitely in their present jobs, the proportion with this prospect before them was as high as four in five for shop assistants, and nearly three in five of the relatively unskilled manual workers, the proportion being somewhat higher for boys than for girls; this assessment applied, however, to only one-quarter of clerical workers, one-eighth of trainees and under one-tenth of apprentices. Substantial proportions, nevertheless, of trainees and, to a lesser extent, apprentices, were fairly likely to continue without promotion; for only apprentices and clerical workers, in fact, were the chances of some change substantially more likely than for others.

Similarly, the majority of skilled and clerical workers were said to be very likely to be upgraded to more skilled work; but less than one in three of boy manual workers, virtually none of the girls and only one in ten of shop workers, had such prospects. Moreover, for nearly one-half of manual workers, boys and girls, up-grading to more skilled work was said to be not very likely, an assessment which hardly applied to other occupations. The chances of promotion to supervisory grades was less frequently certain for all types of employment, though it was more likely for apprentices than for others, since this assessment applied to over one in four of them. The chances were said to be fairly likely, however, for over three-fifths of the sample but again, this assessment less frequently applied to manual workers, for over one-half of whom such promotion was not very likely, though more so for boys than for girls (Table 57).

TABLE 57. Proportion of present workers who could immediately be promoted if opportunity occurred, by type of employment.

| | Apprentice | Trainee | Other manual | | Clerical | Total[a] |
			Boys	Girls		
			(Per cent of total)			
	40	85	35	10	40	39
Total	100	100	100	100	100	100
(Number of workers)	(218)	(61)	(88)	(83)	(164)	647

a Including sales assistants.

Though upgrading to management positions was far less likely to occur than were other types of promotion, manual, shop, and clerical workers were almost entirely excluded from this possibility as were the majority of trainees. Only apprentices had some perspective of this kind before them to the extent that just under one-half were assessed as being fairly likely, eventually, to secure management posts.

Immediate promotion prospects would also seem to have varied according to the type of employment. Employers were asked to assess what proportion of the under-eighteens employed in the jobs described could, if there were appropriate vacancies, be promoted or upgraded. Some immediate movement upwards, presumably to more skilled work, was evidently possible, in principle, for just under two in five of the young people employed; this, however, represented a very high proportion of trainees (over four-fifths), a very low proportion of manual workers (one-third of boys and one-tenth of girls) and less than one-half of other workers.

Size of firm

Promotion prospects, as measured by the likelihood of some upgrading, were evidently more promising for the apprentice in the larger firm. All boys in skilled trades in the firms of over 500 employees were said to be very likely to be promoted to more skilled work, compared with four in five of the boys in smaller firms; one-third of boys in larger firms were also very likely to find their way into the ranks of supervision, compared with only one in ten in smaller firms. Though promotion to management was generally less likely, the chance of this happening was more frequent for boys in the relatively large enterprise than in the small or medium firm. The apparently brighter promotion prospects for boys in large firms was confirmed by a relatively higher proportion also being assessed as ready for promotion if the opportunity occurred.

TRAINING

A series of questions were asked relating to training though, of necessity, these were of a very general character. They were intended to discover simply by whom basic instruction and, where applicable, further training for the job in question, was given; where it took place; how long it took; and whether day release was granted.

By whom basic instruction given

Supervisors were, evidently, by far the chief source of basic instruction, being responsible for instruction on more than two-thirds of the jobs described. But a substantial proportion of jobs were, apparently, taught by more than one person, the teaching of supervisors being supplemented by that of fellow workers or training instructors, though the latter arrangement, as is shown later, operated exclusively in the larger firms. Clerical workers were much less likely than were other workers to be given basic instruction by their supervisors and, with shop workers, less frequently than others received instruction from more than one source. All apprentices and trainees, on the other hand, had been taught, in the first instance, by at least two persons. Though the most constant of these were their supervisors, trainees were, evidently, more likely to have received supplementary training from their fellow workers, and apprentices from instructors. Apprentices and trainees, therefore, would appear to have received, in this sense, the most intensive training, manual workers a generally less intensive one and clerical and shop workers the least.

Where instruction given

The basic instruction for three-quarters of the jobs described was given 'on the job', and it was relatively infrequent for young workers to be taught the initial stages of their work at a school (under one in four), or in a separate training bay or section (one in six). Only a minority of jobs were taught in two stages—first in a school or separate training section and then on the job—and this procedure was much more frequently associated with the training of apprentices and trainees, than with the training of other workers. Girls in other manual and clerical work were the most likely to receive basic training in a separate training section of their work place. This feature was, on further analysis, shown to be associated with the fact that a high proportion of manual and clerical workers were employed in the larger firms where more formal training schemes operated. Boys in other manual jobs and shop workers all received their basic instruction exclusively on the job.

Time taken for basic instruction

For over one in four of the jobs described, basic instruction was completed within three weeks and for over two in five within three months; just under one-quarter of jobs involved an initial training period of between two and five months, and one in five jobs between six and twelve months. The average length of basic training, naturally, varied according to the type of employment. Over two-thirds of manual jobs involved a training period of not more than three weeks and it was these jobs for which the average training time was the shortest (1·8 months). The basic training for most shop work was also completed within three weeks, though the average training time (2·3 months) was a little longer than for manual workers. Clerical jobs were more equally divided between a relatively short training period of under eight weeks and between two and twelve months, the average time being nearly $3\frac{1}{2}$ months. The basic instruction for trainees and apprentices extended over a longer period, the average being seven months for trainees and over one year (13·3 months) for apprentices (Table 58).

Further training

Over two-thirds of the jobs were said to involve further training though this did not apply to the same extent to manual as to other jobs. It is evident, moreover, that some firms did not distinguish, in the case of apprentices, between basic and further training, being of the opinion that apprenticeship training could not be separated in this way. This has the effect of slightly increasing the average length of basic, and slightly reducing the average length of further, training, for apprentices and for the sample as a whole.

The pattern of further training did not differ substantially from that of basic instruction except that it extended over a longer period. Supervisors, other workers, and instructors were involved in almost the same proportions for the two stages of training; apprentices, however, were more likely to receive further than basic training on the job while girl manual workers, on the other hand, were more likely to be trained, subsequently, off the job; neither of these tendencies applied to other jobs. Once again, the length of further training varied according to the type of employment, being shortest on average for manual workers (5·4 months), for two-thirds of whom further training did not extend beyond three weeks; and longest for apprentices and trainees (2½ years), for almost all of whom further training extended for two years or more (Table 58).

TABLE 58. Average time of basic and further training, by type of employment.

	Apprentice	Trainee	Other manual	Clerical	Sales	Total
			(Number of months)			
Basic instruction	13·3	7·0	1·8	3·4	2·3	6·4
Further training	33·0	33·0	5·4	8·2	7·3	21·0
Total training time	46·3	40·0	7·2	11·6	9·6	27·4
Regarded predominantly as learner	45·0	30·0	3·0	9·2	6·0	18·2
Number of jobs[a]	183	45	145	159	33	565
Number of jobs[b]	176	38	88	112	32	446

a Excluding those not answering.
b Workers receiving further training only.

Total training time

The relatively long periods of training which applied to apprentices and trainees, whose jobs together accounted for over two in five of the total described, meant that more than one-third of all jobs were covered by a total training period of up to one year and almost one-half by a period of between two to five years. If the more skilled manual occupations are excluded from the analysis, however, it becomes evident that more than one-third of the remainder of the jobs were covered by a total training period of only up to three weeks, and two-thirds by a period of less than six months. The total average training time was, therefore, more than halved from 27 months when apprentices and trainees were included, to 10 months when they were excluded.

For most of the training period workers were, evidently, regarded, predominantly, as learners, though this general tendency did not apply to the less skilled occupations; in these, workers were regarded, on average, as producers less than half-way through their training.

Day release

Day release for training or for further education was granted for nearly two-thirds of the jobs covered by employers' descriptions, though the proportion varied considerably between occupations. Almost all apprentices and the majority of trainees and clerical workers were covered by day release schemes compared with less than one in four of shop workers and less than one in five of manual workers. Day release for the relatively small proportions of the latter workers was entirely due however to the inclusion in the sample of firms, one large enterprise which had introduced an experimental scheme of day release for certain of its factory operatives, and official or nationalized services. The comparatively high proportion of young workers in day release in the sample compared with that estimated for England and Wales as a whole[11] is also due to the fact that the sample of firms was generally over-representative of large enterprises where day release schemes were much more likely to apply than elsewhere.

Size of firm

As already indicated, training in the larger firms was much more likely to be associated with the employment of full-time instructors, whereas in the smaller firm, boys were taught much more frequently by their supervisors. Boys in larger firms were also more likely to be taught in company training schools or separate training bays or departments, and less likely to be trained on the job. This would be consistent with the picture of rather more favourable training conditions associated with the large firm which, as has been shown,[12] is also associated with a more consistent attendance of apprentices at technical courses and a greater measure of success in examinations. The total training time was not affected, on average, however, by the size of firm but by the nature of their trade; nor did the operation of day-release schemes generally vary by size of firm. The latter is no doubt due to the under-representation of small firms in the sample of jobs described, since other studies have shown that much smaller proportions of day-release students in technical college courses come from small than large firms.[13]

USEFULNESS OF PRESENT JOB EXPERIENCE

Since a considerable proportion of young people change their jobs at least once during their first years at work and many move into different firms as they grow older, it was thought of interest to try to obtain information which would indicate how far the respective job experiences of young people could be regarded as useful assets elsewhere. The employers were, therefore, asked to assess the usefulness of the particular job experiences of

[11] See Appendix I, pages 324-5.
[12] E. Venables, 'Success in Technical School Courses according to size of firm', *Occupational Psychology*, **39**, No. 2, April 1965.
[13] Ibid.

young workers for subsequent employment within their present firms or within similar or different types of enterprise. The replies suggest that while very few jobs could be described as having no value at all for subsequent employment, only just under two in five were regarded as providing experience of a very useful kind for firms differing in the type of industry or service, in the type of work offered and, therefore, in their requirements of young people. The majority of jobs, however, were assessed as being very useful when the experience gained was applied either to present firms or to enterprises of a similar kind (Table 59).

TABLE 59. Usefulness of present job experience as assessed by employers, by type of employment.

Usefulness of present job experience	Apprentice	Trainee	Other manual		Clerical	Total[a]
			Boys	Girls		
In present firm			*(Per cent of total)*			
Very	100	100	88	53	95	91
Fairly	—	—	12	46	5	9
Not very	—	—	—	1	—	—
In similar firm						
Very	100	97	64	23	91	83
Fairly	—	—	11	77	8	13
Not very	—	—	7	—	1	3
In different firm						
Very	55	57	3	—	52	38
Fairly	24	24	7	—	36	25
Not very	21	16	90	100	12	37
No answer	—	3	8	—	—	1
Total	100	100	100	100	100	100
(Number of jobs)	(218)	(61)	(88)	(83)	(164)	(647)

a Including sales assistants.

A rather different kind of assessment, however, applied to the relatively unskilled manual jobs for girls, experience in which was less frequently considered very useful, even in present firms and to an even lesser extent in different firms of a similar type. But almost all these jobs were considered as having very little usefulness when the experience gained in them was applied to firms differing in their processes and in their requirements, a judgment which was made far less frequently of other types of job experience.

On balance, experience in clerical work would seem to have had more frequently useful application elsewhere than had experience in the more skilled manual jobs or work in shops. The negative rating given to experience in the less skilled manual jobs, however, suggests that the skills acquired, particularly for girls, were frequently too highly specialized and non-adaptive.

Size of firm

When the usefulness of the job experience of apprentices was considered according to size of firm, it would appear that the skill and experience in skilled work gained in the larger firm was more frequently considered to be very useful in quite different firms than in present or similar firms. This would suggest that the training given and the type of work performed in the larger firm was of more general application than that in the smaller firm.

PHYSICAL FATIGUE, NERVOUS TENSION, AND HEALTH HAZARDS

Employers were asked to assess how far the jobs described were likely to give rise to physical fatigue, nervous tension, or health hazards to an average, above-average, or below-average degree. Hardly any of the jobs in question were, in fact, considered to give rise to these conditions to an above-average degree; just under one-half and one-third, respectively, were felt to give rise to average and below-average nervous tension. Nearly three-quarters of the jobs were described as having lower than average health hazards, however. The proportions differed somewhat as between types of employment, though the relatively high non-response to some parts of the question makes comparison uncertain.

It would seem that the less skilled manual jobs, particularly for boys, and shop work, were the most likely to produce average physical fatigue while the work of trainees was much more likely to produce less than average physical tiredness. While manual work for boys was considered as less likely to produce average tension, this did not apply to the equivalent type of work for girls, rather higher proportions of such work being described in these terms. Trainees, if anyone, were the most likely to experience above average fatigue though less than one in ten of these jobs were so described; and apprentices, if anyone, were more likely to experience nervous tension—but again only very small proportions were likely to do so.

There was also little difference in the average weekly hours of work, as between different types of employment. Manual workers of all kinds tended to have a slightly longer working week, on average, than non-manual workers, but the difference was not more than 2 hours. Nevertheless, as many as over one-half of clerical workers worked less than a 38-hour week, a condition which did not apply to any other occupational group.

THE QUALIFICATIONS REQUIRED

Having considered some of the characteristics of different types of employment of under-eighteens as these were described by employers, it is perhaps of interest also to consider the qualifications required of young people for different kinds of work. Employers were asked to state the essential qualifications for the jobs in question. Their replies were analysed according to the educational, practical, or personal requirements associated with each main type of employment.

TABLE 60. Qualifications required for different types of employment, as specified by employers.

Qualification	Apprentice	Trainee	Other manual		Clerical	Total[a]
			Boys	Girls		
Educational		*(Per cent of total)*				
G.C.E. 'O' levels	38	12	—	—	43	25
'Minimum' and 'average' standard	22	26	32	36	36	28
Practical ability						
Practical and mechanical ability	23	2	1	—	—	8
Manual dexterity	5	—	—	46	11	11
Ability and willingness to learn	—	—	—	—	18	8
Special aptitudes						
Mechanical	48	67	10	—	—	24
Computational	—	—	—	—	18	8
Scientific	10	—	—	—	—	3
Personal	—	—	—	—	2	1
Clerical	—	—	—	—	2	1
Practical	16	—	6	2	—	6
Personal						
Physical fitness	14	—	12	76	3	17
Reliable, responsible, etc.	14	3	12	46	11	15
Temperament, patience, etc.	—	8	9	46	12	11
Good appearance, speech, manners	1	5	1	8	16	10
Commonsense	3	—	—	2	3	2
Other	34	8	3	16	31	22
No qualifications specified	4	—	42	—	1	7
Total (Multiple replies)	100	100	100	100	100	100
(Number of jobs)	(218)	(61)	(88)	(83)	(164)	(647)

a Including sales assistants.

The analysis showed that educational qualifications, either up to G.C.E. 'O' level or to 'average' standard, and mechanical aptitude, were each more frequently considered essential in regard to the whole range of jobs, than was any other single requirement. However, when qualifications were combined into four main groups, rather more frequent references were made to personal attributes such as appearance, temperament, character, and health, than to any academic qualifications, practical abilities, or special aptitudes (though these three together accounted for the majority of references). This tendency was due, however, to the much more frequent demand for these personal attributes for relatively unskilled manual jobs in which girls were employed, than for any other kinds of employment, including the less skilled manual work performed by boys. In some respects, moreover, the differences in the relative requirements of boys and girls employed in the less skilled manual jobs, were as great as between the requirements for different types and level of employment (Table 60).

It was also evident that rather more requirements in all, were specified for apprenticeships and clerical jobs, than for other kinds of work. Two specifications, the first relating to an apprentice, the second to a comptometer operator, illustrate this:

'A good standard of education—an interest in the trade—integrity—ambition—perseverance—physically fit—willing to travel—parents interested in apprenticeship.'

'Manual dexterity—a liking and aptitude for figures—accuracy and reliability.'

The narrow range of requirements which applied to jobs as trainees, shop assistants, and other manual workers, was associated with rather more frequent emphasis on certain qualifications. Jobs as trainees, for example, were said to need, above all, mechanical aptitude, this requirement applying to over two-thirds of the jobs in this category, compared with less than one-half of apprenticeships and one in ten of boys' other manual jobs.

Appearance, speech, and manners were emphasized for almost all jobs in shops, as the following indicate:

'Smart appearance—pleasant personality.'
'Clean, tidy, and good speech.'

The majority were also said to require an aptitude for figures and a 'general ability and willingness to learn'. None of these requirements was specified, to any marked degree, for any other kind of work.

For girls' jobs in manual work, the most important requirement was, evidently, physical fitness, this being specified for over three-quarters of the jobs in this category. This relatively high proportion is undoubtedly due to the fact that many of these jobs were associated with food preparations and applicants for such work were first required to pass a medical examination before engagement. Manual dexterity, certain temperamental qualities such as patience, obedience, combined with a sense of responsibility and reliability, etc., were also said to be required for almost one-half of the jobs in this category of employment.

A machine feeder, for example, was required to have:

'Good physical health—a temperament suited for high speed machinery—manual dexterity and a sense of responsibility for the product.'

A bench hand:

'A nice appearance—an interest in the work—lively, alert, and willing.'

Such qualities were infrequently stressed for corresponding employment for boys or for other kinds of work for boys or for girls; miscellaneous attributes such as enthusiasm for the job, ambition, alertness, did apply, however, to almost one-third of apprenticeships and clerical jobs. Jobs in the skilled trades and in offices were, however, mainly distinguished from others by the relatively higher frequency with which educational qualifications, particularly G.C.E. 'O' levels or their equivalents, were stressed and by the generally more even frequency distribution of requirements over a wider range.

The distinguishing feature of the requirements specified for other kinds of manual work for boys, was that over two in five were said to require no special qualification, educational, practical, or personal. These jobs were, therefore, associated with far less frequent discrimination than were the corresponding employment for girls, or other types of employment of higher skill and status. By contrast the outstanding feature of the requirements specified for manual work for girls, was the emphasis placed on personal qualities, implying that for these jobs more than for any other, temperamental and physical suitability was more appropriate than were other qualities or skills.

Size of firm and qualifications required

The analysis of the qualifications specified for apprenticeships according to size of firm showed certain striking contrasts in the relative frequency with which certain requirements were specified. Educational qualifications, particularly up to 'O' level, and mechanical ability and aptitude were much more frequently stressed by the larger than by the smaller firms, which, if anything, tended to emphasize personal attributes and qualities or, as in the case of some firms, to make no specific demand.

Previous experience

Relatively few of the jobs described were exclusive to under-eighteens, with the exception of the apprenticeships and about one-third of traineeships. Otherwise, most jobs, manual and non-manual, applied to adults as well as to school leavers. In spite of this, previous experience was rarely required and only specified for about one-quarter of the less skilled and manual jobs in which boys, particularly, were employed.

14

General intelligence

Employers were also asked to assess the range of intelligence required for each job using a five-point scale. Almost two-third of the jobs in question were within the middle range of intelligence, just over one-fifth in the next to top range and one in ten in the next to bottom. There was, however, a tendency for the proportions to vary according to the type of work described; as many as one in three of the less skilled manual jobs were judged to come within the next to bottom intelligence range but virtually none of the others; on the other hand, nearly one-half of apprenticeships were assessed as coming within the next to top range, rather more than applied to clerical jobs, though these assessments, on analysis, applied exclusively to the large firm of over 500 persons.

RECRUITMENT AND SELECTION

All firms normally used more than one method of recruiting young staff; the Youth Employment Service was the method most frequently used, accounting for over four in five of the total employed; but the methods used varied in frequency with the type of employment described (Table 61). Far more frequent reference was made, for example, to the Youth Employment Service, to press advertising and to employee recommendation in regard to clerical than to other types of employment; on the other hand, apprentices were more likely to have been recruited through direct contact with schools or as a result of their inquiries to firms than were other workers. Though notices outside firms were also more likely to have been used to obtain entrants to skilled trades than to other types of manual work, this method was particularly important in the recruitment of staff for shop work, and as frequently used, in their case, as were the official service and press advertisements.

TABLE 61. Methods of recruiting young employees by employers.

	Manual	Apprentice	Clerical, other non-manual	Sales	Total
			(Per cent of total)		
Youth Employment Service	87	80	100	(24)	82
Press advertisements	62	40	96	(24)	59
Employee recommendation	48	50	70	—	48
Direct contact with schools	19	54	39	(2)	35
Gate notices	19	39	2	(24)	25
Other (including self-initiated applications or inquiries)	12	37	7	—	19
Total (Multiple replies)	100	100	100	100	100
(No. of 15–18s)	(232)	(218)	(164)	(33)	(647)

In selecting staff, all young applicants for the jobs described were interviewed by managements, as many as three in five jobs involving some form of test, mainly written. For some jobs, applicants were interviewed by more than one person, either on separate occasions or, as in the case of apprentices, by an interviewing panel, though this method of selection applied only in the medium- and large-sized firm.

Written tests were used much more frequently for trainees, and clerical workers, than for others; manual tests were also generally used for apprentices and clerical workers; in the latter case, they were associated with ability to handle accounting machines. Both written and manual tests applied much more frequently to apprenticeships in the large firm of over 500 persons. The majority of entrants to skilled trades in small and medium firms were not given any formal tests. Only girl manual workers were required to have a medical test, a condition which, as was previously shown, was associated with work on food preparations.

JOBS AND ABILITY

Since the young people themselves presented a range of abilities, and the jobs different requirements, it seemed of interest to discover how many of the under-eighteens in employment were considered by their employers to be correctly placed in terms of their ability. Employers were, accordingly, asked to assess the number of workers in each job described for whom the work performed was consistent with, below or above, the level of their ability. Over two-thirds of the workers were, evidently, judged to be in work which matched their ability, though this applied to a much higher proportion of girls in manual jobs (nine-tenths) than apprentices (three-fifths), or clerical workers (two-thirds).

As many as one in five of boy manual workers, one in six apprentices and one in ten clerical workers were assessed as being in work which was below the level of their ability; but less than one in ten of any occupational group were felt to be in work which was too difficult for them. 'Misplacement' on the basis of employers' assessments, would seem, therefore, to have applied to just over one in five of the workers concerned, but more frequently to apprentices and boy manual workers than to other workers, and more often in terms of under than over-capacity.

WELFARE, SOCIAL, AND MEDICAL FACILITIES
PROVIDED BY FIRMS

In addition to the information from employers about the type of work carried out by under-eighteens, and its training, prospects, and requirements, supplementary data were also obtained showing the extent to which young workers in the sample inquiry were covered by various social, welfare, and medical facilities provided by their firms. This information relates to a larger number of young people than that covered by job descriptions, since the latter were not completed by all firms and did not apply to all young workers employed in the sample firms.

Occupational groups are not distinguished in the analysis since the information obtained applied to all young workers employed by the participating firms. It was, however, necessary to distinguish size of firm since this was directly associated with greater provision of facilities in the large firm and with an almost complete absence of provision in the very small enterprise.

None of the young people employed in firms with a total labour force of twenty-five persons or less, or for that matter employed by small shops, was covered by canteen or medical facilities; none had social or sports clubs within their firms; none of these firms employed Welfare or Training Officers or operated any formal training scheme, day release applying only to apprentices (Table 62).

TABLE 62. Proportion of 15–18s covered by welfare, social, medical, and and training facilities and size of firm.

| Type of facility | Size of firm (Number of persons employed) | | | | |
	Up to 25	26–100	101–500	501 and over	Total
	(Per cent of total)				
Canteen	—	51	76	100	68
Induction/Reception scheme	—	—	2	100	56
Social club	—	16	21	100	63
Sports club	—	11	21	100	75
First-aid room	—	9	43	100	70
Full-time nurse	—	19	16	100	68
Medical officer					
(i) on call	—	14	3	61	41
(ii) part time	—	5	32	38	31
(iii) full time	—	—	—	10	6
Member of local industrial health scheme	—	16	17	22	15
Welfare/Personnel officer	—	17	51	100	73
Training officer	—	—	13	92	60
Senior executive responsible for training	—	29	26	72	53
Day release	4	22	31	67	52
Total (Multiple replies)	100	100	100	100	100
(No. of 15–18s employed)	(43)	(109)	(174)	(548)	(874)
Number of firms (including retail)	17	15	14	20	66

In firms employing between 26 and 100 persons, however, just over one-half of the under-eighteens had canteen facilities, although only a minority were covered by any other provision, though most existed, in some degree. Much higher proportions of young people working in firms of between 100 and 500 persons were covered by the facilities listed: three-quarters had canteens; over two-fifths were in firms with a first-aid room and nearly one-third had the services of a part-time doctor. One-half were in firms which employed a Personnel or Welfare Officer while nearly one-third were covered by training and day-release schemes. In the large firms of over 500 employees, all young workers had canteen facilities, social and sports clubs, and medical services; all were in firms which employed welfare and training officers, where some form of induction and reception scheme applied to new entrants and where day release was granted to some two-thirds of the under-eighteens.

There was thus a very marked tendency for the proportion of young workers covered by welfare, medical, or training facilities to increase sharply with the size of firm, though apart from canteen provision, only minorities were likely to be covered by any facilities, unless they were employed in firms of over 500 persons. Since it has been demonstrated[14] that new entrants to employment are more frequently employed in small rather than large-scale enterprises, and that they are relatively more highly concentrated in small firms than is the adult working population, it follows that they are also less likely than are adult workers to be covered by welfare and medical, if not training, facilities.

EMPLOYERS' OPINIONS ON DAY RELEASE AND FUTURE TRENDS IN THE EMPLOYMENT OF UNDER-EIGHTEENS

In addition to completing job descriptions employers were also asked for their opinions as to the extent to which the young people in their employment were an essential part of their labour force; on the idea of day release for all young workers irrespective of the type of work in which they were engaged; on the advantages to them, or otherwise, of the Industrial Training Act; on the possible effects of a higher minimum school-leaving age on their employment of young people; and on possible changes during the next five or ten years in the employment of school leavers.

It was thought that opinions on such questions might reveal something of prevailing attitudes of employers towards the fifteen- to eighteen-year-old workers. Sixty-six firms completed some, but not all, of these questions and their replies are summarized below.

The role of the young worker in the labour force

This question was answered by just over fifty firms: the majority of their

14 E. T. Keil, D. S. Riddell, and C. B. Tipton, op. cit. and J. Maizels, 1965, op. cit.

replies showed that under-eighteens were regarded as an essential part of the labour force and could not easily be replaced by adult labour. This was chiefly because of the need to train new workers and to replace the skilled labour leaving the firm from time to time, either through retirement or for some other reason. 'To employ young people is the only way to hand on the crafts.' 'School leavers are the only source of new skills.'

In some cases, however, young people were considered essential because otherwise labour costs would rise; because they were quicker than adults to train; or because the work they performed was considered unsuitable for adults. 'These jobs don't need a great deal of strength or intelligence. They're very simple and very suitable for youngsters.' One firm employed young people only because of shortages of skilled adults, and commented: 'We would not train youngsters if we could get trained labour.' Such attitudes were more prevalent among smaller firms; firms who required a boy to sweep up, to run errands and to make the tea; and among firms which did not employ apprentices.

Extension of day release

Sixty firms replied to the question of whether they approved or otherwise of the idea of granting day release to all young workers in their employment, whatever the nature of their work. Only twenty-seven of these gave their unconditional approval, one-half of which were firms employing more than 500 persons, while three were statutory services. Though approval also came from smaller firms (including those employing under fifty employees), one of which considered day release was a 'moral obligation' on employers, the overall tendency was for approval to be more frequent among the large firms, and disapproval and qualified approval more frequent among the small firms.

Qualified approval was given by twenty-one firms: this was usually associated with the view that day release should be granted only for apprentices, or only where it was of obvious vocational value. Other conditions specified included the suitability of the potential student; that it should be confined to boys; that small firms should be safeguarded against the loss of workers after training; and that, in the case of a small shop, day release should be arranged at the beginning of the week when business was slack. Only twelve firms actually disapproved of the idea, and five of these were small shops. The four large firms of over 500 persons tended to feel that day release was not appropriate for the kind of work performed by the young people in their employment, the nature of which required no formal training. The smaller firms felt that release would affect production; would be too costly; or that the initiative should come from the young workers themselves. The balance of opinion was more in favour than against the idea of extended day release, particularly from firms who were already granting day release to some or, as in statutory organizations, to all of their young workers. This tendency reflects, no doubt, the bias in the sample of firms towards the larger enterprise and the employment of apprentices.

Training

Most firms stated that they were satisfied with their present arrangements for training, but fewer were satisfied with arrangements for their particular industries. This was especially true among the smaller firms, some of which commented on the need for group apprenticeship schemes. Uncertainty was expressed about the possible benefits of the Industrial Training Act; some firms were not sure, at the time of inquiry, how their own industry would be affected; others, such as banks, hospitals, and local authorities felt that the Act was not applicable to them. Those who felt that the Act would bring some advantages tended to be the large firm with established apprenticeship schemes.

Future trends

Most firms felt that a higher school-leaving age would not affect their employment of under-eighteens, but these tended to be, again, organizations which recruited entrants at sixteen, which had apprenticeship or other training programmes, and found little difficulty in attracting suitable applicants. The firms which foresaw shortages in the supply of school leavers, and greater difficulties in finding young people to do routine work, tended to be those with less-skilled employment to offer and with a higher labour turnover. 'There'll be fewer applicants and they'll want something better' was a comment reflecting anxiety about the effect of the proposed higher school-leaving age.

Similarly, firms with training programmes were more inclined to comment on possible trends in the coming five or ten years. Their predictions included changes in training methods; improved training facilities; reductions in apprenticeship training time; an extension of automation to routine work, including office work, now performed by school leavers; and higher educational standards of entrants to industry and commerce. 'A two to three years apprenticeship course will be quite adequate'; 'A lot of training will be taken right out of the workshop and concentrated in training schools'; 'Young persons will be regarded as trainees and be much less involved in production work'; were some of the forecasts made. One employer saw the sixteen- to seventeen-year-old of the future as 'intelligent and adaptable, educated not so much with information as with the ability to adapt to new techniques and new ideas'.

Thus higher standards, in education, training, selection, and working conditions, represented the general trend of comment in regard to possible changes in the employment of young people in the coming years. Nearly one-half of the firms questioned did not reply to this question, perhaps because they did not view the future with such optimism. The outlook of those who did reply, however, suggests that they represent the firms which, in anticipating change, are in some ways preparing for it.

While these replies cannot be regarded as necessarily typical of employers in general, they indicate nevertheless the contrast in attitudes between the large and small firm and between the firms which provide training programmes and for day release, and those which do not. It would appear that the more the worker is treated as a producer and the less that is invested in his training, the more likely it is that his employer will regard future changes as likely to reduce the supply of suitable and relatively cheap labour. In contrast, the more the worker is regarded as a learner and the more that is invested in his training, the more likely it is that employers may anticipate or accept changes which would raise the skill, status, and conditions of young workers. For these changes to apply to all young workers, however, would mean a much wider acceptance, on the part of employers, of the adolescent at work not so much as a worker but as one who is learning to work and, at the same time, developing his mind and widening his technical, social, and personal horizons.

SUMMARY

The job descriptions completed by employers provide an indication of the very great contrast in conditions which apparently exist between different types of employment in regard to their job characteristics, methods of training, opportunities for promotion, and the usefulness of the job experience. At the higher end of almost every favourable condition are apprentices, particularly those employed in the large firm. They, more than any other occupational group considered in the present inquiry, were in jobs which were frequently described as interesting, varied, skilled, and responsible and which frequently involved the use of thought and initiative. Apprenticeships were also likely to provide for intensive and prolonged training, during most of which the worker was more usually regarded as a learner than as a producer; skills and experience gained in this kind of work were likely to be useful when applied elsewhere; promotion prospects of some kind were almost certain. In specifying the requirements for such work, the need for educational qualifications and mechanical aptitudes predominated.

At the other extreme were the relatively unskilled manual workers. Their jobs, particularly for girls, were more frequently than others described as requiring little skill and offering only limited interest, variety, responsibility, or mental exercise. Training for most of these jobs was, on average, completed in a matter of weeks and most workers were expected to be fully productive before the total training period was ended. They were, in any case, more likely than were other workers, to be kept busy at their work on processes which for girls, particularly, were predominantly routine and monotonous. Experience in this type of work was rarely considered useful elsewhere, and promotion prospects were far less certain than was the likelihood of indefinitely continuing in much the same kind of work. In describing the qualifications required for such work, the need for personal and temperamental qualities were emphasized more frequently than were educational achievements or special aptitudes.

Between these two extremes, though nearer in most respects to the skilled than the unskilled jobs, were trainees, clerical workers, and shop assistants. Trainees tended to follow in the footsteps of apprentices, sharing with them many similar job characteristics and training methods, though their long-term promotions prospects were not as good. Clerical and sales jobs had also a number of similar characteristics; clerical work was particularly associated, however, with lower 'scores' on positive interest factors, but with a more intensive and lengthy training, more frequently useful job experience and less frequent pressure to be kept busy at work.

Supplementary data were also obtained which showed the extent to which young workers, irrespective of their occupations, were covered by various welfare, medical, and social provisions. The proportion of young workers to whom canteens, sports and social facilities, medical services, day-release schemes, welfare, personnel, and training departments applied, increased sharply with the size of firm. These services applied to all or most of the young workers in firms of 500 persons or more, but to virtually none of those employed in firms of under twenty-five persons, and only to small minorities (except in regard to canteens) in firms employing between 25 and 100 persons. Since new entrants to employment have been shown to be more frequently employed in small rather than large scale enterprises, and relatively to the adult working population, are more concentrated in smaller firms, it follows that they are also less likely than are adult workers to be covered by welfare, social, and medical facilities.

CHAPTER XIII

PRESENT EMPLOYMENT, AS DESCRIBED
BY YOUNG WORKERS

INTRODUCTION

The young people interviewed were also questioned about the characteristics of their work, the method and length of their training, and their promotion prospects. They were also asked to give their opinions regarding their supervisors, firms, and further education; to comment on particular features of their work that were liked or disliked; and to assess how they felt about their present jobs. Supplementary questions related to their journey to work, work accidents, and absences.

The information obtained relates to a smaller number of under-eighteens at work than that obtained from employers (330 as against 647). A comparison between the two sets of opinions is given in Chapter XVII.[1] The purpose of this and Chapters XIV to XVI is to present only the opinions of the 330 young people interviewed.

Method of analysis

The analysis first distinguishes five occupational groups—apprentices, trainees, other manual workers, clerical workers, and sales assistants. Since the numbers in each occupational group were relatively small, it was not always possible to distinguish according to sex for 'other manual' and clerical workers, though where boys and girls in these occupations differ substantially from each other in their views or experiences, due reference is made in the text. The opinions of apprentices and trainees relate almost exclusively to boys, and of shop assistants to girls.

The present chapter examines the characteristics of their jobs, their likes and dislikes, their promotion prospects, their accidents at, and absences from, work, according to the type of occupation followed. Likewise, Chapter XIV discusses their training and further education, including their assessment of day and evening classes and their attitudes to further education. Their impressions of supervisors and firms have been recorded in Chapter XV, while Chapter XVI looks at their job satisfaction and at some of the factors associated with their feelings. Since the dissatisfied

---

[1] To make a valid comparison it was necessary to confine the analysis to those job descriptions and interview schedules relating to identical jobs.

numbered so few, only the 'very' and the 'moderately' satisfied are distinguished in the analysis. The relatively small size of the sample of young people interviewed made it impossible, without refined statistical techniques, to assess which of the several inter-related variables considered was the most important influence on attitudes to work. Similarly, the uneven distribution of the sample in regard to size of firm made it difficult to assess its particular influence.

JOB CHARACTERISTICS

Young people were asked to select from a check list of twenty-six items those which most closely applied to their present jobs. The items were adopted from a N.I.I.P. study[2] and were virtually identical with those submitted to employers. The replies were divided into four main groups corresponding approximately to 'interest', 'demand', 'physical', and 'social' factors associated with each job.

Most items, on the check list, favourable or otherwise, received a relatively low score. Only one item—that associated with working with a good crowd—was selected by a majority of boys and girls (almost two-thirds), and only one other item—that associated with being kept busy—by more than one-half of the girls. It also appeared that items relating to pay, security, and certain social aspects of their present jobs received a higher score, on average, than did those items relating to positive interest factors, particularly for girls. Moreover, though the majority of boys were in manual and girls in non-manual work, their opinions were remarkably consistent, though girls were less inclined, on average, to select positive interest items.

Interest factors

Seven items were included to indicate characteristics likely to increase and four as likely to diminish, the interest of young workers in their jobs. Though two in three young workers referred to at least one positive interest item, the relatively low frequency with which these items were selected, suggest that only minorities regarded their jobs as interesting, varied, or skilled.[3] About one-half of the boys, but fewer of the girls, referred to their jobs as interesting; smaller proportions (about one-third) as providing a chance to use their initiative[4] or requiring concentration; while less than one-third of the boys and only one-fifth of the girls stated that their jobs were varied or used the brain, or were associated with an interesting product or service (Table 63).

[2] J. D. Handyside, op. cit.
[3] Work requiring special skill or training was one of the most important job characteristics selected by boys in the Veness inquiry. (See T. Veness, op. cit.)
[4] In the Veness study, this characteristic did not appear to be an important aim for most school leavers (ibid.).

TABLE 63. Interest characteristics of jobs as
described by young workers.

	Boys	Girls
	(Per cent of total)	
Positive		
Interesting	49	40
Chance to use initiative	36	30
Have to concentrate	33	34
Interesting product/service	32	21
Varied	32	21
Uses brains	29	22
Skilled	19	4
Negative		
Too routine	15	14
Not enough skill	12	5
Monotonous	12	7
Boring	10	10
Total (Multiple replies)	100	100
(No. of 15–18s)	(183)	(147)

On the other hand, much smaller minorities described their jobs as too routine (one in seven); fewer still as requiring not enough skill or being monotonous; and only one in ten as boring. Nevertheless, as many as one in five of the boys, and one in three of the girls, made no reference at all to any positive interest item associated with their jobs. Positive interest items were, however, more frequently selected than were negative ones but the only item to exceed the half-way 'score' was that the job was interesting and this only when selected by apprentices and trainees. Boys in skilled trades were much more likely to refer to positive interest items than were other workers but, in fact, only minorities did so. Clerical and shop workers were, on the whole, less likely to regard their jobs as having as much interest, variety, skill, or mental exercise; manual workers, particularly girls, did so to an even lesser extent. In fact, the proportion of girls in manual jobs who selected any positive interest item was at least half that of the corresponding group of boys for almost every item except the need for concentration (Table 64).

Surprisingly enough, relatively more apprentices than other workers felt their jobs were monotonous (one in eight) and that not enough skill was required. They were less inclined than were others, however, to refer to their jobs as too routine and with trainees as boring. Clearly, most young workers did not refer to their jobs in these terms.

TABLE 64. Interest characteristics of jobs, by type of employment, as described by young workers.

	Apprentices and trainees	Other manual	Clerical	Sales
	(Per cent of total)			
Positive				
Interesting	54	37	42	(15)
Uses brains	37	13	20	(4)
Chance to use initiative	44	19	42	(6)
Have to concentrate	38	36	28	(6)
Skilled	32	6	2	(5)
Interesting product/service	40	20	28	(4)
Varied	44	17	31	(5)
Negative				
Monotonous	12	7	9	(4)
Not enough skill	9	14	5	(2)
Too routine	14	11	18	(4)
Boring	6	16	10	(2)
Total (Multiple replies)	100	100	100	..
(No. of 15–18s)	(97)	(104)	(99)	(30)

TABLE 65. Demand and physical characteristics of jobs as described by young workers.

	Boys	Girls
	(Per cent of total)	
Demand		
Keeps you busy	43	53
Pause when you want to	39	32
Responsible	26	20
Difficult	4	3
Physical		
Mainly indoors	49	33
Dirty	28	6
A lot of moving about	25	18
Clean	18	33
Mainly sitting	18	27
Noisy	15	10
Badly organized	11	4
Total (Multiple replies)	100	100
(No. of 15–18s)	(183)	(147)

Demand factors

These items, four in all, were intended to indicate the physical and other demands on young workers of the jobs performed. The most frequent reference was to being kept busy, which applied to just under one-half of the sample. Occupations would not appear to have been associated with any substantial differences in the frequency with which this or other demand characteristics were selected. Apprentices were a little less likely to be kept busy and trainees a little more likely to regard their work as difficult. Girls in manual work were less inclined to feel they could pause when they wished, only one in five selecting this item compared with under two-fifths for the sample as a whole. Not more than one in four young workers felt their jobs were responsible and fewer, particularly girls in manual jobs, that they were difficult (Table 65).

Social factors

In this category five items were distinguished to indicate characteristics associated with pay, prospects, and social aspects of the job. A much higher score, on average, applied to all these items than to any other categories of job characteristics. The majority of young workers—nearly two-thirds—felt that they worked with a 'good crowd'—and this, as already mentioned, was the only item to receive such a high rating. Substantial minorities—over two-fifths of the boys, and over one-third of the girls—felt their jobs were steady ones and that they were learning something useful: fewer, evidently, worked with their own age group, and fewer still felt their jobs offered promotion prospects[5] or were well paid, though in this last respect, rather more girls than boys had favourable views (Table 66).

TABLE 66. Social characteristics of jobs as described by young workers.

	Boys	Girls
	(Per cent of total)	
Work with a good crowd	64	64
A steady job	47	36
Teaching me something useful	44	34
Work with own age group	33	27
Offers promotion prospects	26	20
Well paid	22	31
Total (Multiple replies)	100	100
(No. of 15–18s)	(183)	(147)

[5] This, with skill and training, was one of the most important of the characteristics selected by boys and girls in the Veness inquiry. (See T. Veness, op. cit.)

There were certain differences, however, according to occupation. Working with a good crowd was much more frequently selected by apprentices (three-quarters), and much less frequently by 'other manual' workers, particularly girls. Apprentices were also more likely than other workers to feel that their jobs were teaching them something useful, a characteristic which applied to less than one in four of 'other manual' and shop workers, and to only one in seven of boys and girls working in offices. The office workers were also the least likely to be working with their own age group. Occupational groups hardly differed in the frequency with which jobs were regarded as steady, except for girls in manual jobs who were the least likely to be of this opinion: these girls were the most likely however, to feel that they were well paid (though only just over one in three did so). Clerical workers, with trainees, were more inclined than others to feel their jobs had promotion prospects, in contrast to hardly any of the girls in manual jobs who had such views.

Physical factors

There were seven items relating to the physical environment of work (Table 66), and these were found to be associated with occupation, mainly according to manual or non-manual jobs. Thus hardly any clerical or shop work was regarded as dirty or noisy though these characteristics applied to as many as one in three and over one in four respectively of apprentices; manual workers were more likely to be involved in a lot of moving about in their work but clerical workers were likely to be mainly sitting. Badly organized work was also less likely to affect clerical and shop workers than manual workers, though only one in seven of manual workers were so affected.

COMPARISON WITH THE RESULTS OF THE N.I.I.P. INQUIRY

The relatively low score for most items relating to jobs is consistent, however, with the results obtained in the N.I.I.P. inquiry.[6] Since the check list of items used in the present inquiry was based on that used in the N.I.I.P. study, it was thought of interest to compare the two sets of results. This comparison, which relates to the two samples irrespective of age, sex, or occupational differences, shows that the results of the present inquiry, though not identical in all respects, were not greatly at variance with those of the N.I.I.P. sample (Table 67).

Virtually equal proportions of both samples, for instance, felt that their jobs used their brains, required them to concentrate, kept them busy, were clean or dirty; not very dissimilar proportions also felt that their jobs were too routine, boring, and associated with working with their own age group. The under-eighteens in Willesden, however, were more likely to

---

[6] J. D. Handyside, op. cit.

have a higher score than workers in the N.I.I.P. study for certain interest and social factors.[7] Many more of them, proportionately, felt that their jobs were interesting, provided them with a chance to use their initiative and were well paid; they were also a little more inclined to describe their jobs as varied, and associated with interesting products. The N.I.I.P. sample of workers, however, more frequently felt that their jobs allowed them to pause when they wanted to, were responsible, steady but noisy, skilled but monotonous.

TABLE 67. Job characteristics: a comparison of the results of the N.I.I.P.[a] and present inquiries.

	Present inquiry (1)	N.I.I.P. inquiry (2)	(1) as ratio of (2)
1. *Interest factors*	*(Per cent of total)*		
(a) *Positive*			
Interesting	45	30·1	1·5
Chance to use initiative	33	18·7	1·8
Have to concentrate	32	34·3	0·9
Varied	29	21·5	1·3
Interesting product/service	27	17·1	1·6
Uses brains	26	28·5	0·9
Skilled	12	18·4	0·7
(b) *Negative*			
Too routine	15	10·8	1·4
Boring	10	13·1	0·8
Monotonous	10	16·3	0·6
2. *Demand factors*			
Keeps you busy	47	46·9	1·0
Pause when you want to	36	42·4	0·8
Responsible	23	34·6	0·7
3. *Physical factors*			
Clean	24	27·2	0·9
Dirty	18	19·8	0·9
Noisy	13	22·9	0·6
4. *Social factors*			
Work with good crowd	64	56·2	1·1
A steady job	41	57·9	0·7
Work with own age group	30	25·3	1·2
Well paid	26	11·0	2·4
Total (Multiple replies)	100	100	
(No. of workers)	(330)	(1000)	

a J. D. Handyside, op. cit.

[7] J. D. Handyside, op. cit.

JOB CHARACTERISTICS LIKED AND DISLIKED

Asked what they particularly liked about their present jobs, most young people commented on one or other feature of their work which had a special appeal for them. Girls' 'likes' tended to be concentrated on relatively fewer items than were boys', and they were more inclined to like some special process or duty associated with their work. 'I like arranging the counter and putting the new stock out'; or the people with whom they worked: 'I like the people I work with—they're friendly and helpful.' Of girls' comments, one in three and one in four, respectively, were in these categories, compared with only one in six of the boys who referred to such features. Just as many of the boys, but relatively fewer of the girls, liked their jobs because they offered interest, variety and because they felt they were learning something. 'There's always something different to do and I move around on different jobs and get variety.' 'You feel you're learning something all the time.' Boys also more frequently commented with favour on the leniency of discipline: 'They're strict but not rigid.' 'No-one nags at you all the time.' Other aspects of their work commented on, but only by relatively few boys and girls, included their training: 'They give you a fair course of training here'; and their hours, holidays, and conditions. 'You get free meals and lots of amenities. We play table-tennis most dinner breaks.' (Table 68.)

TABLE 68. Characteristics of job particularly liked by young workers.

	Boys	Girls
	(Per cent of total)	
Job itself interesting	17	12
People	17	24
Nothing in particular	16	13
Some specific aspect or process of job	15	33
Not too much discipline	13	3
Training	8	3
Hours, holidays, conditions	7	6
Everything	5	3
Pay	3	3
Other	6	5
Don't know	1	2
Total (Multiple replies)	100	100
(No. of 15–18s)	(183)	(147)

Opinions were not found to vary according to the type of employment as much as might have been assumed. Apprentices were much more likely than other workers to comment on their training and on the intrinsic interest of the job; they were less likely, however, as were other manual

15

workers, to find any special process or part of their job attractive. Manual workers, however, more so than others, were inclined to feel that their work had no particularly attractive feature. Only in respect of the popularity of training, however, were these differences at all substantial.

A rather different pattern of replies emerged in relation to unpopular features of their work. First, as many as two in five young workers found nothing particular to dislike; second, the only difference between the views of boys and of girls was that girls were much more likely to dislike a duty or task associated with their jobs. 'I don't like the rush when someone wants something quickly and I have to run about for them' or 'I don't like getting the grease off because that's a very dirty job.' A few young workers, not more than one in ten, complained that their work was dull or boring; ('It's only repetition work—the same routine every day.)' Some found the pay insufficient; the hours too long or inconvenient and some referred to the buildings in which they worked: 'It's such an old office—drab and depressing.' In some cases discipline was considered too strict. 'The authorities take things too far'; or the job was unpleasant in some other way. Only small minorities referred to difficulties with their own work associates or to uncertainties about prospects. 'There's no chance of anything better here.' (Table 69.)

TABLE 69. Characteristics of job particularly disliked by young workers.

	Boys	Girls
	(Per cent of total)	
Nothing in particular	39	40
Job dull: not learning anything	12	10
Some aspect of job process	9	21
Pay	8	1
Hours, conditions, etc.	8	5
Job unpleasant, dirty, heavy, etc.	8	6
Being given the odd jobs	6	6
Discipline	3	3
Training	2	—
Other	11	8
Don't know	—	1
Total (Multiple replies)	100	100
(No. of 15–18s)	(183)	(147)

Occupation, as such, would not seem to have been associated with much variation in the replies though only manual workers referred to too strict discipline and apprentices to dissatisfaction with training; trainees were the most likely to refer to their work as dull and clerical workers the least likely to refer to any unattractive feature of their work.

Most young workers, while regarding their jobs as having both attractive and unattractive features, were rather more inclined to like than to dislike particular aspects of their work. This would be consistent with the theory that job satisfaction is, in any case, a process of balancing one thing against another rather than satisfaction with every aspect. Relatively few workers were non-committal; but no one feature, however, either positive or negative, applied to more than a small minority of workers, irrespective of their occupation.

CHANCES OF PROMOTION

In their selection of certain job characteristics, just under one in four of the total sample of young people interviewed referred to their present jobs as having promotion prospects.[8] In order to see more precisely how they assessed their own chances of promotion if they remained in their present firms, a five-point scale was prepared with provision for those who did not know what their chances might be. The replies showed first, that only a small minority of boys, and even fewer girls, assessed their promotion prospects as extremely or very good (Table 70). Second, that substantial proportions particularly of girls, and of the less-skilled manual workers, among the boys, did not know what their prospects were. Third, that boys were much more frequently confident about their chances than were girls, as were apprentices and non-manual workers compared with trainees and other manual workers.

TABLE 70. Chances of promotion as assessed by young workers.

	Boys	Girls
	(Per cent of total)	
Extremely good } Very good }	16	7
Fairly good	36	16
Not very good } Not at all good }	18	27
Don't know	23	43
No answer	7	7
Total	100	100
(No. of 15–18s)	(183)	(147)

Only one in six of the boys, for instance, felt that their chances of promotion were extremely or very good and just over one in three, that they were fair; but the proportions were twice as high as among the corresponding groups of girls. In fact, among the girls, almost as many did not

[8] See page 206.

know what their prospects were as were able to assess their chances, and of those who did make an assessment, more placed a low rating on their chances than estimated them as good or fair.

There were some sharp contrasts between occupations. The majority of boys in non-manual occupations assessed their chances as fairly good or better, hardly any gave a low rating and only one in ten were uncertain. (The explanation of this tendency may well have been the fact that many of these boys were employed in the clerical grades of government services with established and recognized promotion procedures.) Apprentices were the next most likely to rate their chances as fair to good but rather more of them than of non-manual workers were uncertain. None of the trainees expressed uncertainty, but far fewer than of apprentices felt their chances were good, and as many (as did other manual workers) placed a low rating on their prospects. The unskilled and semi-skilled workers were much more likely than other groups, not to know what their prospects were.

The main contrasts between girls' occupations were that office workers, who more frequently than others assessed their chances as good or better, also more frequently rated their prospects as poor. The majority of manual workers did not know what their prospects were, and virtually none felt that their chances were better than fairly good.

Job or status hoped for

The tendency for boys to be rather more frequently optimistic about their chances of promotion than girls was made more evident in their replies to the question as to what kind of work, status, or position they hoped for, assuming they remained in their present jobs. Far more boys, proportionately, than girls felt that there was some chance that they might eventually progress to higher technical or supervisory positions or to jobs of higher skill, while far fewer felt that their jobs led nowhere, or that they could not say what their future might be. The most frequent reply from the boys was a reference to jobs with higher skill; the most frequent from the girls was that they did not know where their present jobs would lead.

Future hopes were also strongly associated with the type of employment followed. More than one-half of the boys in the less skilled manual jobs felt either that they were likely to remain in the same jobs as now or that they did not know where their jobs might lead.

Trainees and apprentices, on the other hand, were the most confident of obtaining higher status, particularly in technical appointments. Apprentices, to a more frequent extent than trainees, also expected to follow the same trade as at present employed though at a higher level of skill: trainees were more inclined to hope for some promotion without specifying its nature.

Of the girls in offices, nearly two in five expected to reach a higher grade in clerical work; they were also more inclined than other girls to feel that their present jobs led nowhere but less inclined to feel uncertain. The girls in manual work were the most uncertain of all workers, nearly three in five not knowing what their vocational future might be, assuming they remained in their present job.

It seemed logical to assume that relative newcomers to a firm might feel less certain about their promotion prospects. The replies were, therefore, analysed according to the length of time spent in their present jobs. The analysis showed that there was a tendency among the boys who had been at work for longer than six months to be more optimistic about their chances and surer as regards their chances of promotion. A different pattern appeared for the girls, however. While the newcomers were less likely to predict their chances as very or extremely good and more likely to be uncertain, employment of over six months duration was associated with a much higher proportion who assessed their chances as poor, and with smaller proportions who felt their prospects were 'fairly' good.

Actual promotion

Girls' assessment of their chances would appear to have been rather more realistic than were boys' if the proportions actually promoted are compared with those who estimated such prospects for themselves. One in five of the girls had been promoted or upgraded since first starting work in their present firms, compared with just under one-quarter who had assessed their chances of promotion as fair or better. Over one-half of the boys had made such an assessment but in fact only one in ten of them had been promoted. Again, logically enough, promotion was more frequent among those who had been in their jobs for a year or more and further analysis also showed that clerical workers, particularly girls, had more frequently moved upwards than had other workers. Indeed, the relatively higher proportions of girls in the sample as a whole who had done so reflected, mainly, the promotion of almost one in three of the girls employed in offices who had moved from junior positions to jobs as typists, machine operators, etc. Though a tendency to move upwards also applied to boys in non-manual occupations, their numbers were very much smaller in relation to the total sample (Table 71).

On the basis of the average length of time in which boys and girls had been in their present jobs, the rate of promotion for girls was, therefore, twice that of boys, representing just under one in five and one in nine per year, respectively. Though girls were more likely than boys to have been promoted, they were also more likely to have remained in the same jobs while with their present firms. Some two-thirds of them, in fact, were still in the type of work in which they had first started their employment with their present firms, compared with only one-half of the boys. Boys were more likely, therefore, to have varied experience though not quite one in three had had three or more jobs within an average period of service of just under one year; changes were more frequent the longer the time spent in the firm. Most of the job changes had occurred on the initiative of management, only one in ten of the boys' and one in five of the girls' job changes having occurred on their own request for a transfer or promotion. Thus, only a minority were actually promoted; only a minority believed they had a good chance of promotion; and more than one-half of the workers had performed more or less the same kind of tasks during a year's employment.

TABLE 71. Change of job, promotion, and upgrading within present firm.

	Boys	Girls
	(Per cent of total)	
Number of jobs within present firm		
1 only	51	65
2	19	18
3	22	17
4 or more	8	—
Total	100	100
(No. of 15–18s)	(183)	(147)
Proportion of sample having been promoted or upgraded	10	20
Proportion who		
(i) asked for change	10	21
(ii) were requested by management to change	90	79
Average length of time in present job	Months	
	11·1	11·3

OTHER ASPECTS OF EMPLOYMENT

Starting work for most school leavers involves them in a longer working day than at school; the distances travelled to work may also be greater; home may no longer be accessible enough for the mid-day meal and the factory and office do not always provide a canteen. It was thought of interest to discover from the school leavers seen in the present inquiry, therefore, how far they felt fatigued by their jobs; the time taken for their daily journey to and from work; and the regularity and place of a cooked, or other, type of mid-day meal. Since school leavers, partly because of their relative inexperience, are also exposed to new risks of physical injury and ill-health, they were also asked about any accidents sustained by them while at work and for details as to the length and reason for any absence from work.

Tiredness

Though nearly one-half of young workers felt their jobs kept them busy, and only a minority that they could pause when they wanted to, tiredness was, evidently, not a consequence. Asked how tired they felt at the end of the working day, two in five young workers replied that they were hardly tired at all, and almost one-half that they were only moderately tired. Only a minority—less than one in ten—felt very tired when it was time to go home, and even fewer were tired by the middle of the day, or most of the time. Curiously enough, the proportions feeling most tired were highest among non-manual workers, as far as boys were concerned, but for the girls the manual workers and shop assistants were more likely to feel this way.

Tiredness, even moderate, was not associated with the average time spent in travelling to and from work, though rather more of those who felt 'moderately' or 'very' tired lived outside the borough; nor was it associated with whether or not a regular cooked meal was taken at mid-day, nor were relative newcomers to work any more likely than others to feel tired. There was, however, a tendency among the boys for those who felt least tired to be more frequently enthusiastic than others about their present jobs; this hardly applied, however, to the girls.

The journey to work

As was to be expected, school leavers who lived and worked in the borough were involved in much shorter travelling times, on average, than those living outside the borough, who, on average, spent over twice as long on their daily journeys.

For almost three in five of the sample, the journey to work took 20 minutes or less, while for more than three in four, it took no longer than 30 minutes. These proportions are considerably higher than those given in Liepmann's study,[9] suggesting that school leavers in the present inquiry were involved in far shorter travelling times, on average. There were, however, differences according to the type of employment followed, partly because much higher proportions of workers in relatively unskilled manual work lived and worked in the borough (over two-thirds) than did apprentices (just over one-quarter), trainees or non-manual workers (under one-half). Thus, for boys in less skilled manual work, more than one-half travelled to work within 15 minutes, whereas only just one-quarter of apprentices reached work within this time and almost as many took 40 minutes or longer. Almost all the girls in manual work started work within 25 minutes of leaving home and nearly one-third within 10 minutes or less. Most girls in offices, however, tended to be involved in journeys of between 20 and 30 minutes, and relatively few were shorter or longer than this.

[9] K. Liepmann, The Journey to Work, Routledge and Kegan Paul, 1944.

On average, and allowing for the journey home as well as to work, boys in less skilled manual jobs spent the shortest time in travelling (just under half an hour), and boys in non-manual work, the longest (nearly one hour a day). The average for other workers was between 30 and 40 minutes. The shortest average for all workers, however, was for boys living in the borough and working in small firms of fifty employees or fewer, who spent not much more than 20 minutes per day getting to and from work, whereas for boys living outside the borough and working in the largest firms the average daily travelling time was at least one hour.

The mid-day meal

School leavers were asked how regularly they ate a hot meal at mid-day and where the meal, whatever its nature, was normally taken. Their replies showed that less than one-half took a cooked meal every working day; the proportion who did so varied, however, according to whether they ate at home, or in a canteen, café, or the workshop; where they ate their meal was also associated with the size of firm in which they were employed. Moreover, as many as over one-third rarely or never had a cooked meal at mid-day, relying, therefore, on cold snacks or sandwiches (Table 72).

TABLE 72. Regularity and place of cooked
mid-day meals.

	Boys	Girls
	(Per cent of total)	
Frequency of cooked mid-day meal		
Every working day	52	44
Most working days	4	3
Some working days	12	10
Rarely or never	32	43
Place of mid-day meal		
Canteen	58	46
Workshop	21	21
Home	11	18
Café	10	15
Total	100	100
(No. of 15–18s)[a]	(180)	(142)

a Excluding those not answering.

Though relatively few young people went home at mid-day, almost all the boys who did so had a cooked meal on most working days; home was, therefore, associated in their case, with regular cooked meals. Over one-half ate their mid-day meal in a canteen, but as many as one in five used a canteen only for snacks or sandwiches. Cafés were more frequently used for the occasional, than the regular, cooked meal; the workshop, however, was the chief eating place for boys who never or rarely had a cooked meal at mid-day.

The proportion who went home, however, was much higher among those who were employed in small firms (fifty persons or fewer), and home was used more frequently than canteens, among this group of young people. This reflected the fact that the majority of boys employed in small firms lived in the borough, and that fewer small firms provided canteens. Boys in small firms also tended to eat in the workshop a little more frequently than did other workers.

In the larger firms, a different pattern applied. Hardly any boys went home for a mid-day meal; the great majority used canteens and small proportions, though still about one in six, ate in their workshops. Among the large firms (more than 500 people), cafés were rarely used: in small and medium firms they were used by one in six of the boys.

Regular cooked meals at mid-day were much more frequent, therefore, the larger the firm in which boys were employed (and the shorter the journey to work) the proportions always or mostly having such meals steadily rising from just under two-fifths in the small firm to nearly two-thirds in the large enterprises. Conversely, occasional cooked meals were less frequent the larger the firm.

Similar tendencies applied to the girls, though relatively few were employed in the small firms; but the larger the firm the more frequent was the regular cooked meal and the use of the canteen, and the more likely a cooked meal was taken on all, or most, working days. A rather higher proportion of girls than of boys lived in the borough so that small proportions from the larger firms also went home. Home, however, was almost as frequently used for snacks as for cooked meals, as far as girls were concerned.

Accidents

Concern is frequently expressed in Annual Reports of H.M. Chief Inspector of Factories[10] at the increasing number of accidents occurring to young persons under eighteen. In 1966 nearly 14000 boys and over 4000 girls were injured in industrial accidents, a higher figure than in previous years. The Chief Inspector comments in the 1966 Report:[11] 'The year under review saw little abatement in the number or seriousness of accidents to young persons in industry. I have in past reports written at some length on this question and have pointed out that the high accident rate amongst young persons not only shows a wanton disregard of moral responsibility to the young but is also a patently bad investment for the future.'

[10] See, for example, the *Annual Report of H.M. Chief Inspector of Factories 1966*, H.M.S.O., page 90, fig. 14.
[11] Ibid., page 9.

Accidents which are brought to the attention of the Factory Inspectorate are only those which occur in premises (or on processes) covered by the Factories Act of 1961, and which cause loss of life or disable a worker for more than three days from earning full wages at the work at which he or she was employed (though certain dangerous occurrences must also be reported even if no injury is caused). The official statistics do not include, therefore, accidents which have relatively slight consequences, or which happen to persons employed in organizations or on processes not covered by the Act.

In the present inquiry, young people were asked about any type of accident that had occurred, however slight the injury. The replies showed that just over one in four had, in fact, experienced some kind of accident while at work, though—as was to be expected—the proportions were higher for manual than for non-manual workers and, within manual occupations, higher for those in the less skilled occupations.

The incidence of accidents in the sample, if related to the average period during which young people had been at work, indicates an annual incidence of 21·6 per 100 employees. Since this includes all types of accidents and is related to all occupations it cannot be compared with the 1966 incidence rate for reportable accidents of 1·5 per 100 employees applying to all age workers in north-west London, covered by the Factories Act.[12] Most accidents to the young people interviewed in the present inquiry did occur, however, to manual workers covered by the Act. The contrast between the official and the all-inclusive rate is such as to strengthen the argument of the H.M. Chief Inspector of Factories for alternative means of evaluating accident statistics. In his opinion 'the varying and unknown factors which cause a given incident to become a reportable accident are of such significance that the total number of reportable accidents can no longer by themselves be accepted as a reliable guide to accident prevention performance'.[13] He suggests that one way in which statistics might be put into better perspective would be 'to supplement them by figures of the cases attending works surgeries for first-aid treatment'.

The injuries

Most of the injuries sustained in accidents were cuts and bruises, chiefly to fingers, hands, and arms, though among the boys there were also some fractures and burns. Among the girls, most injuries were evidently slight, the majority having received little or no medical treatment. Almost one-half of the boys' injuries, however, had required hospital treatment (frequently stitching) though mostly on a casualty or outpatient basis. Relatively few had involved more than one week of absence from work, the

12 Ibid., page 148.
13 Ibid., 1965, page 70.

most serious being one in which the boy concerned had had both legs crushed while loading vans and had spent four months in hospital.

Machinery and hand tools were chiefly associated with accidents though falling objects were also a hazard. A mis-directed hammer caused a squashed thumb; a slipped file, a bruised nose; a piece of falling sheet metal, a cut toe; falling over a truck, scalded legs; an unseen hoist, a hit on the head; an obstinate nut, a wrenched hand. These were typical of many of the accidents described.

The mid-day meal

It might have been assumed that accidents were more likely to occur the younger and less experienced the worker, the less intensive the training, and the smaller the firm. No such tendencies, however, were apparent in the sample of young people interviewed. If anything, accidents were a little more frequent among older and more experienced workers; just as frequent among those who were still learning their jobs and a little less frequent the shorter the average basic training time; a little more frequent in the medium firm than in the small or large firm. Such differences as these, however, were all very slight. Nor did further analysis reveal accidents to be associated with tiredness after work, with the average daily travelling time or with the degree of job satisfaction. The only factor of those examined, other than occupation, which did seem to be positively associated with the incidence of accidents among boys[14] was the type and place of the mid-day meal. There were proportionately fewer accidents where a cooked meal was always or mostly taken, and more where a cooked meal was rare or absent (Table 73).

TABLE 73. Frequency of accidents and place of cooked mid-day meals.

	Percentage of boys sustaining accidents	Total number of boys
Frequency of cooked mid-day meal		
(i) All or most days	21	99
(ii) Seldom, rarely, or never	33	79
Total		178
Place of mid-day meal		
(i) Home or canteen	20	127
(ii) Workshop or café	45	51
Total		178

[14] There were too few girls for a similar analysis to be considered.

This tendency applied even when non-manual workers were excluded from the analysis (since their accident rate was so much lower than for others), though it operated differently for the less skilled manual workers than for trainees and apprentices.

Though the numbers in each category were small, the results, nevertheless, suggest that accidents were much more likely to occur if the meal was eaten in the workshop or café but much less likely if taken at home or in a canteen. How far these tendencies were due to accidents arising as a result of 'play' in the workshop, for instance, could not be ascertained.

Absence from work

Nearly one-half of the young people interviewed had some period of absence from work during the three months preceding the interview.[15] The proportions did not vary particularly according to the type of employment, except that a relatively smaller proportion of sales assistants were away from work as were workers in small firms.

Colds, gastric complaints, and influenza were the chief reasons given for absences, though other reasons included other illnesses, surgical operations, and recovery from accidents, road and industrial. Relatively few young people had been absent for any non-medical reason. Absence from work was rarely longer than one working week and in the majority of cases no longer than three days, the average being 4·5 working days for boys and 4·2 for girls. For the sample as a whole, this represents an annual rate of absenteeism, mainly through illness, of 8·8 working days for boys and 8·0 days for girls. This is equivalent to the loss on average of just under two working weeks per year through absenteeism by the 330 young people interviewed.[16]

SUMMARY

It was evident from the replies of young workers to a check list of items relating to job characteristics, that, in contrast to the employers' views, only a minority regarded their jobs as interesting, varied, or skilled, requiring the use of their brains, initiative, or concentration; or felt that their jobs taught them something useful, had promotion prospects, or were well paid. By contrast, the majority felt they worked with a good crowd and few described their jobs as monotonous, boring, or routine. School leavers varied somewhat in their replies according to the type of employment followed and items associated with interest of the job was most frequently selected by apprentices and trainees and least frequently by girls in manual

[15] The three months did not relate to the same period of time.

[16] The number of days of certified incapacity for the population of England and Wales for 1964–5 was 14·3 for men and 16·3 for women. (See the *Annual Report of the Ministry of Social Security* for 1966, Table 19, pages 155–8.)

work, who were also the least inclined to refer to their jobs as responsible, difficult, having promotion prospects, or as well paid.

Boys were more inclined to like their job because of the interest and variety it offered and girls because of some special aspect of the work or their fellow workers which appealed to them. No one feature was felt to be attractive to more than a small minority of young people and most young workers regarded their work as having both attractive and un-attractive characteristics. This is consistent with the majority feeling well or moderately satisfied with their present jobs and with the theory that job satisfaction is a process of balancing one thing against another, rather than satisfaction in every respect.

Asked to assess their promotion prospects, only small minorities of workers felt their chances were extremely or very good and substantial proportions, particularly of girls, did not know what their prospects were. There were sharp contrasts according to occupation, workers in the less skilled manual jobs being the least confident, and apprentices and boy clerks, being the most. The tendency for boys to be more frequently optimistic about their chances were again evident in their reference to the kind of job, status, and position hoped for if remaining in the present firm. Far more boys than girls felt that they would eventually progress to higher technical or supervisory positions or to jobs of higher skills, and far fewer felt their jobs led nowhere or were uncertain, than was the case among girls among whom uncertainty was typical of their replies. Future hopes were strongly associated with the type of employment followed, however, and manual workers, particularly, were much more frequently uncertain where their jobs would lead or convinced there were no prospects for them.

Though nearly one-half of young workers felt that their jobs kept them busy and only a minority referred to their being able to pause when they wished, relatively few felt tired at the end of their working day. Nor was there any association between the degree of tiredness felt and the journey to work. Most young workers spent less than one hour in the daily journey to and from work, but it was evident that boys in unskilled manual jobs were much more likely to live near their work than were boys in skilled or non-manual jobs. This was shown to be associated with the size of firm, the tendency being for boys employed in other manual work in small firms to live fairly near their work. Distance from home and the size of firm was also associated with the place, frequency, and type of the mid-day meal. Thus boys employed in the small firms tended to go home for a mid-day meal while boys in the larger firms tended to have their meals in canteens.

Asked for details of any accident occurring while at work, the replies indicated an annual incidence of 21·6 per 100 young workers. Though injuries were usually slight in the case of girls, as many as one-half of those sustained by boys had involved hospital treatment (chiefly outpatient or casualty). Of several factors examined for a possible association with the incidence of accidents only the type and place of the mid-day meal seemed relevant. As far as boys were concerned, accidents were more frequent when meals were taken in the workshop or when a cooked meal was rarely or never eaten, and less frequent where the meal was taken in a canteen and a cooked meal eaten on all or most days.

CHAPTER XIV

TRAINING AND FURTHER EDUCATION

INTRODUCTION

It is widely recognized that the customary training provided for many young people in industry is the casual and unsystematic learning of new tasks through watching and imitating an experienced worker; and even apprenticeship training has been shown to be inadequate in many important respects.[1]

It was for the purpose of making better provision for training, including that of apprentices, that the Industrial Training Act of 1964 came into being. The Act shifts the emphasis of ultimate responsibility for training from employers to the State; it provides for a series of Industrial Training Boards, one for each industry,[2] responsible for the training and retraining of the persons employed in the industry, though their main concern is with young people, whether or not they are apprentices. Each Board is required to determine the length and content of training appropriate for the occupations within their industry, and empowered to place a levy on firms; those making satisfactory training provision receive a grant in return, the remainder of the levy then being used to provide for new training facilities.

Some doubts exist, however, as to whether the provision of separate training programmes for each industry may not result in narrow training in limited skills when, in order to keep up with technological change, training in broad skills may be required; and whether the under-representation on the Boards and Central Training Council of those professionally concerned with further education, may not result in an emphasis on training to the detriment or exclusion of non-vocational education. According to Carter,[3] the new system 'allows the employers and trade unions in particular industries to determine the character and coverage of industrial training and further education of young workers' when, in his view, these are matters for the community as a whole to decide.

Non-vocational education extends to even fewer young people than does industrial training;[4] many vocational training courses provide for arts subjects, liberal studies, and current affairs; but the majority of boys and

---

[1] G. Williams, op. cit., K. Liepmann, op. cit.
[2] By mid-1969 there were 26 Industrial Training Boards.
[3] M. Carter, 1966, op. cit.
[4] *Day Release*: The report of a committee set up by the Minister of Education, op. cit.

girls in occupations where no formal or extended training schemes exist are outside day-release schemes and do not attend evening classes. For these young people, education in the formal sense stops when they leave school, though this was not the intention of the Education Act of 1944, which provided, through the establishment of county colleges, for such further education as would 'enable young people to develop their various aptitudes and capacities and prepare them for the responsibilities of citizenship'.

It was to be assumed, therefore, that only some of the young workers interviewed in the present inquiry would have received formal training or be attending day or evening classes. Since they represented a variety of occupations, industries, and enterprises, it was also to be assumed that they would represent a diversity of experience. The detailed examination of training methods was, in any case, outside the scope of the present inquiry. For present purposes, what was required was some general view of how they had learned to do their present work and some opinions about further education.

The questions relating to training and further education covered, therefore, where and by whom they were taught their present jobs; the time required for them to learn; attendance at classes; the usefulness or otherwise of the subjects taken; and, finally, a check list of items containing assorted statements about further education from which the young people interviewed selected those which corresponded closest to their own opinions. Where it seemed relevant, their replies were analysed according to type of employment, size of firm, and attitudes towards leaving school.

BY WHOM TAUGHT

Over one-half of the young people seen felt that it was their fellow workers who had been wholly or partially responsible for showing them how to perform their present jobs. In the case of boy apprentices, and to a lesser extent trainees, this meant being taught chiefly by a skilled worker. In other occupations, it meant, evidently, 'sitting by Nellie' who, in the case of girls, was more likely to be of their own age group than a senior (Table 74).

Next in importance were supervisors, referred to by over one in three of the girls and one in four of the boys, but to a less frequent degree by trainees and not at all by boys in non-manual work for whom senior management were chiefly responsible. Management was also responsible for the initial instruction of all the girls in department stores. Training instructors were mentioned by less than one in ten leavers and were more likely to have taught clerical, but hardly any manual, workers. Very few had not been shown by anyone what to do or felt they were expected to learn just from watching others.

TABLE 74. Instruction in present job.

Shown by	Boys	Girls
	(*Per cent of total*)	
Fellow worker		
(i) skilled	27	—
(ii) senior	24	26
(iii) contemporary	13	30
Supervision	26	34
Senior management	9	24
Training instructor	9	5
No-one in particular	2	1
No answer	10	5
Total (Multiple replies)	100	100
(No. of 15–18s)	(183)	(147)

Boys and girls in relatively unskilled manual work would seem to have had a less intensive training than others, in the sense that they made a smaller total number of references to their instructors at work. Their training would also seem to have been more frequently concentrated in the hands of supervisors and experienced, but not necessarily skilled, fellow workers. The higher the level of skill ultimately expected of manual workers, however, the more likely it was that senior skilled workers were involved as well as senior management and instructors. The same tendency was true, though not in the same degree or in all respects, for clerical workers.

Size of firm

The main contrast as between training practices in firms of different sizes, appeared to be that almost all the training instructors were employed by larger firms (having over 500 employees), whereas more than one-half of the boys who were instructed in their jobs by senior management were in smaller firms, particularly those employing fewer than fifty people.

WHERE TAUGHT

Almost all young workers learned their present work 'on the job'; only small minorities of boys, and even fewer girls, referred to their having attended training schools, and this was chiefly during their period of initial training; some, particularly in communications and statutory services, had attended schools for a short period of training before starting work. Only trainees, and relatively few of these, had been taught in a separate training bay or department. These proportions were not much affected by the type of employment followed, though it was evident that

16

girls in manual work were the least likely to have had any training, other than at the machine or bench.

Day release

In addition to the training received at work, over one-half of the boys, but less than one-fifth of the girls, were attending classes, predominantly vocational and associated in the case of boys with apprenticeships, and of girls with commercial courses. The proportions actually in day release were rather smaller (just over two-fifths and one-tenth respectively) while as many as one-third of the boys (but less than one in ten of the girls) were attending evening classes, mostly in addition to day-time attendance. In fact, the typical attendance pattern for most boys was of one day and two evenings each week. Less than one in ten of the boys were in block release or other education and training schemes (Table 75).

TABLE 75. Attendance at training or further
education classes.

	Boys	Girls
	(*Per cent of total*)	
Proportion attending classes	56	18
Proportion attending		
Day release	44	11
Evening	32	9
Other	8	1
Total (Multiple replies)	100	100
(No. of 15–18s)	(183)	(147)

There was considerable variation, however, according to type of employment. All but six of the apprentices were attending classes, two-thirds of them being in day-release or other schemes as were one-half of trainees and non-manual workers. Less than one in eight of the boys in manual work were granted day release, however, and even this proportion was mainly due to a number of manual workers being employed by government services, where day release and further education is a matter of general policy. Far fewer girls were involved in day-release schemes, and manual workers far less so than were clerical workers (many of whom were also employed in statutory services), and shop workers not at all.

TIME TAKEN TO LEARN THE JOB

Young workers were asked to assess the times taken for them (a) to learn their present job, and (b) to know it well enough to do it easily and confidently. In replying to the first of these questions, as many as one-half of the boys felt that they were still in the learning stage; but this proportion was partly accounted for by the fact that all the apprentices and the majority of trainees regarded themselves as learners and these boys constituted more than one-half of the total number of boys interviewed. None of the boys in non-manual occupations, and less than one in seven of other manual workers felt that they were still at the stage of basic instruction; and, of the minorities still learning their jobs, some boys and girls were relative newcomers to their present work.

The variety of occupations represented in the sample of young people seen produced a wide range in the assessments made of initial learning times. More than one in ten of the boys, and one in six of the girls, felt that they had mastered the elements of their jobs in less than one week (over one-half of these had learned their jobs within the first day). Some felt that they had learnt what was required within a few hours. The shortest time stated was 'a minute', which was the reply of a girl whose job was to work a press which stamped the trade name on tablets of soap.

There were only marginal differences, among the boys, between manual and non-manual workers, the majority in both categories having completed their training within seven weeks, and substantial proportions in under one week or between one and three weeks. Among the girls, manual and shop workers were much more likely, than were girls in offices, to have learned their jobs within a few days, but the majority of all girls, like the boys, felt that within seven weeks they had mastered what was required of them. Very few girls in manual and shop occupations felt that their jobs had taken longer than eight weeks in all to learn, compared with sizeable proportions of girls in offices, and boys in manual and non-manual occupations (between one-quarter and one-third) who were of this opinion.

On average, however, basic learning time (excluding apprentices and trainees) was higher for other manual than for non-manual boys (2·1 months as against 1·5 months), and higher for manual and clerical girls than for shop assistants (1·7 and 0·7 months respectively). It was also higher for boys (2·3 months) than for girls (1·2 months) (Table 76).

Rather more time, on average, was, naturally, required to gain proficiency in the job than to master its basic elements. This was particularly marked for boys in non-manual occupations. By combining the length of the initial training period with that required to become efficient and confident, a total 'learning' time was estimated. This, on average, varied considerably for boys according to occupations, being only 7½ months on average, for semi-skilled and unskilled manual and ten months for non-manual employment, but as long as 55 months for apprentices and 37 months for trainees. Among girls, however, the average total learning time was much shorter, being just over 4 months for manual workers, 5.3 months for shop assistants and 6.2 months for office workers.

TABLE 76. Average learning time.

	Boys					Girls			
	App.	Trainee	Other manual	Non-manual	Total	Other manual	Clerical	Sales	Total
					(Months)				
Basic learning time —		4·6	2·1	1·5	2·3[b]	1·7	1·7	0·7	1·2
Time to acquire proficiency and confidence	—	32·4	5·4	8·5	13·9[b]	2·6	4·7	4·8	3·7
Total learning time	55	37·0	7·5	10·0	32·5	4·1	6·2	5·3	4·9
Total number of 15–18s [a]	54	36	42	24	156	33	68	28	129

a Excluding apprentices not answering, don't knows, and 'indefinites'.
b Excluding apprentices.

Even so, there were still substantial proportions of young workers who felt that they had become proficient in their jobs within a few weeks, particularly among manual workers, one in five of the girls being in this category. Higher proportions felt that they could do their work easily within seven weeks of first learning it, and as many as one in four of the boys, and over one-half of the girls, made this assessment.

The replies of all apprentices and most trainees were clearly influenced by the fact that their jobs were associated with established periods of training. They were not asked to re-assess these in the light of their own experiences, since most were, in any case, about half-way through their total training programme. Their replies were, therefore, accepted as representing the total learning period without regard for possible individual variations. The replies of other young workers, however, showed that there was considerable variation, even among workers on identical or closely similar jobs, both in regard to the time required to learn the elements of the job and to become proficient in it.

It was not possible to verify how well jobs had been learnt or the standards of proficiency reached. The replies suggest however, that the subjective assessments of young workers themselves of the time required to learn their jobs, were considerably less standardized than were the various tasks they performed. This individual variation in response to the learning of work activities would seem to be an important consideration in the planning of training programmes.

COURSES, SUBJECTS, AND EXAMINATIONS TAKEN

The great majority of boys were studying for the Ordinary National Certificate, or the City and Guilds of London Institute and were, therefore, involved in a variety of technical courses. The non-manual workers tended to be studying for qualifying examinations of various kinds, and as many as one in five were preparing for G.C.E. or equivalent examination. After technical theory and practice, English and mathematics were the subjects most frequently studied by boys. Since most of the girls were attending commercial courses, shorthand and typewriting predominated in their case, followed by English. Languages, history, geography, art, liberal, and general studies were all mentioned, but by relatively small proportions.

The boys had already spent, at the time of interview, an average of just over three and a half terms, and girls an average of two, in attending training or further educational courses; they were relatively new to their courses, therefore, and for the sample as a whole, an average of nearly seven terms was still to be completed. Virtually all boys and girls receiving further education were preparing for examinations, the passing of which was regarded as a means of attaining higher skill and status levels. One in five of the boys and one in six of the girls, however, had some specific job in mind for which particular qualifications were required.

Whether encouraged to learn

Young people were also asked whether they felt encouraged to learn by anyone in their present firm. As was to be expected, there were considerable contrasts between certain occupations in the extent to which encouragement of this kind was given. Only a small minority—less than one in five—of boys in the less skilled manual jobs felt encouraged, compared with between two-thirds and three-quarters of boys in more skilled and non-manual work. The differences between boys and girls were not so substantial, though nevertheless present: girls were more likely than boys, however, to feel uncertain and not to know what to reply to the question. It was also evident that girls, if encouraged, were less intensively so than were boys, for though the girls' chief source of encouragement was their supervision, boys nearly as frequently also felt encouraged to learn by their management and, to a much more frequent extent than girls, by senior and skilled workers, and by their fellow workers.

ASSESSMENT OF CLASSES

Young people who were, at the time of inquiry, attending classes were asked whether there were any subjects which were felt to be more or less useful than others; whether the course could be improved and if so, in what way. Of the boys, one in three felt that there were subjects which were more useful for them than were others, while rather more than one-half felt that there were subjects which were less so. Hardly any of the girls, however, made such observations. Among the subjects considered most useful by boys, workshop practice, technical theory, and mathematics, were the three most frequently mentioned: among the least useful, liberal and social studies predominated, followed by aspects of technical theory and English. Over one-half of boys and girls felt that the courses could be improved, most of all by changes in syllabus, but also by improvements in the methods and standards of teaching.

Positive attitudes to subjects were associated with the degree to which they were felt to supplement or relate directly to what was being learnt at work: some boys welcomed technical theory and mathematics because of this, and workshop practice was popular where it provided the opportunity to extend the learning of new skills. Negative attitudes arose when subjects seemed to have little connection with specialized studies; certain theoretical aspects did not always seem to young people as applicable to their particular trade. Workshop practice, for example, was sometimes felt simply to duplicate the tasks they were on at work; liberal and social studies were, particularly, felt to be superfluous since these were intended, presumably, to improve their minds rather than their skills or technical understanding. Since many boys were, in any case, working a four-day week, spending two evenings a week at school and preparing for examinations, any subjects which seemed to lie outside their specialized interests were particularly unwelcome. The following comments illustrate this point of view.

'Liberal studies are just a waste of time. Everyone feels this—they should be knocked out of the course as no work is involved and no exam.'

'Social studies are a waste of time. People can learn that sort of thing for themselves.'

'Liberal studies are supposed to broaden the outlook, but they're really a waste of time. They're not very useful and I can't see the connection.'

The pressure of time on part-time students is indicated in comments such as:

'We're expected to do too much in the time. We have to get our homework done by the next evening and we have only two hours then.'

'We could do with more time. It's hard doing things part-time—we have to go through the subjects too quickly.'

'Too much work is crammed into too short a time. We have to do two years' work in one.'

The unpopularity of liberal studies would be regarded as a healthy reaction by R. S. Neale,[5] who considers that students most responsive to

---

[5] R. S. Neale, 'On Liberal Studies', *The Vocational Aspect of Secondary and Further Education*, No. 41, Autumn 1966, Vol. xviii, Pergamon Press.

the kind of studies as generally taught, are probably those most lacking in initiative, independence, or a questioning mind. In a critical review of present aims and approach, he argues that liberal studies are largely a waste of students' time, since the aim is to change the very attitudes which, for many working-class youths, are their only protection against the 'do gooder' and conventionalized values, in the criticism of which, in his view, 'lies their only hope of intellectual development'.

Improvements in courses

Nearly one-half of the suggestions made for improving training and further education courses related to changes in the syllabus. Though this sometimes meant that theoretical rather than practical subjects were wanted, or *vice versa*, it much more frequently meant the removal from the syllabus of liberal and social studies. This opinion was expressed, moreover, not only by apprentices, but by clerical and other workers, some of whom were in non-vocational courses.

Next in order of frequency were improvements in methods and standards of teaching; references were made to teachers being out of date and out of touch with modern industrial methods, and to their teaching being unsatisfactory. ('The teachers haven't had experience of the latest methods'; 'They put things over so badly. We have one good one out of four.') There were also some young workers who were critical of the timetable, particularly when current affairs or liberal studies were given during day-time sessions and science, physics, mathematics in the evening, when they felt tired and found it harder to concentrate. These young people felt that if non-technical subjects were to be included, they should at least be given during evening sessions. Other improvements related to the need for more block release, to better teaching, equipment, buildings, and smaller classes. Thus, as students elsewhere, school leavers in technical courses had varied ideas and suggestions which they felt, if implemented, would make their training more satisfactory.

These criticisms and suggestions chiefly reflect the views of young people in vocational courses, however, since apprentices and trainees formed the majority of part-time students in the sample of young people interviewed. The opinions of a group of twelve young manual workers employed in two separate establishments of a government service, and attending the same non-vocational course are, therefore, of special interest. Even the most critical vocational student still felt that he was learning something from his course, would have liked more rather than fewer sessions, and more rather than less time to specialize. By contrast, almost all the twelve young boys in the non-vocational course would gladly have given up their day release, were extremely critical of the course and felt that, in terms of the subjects taught, the level at which they were taught and their treatment by the teachers, it was like being back at school. They complained:

'They teach us the same as we learnt at school—we're just treated like kids—we're not learning anything.'

'Teachers don't take enough interest. There's nothing new. It's just like we had at school.'

'There's too many in the class; not enough time to teach you anything. Don't get anything out of it.'

REASONS FOR DISCONTINUING CLASSES

There were a number of boys and girls who, though at the time of inquiry were not attending classes, had once done so. Among the boys, nearly one-quarter were in this category, and among the girls, one in eight. The boys were mainly employed as trainees or other manual workers, the girls in offices.

Asked for their reasons for giving up classes, boredom with the subjects, course, or teaching was the most frequent explanation given, leavers being more frequently critical in these respects than was evident in the Social Survey inquiry.[6] Typical comments included:

'I went for six months for English and maths, but then it began to get boring.'

'I went for English and Maths for two weeks but I didn't like the teaching and it was very dull.'

'I went to day release for one term, but I wasn't learning anything new, so I didn't think it was worth while going anymore.'

Completion of studies was the reason offered by one in ten ex-students, while a similar proportion had been affected by changes in employment. Some boys and girls left because they felt they were not making progress or because they failed to pass examinations. 'I got disheartened after failing my exam.' Others found the attraction of alternative activities greater: 'I went for three to four months, but then the classes got in the way of my going out, and there were too many things I wanted to do.' In a few cases, day release had ended because the employers felt that insufficient progress was made.

There seems to have been an attempt on the part of some boys and girls to register for classes, particularly in English and Mathematics, on leaving school with the intention of either qualifying themselves for better jobs, or to make good what they felt they had missed in their education. One boy, for instance, actually attended evening classes for four evenings a week for one year in the hope that he would be able to move from relatively unskilled work to a skilled trade. When the results of his efforts were not as good as he had hoped for, he felt that there was little point in continuing.

[6] *15–18*, op. cit.

His case was typical of those who started and then discontinued their classes, discouraged by their failure to improve either their academic standards, or their vocational opportunities. Further education brought to them, as for the twelve boys who went unwillingly to day-release classes, repetition of school experiences and, chiefly on this account, was ultimately rejected.

REASONS FOR NEVER HAVING ATTENDED CLASSES

It seemed important to discover why it was that some young people had never attended any further education classes. Since more than one-half of the boys were, at the time of inquiry, in some form of continued education, and a further one-quarter had been so at one time or another, those whose education had ended when they left school were predominantly girls. In fact, two-thirds of the girls were in this category compared with only one in five of the boys.

The pilot study had shown that replies to direct questioning about further education were likely to be influenced by the feeling on the part of some young workers that attendance at classes represented socially approved activities. Though the extent to which this applied in the present inquiry could not be verified, it was felt that some alternative to direct questioning should be used. A check list of items was, therefore, prepared, representing a variety of statements about further education based on opinions in group discussions during the pilot stage. Those who had never attended classes since leaving school were asked to select from the list those statements which corresponded closest to their own views.

Direct questioning showed that as many as one in five young people replied that they intended to register for classes in the coming session or expected to be in day release. The remainder felt, however, either that classes were unnecessary for them, that further education did not interest them, that they had too many other interests, or that they had never really seriously considered the matter. Girls were more likely than boys to feel that classes were unnecessary, and boys to feel that they had too many other things to do. Only boys, though few of them, felt that there was no point for them since they were not the 'brainy type'. Some young people had tried to register for classes, but found that they were either too late or that the classes they wanted were full.

The response to the check list of statements revealed rather a different pattern of replies, however, and it was possible to distinguish a variety of attitudes which ranged from the wholly negative to the conditionally approving. Moreover, it appeared that attitudes varied in some degree according to how they had felt about leaving school and, among girls, according to the type of employment followed.

Four groups of responses could usefully be distinguished, namely, those approving further education conditionally; those wholly disapproving; those preferring alternative pursuits for leisure time; and a miscellaneous group (Table 77).

TABLE 77. References to further education.

| | Total | Boys and Girls How much wanted to leave school | |
		Very much. Quite a lot.	Didn't mind. Not very much. Not at all.
		(Per cent of total)a	
Conditional approval			
Depends on whether classes useful for my job	45	52	38
Would go if firm sent me one day a week	22	32	10
Would like to go to classes for some things	15	20	8
Would go if my friends went too	12	17	4
Disapproval			
Had enough of school	23	38	5
Waste of time	16	7	25
School put me off wanting any more education	13	..	..
More learning would be boring	10	13	5
Alright for brainy ones	10	..	..
Alternatives preferred			
Learn a lot from talking to people at work	28	..	..
Too many things to do in spare time	16	24	8
Prefer to read books if I want to know anything	12	17	7
Prefer sport	9	..	..
Other			
Too tired after work	19	15	24
Ought to be taught all you need at work	16	..	..
Don't know of any classes to interest me	15	..	..
Would like to know more than I do	11	..	..
Haven't been able to find the right classes for me	6	..	..
No evening classes in my neighbourhood	3	..	..
Total (Multiple replies)	100	100	100
(No. of 15–18's)	(130)	(71)	(59)

a Percentages shown only where differences are at least 8 percentage points.

Conditional approval

The largest group among those not receiving further education (nearly one-half), felt that their attendance at classes depended on whether these would be useful or otherwise for their present or intended jobs; while one in five felt they would go to classes if sent by the firm on day release. In both instances rather more boys were of these opinions than were girls. Smaller proportions also indicated that they were interested in classes for certain subjects or activities or they would attend if their friends went too. Interestingly enough, conditional approval in all these respects was much more forthcoming from enthusiastic than reluctant leavers; this would indicate that an important minority group which had not done well at school and had been eager to leave, was, nonetheless, not averse to the idea of further education; but to be acceptable, such education had to have a clear purpose.

Disapproval

There were also some young people who were not at all attracted to the idea of further education and whose selection of statements indicated that there was some association in their minds between that idea and unfavourable memories of their school days. Nearly one in four, for instance, felt that they had had enough of school; one in eight that school had put them off wanting any more education; one in six that it was a waste of time and one in ten that more learning would be boring; a similar proportion felt that it was all right for the 'brainy' ones, but, by implication, not for them. There were only marginal differences between boys and girls but much higher proportions of enthusiastic than unwilling leavers felt that they had had enough of school and that more learning would be tedious; the latter viewpoint was also more prevalent among girls in manual than in clerical occupations. The essential characteristic of this group was, therefore, that their attitudes to further education were a reflection of their unfavourable school experiences.

Preferred alternatives

Attitudes to further education also seemed to be influenced by the degree to which other activities were regarded as more interesting and satisfying. As many as one in six of the young people questioned indicated that they had too many other things to do with their spare time and just under one in ten, chiefly boys, that they preferred sport to educational activities. One in eight felt that if they wanted to know anything, they would prefer to read books rather than attend classes. A substantial proportion (one in four), also felt that they had learnt a lot since leaving school simply from talking to people at work. Young people who had been keen to leave school were much more likely than others to feel there were too many other things to do and to prefer to consult books. There were relatively few differences between boys and girls in these attitudes.

Other opinions

Small minorities also expressed other points of view. One in six, for instance, felt that young people ought to be taught what they needed while at work and rather more, one in five, that they were too tired after work to attend classes; the latter opinion was more prevalent among manual workers. There were also boys and girls who did not, for one reason or another, know of any classes that would interest them either in their neighbourhood or elsewhere; or who had not been able to find the right kind of classes for themselves. As many as one in ten referred to their wanting more knowledge, frequently on a special subject, though sometimes of a more general character; this need was more frequently expressed by boys than by girls.

For many school leavers outside schemes of formal training which involved attendance at technical school or college, further education was not, therefore, a matter to be given serious consideration. It had proved boring and irksome for those with some experience of it; it seemed to serve little useful purpose as far as their jobs were concerned; to promise little more than a repetition of what they felt they had suffered at school; and to offer a prospect far less enjoyable or interesting than the pursuit of their own independent activities. School experiences would seem to have played some part in influencing these attitudes in so far as formal education was identified in the minds of certain young people with their unfulfilled needs and aims.

SUMMARY

Questioned about the method of learning their present jobs, most young people referred to their being taught by fellow workers or supervisors and relatively few by training instructors. The higher the level of skill, however, the more intensive the training and the more frequently other workers, supervisors, and instructors were involved. Almost all the training took place on the job; and apart from apprentices and trainees whose training extended over several years, average learning times, as assessed by young workers, amounted to nine weeks at the most and just over three weeks at the least; there were some jobs which, in the opinions of the workers concerned, had been learned in a matter of minutes. Most workers felt that further time was required in order to perform the work easily and confidently. Average total training times were estimated by boys to be between 7 and 10 months and by girls between 4 and 6 months; shorter times, on average, applied to manual than to non-manual workers.

A rather higher proportion of young people (one-half of the boys and one-fifth of the girls) were in day release schemes than generally applies to under-eighteens at work; almost all apprentices and a high proportion of trainees were covered by such schemes, but only those manual workers employed in large firms or nationalized services. Those attending day or evening classes were asked about their courses; liberal and social studies were frequently regarded by young people as the least useful of the subjects studies, because they were felt to have little relationship to their specialized studies. Most suggestions for improving further education centred on the removal of these particular subjects from the curriculum; other suggestions included improvements in methods and standards of teaching; rearrangements of time-tables; better teaching equipment and buildings, and smaller classes.

Boys attending non-vocational classes were particularly critical of the level of teaching and of their treatment by the staff, which in their view, were reminiscent of unsatisfactory school days. School leavers who had given up attending classes were asked for their reasons for doing so. Boredom with the subject, course or teaching was the most frequent explanation offered, though there were other school leavers who had become discouraged when they did not make the progress hoped for. School leavers who had never attended classes tended to feel that further education was unnecessary in their case; but when selecting from a check list of statements those which most closely corresponded to their own views, substantial proportions indicated that they would attend classes if these were useful to their present jobs or if they were sent by their firms on day release. There was some indication that entirely negative views towards further education were associated with unfavourable impressions of school; other leavers felt that sports, hobbies, and other activities were more interesting and satisfying than was the prospect of attending classes.

CHAPTER XV

IMPRESSIONS OF SUPERVISORS AND FIRMS

INTRODUCTION

It will be recalled that in order to obtain from school leavers some impressions of their teachers and schools, check lists of items adapted from a N.I.I.P. methodological study of job satisfaction[1] were used which allowed young people to select those which most clearly corresponded to their recollections. The same method was used to elicit opinions about their present supervisors and firms.[2] This technique seemed particularly appropriate to use in the interviewing of young people in their place of work since it provided them with a wide choice of response and enabled them to select as few or as many items as they wished.

For the purpose of the analysis, the items selected by young people were divided into favourable and unfavourable comment; further distinction was also made between items associated with the supervisory function as such, and those reflecting purely personal qualities; and between items relating to the social aspects of firms and those relating to their technical efficiency.

REFERENCES TO SUPERVISORS

Even allowing for the fact that the check list of items contained rather more favourable than unfavourable references (19 as against 12), the former were more frequently selected by both boys and girls, and by all occupational groups. Almost one-half of young people made no unfavourable references at all, whereas only one in eight made no favourable comment.[3] Nevertheless, only a minority selected the most favourable references, a tendency which was more marked for the girls than for the boys.[4]

The most frequently selected reference, for both boys and girls, was that their supervisors were helpful, just over one-half being of this

---

[1] See Chapter IV.

[2] A comparison between the results of the N.I.I.P. and the present inquiry is described on pages 247–8 and included in Tables 79–81.

[3] See Chapter XVI, pages 258–60 for the association between job satisfaction and references to supervisors.

[4] Boys made, on average, 5·5 favourable references to supervisors and only 1·0 unfavourable references: for girls, the corresponding figures were 4·5 and 1·0.

opinion. Almost as many felt that their supervisors were good to work under and of boys, that they were fair; just under one-half also felt that they knew their job (Table 78). Rather smaller proportions felt that their supervisors explained things clearly, treated them like human beings, listened to what they wanted to say, or were pleasant. Not more than one in four of the boys, and fewer of the girls, referred to the people in charge of their work as encouraging, efficient, reliable, clever, or praising them when they did well; even fewer as kind or sincere. Only three of the nineteen favourable items were selected by as many as one-half of the boys and only one by a corresponding proportion of girls.

TABLE 78. Favourable references to supervisors.

	Present inquiry			N.I.I.P.[a] inquiry
	Boys	Girls	Total	
	(Per cent of total)			
Functional				
Good to work under	51	49	50	35·2
Knows his/her job	49	43	46	38·3
Explains things clearly	38	28	33	18·2
Listens to what I want to say	33	28	30	34·2
Encourages me	24	16	20	..
Efficient	24	11	18	20·3
Praises me when I do well	20	28	19	10·5
Clever	20	7	14	..
Full of ideas	18	10	15	10·4
Personal				
Helpful	52	52	52	30·7
Fair	51	37	44	45·9
Treats me like a human being	34	27	30	25·6
Pleasant	30	38	34	26·5
Considerate	29	23	26	25·9
Reliable	24	16	20	16·6
Confident	20	11	16	11·7
Kind	12	14	13	..
Sincere	11	11	11	14·3
Always keeps promises	9	4	7	11·2
Total (Multiple replies)	100	100	100	100
(No. of workers)	(183)	(147)	(330)	(1000)

a J. D. Handyside, op. cit.

On the other hand, negative comment was made by only very small minorities of school leavers. Less than one in five of the boys and fewer, proportionately, of the girls felt that their supervisors nagged them, were moody, or expected too much; less than one in ten referred to them as being strict, disinterested, or sarcastic. As many as one in seven of the girls, however, found their supervisors frightening, though virtually none of the boys were of this opinion (Table 79).

TABLE 79. Unfavourable references to supervisors.

	Present inquiry			N.I.I.P.[a] inquiry
	Boys	Girls	Total	
	(Per cent of total)			
Functional				
Expects too much	12	10	11	11·8
Strict	9	7	8	..
Has favourites	9	8	9	18·9
Doesn't seem interested	7	9	8	..
Muddled	5	7	6	..
Personal				
Nagging	18	8	..	..
Moody	16	11	14	20·1
Sarcastic	10	3	8	13·6
Too old	9	11	..	..
Interfering	7	10	11	11·0
Frightening	1	14	..	..
Too young	1	3	..	..
Total (Multiple replies)	100	100	100	100
(No. of workers)	(183)	(147)	(330)	(1000)

a J. D. Handyside, op. cit.

Relatively more boys than girls, proportionately, referred to their supervisors as fair, reliable, confident; boys would appear to have been more frequently impressed than were girls with the certain 'professional' qualities, being more inclined to describe the people over them as encouraging, efficient, clever, and able to explain things clearly. Boys were also more likely to feel that they were nagged, however, while girls, as has been shown, were much more likely to find their supervisors frightening.

When occupational differences were distinguished, favourable comment in most respects came more frequently from trainees than from other workers, particularly in regard to the 'professional' merits of supervisors. Boys in relatively unskilled manual work, however, were the most likely of all to feel that their supervisors were fair, and apprentices that they knew their jobs. Boys in less skilled manual jobs were less likely than others to describe the people over them as sincere, keeping promises, encouraging, or efficient. Girls in corresponding jobs, while more frequently than others referring to their supervisors as pleasant, tended to be the least likely to find them explaining things clearly, efficient, or treating them like human beings; they were more likely than others, moreover, to feel that their supervisors were frightening (over two-fifths of them selecting this item), disinterested, and muddled. Among the boys, it was the manual workers and apprentices who, if anyone, were inclined to select unfavourable aspects of the supervisory function, while among girls it was only the manual workers who showed this tendency. Trainees and apprentices, however, had the highest average number of total comments, favourable and unfavourable.

REFERENCES TO FIRMS

Similar tendencies were apparent for the references of young people to certain aspects of their firms. Favourable far outnumbered unfavourable, even allowing for more favourable than unfavourable items (thirteen against ten), on the check list. Almost two in five young workers made no unfavourable comment at all and only one in ten no unfavourable comment.[5] Once again, the 'score', particularly for girls, was relatively low. It was evident, moreover, that young people stressed the social rather than the technical characteristics of the firms in question (Table 80).

TABLE 80. Favourable references to firms.

	Present inquiry			N.I.I.P.[a] inquiry
	Boys	Girls	Total	
Technical efficiency	(*Per cent of total*)			
Good reputation	38	28	34	33·7
Serves customers well	32	24	28	20·7
Good product or service	26	18	22	32·6
Efficient	19	14	17	13·0
Up to date	18	18	18	19·6
Honest	17	16	16	14·3
Social				
Friendly	47	57	51	27·8
Good to work for	45	46	45	46·1
Offers secure job	40	31	36	23·2
Nice class of worker	39	31	35	16·6
Right size of firm	31	34	33	··
Easygoing	24	18	22	18·5
Good welfare	9	16	20	36·2
Total (Multiple replies)	100	100	100	100
(No. of workers)	(183)	(147)	(330)	(1000)

a J. D. Handyside, op. cit.

[5] For frequency of reference to favourable and unfavourable items according to degree of job satisfaction, see Chapter XVI.

The most frequently selected reference to firms was that they were friendly; nearly one-half of the boys and just under three-fifths of the girls were of this opinion. Next in order of frequency was that firms were good to work for,[6] just under one-half of all school leavers selecting this particular item. Almost as many boys, but fewer girls, referred to their employers as having a good reputation, offering secure jobs, and employing a nice class of worker. Boys and girls, in almost the same proportions (nearly one-third), also felt that they were working in the right size of firm; only between one-fourth and one-fifth, however, felt that their firms were associated with a good product or service, or were easy going; even smaller proportions described their employers as efficient, up to date, honest; and not more than one in seven felt that good welfare applied.

Of the thirteen favourable items relating to firms, therefore, only one was selected by more than one-half of the school leavers seen and then to this extent only by the girls; four items were selected by about one-third and five by not more than one in four.

TABLE 81. Unfavourable references to firms.

	Present inquiry			N.I.I.P.[a] inquiry
	Boys	Girls	Total	
	(Per cent of total)			
Technical efficiency				
Not enough training	18	9	14	..
Old fashioned	16	11	14	..
Needs fresh people at top	14	10	12	14·9
Too set in ideas	12	5	9	11·7
Social				
Strict about time-keeping	37	34	36	32·4
Too many rules and regulations	12	10	11	13·2
Too much class distinction	9	3	5	15·7
Only out to make money	9	4	6	14·1
Too small	8	1	5	..
Too big	3	4	3	..
Total (Multiple replies)	100	100	100	100
(No. of workers)	(183)	(147)	(330)	(1000)

a J. D. Handyside, op. cit.

Only very few school leavers commented on any unfavourable aspect of their firms and girls did so to a much less extent than boys (Table 81).

[6] L. T. Wilkins found that most satisfaction was expressed by young workers who believed that they worked for a 'good' firm. (L. T. Wilkins, op. cit.)

The most frequently selected item here was that their firms were strict about time keeping; as many as one-third of the school leavers seen referred to this, representing a far higher proportion than selected any other unfavourable item. The next in order of frequency for boys was that not enough training was provided, though less than one in five were of this opinion. Even smaller proportions described their employers as old fashioned, needing fresh people at the top, or as too set in their ideas.

Occupational differences in the frequency distribution of comment were few and such as there were applied almost exclusively to boys and girls in relatively unskilled manual work. Boys in such jobs were less inclined, for instance, to feel that their firms had a good reputation and girls that their firms were friendly or efficient. Hardly any of these boys referred to their working with a nice class of worker and, even among the girls, the proportions with this point of view were much smaller for manual than for non-manual workers. Boys in less skilled manual jobs were also more likely to feel that there were too many rules and regulations and that their firms were too small and old fashioned; they were less likely, however, to feel that their employers were strict about time keeping; no such differences were evident among the girls.

The relatively low frequency with which school leavers selected favourable aspects of their supervisors and firms suggests that, in general, they did not rate their employers, or the people in charge of their work, very highly. A positive response towards the firms in which they were employed and the people who were their immediate superiors, was evoked from as many as one-half of young workers in only a few respects, and in most instances from less than one in three. The relative infrequency of adverse comment, however, suggests that the replies reflect a working environment characterized for them by the absence of negative rather than the prevalence of positive conditions. Within the limits set by the check-list of items (which clearly did not provide for all aspects of employment to be considered), the analysis suggests that favourable conditions were infrequent rather than general.

It could be argued, however, that in the selection of items, young people were influenced in some degree by the fact that interviews were conducted at work. Even with the assurance of confidentiality and anonymity, there may well have been some reluctance on the part of young people to commit themselves, albeit in non-verbal responses, to comments, adverse or otherwise, about their supervisors and firms. This assumption was strengthened when comparison was made of the relative differences with which school leavers regarded their teachers and supervisors, for it was evident that supervisors evoked far less frequent critical comment than did teachers.[7]

[7] M. Speak found that, on the whole, people wanted to say nice things about their jobs, bosses, and firms. (See M. Speak, *Occupational Psychology*, **38**, July and October 1964.)

TEACHERS AND SUPERVISORS

When the frequency of favourable comment about teachers is compared with that relating to supervisors, the similarity in most of the replies seems to convey a view of adults as symbols of authority, irrespective of the differences in their respective roles. Only in four of the nineteen favourable items, for instance, did the boys' replies concerning their teachers differ substantially from those relating to their supervisors, and all these were associated with the 'professional' aspects of teaching or supervising; for girls, differences were apparent in five items, only three of which were associated with 'professional' and two with personal qualities. Thus supervisors were much less likely than were teachers to be regarded as encouraging, explaining things clearly, or, as far as boys were concerned, praising them when they did well. There would seem to be some logic, however, for young people failing to experience in the same degree as at school, explanation, encouragement, or praise in the learning of new tasks, or in work performed, since supervisors are not necessarily trained in the principles or methods of teaching.　—

It is possible that the contrast between teachers and supervisors, in these specific respects, is one of the more difficult areas of adjustment between school and work for certain newcomers to commerce and industry. But if supervisors were more likely to be deficient in these qualities, they were much more likely, particularly by girls, to be felt to be good to work under than were teachers. In all personal respects, however, views about supervisors were almost identical with those about teachers, though girls felt their teachers to have been more frequently kind and to have kept their promises, than were their supervisors at work (Table 82).

TABLE 82. Differences in the frequencies of favourable references to teachers and supervisors.

| | Boys | | Girls | |
	Teachers	Supervisors	Teachers	Supervisors
	(Per cent of total)			
Explains things clearly	50	38	38	28
Encourages me	41	24	40	16
Praises me when I do well	31	20	..	..
Good to work for	30	51	18	49
Kind	..	..	22	14
Always keeps promises	..	..	12	4
Total (Multiple replies)	100	100	100	100
(No. of 15–18s)	(183)	(183)	(147)	(147)

Teachers, however, were more frequently criticized than were supervisors. This was particularly marked in regard to strictness, associated with teachers by nearly two-fifths of the boys, and one-third of the girls, but with supervisors by less than one in ten leavers; in regard to having favourites, associated with teachers by over one in three young people, but with supervisors by less than one in ten; and in regard to being sarcastic, associated with teachers by one in five leavers, but with supervisors by not more than one in ten (Table 83).

TABLE 83. Differences in the frequencies of unfavourable references to teachers and supervisors.

| | Boys | | Girls | |
	Teachers	Supervisors	Teachers	Supervisors
	(Per cent of total)			
Strict	39	9	31	7
Has favourites	33	9	41	8
Sarcastic	22	10	23	6
Muddled	..	..	23	7
Too old	17	9	15	5
Too young	15	1	14	3
Nagging	..	..	18	8
Frightening	9	1	..	..
Total (Multiple replies)	100	100	100	100
(No. of 15–18s)	(183)	(183)	(147)	(147)

SCHOOLS AND FIRMS

There were relatively few items common to schools and firms. Nevertheless, it was evident that the latter were regarded more frequently as friendly (particularly by the girls), easy going, and as requiring fresh people at the top; but less frequently as efficient and up to date than were schools. They were also associated, however, with rather less frequent references to strict time keeping, to too many rules and regulations and, by girls, to being too big (Table 84).

These results, at first glance, suggest that young people were more reluctant to make adverse comment about their supervisors and firms, than about their teachers and schools. But other interpretations are possible. The influence and authority of teachers extends beyond the area of formal education to that of the social behaviour, attitudes, and moral values of school children; this is sometimes resented and resisted by the children themselves. The authority of supervisors, on the other hand, is much more closely applied to the task in hand; supervisors themselves may come from the same social background as the people whose work they oversee, and may have started their working lives in the same way as the young people themselves. Moreover, they frequently have in their charge, not only the work of young newcomers but that of adults as well. Their authority is, therefore, likely to be felt as far less pervasive than that of teachers and in some respects more acceptable. It is perhaps for this reason that certain unfavourable aspects made less impact than did similar characteristics of teachers, and partly accounted for the relatively low frequency of critical comment.

TABLE 84. References to certain common features of school and firm.

| | Boys | | Girls | |
	School	Firm	School	Firm
	(Per cent of total)			
Favourable				
Up to date	40	18	31	18
Friendly	34	47	31	57
Efficient	30	19	..	..
Just the right size	..	..	17	34
Unfavourable				
Strict about time-keeping	45	37	46	34
Too many rules and regulations	21	12	21	10
Too big	6	3	17	4
Total (Multiple replies)	100	100	100	100
(No. of 15–18s)	(183)	(183)	(147)	(147)

There is also the argument that children in school, after all, are a captive population and as such have to endure any characteristic of their teachers which displeases them, a factor which in itself may strengthen unfavourable impressions. Difficulties in relationships which arise at work, on the other hand, can sometimes be resolved by finding fresh employment. It seems unlikely, given opportunities for job change, that unfavourable comment would have been forthcoming in the present inquiry except from small minorities.[8] This assumption would seem to be confirmed when the results in the present inquiry were compared with those obtained in the N.I.I.P. study of job satisfaction[9] and when the favourable opinions of school leavers concerning their supervisors and firms were found to be associated with the fact that a high proportion of them (nearly three-fifths) were very satisfied with their present jobs. This suggests that the results of the inquiry reflect the actual experience of young workers rather than any reticence on their part to criticize their supervisors and firms.

[8] Wyatt and Marriott found that the most dissatisfied workers left while they were young and those who remained became increasingly resigned as they grew older. (S. Wyatt and R. Marriott, *A Study of Attitudes to Factory Work*, H.M.S.O., 1956.)

[9] J. D. Handyside, op. cit.

THE PRESENT INQUIRY AND THE N.I.I.P. STUDY

The N.I.I.P. study was essentially a methodological one, carried out to explore the advantages and disadvantages of self-completing questionnaires and interview methods. It was based on a sample of 4000 employees of all ages drawn from five firms, who were approached at work and asked to complete questionnaires. Supplementary interviews with employees at their place of work were also carried out. A number of questions in the present inquiry were adopted from those used in the N.I.I.P. study; it is possible, therefore, to compare some of the results obtained, particularly relating to opinions about supervisors and firms. Since, in these respects, the N.I.I.P. results did not distinguish between age, sex, or occupation, it was necessary, for comparative purposes, to combine the replies of boys and girls in the present inquiry. It is possible, however, that some of the differences in the results of the two inquiries may reflect the age factor. Job satisfaction was found to be higher for new entrants to work, particularly girls, in the N.I.I.P. study, and for boys in the present inquiry.[11]

School leavers in the present inquiry were much more likely than were workers in the N.I.I.P. study, to feel that their supervisors were good to work under, explained things clearly, and were helpful; they were also a little more likely to feel that they knew their job and praised them when they did well. In most other favourable respects, however, the replies of the two samples were closely similar and almost identical proportions considered their supervisors to be fair, considerate, and efficient (Table 78). Of the four unfavourable items which could be compared, rather more of the N.I.I.P. sample assessed the people in charge of their work as moody, sarcastic, and having favourites than applied to the young workers in the Willesden inquiry, though roughly similar proportions in each sample felt too much was expected of them. But, as in the present inquiry, only minorities commented adversely on their supervisors (Table 79).

Workers in both inquiries had certain similar views about favourable aspects of their firms, more or less equal proportions feeling that their firms had a good reputation, were efficient, up to date, honest, good to work for, and easy going. The enthusiasm of being out at work for the first time was perhaps responsible for the higher proportions of young workers who felt that their firms were friendly, offering secure jobs, and associated with a nice class of worker. Fewer school leavers, proportionately to the N.I.I.P. sample of workers, however, felt that their firms offered good welfare or considered that the product associated with their firms was a good one (Table 80).

There was further consistency in the replies of both samples to certain unfavourable aspects of their firms. Almost equal proportions of each, for

[10] Ibid.
[11] See Chapter XVI.

instance, felt that their employers were strict about time keeping and too set in their ideas; that there were too many rules and regulations and that new people were required at the top. Workers in the N.I.I.P. study were more inclined than were school leavers, however, to feel that there was too much class distinction and that their firms were only out to make money. Again, only small minorities expressed such opinions (Table 81).

The main conclusion to be drawn from the general consistency of the replies of the two samples of workers, would appear to be that the views of relative newcomers to industry or commerce were not greatly at variance, in most respects, with those who had had longer working lives. This seems to suggest that the working environment, in so far as it was influenced by the qualities of supervision, the efficiency of organization, the kind of social atmosphere, and by training and other facilities, was not very different for young workers who were still in their formative years, than for experienced adult workers who were, perhaps, more set in their skills and in their ways. This environment would not seem to have provided, on the whole, conditions that were likely to evoke a positive response from more than a minority of workers, irrespective of the length of time at work. On the other hand, it seems evident that school leavers, in particular, found their working environment to be far less restrictive than that of their later school years. For those who had found the authority of their teachers too strict or their school life too regulated, work—in spite of its negative aspects—appears to have brought a new sense of freedom.

ATTITUDES TOWARDS LEAVING SCHOOL

It was thought of interest to relate differences in opinions regarding teachers and supervisors, to attitudes towards leaving school. It was hoped to show the extent to which differences between the eager and the reluctant leavers in their opinions of teachers and schools were repeated in respect of their supervisors and firms; and the extent to which favourable impressions of school were associated with subsequent impressions at work.

Rather different tendencies emerged for boys and for girls and several of the original differences between eager and reluctant leavers in regard to their opinions about teachers were not subsequently repeated in their opinions about supervisors.

Fewer of the enthusiastic than of the reluctant leavers, for instance, had felt that their teachers knew their job, encouraged them, or treated them like human beings; but much higher proportions of them than of the less willing leavers now referred to their supervisors in these respects. On the other hand, while equal proportions of enthusiastic and reluctant leavers recalled their teachers as having listened to them and praised them, higher proportions of former enthusiastic leavers now felt this about their supervisors than did those who had been less willing to leave school.

A much higher proportion of boys who had been eager to leave school also felt that their supervisors were good to work under, than was the case with other boys.

TABLE 85. Attitudes to leaving school and differences in the frequencies of references to teachers and supervisors: boys.

| | How much wanted to leave school | | | |
| | Very much Quite a lot | | Didn't mind Not very much Not at all | |
	Teachers	Supervisors	Teachers	Supervisors
	(Per cent of total)			
Knows his/her job	44	58	57	41
Encourages me	..	..	51	19
Treats me like a human being	30	40	38	29
Listens to me	31	42	31	25
Praises me when I do well	31	23	31	16
Good to work under	31	60	25	43
Total (Multiple replies)	100	100	100	100
(No. of 15–18s)	(90)	(90)	(93)	(93)

A similar tendency was evident in regard to opinions about schools and firms: most original differences did not persist but more, proportionately, of the boys who had wanted to leave school now felt that their firms had a good reputation, were good to work for, and offered secure jobs, than of boys who had been less eager to finish their school days (Table 85).

Among boys, therefore, supervisors were, generally, regarded more favourably than teachers (and firms more favourably than schools) by the enthusiastic leavers, and less favourably by those who had been non-committal or reluctant about leaving school. Experiences of school and work were by no means consistent, and a positive response to certain aspects of work was more likely the less favourable the experience of school, and *vice versa*.

Girls' experiences were more varied than were those of the boys (Table 86). If anyone, it was the less willing school leavers who were likely to repeat, or to improve on, their favourable experiences of school, though not in every aspect. The improvement for enthusiastic leavers arose mainly because they discovered work to be less unfavourable than school in certain respects. There was thus a greater contrast, in this sense, for them than for other leavers, between school and work. But for all girls, the main improvement was that they found their supervisors were less strict than had been their teachers.

TABLE 86. Attitudes to leaving school and differences in the frequencies of references to teachers and supervisors: girls.

| | How much wanted to leave school | | | |
| | Very much Quite a lot | | Didn't mind Not very much Not at all | |
	Teachers	Supervisors	Teachers	Supervisors
Favourable	*(Per cent of total)*			
Explains thing clearly	38	32	38	44
Treats me like a human being	34	24	21	31
Listens to what I want to say	32	24	..	..
Good to work under	18	44	18	57
Unfavourable				
Strict	31	10	31	1
Expects too much	..	..	21	31
Interfering	3	10	3	1
Total (Multiple replies)	100	100	100	100
(No. of 15–18s)	(82)	(82)	(65)	(65)

SUMMARY

School leavers were asked to select from a check list of items those which most closely applied to their supervisors and firms. Even allowing for the fact that the check lists contained more favourable than unfavourable items, favourable references were far more frequently selected than were unfavourable ones, by both boys and girls and by all occupational groups. It might have been assumed that this reflected some reluctance on the part of young people to commit themselves to adverse comment while being interviewed in their place of work, an assumption which was strengthened when it became evident that supervisors evoked far less critical comment than did teachers. However, the consistency of many of the replies of school leavers with those obtained in a much larger inquiry among all-age workers conducted by the N.I.I.P., and the fact that relatively few young workers in the present inquiry were dissatisfied with their present jobs, suggests that their comments, favourable and otherwise, could be regarded as reflecting their actual experiences rather than their reticence to criticize.

A relatively low frequency applied to most favourable references, however, particularly as far as girls were concerned. Only three of the eighteen favourable items relating to supervision—that they were helpful, fair, and good to work under—were selected by as many as one-half of the boys and only one—that of helpful—by a corresponding proportion of the girls. Similarly, of the thirteen favourable items relating to firms, only one, that of friendliness, was selected by more than one-half of the girls and just under one-half of the boys. On the other hand, adverse comment was made by even fewer school leavers; less than one in five referred to their supervisors as nagging, moody, or expecting too much, and much smaller proportions selected any other unfavourable aspect; strictness about time keeping was more frequently selected (by one in three), than was any other unfavourable item for firms, the next most frequent (from one in five of the boys), was that referring to insufficient training.

The relative infrequency of adverse comment and the relatively low score given to most favourable references to supervisors and firms, suggests not only that school leavers did not rate either their employers or their supervisors very highly, but that the environment of work for them was characterized more by the absence of negative than the prevalence of positive conditions. Within the limits set by the check lists, the analysis suggest that favourable conditions, in most respects, were infrequent rather than general. It seems evident, however, that school leavers, in general, found their work environment to be less restrictive than that of school and for those who found the authority of their teachers too strict or their school life too regulated, work, in spite of its negative aspects, brought a new sense of freedom.

CHAPTER XVI

JOB SATISFACTION

INTRODUCTION

The very extensive literature relating to British and American studies of job satisfaction (and dissatisfaction) reveals the complexity of the subject.[1] Many studies have sought to discover the chief sources of satisfaction; others, its chief determinants. It has been shown to vary according to type of work and skill; to factors such as age, sex, social class and status, expectations, and interests; and to be influenced by the extent and quality of social relationships at work. In the interpretation of findings, however, there is some controversy as to whether job satisfaction is unitary or multi-dimensional in character; whether it represents a state of mind or assumes that the individual can separate elements such as job, pay, and supervision, and assign relevant degrees of satisfaction to them. Doubt is also expressed as to whether the assessment of satisfaction is meaningful if the worker is not aware of alternative possibilities of work, or of his potential; if dissatisfaction with work is felt to be associated with social failure; or if, as seems increasingly likely, work is regarded not as a source of positive satisfaction, but only as a means of obtaining greater satisfaction through the purchase of goods and services.

Because of the difficulties involved in devising valid questions and in interpreting replies about attitudes to work, it seemed preferable in the present inquiry to use questions which had been applied successfully in other, larger scale, inquiries. Some of the questions used were based on the N.I.I.P. methodological study of job satisfaction,[2] some of whose conclusions are of special interest. Results were obtained from factor analysis which indicated that job satisfaction is multi-dimensional, consisting of a number of independent factors associated with work and its conditions, rather than with any factors associated with attitudes—neurotic or other—to life in general. Moreover, job satisfaction also appears to be a dynamic process of balancing one factor against another, rather than a static condition of a particular level of overall satisfaction.

If these conclusions apply to the sample of school leavers seen in the present inquiry, it seems likely that their attitudes to work were derived more directly from their work experience than from other experiences of

[1] A recent unpublished bibliography lists nearly 150 post-war studies in this field.
[2] J. D. Handyside, op. cit.

life. Moreover, their attitudes, at the time of inquiry, were not reliable predictors of continued satisfaction with work, since any modest change in the balance of factors could well have changed the 'very' to 'moderately' satisfied, and the 'moderately' satisfied to 'dissatisfied', and *vice versa*.

DEGREE OF JOB SATISFACTION

School leavers were asked to assess their feelings about their present jobs according to an eleven-point rating scale.[3] Their replies showed a distribution which covered almost every point of the scale, though the majority were well towards the top (Table 87). The alternative 'On the whole I like it' attracted more ratings from the boys (just under one-third) than did any other, and 'I like it very much' the most from the girls (over one-quarter). Very few 'loved' their jobs, but even fewer wholly disliked them. By grouping the replies into three main categories, the 'very' and 'moderately' satisfied and the 'dissatisfied', it was evident that most boys and girls were very satisfied with their jobs (over one-half and three-fifths, respectively), and substantial proportions moderately satisfied (between

TABLE 87. Degree of job satisfaction.

	Boys	Girls
	(Per cent of total)	
Very satisfied		
I love it	5	7
I am enthusiastic about it	14	9
I like it very much	23	29
I like it a good deal	11	15
Sub-total	53	60
Moderately satisfied		
On the whole I like it	30	19
I like it fairly well	9	14
Sub-total	39	33
Dissatisfied		
I like it a little	4	3
I am indifferent to it	2	—
On the whole I don't like it	1	1·5
I dislike it	1	1·5
I hate it	—	1
Sub-total	8	7
Total	100	100
(No. of 15–18s)	(183)	(147)

[3] Devised by Robert Hoppock, op. cit.

one-third and two-fifths). Girls were less likely than boys to be 'enthusi-astic' about their jobs, but rather more of them, proportionately, indicated that they 'liked them very much' or a 'good deal'. The differences between the ratings of boys and girls were not, on the whole, substantial.

When compared with the results shown by the N.I.I.P. sample, a very much higher proportion of school leavers in the present inquiry were very satisfied with their present jobs (nearly three-fifths) than applied in the (all age) N.I.I.P. sample (over one-quarter) (Table 88). This seems to be partly due to the tendency revealed in the latter inquiry for the youngest employees and newest entrants, who in total form a small proportion of the N.I.I.P. sample, to be in the upper ratings of the job satisfaction scale.

TABLE 88. Degree of job satisfaction: a comparison of the results of the N.I.I.P. and present inquiries.

	Present inquiry	N.I.I.P.[a] inquiry
	(Per cent of total)	
I love it I am enthusiastic about it	18	6·7
I like it very much I like it a good deal	40	21·6
On the whole I like it I like it fairly well	36	57·2
I like it a little I am indifferent to it On the whole, I don't like it I dislike it I hate it	6	14·5
Total	100	100
(No. of workers)	(330)	(1000)

a J. D. Handyside, op. cit.

Wilensky[4] also found that job satisfaction shows a chronology linked to the family life cycle and work history, being lower among young people in their twenties, higher in middle age and falling with the approach of retirement, being similar in terms of variation to studies of ageing and social participation. In his view, job satisfaction is a function of disparity between rewards of work (income and status) and aspirations and expec-tations (status, goods and services wanted). The relatively high proportion of young workers in the present inquiry with positive feelings about their present jobs (even when age, type of employment followed, and length of

[4] H. L. Wilensky, 'Work, Careers, and Social Integration', *International Social Science Journal*, No. 4, 1960.

service were taken into account),[5] may have been partly due to factors associated with being at work as such. Leaving school and starting work may have been a time, however brief, when parity between rewards and expectations was at its closest. Whatever satisfaction was derived from the job itself, was further enhanced, perhaps, by the experience of acquiring, for the first time, the status and rewards of a wage earner. This, for the newcomer, may have been sufficient to satisfy immediate, though not long-term, expectations. There is also the possibility that because, generally, little was expected from work by the young people interviewed, their degree of job satisfaction was consequently higher.[6]

SOME FACTORS INFLUENCING JOB SATISFACTION

It was not possible, in the present inquiry, to study the nature of job satisfaction as such, or the extent to which school leavers' attitudes were associated with their expectations; brief examination was made only of the extent to which job satisfaction was associated with the type of employment followed, the characteristics of the job performed, the impressions of supervisors and firms, the length of service, and the assessment of promotion prospects. In all these respects, job satisfaction was found to vary to a greater or lesser degree.

Type of employment

A number of studies have shown that job satisfaction tends to vary with occupation. In the present inquiry, the pattern of job satisfaction differed significantly as between broad occupational groups (see chi-squared results in Table 89). Job satisfaction ratings for boys differed appreciably between apprentices and non-manual workers on the one hand, and other

TABLE 89. Degree of job satisfaction and type of employment.

How satisfied with present job	Apprentices	Trainees	All other manual	All non-manual
	(Per cent of total)			
Very	63	48	43	62
Moderately	36	38	37	33
Dissatisfied	—	14	20	5
No answer	1	—	—	—
Total	100	100	100	100
(No. of 15–18s)	(55)	(42)	(99)	(134)

$$\chi^2 = 24.54; \text{ d.f. } = 6; p < 0.001$$

[5] See pages 262–3.
[6] See M. Carter, 1966, op. cit.

manual workers on the other; for girls, the main difference was between office and other occupations. More than three in five of boy apprentices and girl office workers were very satisfied with their present jobs, and almost all the remainder moderately so; much smaller proportions of other workers, however, felt very satisfied and relatively more of them felt dissatisfied.

Characteristics of the jobs
Interest factors

One of ten relatively independent factors found in the N.I.I.P. study, to be correlated with job satisfaction was the intrinsic interest of the job performed.[7] In the present inquiry, it was evident that even between the 'very'

TABLE 90. Degree of job satisfaction and characteristics of present job: boys.

	How satisfied with present job		Ratio of (1) and (2)
	Very (1)	Moderately (2)	
Interest factors	*(Per cent of total)*		
Chance to use initiative	54	22	2·8
Have to concentrate	44	21	2·1
Skilled	26	14	2·0
Uses brains	40	20	2·0
Interesting	69	36	1·9
Interesting product/service	40	28	1·4
Boring	2	14	0·14
Too routine	5	21	0·2
Monotonous	6	18	0·3
Prospects, pay, etc.			
Teaching something useful	61	31	2·3
Well paid	24	17	1·4
Work with a good crowd	76	58	1·3
Physical			
Noisy	20	11	1·8
Dirty	34	18	1·6
Sitting	11	24	0·4
Demand			
Responsible	33	21	1·7
Keeps you busy	45	31	1·4
Total (Multiple replies)	100	100	
(No. of 15–18s)	(96)	(71)	

[7] J. D. Handyside, op. cit.

and the 'moderately' satisfied, the differences in the frequency with which positive interest items were selected were considerable, particularly among the boys (Tables 90 and 91).

TABLE 91. Degree of job satisfaction and characteristics of present job: girls.

	How satisfied with present job		Ratio of (1) and (2)
	Very (1)	Moderately (2)	
Interest factors	*(Per cent of total)*		
Interesting product	28	12	2·4
Interesting	53	23	2·3
Have to concentrate	40	21	1·9
Varied	24	14	1·7
Uses brains	26	16	1·6
Chance to use initiative	35	25	1·4
Monotonous	1	14	0·1
Boring	2	18	0·1
Skilled	6	..	..
Too routine	7	27	0·3
Prospects, pay, etc.			
Offers promotion prospects	26	14	1·8
Well paid	34	25	1·4
Physical			
Badly organized	1	8	0·1
Demand			
Keeps you busy	24	14	1·7
Difficult	4	..	..
Total (Multiple replies)	100	100	
(No. of 15–18s)	(89)	(48)	

About twice as many of the 'very' than of the 'moderately', satisfied, for instance, felt that their jobs were interesting, required concentration, used their brains, and were skilled. There was an even greater difference between the proportions in each category who felt their jobs provided them with a chance to use their initiative. By contrast, it was the moderately satisfied who were much more likely to refer to their jobs as boring, too routine, or monotonous.[8] Similar tendencies applied to the girls, though the differences between the 'very' and the 'moderately' satisfied were not,

[8] T. Veness shows that monotony, repetitiveness, and routine were frequently given by school leavers interviewed before entering employment, as features of work that they expected to dislike. (T. Veness, op. cit.)

on the whole, so substantial. Clearly there was an occupational factor influencing these results, since apprentices and girl office workers were more
likely than others to have a higher score on positive interest items,[9] and
were also more likely to be very satisfied with their present jobs. But since
the differences according to job satisfaction were much greater than
according to the type of employment followed, it would seem that, quite
apart from the occupational factor, job satisfaction was associated with the
interest appeal that certain jobs had for certain individuals. Though skilled
were more likely than unskilled jobs to be interesting, apprentices varied
in the degree to which they found them so, and some were less satisfied
with their jobs in this respect than were some of the workers engaged in
more routine tasks, which were generally associated with offering far less
in the way of intrinsic interest. Apart from any subjective factors which
influenced the way young people regarded their jobs, each type of employment must have included jobs which varied considerably from each other
in a number of respects. Since the sample of young people was relatively
small, it was not possible however, to examine either attitudes or jobs
except in regard to broad categories of employment.

Other characteristics

Differences between the 'very' and the 'moderately' satisfied in regard
to other job characteristics were not so great as for interest items, though
the very satisfied among the boys were more likely than others to feel that
they were learning something useful, that they worked with a good crowd,
and that their jobs were responsible; and girls to feel that their jobs
offered promotion prospects. Both boys and girls with the highest ratings
for job satisfaction were also more inclined to feel that they were well paid
and that their jobs kept them busy. References to physical factors varied
only among the boys, however, the very satisfied being more likely to
describe their jobs as noisy and dirty but less likely as mainly sitting.
Occupational factors probably biased these references, however, since
apprentices, who were more likely than others to feel very satisfied with
their jobs, were also more frequently exposed to dirt and noise and were
less frequently in sedentary work.[10]

References to supervisors and firms

The assumption that attitudes to supervisors and firms were not carried
over from school experiences, nor the result of undue reticence on the part
of school leavers to make adverse comment, was further confirmed when
their opinions were analysed according to the degree of satisfaction
expressed with their present jobs. The Handyside study[11] has shown that

[9] See Chapter XIII.
[10] See Chapter XIII.
[11] J. D. Handyside, op. cit.

satisfaction with supervision and evaluation of the firm were two of the ten relatively independent factors correlated with satisfaction at work. These two factors were also operative in the present inquiry though to a much greater extent for boys than for girls. Opinions on supervisors and firms varied considerably even between the moderately and the well satisfied, though substantial differences according to the degree of job satisfaction only applied to favourable and not to unfavourable comments, as far as opinions on supervision were concerned (Table 92).

TABLE 92. Degree of job satisfaction and favourable references to supervisors.

| | How satisfied with present job | | Ratio of |
	Very (1)	Moderately (2)	(1) and (2)
	(Per cent of total)		
Boys			
Always keeps promises	16	1	16·0
Kind	21	7	3·0
Praises me when I do well	27	11	2·5
Reliable	34	14	2·4
Explains things clearly	53	47	1·9
Efficient	32	18	1·8
Encourages me	32	18	1·8
Considerate	33	18	1·8
Clever	25	16	1·6
Confident	25	34	0·7
Girls			
Encourages me	22	8	2·8
Kind	24	14	1·7
Considerate	26	19	1·4
Listens to what I want to say	33	23	1·4
Explains things clearly	43	31	1·4
Treats me like a human being	31	23	1·3
Total (Multiple replies)	100	100	
(No. of 15–18s) (boys)	(96)	(71)	
(girls)	(89)	(48)	

Thus, for boys every favourable item with only two exceptions—fairness and sincerity—was selected by higher proportions of the relatively enthusiastic than of those who were less satisfied with their jobs. In some respects the differences were very marked, the most striking contrast arising from the differences between the moderately and the well satisfied in the proportions who felt that their supervisors always kept promises. Virtually none of the moderately satisfied were of this opinion compared with one in six of the very satisfied. Much higher proportions of the very satisfied

workers also described their supervisors as kind, praising them when they
did well, reliable, explaining things clearly, considerate, efficient, and
encouraging than applied to the moderately satisfied workers. Moreover,
the contrasts between the really enthusiastic and the dissatisfied were even
greater, since for many items, few or none of the latter referred to their
supervisors in these terms. The opinions of boys in the present inquiry
would appear, therefore, to be consistent with those of students in the
Venables study[12] for whom the most valued adult was one who kept
promises and showed 'fairness to the men in all respects'. The important
things evidently, for them, were that 'the boss should be a nice man';
'there should be good chaps to work with' and 'decent supervision to talk
to and rely on'. Favouritism, class distinction, lack of interest, and being
given the jobs that others did not want to do themselves were, in their
case, the chief source of complaints and dissatisfaction.

TABLE 93. Degree of job satisfaction and favourable
references to firms.

	How satisfied with present job		Ratio of (1) and (2)
	Very (1)	Moderately (2)	
Boys	(Per cent of total)		
Up to date	24	11	2·2
Good welfare	29	18	1·6
Good to work for	57	35	1·6
Honest	23	13	1·6
Nice class of worker	47	32	1·5
Offers secure job	48	32	1·5
Friendly	56	39	1·4
Efficient	24	17	1·4
Serves customers well	37	27	1·4
Good reputation	44	31	1·4
Girls			
Up to date	21	14	1·5
Total (Multiple replies)	100	100	
(No. of 15–18s) (boys	(96)	(71)	
(girls)	(89)	(48)	

Differences were also apparent between boys in their comments about
firms but the contrast between the very satisfied and others were not so
great as in their respective references to supervisors. A higher proportion
of workers who liked their jobs most, felt, among other things, that their
firms were up to date and efficient; honest and good to work for; offered

[12] 1965, op. cit.

secure jobs and good welfare (Table 93). It was the less satisfied leavers who tended, among other things, to feel that their firms required fresh people at the top; were too set in their ideas; had too many rules and regulations; were old fashioned and only out to make money; and did not provide enough training.

TABLE 94. Degree of job satisfaction and unfavourable references to firms.

	How satisfied with present job		Ratio of (1) and (2)
	Very (1)	Moderately (2)	
Boys	(Per cent of total)		
Needs fresh people at the top	8	22	0·3
Too set in ideas	8	17	0·5
Too many rules and regulations	10	18	0·5
Only out to make money	9	15	0·6
Not enough training	13	21	0·6
Old fashioned	17	25	0·7
Girls			
Not enough training	..	12	..
Only out to make money	2	16	0·1
Too many rules and regulations	6	21	0·3
Too small	7	16	0·4
Total (Multiple replies)	100	100	
(No. of 15–18s) (boys)	(96)	(71)	
(girls)	(89)	(48)	

In these respects, their opinions were again consistent with the students in the Venables study[13] who were also more likely to be dissatisfied with their firms if some of these conditions applied.

Similar tendencies applied to the sample of girls though the differences between the 'very' and 'moderately' satisfied workers were not so great or as frequent as for the boys. The more satisfied girls, however, were, like the boys, more likely to refer to favourable aspects of their supervisors and firms and less likely to refer to unfavourable characteristics. The more important factors for the satisfied girls, were, evidently, the extent to which they found their supervisors encouraging and kind and their firms up to date. Only less satisfied girls referred to the lack of training; and, like the corresponding boys, were more inclined to feel that their firms had too many rules and regulations and were only out to make money (Table 94).

[13] Ibid.

Age and length of service

Several studies have shown that job satisfaction tends to increase with age[14] though this may reflect certain special aspects of the job role in relation to age and the seniority and responsibility associated with older workers.[15] One study of factory workers,[16] however, found that satisfaction increased with age because the most dissatisfied left when young and those who remained became increasingly resigned as they grew older. Super[17] and Wilensky[18] suggest that job satisfaction varies with age but shows cyclical changes. There is also some evidence[19] to indicate that older groups derive satisfaction more frequently from the social and technical environment, while for younger workers the intrinsic nature of the job is of greater importance.

In the present inquiry, job satisfaction varied only slightly with age as far as boys were concerned, the older leavers being a little less likely than others to be very satisfied with their jobs: no such difference applied to the girls. In any case, age differences spanned only a period of three years and were also closely related to length of service. Relatively few of the fifteen- and sixteen-year-olds had been in their present jobs for longer than one year, compared with more than one-half of the seventeen- and eighteen-year-olds. The variation in job satisfaction would thus appear to be more related to the time spent in the job, for when allowance was made for age and for occupational bias, there was some association evident between length of service and feelings about the job.

The association was different for boys than for girls. For the boys, the proportion 'very' satisfied was lower among those who had been longest in their jobs than were those who had been at work for six months or less: the opposite tendency applied to the girls, relatively more of those who had been in their jobs longest being 'very' satisfied than of the newcomers. On the other hand, there were fewer dissatisfied workers among the boys at work for longer than six months; and, in contrast, rather more dissatisfied girls whose length of service exceeded six months. It was not possible in view of the size of the sample and the inter-dependence of the many variables associated with job satisfaction to discover the exact reason for these contrasting tendencies. Nor was there any evidence from which to discover the extent to which more boys than girls may have started work with high expectations only to become disillusioned in time. Lady Venables was left in no doubt, apparently, that many of the boys in her sample of technical course students found the transfer to work a disillu-

---

[14] In particular, see S. Wyatt and R. Marriott, op. cit.

[15] J. R. Dale, *The Clerk in Industry*, Liverpool University Press, 1962.

[16] S. Wyatt and R. Marriott, op. cit.

[17] D. E. Super, 'Occupational Level and Job Satisfaction', *J. Appl. Psychol.*, **23**, No. 5, 1939.

[18] H. L. Wilensky, op. cit.

[19] F. Friedlander, 'Underlying Sources of Job Satisfaction', *J. Appl. Psychol.*, **47**, 1963.

sioning process. In her view, this was because of a tendency for adults to make promises that they did not, or could not, fulfil.[20] This tendency may operate more frequently in the case of boys than of girls because of the differences with which their respective long-term career interests are regarded, both by themselves and by others.

It is possible that part of the explanation for the particular relationships found in the present inquiry between job satisfaction and length of employment lies in the fact that rather more girls than boys, proportionately, were promoted or upgraded.[21] Promotion was itself associated with length of service[22] and, in the case of girls, with job satisfactions, higher proportions of the 'very' than of the 'moderately' satisfied having been promoted and, likewise, relatively more of those who had been promoted being the most satisfied (though these tendencies applied mainly to office workers).

Promotion prospects

It seemed logical to expect that where the chances of promotion were assessed as very good, job satisfaction would be higher.[23] This in fact was the tendency among the boys, and almost twice as many of the 'very', than the 'moderately', satisfied assessed their prospects as extremely or very good and, conversely, twice as many of the moderately, than the very, satisfied assessed their prospects as fair. This tendency was partly due to the apprentices in the sample who were more likely than others to be very satisfied with their jobs and much more likely than trainees or other manual workers to feel their prospects of promotion were good. Girls were not, apparently, affected in their feelings for their jobs by promotion prospects and were only a little more likely to feel they had little or no chance of promotion if moderately, than very, satisfied. Girls who had actually been promoted were much more likely to be very satisfied than those who had not—but the opposite tendency applied to boys. None of the dissatisfied boys or girls, however, assessed their prospects as more than fair, or had experienced any upgrading or promotion.

Size of firm

No association between job satisfaction and size of firm appeared evident, partly because the number of young people in the sample seen was too small to allow for detailed analysis of job satisfaction, occupation, and size of firm. Though attitudes to supervisors appeared to differ according to size of organization, this was subsequently found to be chiefly influenced by occupational bias. Occupations were not evenly distributed between

---

[20] E. Venables, 1965, op. cit.

[21] See Chapter XIII, page 213.

[22] See Chapter XIII, page 213.

[23] In the Veness inquiry, promotion as expressed in the job characteristic 'My work should give me the chance to get right to the top of my job' was one of the two most important selected.

firms of different sizes; the fact, therefore, that boys in smaller firms (employing 500 persons or fewer) and girls in larger firms (employing over 500 persons) tended to have a more favourable view of their supervisors in many respects, was found to be largely due to the relative concentration of certain categories of occupations (apprentices and clerical workers), with more positive opinions, in these firms. This was not so much the case, however, in regard to opinions on firms. The larger firms, irrespective of occupation, were associated with rather more frequent references to good welfare, security of employment, and efficiency, but also with rather more frequent references to too many rules and regulations, and strictness about time keeping. Though rather more boys in small firms than in large referred to their organizations being the right size, as many as one in eight employed in small firms also considered their firms too small. Boys in small firms were also more likely to feel that they were not getting enough training.

Similar tendencies were apparent in the Venables study.[24] Students valued the large firm because of its organization, sports and welfare arrangements, amenities and subsidized meals. The dissatisfied workers complained, however, that the larger firms were too impersonal and prone to favouritism. Outright dissatisfaction was, evidently, greatest with the medium-size firm, the most frequent complaint being that these were old fashioned, out of date and lacked proper training; the small firms were redeemed by their closer personal relationships.

AIMS AND ATTAINMENTS

As was shown in Chapter IX, as many as one in three school leavers were in employment which did not correspond with their original aims and the proportions were even higher—one-half of the boys and three-fifths of the girls—for those in relatively unskilled manual work. In so far as the employment obtained proved acceptable and, in time, was regarded as a wiser choice than the original job preference, modification of original aims was by no means necessarily associated with disappointment or regret. The fact of obtaining a job in accordance with original aims did not always mean that young people were satisfied with their jobs; some in fact changed to other types of employment when they found their first jobs unsuitable and not up to their expectations. Nor did it follow that leavers who obtained work other than that which they would have preferred were necessarily dissatisfied. There was, in fact, only a very slight tendency for the young people who were very satisfied with their present jobs to be in work which corresponded more or less exactly with their first preferences, or for more of those in jobs which differed from their original aims to be among the moderately satisfied.

[24] E. Venables, 1965, op. cit.

It was the extent to which they still felt committed to their original choice which seemed to be more strongly associated with their present attitudes, particularly for girls. More, proportionately, of the moderately satisfied now felt that their first preferences had had to be relinquished than applied to the very satisfied; among the girls, twice as many of the less satisfied workers felt this way than of the most satisfied. Similarly, those who now felt that their present employment had involved giving up their original aims were much more likely to be among the dissatisfied, as well as among the moderately satisfied, workers.

REGRETS ABOUT PRESENT JOB

Relatively few workers had any regrets about having taken up their present jobs, and only small minorities were uncertain as to whether they had made the right decision. Regret or uncertainty more frequently occurred among the less satisfied workers and was more pronounced among relative newcomers, as far as girls were concerned, and among boys who had been at work between six and twelve months. Occupation as such made little difference to attitudes in this respect. It may be recalled, however, that though the majority of boys and girls had no regrets about leaving school, mainly because they were now happy to work and found work better than being at school, those with regrets or uncertainties about their school-leaving decision were less likely to be satisfied with their present jobs.[25] They were also less likely to have fulfilled their original vocational ambitions and to have found, if boys, work in semi- or unskilled manual occupations. They were also more likely now to regret, or to be uncertain about, their present jobs though this feeling was not exclusively theirs. It is not possible to know, however, from the evidence available, how far their present regrets were due to the actual work they were doing, or to the fact that their work was different from that originally wanted, or to any divergence between their attainment and their original hopes.

Logically enough, the more satisfied the workers the less frequently had serious thought ever been given to any change of employer and the more settled they felt in their present job. Though most workers had rarely or never seriously contemplated a change, the proportions were much higher among the 'very' than the 'moderately' satisfied. Among the boys, however, apprentices influenced the situation, since on the one hand they tended to be more frequently satisfied with their jobs and, on the other, were much more likely never to have considered any change during their training. Were it not for the apprentices, boys would have shown the same tendency as girls—namely, that rather more of those with longer service would have occasionally considered a change than among relative newcomers.

[25] See Chapter VI.

WORK AND LEISURE

The last of the questions relating to present employment was intended to discover from young people whether they derived greater satisfaction from their work or after-work activities. The majority of leavers—nearly three in five—responded to the question by saying that neither activity predominated; less than one in five referred chiefly to their work and slightly more—one in four—to leisure interests.

The proportions referring to work as the chief source of satisfaction were much higher, however, among the most satisfied than among the less satisfied workers; and the less satisfied the worker, the more likely that leisure rather than work activities brought greater satisfaction. Since it was the boys and girls in relatively unskilled work who were the least likely to be very satisfied in their work, they were also the ones who, if work and leisure were not equally balanced, found greater satisfaction in the activities pursued after work was done.[26]

SUMMARY

By grouping the replies of school leavers to an eleven point rating scale relating to their feelings about their present jobs, it was evident that over one-half of the boys and three-fifths of the girls were 'very' satisfied; between one-third and two-fifths 'moderately' so; and less than one in ten, dissatisfied. Boy apprentices and girl office workers were much more frequently well satisfied than were other workers, while leavers in the less skilled jobs, particularly girls, were the most frequently dissatisfied. It was also evident that even between the 'very' and the 'moderately' satisfied, the differences in the frequency with which positive interest items were selected was considerable.

Far more of the 'very' than of the 'moderately' satisfied, felt their jobs were interesting, required concentration, used their brains and were skilled; by contrast, it was the moderately satisfied who more frequently referred to their jobs as being too routine and monotonous. Similar tendencies applied to the girls though the differences were not so substantial. Though there was an occupational factor influencing these results, since apprentices and clerical workers had a higher score than did other workers on positive interest items, and were more frequently 'very' satisfied with their jobs, the differences according to job satisfaction were much greater than according to the type of employment. Though skilled and non-manual jobs were associated with being more interesting, it was evident that job satisfaction was more strongly associated with the interest appeal that certain jobs had for certain individuals. Apprentices, for instance, varied in the degree to which they found their work had intrinsic interest

[26] Leisure activities are more fully described in Chapter XIX.

for them, as did other manual workers in regard to the monotony or boredom of their jobs.

Attitudes to supervisors and firms were also found to vary with the degree of job satisfaction, though chiefly more on favourable than on unfavourable items. Almost every favourable aspect of supervision received a higher score from the more, than from the less, satisfied workers, particularly among the boys; the same tendency applied to favourable comments about firms, though the contrast between the well and the moderately satisfied workers was not so great or so frequent. When allowance was made for age and occupational bias, there was also some association evident between length of service and present feelings about jobs, the tendency being for boys with the longest service to be more frequently 'moderately' than 'very' satisfied; the opposite tendency applied to girls, however, and rather more of those who had been in their jobs longest were 'very' satisfied than of relative newcomers.

Job satisfaction was rather more frequent, among the boys, where the chances of promotion was assessed as very good, though this was partly due to the apprentices in the sample who were more likely than others to be very satisfied with their work and also to be more confident of their prospects. Though as many as one in three school leavers failed to find the type of employment which corresponded to their original aims, there was only a very slight tendency for more of those in jobs which differed from their early hopes to be, 'moderately', satisfied or for more of the 'very' satisfied to be in work which was consistent with their first preferences. But those who now felt that their present employment had involved giving up their original aims were much more likely not only to be among the moderately satisfied, but among the dissatisfied workers. Nonetheless, relatively few young people had any regrets about having taken up their present jobs and even fewer doubted whether they had made the right decision.

Regret or uncertainty was more frequent, however, among relative newcomers as far as girls were concerned and among boys who had been at work between six and twelve months. Those with regrets and uncertainties about their present jobs included rather more of those who had similar feelings about their school-leaving decisions. It is possible that this was due to the fact that regret and uncertainty about leaving school was associated with less frequent satisfaction at work. Most young workers, evidently, derived equal satisfaction from work and their leisure interests, but the proportions referring to work as the chief source of satisfaction were much higher among the 'very' than among the 'moderately' satisfied; the less satisfied the worker, moreover, the more likely that leisure rather than work brought the greater satisfaction.

Those factors which emerge in the present inquiry as having some relevance to attitudes to work are consistent with the results in the N.I.I.P.

study. It would appear that for school leavers, as for adults, the type of employment followed, the intrinsic interest of the job performed, the quality of the supervision and the evaluation of the firm in relation to efficiency, training facilities, and disciplinary regulations, were all important factors associated with the degree of job satisfaction.

CHAPTER XVII

A COMPARISON OF THE VIEWS OF
EMPLOYERS AND YOUNG WORKERS

INTRODUCTION

Since employers and young people were asked identical questions concerning the characteristics of jobs and the method and length of training, it was thought of interest to compare their respective replies. As there have so far been relatively few objective job studies, employers represent the chief source of information about available employment for official and other types of vocational advice. It is they who advertise, who notify youth employment bureaux and other agencies of their requirements and conditions of employment; and who supply information to interested applicants. The attempt to give young people accurate and realistic information about employment could, therefore, be frustrated if there is undue bias in the employers' concept of what particular jobs involve; if certain characteristics are under- or over-emphasized; or if the prospects are held to be better than is, in fact, the case. Moreover, school leavers themselves are likely to feel disappointed, if not disillusioned, if the jobs they enter do not correspond in practice with what they were told or led to expect.

To make a valid comparison between the replies of employers and school leavers, it was necessary to confine the analysis to those job descriptions and interview schedules relating to identical jobs. This gave comparable data for 144 jobs for boys and 108 jobs for girls, representing three-quarters of the sample of young people actually seen and two-fifths of the total number of jobs described by employers.

JOB CHARACTERISTICS

The comparison showed that employers, generally, placed more emphasis on positive and less emphasis on negative features of the job described, than did young workers. More than twice as many boys' jobs were referred to as skilled and of girls' as providing a chance to use initiative by employers than by the workers who performed them (Tables 95 and 96). Employers also, more frequently than their employees, described jobs as having other positive interest characteristics, as being responsible, allowing a pause when wanted, as steady and well paid; and, as far as boys' jobs

TABLE 95. Job characteristics as selected by employers and
young workers: boys.[a]

	Selected by		Ratio of (1) and (2)
	Employers (1)	Boys (2)	
Positive interest	*(Per cent of total)*		
Skilled	50	21	2·5
Varied	62	34	1·8
Uses brains	55	33	1·7
Chance to use initiative	56	38	1·5
Interesting product or service	42	31	1·3
Negative interest			
Routine	3	14	0·4
Monotonous	8	13	0·6
Not enough skill	30	7	4·3
Total (Multiple replies)	100	100	
(No. of jobs)	(144)	(144)	

a Excluding items for which ratio of employer's to workers' percentages was between 0·7 and 1·2.

TABLE 96. Job characteristics as selected by employers and
young workers: girls.[a]

	Selected by		Ratio of (1) and (2)
	Employers (1)	Girls (2)	
Positive interest	*(Per cent of total)*		
Chance to use initiative	59	26	2·3
Varied	43	35	1·3
Uses brains	45	34	1·3
Interesting	31	40	0·7
Interesting product	18	32	0·6
Negative interest			
Not enough skill	33	9	3·7
Monotonous	27	6	4·3
Total (Multiple replies)	100	100	
(No. of jobs)	(108)	(108)	

a Excluding items for which ratio of employers' to workers' percentages was between 0·7 and 1·2.

were concerned, as difficult and teaching them something useful and girls', as associated with working with a good crowd. The contrast between the employers' and young workers' views as regards promotion prospects was particularly striking, since only one in four of the boys and one in three of the girls referred to this item, compared with seven in ten of the employers. An even sharper contrast applied to girls' jobs, two-fifths of which were felt by employers to require nimble fingers, compared with only one in twenty of the girls themselves who were of this view (Tables 97 and 98).

There was agreement between employers and boys in so far as jobs were considered interesting, mainly indoors, sitting and having a good crowd to work with; and with girls, in so far as the work was considered routine, noisy, associated with a lot of moving about, and teaching them something useful.

Only a few items were referred to more frequently by young workers than by their employers; boys, for instance, were more likely to describe their jobs as routine, monotonous, and dirty; but girls were rather more inclined than were their employers, to feel that their jobs were interesting and associated with an interesting product or service.

TABLE 97. Job characteristics as selected by employers and young workers: boys.[a]

	Selected by		Ratio of (1) and (2)
	Employers (1)	Boys (2)	
Demand	*(Per cent of total)*		
Difficult	23	6	4·0
Responsible	55	28	1·9
Keeps you busy	66	47	1·4
Pause when you want to	53	39	1·3
Physical			
Clean	45	20	2·3
A lot of moving about	37	25	1·5
Dirty	8	24	0·3
Social, pay, prospects, etc.			
Offers promotion prospects	70	27	2·6
Well paid	28	19	1·5
A steady job	74	51	1·4
Teaching something useful	65	45	1·4
(No. of jobs)	(144)	(144)	

a Excluding items for which ratio of employers' to workers' percentages was between 0·7 and 1·2.

TABLE 98. Job characteristics as selected by employers and
young workers: girls.[a]

	Selected by		Ratio of (1) and (2)
	Employers (1)	Girls (2)	
Demand	*(Per cent of total)*		
Needs nimble fingers	41	5	8·2
Responsible	59	22	2·7
Pause when you want to	40	27	1·5
Keeps you busy	79	56	1·4
Physical			
Dirty	..	8	..
Clean	69	39	1·8
Mainly sitting	44	25	1·8
Social, pay, prospects, etc.			
Well paid	68	29	2·3
Offers promotion prospects	66	31	2·2
A steady job	76	38	2·0
Work with a good crowd	74	54	1·4
Total (Multiple replies)	100	100	
(No. of jobs)	(108)	(108)	

a Excluding items for which ratio of employers' to workers' percentages was between 0·7
and 1·2.

Types of employment

The opinions of employers and young workers and the differences
between them varied considerably according to the type of employment
described. The employers differed from their apprentices on questions
associated with the skilled nature of the job and with job security, pay,
and prospects, referring to these items more frequently than did the
apprentices themselves; the contrast was particularly sharp in regard to
the skill of the work and to promotion prospects, employers' references in
this latter regard outnumbering those of apprentices by four to one. A
similar tendency applied to other manual workers' jobs, some of which
were more frequently described by employers as varied, using the brain
and initiative and others as monotonous and requiring little skill.

Office girls were far less frequently inclined than were their employers
to regard their jobs as having positive interest characteristics; but in the
case of girls' manual jobs, a different tendency applied, since their monotony and lack of skill were stressed by employers rather than by young
workers. Thus, clerical workers appear to have found their work less

interesting, and manual workers their jobs less monotonous, than was the belief of their respective employers. Girls in clerical work, as apprentices, were also the more likely to differ from their employers on questions of pay, prospects, or steadiness of the job.

Aspects of work liked and disliked

It was evident that employers tended to over-emphasize the popularity of some features and to under-estimate the unpopularity of others. Employers were also less likely to know about unpopular aspects, since higher proportions of them were uncertain in this regard than in relation to attractive features. A higher proportion of employers, for example, believed that employment conditions (hours, holidays, facilities, etc.) were popular than was, in fact, the case among young workers. Similarly, a higher proportion believed that girls in their employment found a particular process of task attractive to them or that they liked their fellow workers, than actually applied to the girls concerned. Moreover, employers tended to over-emphasize inadequate pay and conditions and, as far as boys were concerned, dissatisfaction with training and uninteresting work, as unpopular features. They were less inclined, however, than were the workers, to specify the popularity of lenient discipline, or the unpopularity of tea making and carrying out the 'odd jobs', both of which were regarded unfavourably by young workers.

TRAINING

There were also differences between employers' and young workers' replies in regard to methods and length of training. Employers, rather more frequently than workers, stated that instruction was given by supervisors and training instructors and far less frequently by fellow workers, than was the view of the girls. Young workers, on the other hand, were more inclined than were their employers to state that their training had been given on the job and did not so frequently refer to training schools or departments.

How far this was due to new entrants being unable to distinguish, in the early weeks, the status of one adult in authority from another, could not be ascertained. There is also the possibility that training schedules were not being kept to by the firms in question.

Employers' assessments of the time required to learn the basic elements of the jobs in question tended to be slightly longer, on average, than that of boys (4·9 months compared with 4·3 months), and more so than that of the girls (3·4 months compared with 1·9 months). Average training times varied, however, according to the type of employment described, the estimates of girls in offices, and boys in less skilled manual work, being the most frequently at variance with those of their employers.

THE PATTERN OF VIEWS

The differences between the views of employers and their young workers arose mainly because of a tendency for employers, generally, to place relatively more emphasis on positive features and relatively less emphasis on negative features. Overall, however, the pattern of views was not very different, except for some occupations and for some particular aspects of employment. The most striking of these differences was the contrast between the relatively high proportion of employers and the low proportion of workers who stressed the skill and promotion prospects of apprenticeships; the job security, pay prospects, and positive interest factors of office work for girls; the negative jobs interest factors of office work for girls; the negative jobs interest factors of the less skilled manual workers; and the need for finger dexterity for girls in clerical and manual work.

A degree of disagreement was to be expected. Employers may have seen certain aspects of the work they offered in more positive terms than was justified because of the nature of the inquiry and its interest in opportunities for adolescent workers. Some of the management representatives may have begun their work in similar jobs and their judgment may have been influenced by their own subsequent progress and achievements. In some instances, management may have failed to convey the actual prospects to young workers, or young workers may have failed to discover these for themselves, particularly, perhaps, in the larger firms which specified favourable conditions, including promotion prospects, for all or most of their apprentices. The results may also reflect possible areas of disagreement between managements and workers, between generations and, as far as attitudes to certain types of work are concerned, between social classes. In any case, it was to be assumed that the feelings derived from direct experience would not correspond, in any precise degree, with those derived from the observer's concept of this experience.

If the tendency of employers to place greater emphasis than their employees on the more favourable aspects of employment applies more generally, then some doubt would seem to arise as to the validity of using information about available employment obtained from employers alone, for vocational advice purposes. This would suggest not only that objective job studies of individual jobs are required, but also that there is need to draw on the direct experience of young workers themselves and to recognize its relevance for vocational advice given to school leavers.

CHAPTER XVIII

THE CONCEPT OF SUITABLE EMPLOYMENT

INTRODUCTION

In the vocational guidance setting, 'suitable employment' generally means that which allows for the closest matching of individual abilities, aptitudes, and interests with the requirements and characteristics of particular occupations. The 'talent matching' model of vocational guidance is essentially market-orientated. It tends to ignore the concept of individual need, fails to incorporate motivation as an influential variable and emphasizes selection for the job according to the value of qualities which have an exchange value in the labour market. To the extent that the 'saleable' qualities correspond with market requirements, so a 'match' is achieved.

Since few occupations allow for the full use of talents, while a large proportion of jobs for adolescents, as for adults, require little technical or other skill, any match achieved is minimal. In many cases, it depends on the capacity of the individual to modify his inclinations, and to function with many of his known and unknown talents dormant. The fact that prevailing attitudes imply that work, for most individuals, is rarely a source of pleasure or satisfaction, discourages the idea that it might be an activity to be enjoyed or a means of self-development, and strengthens the assumption that the meagre correspondence between the distribution of ability and the job preferences of young people, on the one side, and the occupations available, on the other, is a regrettable but inevitable necessity in an industrial society.

Allied to this is the belief that because post-war educational reform has extended entry into selective and higher education to working-class children, the present distribution of young people at various occupational levels approximates to the distribution of the existing 'pool' of ability, the size of which is unlikely to be increased.

It has been demonstrated, however, that within broad limits the amount of talent among young people—or in the nation as a whole—is not fixed but is, rather, a variable subject to the influence of certain environmental factors.[1] The intellectual reserves of a nation can rise or fall depending on the extent to which official policies, the educational system and the strength of individual motivation, favour the development of potential talent. The educational system and the population respond to new demands for an

[1] J. E. Floud, op. cit.

increase in the supply of talent, and where there is a need for more educated persons, more persons are found to qualify for further and higher education. Moreover, as Halsey and others have argued, there is also the need to define ability not in the singular, but 'as a whole range of human skills and excellences, literature, numerate, and manual'.[2] Any change that society puts upon its members reveals new abilities among them, so that programmes and policies designed to develop talent would seek and find new abilities and skills.

In most countries, there is a waste of potential skill, either because of low levels of economic development or, as in the case of economically developed countries, of the influence of social and cultural factors on the nature and development of ability. In the latter case, as has been shown in studies by Jean Floud, the gap between the demands and assumptions of schools, and the skills and assumptions that children bring with them to school, widens as the social composition of secondary schools becomes increasingly representative of the population at large, and contains substantial proportions of working-class children. 'The existence of social class differences in ways of life, values, attitudes, and aspirations as well as material circumstances are expressed in different responses to schooling, even at the same level of measured intelligence.'[3] There is a social, as distinct from an academic, process of selection which operates in favour of children whose cultural background is consistent with, and against children whose background does not correspond to, the expectations of the school. The present distribution of young people according to occupation does not, therefore, represent the result of 'talent' finding its own level, for ability, educational opportunity, and performance are nothing like in perfect relationship.

In the light of these factors, the present concept of suitable employment would seem to have little meaning. Setting aside all other considerations mentioned, and on the assumption that the minds of most young workers are capable of further development, quite apart from the considerable reserves of talent among them, then only that employment which offers the opportunity for continued development of the individual can properly be regarded as 'suitable'.[4]

AN ASSESSMENT OF SUITABILITY

Using this concept as a basis, an attempt was made to assess the suitability of the employment of the under-eighteens as recorded in the present inquiry. As purely illustrative criteria, the following six conditions were assumed to be necessary to favour such development:

[2] Ibid.

[3] See Jean Floud, op. cit.

[4] It could be argued that suitability, in the last analysis, can be satisfactorily defined only by the individual concerned.

(a) formal and prolonged training extending at least until the age of eighteen;

(b) attendance through day release at vocational and non-vocational courses;

(c) the acquisition of varied skills and experience useful in other types of employment;

(d) good prospects for promotion, at least to more skilled and responsible work;

(e) interesting and varied work which provided for some independent control, initiative, and thought; and

(f) the existence of a delegated person in the employing firm responsible for the general welfare and training of young persons.

These conditions cannot, of course, be regarded as covering all those necessary to ensure the development of the individual; a more precise study of the work environment than was possible in the present inquiry would be required to establish definitive criteria, to assess their relative importance and to explore the more intangible influences of social relationships and types of organization, on the development of young workers. Taken in the aggregate, however, they served the immediate purpose of providing, on a provisional basis, some measure by which the jobs included in the inquiry could be considered as suitable or otherwise for the young people engaged on them.

On the basis of the employers' descriptions, the majority of apprenticeships could be regarded as suitable employment, since the criteria suggested above applied to most of these jobs. A substantial number of jobs as trainees, though not the majority, could also be said to qualify, though fewer trainees than apprentices were covered by day release, extended training or the appointment of welfare or training officers. Few of the non-manual jobs complied with all the conditions, though the majority were covered by good promotion prospects, very useful job experience, varied work and welfare, and training provisions. Most other manual jobs for boys, however, and virtually all those for girls, were assessed as unsuitable, since most failed to qualify on day release, none on extended training, and few were covered by any one of the other conditions assumed to be necessary. On balance, more than one-half of the jobs considered, predominantly the less skilled manual, would appear to have failed to qualify on the criteria adopted, and could be assessed, therefore, as unsuitable.

For the sample of jobs described by young workers (many of which were also described by their employers), only a minority of apprenticeships, and fewer, proportionately, of jobs as trainees or non-manual workers, qualified, chiefly because only small proportions assessed their promotion prospects as good, while much lower ratings, compared with the employers, were given to the various interest items associated with their work. A generous estimate, even leaving out of account promotion prospects, on which there was a fair degree of uncertainty, is that not more than one in five of the jobs, as described by young workers, complied with the remainder of the assumed criteria. The majority, therefore, could be assessed as unsuitable.

If a measure is taken somewhere in between these two assessments, it would appear that at least three in five of the jobs considered would fail to qualify as suitable employment for young people under eighteen. This proportion is high enough to suggest, at first glance, that the criteria used here might form only a part of all those which would be required if the objective was to give a predominantly educational influence to the work environment and to make work a means for the fuller development of the individual.

The extent of unsuitable employment, as shown in the present inquiry, reveals a situation which for too long has been accepted with complacency, namely, a disregard for the educational needs, in the broadest sense, of the majority of young adolescent workers and a failure to discover or to develop their potential abilities and aptitudes.

PART V

OTHER ASPECTS
OF THE TRANSITIONAL YEARS

CHAPTER XIX

OTHER ASPECTS OF THE TRANSITIONAL YEARS

INTRODUCTION

It was not the intention of the present inquiry to examine in detail any other aspect of the transitional years. To have done so would have unduly prolonged the inquiry without adding greatly to existing information. A great deal of research, for example, has been undertaken in recent years into the leisure activities of young people and interest has grown in the question of interpreting and providing for their social needs;[1] perhaps, because the social life of young adolescents is a sphere in which they may more easily and conspicuously assert their independence than is possible in school or at work. It was felt useful, however, to include in the present inquiry some questions relating to leisure interests and activities and to trace the extent to which interests and opinions varied according to school experiences, the type of employment followed and the degree of job satisfaction expressed.

Many writers have argued[2] that the period of transition between school and work is a crucial stage in the development of adolescents and a time when they need particular guidance, reassurance and encouragement. The pilot study had shown that young people had experienced difficulty in one or more of the situations that had faced them since leaving school and would have liked more help than was available to them. It was, therefore,

---

[1] In particular, these include:

M. Abrams, 'The Younger Generation', *Encounter*, May 1956.

K. M. Evans, *Club Members Today*, National Association of Mixed and Girls' Clubs, 1960.

P. Jephcott, *Some Young People*, Allen and Unwin, 1953.

—, *Time of One's Own*, Oliver and Boyd, 1967.

J. W. Reeves and P. Slater, 'Age and Intelligence in relation to Leisure Interests', *Occ. Psych*, **21**, No. 3, July, 1947.

M. Stewart, 'The Leisure Interests of Grammar School Children', *Brit. J. Ed. Psych.*, **20**, Part II, 1950.

L. T. Wilkins, op. cit.

—, *The Youth Services in England and Wales*, op. cit.

15–18, op. cit.

[2] These include:

M. Carter, op. cit.

T. Ferguson and J. Cunnison, op. cit.

M. E. M. Herford, 1957, op. cit.

L. Paul, *The Transition from School to Work*, Industrial Welfare Society, 1962.

Report of the Director-General, Part I, Youth and Work, International Labour Organisation, 1960.

T. Veness, op. cit.

considered necessary in the present inquiry to discover from larger numbers what these situations were: how they were now assessed; which were considered to be the most important in the lives of young people; and those on which advice and information was felt to be most required. Some of these questions were also considered in the light of attitudes to school and work. It was hoped that this information would help in assessing the extent to which existing community services for young people might be improved or extended.

CHIEF LEISURE ACTIVITIES

Chief activities

Young people were first asked what were their main leisure activities; how they had spent the previous evening;[3] whether they belonged to a club; and whether they ever felt bored or uncertain as to what to do after work.

Boys' leisure interests contrasted sharply with those of girls', when they each described how they spent most of their spare time. Boys' activities, for example, were concentrated, particularly, on sports[4] and one in three referred to outdoor games such as football, and to cycling or athletics; and one in seven to indoor interests, such as wrestling, swimming, table tennis, etc. Outdoor sports were hardly mentioned by girls, however, and though they were just as likely as boys to refer to indoor games, their chief activities were social, chiefly dancing.[5] This activity alone accounted for over two in five of their replies. Though dancing, with crafts, was second in importance for boys, less than one in five referred to it as one of their chief pursuits.

Third in importance for boys, but second for girls, were spectator activities, chiefly the cinema;[6] relatively more girls than boys referred to this, as they also did to listening to radio and records. Girls were also much more inclined than boys to be involved in reading and in domestic chores, and to refer a little more frequently to courting.

The preceding evening

Naturally enough, far fewer young people were actually involved in any one activity on the evening previous to their interview. Hardly any of the boys, for example, were involved in sports, outdoors or indoors; very few

[3] The week-night immediately preceding the interview, which included Friday but not Saturday or Sunday.

[4] This is consistent with other studies, e.g. Wilkins found that 61 per cent of young men named sport as a strong interest. (See L. Wilkins, op. cit.)

[5] Dancing was found to be particularly high for modern school girls in the Social Survey for the Crowther Report and by M. Stewart, op. cit.

[6] The Social Survey of the Crowther Report also found the cinema to be an important activity for girls. (See 15–18, op. cit.)

girls, or boys, had gone dancing or visited the cinema. Spectator activities, particularly television viewing, were the most frequently described and as many as one in three of the boys and almost one-half of the girls had spent the evening in question at home.[7] There were relatively few differences, moreover, in the respective activities of boys and girls, though more boys, proportionately, had spent the evening studying, at classes or doing their homework, or had been with friends; and relatively more girls had been busy with domestic tasks or were uncertain as to how to describe their time.

Some contrast between overall interest and one evening's activities was to be expected; it is possible that weekend activities might have shown a closer relationship to the chief leisure occupations than did any one evening during the working week. It is also possible that in describing their chief interests, young people had in mind how they spent their time at weekends; or they may have been inclined to describe popular, but nevertheless infrequent, activities. Whatever the reason, their descriptions of how they spent the previous evening suggest that a typical week night for substantial proportions of under-eighteens, was an evening at home, watching television, listening to the radio or records, washing their hair, mending their bikes, chatting to the family and going to bed early. Relatively few of those who had been out for the evening, evidently, were involved in any organized entertainment or activity.

The pattern of leisure activities, both in general and on one particular evening, did not appear to be markedly related to attitudes to leaving school, type of occupation, and job satisfaction. Enthusiastic leavers seemed less likely than others to refer to social activities with friends and, as far as girls were concerned, more frequently to courting; enthusiastic leavers among the girls had also more frequently than others spent the previous evening away from home and had less frequently watched television. The only difference among the boys, however, was that those who had been the most eager to leave school tended to refer to rather fewer activities, on average, than did the less willing school leavers.

As regards occupational differences, girl manual workers were more likely than others to refer to domestic tasks, to courting, to the cinema, and to a lesser extent, to dancing; they were also more frequently engaged in home activities, such as domestic chores, watching television and reading on the previous evening. Among the boys, apprentices were more likely than others to be involved in watching sport, while manual workers were more frequently involved in social activities with their friends; apprentices were also the only group to refer to studying.

It may be recalled that there was a tendency for the young people who were the least satisfied with their jobs to be the ones who, if work and

[7] Similar proportions were also found to have spent the previous evening at home in the Jephcott inquiry. (See *Time of One's Own*, op. cit.).

leisure were not equally satisfying, found greater satisfaction in the activities pursued after work was done. Job satisfaction, as such, however, would not seem to have been associated with any very different pattern of leisure activities; moderately satisfied girls were more inclined than others to refer to dancing and going out with friends as their chief activities, and to watching television on the evening previous to their interview. No such differences were apparent among the boys.

Club membership

Young people were asked if they belonged to any kind of club or society. No distinction was made in the analysis of their replies between youth clubs, religious or uniformed organizations or hobbies groups, or in the number of clubs or organizations to which young people belonged. Just under one-half of the boys, and one-third of the girls, were members of some organization; of those who were not, one in three had, at some time or another, belonged to one but had lapsed from membership.[8] The proportions belonging to a club or society were considerably higher than found in other inquiries. This may have been due to the fact that the sample in the present inquiry contained boys and girls who were in further education, a factor which in the Social Survey for the Crowther Committee,[9] was shown to be associated with higher club membership. The Cardiff survey also concluded that the educational flavour of youth clubs sometimes made them unattractive for those who wished to leave their school setting behind them; and that clubs were sometimes organized in such a way as to make it easier for those with grammar school backgrounds and more social skills to use them. The Social Survey[10] also found club membership higher among grammar and technical school leavers than among modern; and the National Service Survey[11] (also for the Crowther Committee), that club membership was associated with selective schooling and higher intelligence. The tendencies in the present inquiry for club membership to be higher among the reluctant than the enthusiastic leaver, among the selective than the secondary modern school boy and among non-manual workers and the sons and daughters of non-manual workers, might be related to these factors.

Such factors were not directly apparent, however, in the reasons offered for not being members of clubs or other organizations, though some of these might be so interpreted. One in five of non-members felt clubs were not

[8] The higher proportion of boys, than of girls, who were members of clubs is consistent with the findings of other studies. Research in Cardiff and Sheffield found, for example, that membership declined after the age of sixteen, in the first months after leaving school, and more rapidly among girls than boys. (See A. Crichton and E. James, 'Youth and Leisure in Cardiff, 1960', *The Sociological Review*, **10**, No. 2, July, 1962 and M. Carter, op. cit.)

[9] *15–18*, op. cit.

[10] Ibid.

[11] Ibid.

suitable for them—they preferred to go about with one or two friends, following their own interests, making their own entertainment, without being organized or controlled; or they associated clubs with being too rough, too crowded, or offering restricted activities; or membership of the clubs they knew about was conditional on attending a church. As many as one in five also said that they knew of no suitable club in their neighbourhood.

Lapsed membership was associated with more direct criticisms of the management of clubs, activities, and members. Managements were felt to have been too strict and controlling; the activities boring and 'dreary'; the members rough or too young;[12] the club's reputation dubious. Over two in five of the replies of one-time club members were of this nature. Finding a 'regular' boy or girl friend was the reason offered by one in five for having left their clubs and a similar proportion stated that their clubs had closed down; almost as many had found that they were too busy. A very small proportion—about one in twenty—had been asked to leave (or in their own words, had 'been chucked out').

Boredom

Relatively few young people, evidently, experienced at all frequently the feeling of boredom with, or uncertainty as to how to spend, their spare time. Substantial proportions, though relatively more girls than boys, were sometimes bored; comparable numbers, however, though rather more boys than girls, never experienced this mood. The frequency of boredom appeared to vary in some degree with attitudes to leaving school, present occupation, job satisfaction, and club membership, but the variation was not consistent for boys and for girls. It was only the enthusiastic boy leavers, for example, who were less likely than others to be frequently bored and more likely never to feel this way; it was only the boys who were very satisfied with their employment who were also less likely than others to feel frequently fed up or uncertain, and more likely never to be in this mood; it was only the manual workers among the girls who more frequently than others experienced some boredom in connection with their leisure. Moreover, in so far as club membership appeared to be associated with the frequency of boredom, the association only applied to boys, who were far less likely to experience frequent boredom and much more likely never to do so if they were club members than if they were not.

Curiously enough, girls who were never bored tended, as did the corresponding boys, to refer much more frequently than others to spending the previous evening at a club, but only boys showed this same tendency when describing their chief activities, relatively more of those who were never fed up or uncertain what to do referring to club activities.

[12] P. Jephcott found that older adolescents were deterred from joining clubs if there were too many fourteen-year-old members. (See Some Young People, op. cit.)

There were few other differences between those sometimes, and those never, bored in regard to their leisure activities, though girls who were never bored were more inclined than others to refer to indoor sports and to studying, and less inclined to refer to the cinema when describing their chief interests; they were also much more likely to have been involved in crafts (knitting, sewing, embroidery), and to have been at home when describing their previous evening. Both boys and girls who never experienced boredom were also more inclined than others to refer to a greater number of activities on average, though this was more marked for girls than for boys.

Friendships

Since social activities are, to some extent, related to friendships, it was decided to ask young people how many close friends they had. Boys tended to have either relatively few—under four—or six or more; the replies of girls tended to be relatively concentrated between one and three; they were more likely than boys, however, to have none and as many as one in ten were in this category, compared with one in twenty of the boys. The average number of close friends—six—did not vary, however, according to sex or to occupation, social class, or job satisfaction. Work was not the main source of close friendships and only one intimate friend, on average, was said to derive from work. Two-fifths of the boys, and over one-half of the girls said that they had no close friend at work, and between one in four and one in five only one. Friendships at work were no doubt associated with the size of firm, and the extent to which young people worked with their own age group. There was a tendency, however, for manual workers to be more likely than others to have more than one close friend at work; this may have been associated with the fact that rather more of the relatively unskilled manual workers lived close to their work which may, in itself, have encouraged close friendships; and with the fact that some of the girls in manual work had found employment in the same firm as a close friend.

In addition to their close friends, one-third of the boys and one-half of the girls also said that they were going 'steady' with one regular friend of the opposite sex and, of these, similar proportions were either engaged to be married or were planning to become so in the near future; many more boys, proportionately, were contemplating, than had actually committed themselves to, engagement. Most of the girls who were engaged, or expecting to be, planned to marry before they were twenty, but most of the corresponding boys not until twenty-one or later. Less committed young people tended to plan to marry at a later age, the average age anticipated by the girls being 21·4 years, and by the boys, 23·6 years.[13] Engagement, actual

[13] For both boys and girls, the average anticipated age of marriage was somewhat lower than the actual average for all first marriages in England and Wales in 1965 (girls 22·0 years, boys 24·5 years). *The Registrar-General's Statistical Review, 1965,* H.M.S.O.

or planned, thus brought nearer the age at which young people hoped to marry.

FUTURE HOPES

As in the Veness and Wilkins inquiries,[14,15] references to marriage and children dominated the replies of girls to the question of what they hoped to be doing by the age of twenty-five. Though, in many cases, references were also made to continuing in work until the arrival of children or, in some cases, to the return to work when children were older, two in three referred exclusively to their hope for a family life. Those who commented on their future employment tended to assume that this meant remaining in the same kind of work, few assuming that any promotion was likely. A few girls talked of their wish to travel; two did not want to marry at all; and as many as one in six were uncertain about their hopes for the future.

By contrast, boys' hopes were almost exclusively vocational, and their references related chiefly to specific jobs or positions of higher skill and responsibility. Though this did not mean that hopes of marriage were not expressed, far fewer references were made to family life, as such, than among the girls, and these followed rather than preceded, their references to work. Over one-half of the boys expressed the hope that by the age of twenty-five they would be in more skilled and responsible work than at present. In most cases (two in five), this meant remaining in the same kind of work; in the remainder, particularly boys in other manual jobs, different work was anticipated, chiefly through changes of employer. One in eight made no reference to the type of work, as such, but to their hopes for a 'good job', 'good prospects', 'earning good money'; an equal proportion were hesitant and uncertain as to what their future might be or what they might be doing. Very few spoke of possible emigration, travel, joining the Armed Services, or of becoming self-employed.

Most boys in the present inquiry, therefore, hoped for personal advancement and, in this sense, could be regarded as 'ambitious'. That the girls appear to have been less so is presumably a reflection of their greater preoccupation with marriage, and their belief that their future achievements lay in this direction. Unlike the boys in the Veness inquiry, 'ambitiousness' did not vary according to educational background, though technical school leavers were not separately distinguished;[16] nor with attitudes to leaving school. Trainees and apprentices, however, were much more likely to foresee skilled work for themselves while clerical workers hoped for jobs with more senior responsibility and status. Other manual workers,

---

[14] Marriage was mentioned by 94 per cent of the girls and 67 per cent of the boys in their life histories. (See T. Veness, op. cit.)

[15] L. T. Wilkins, op. cit.

[16] Technical school leavers had a higher score than other leavers on the eight items used in a scale of ambitiousness. (See T. Veness, op. cit.)

on the other hand, were the most likely to hope that by changing their jobs they would obtain work of higher skill. Job satisfaction as such did not appear to influence the future hopes of boys, but higher proportions of the 'moderately' than of the 'very' satisfied girls referred to their hopes for marriage and family life.

SITUATIONS FACED SINCE LEAVING SCHOOL

One of the methods used in the Veness inquiry to yield information as to what seemed to be the most satisfying or impressive event in the lives of school leavers was to ask them to write about the one which they considered to be the 'best moment in their lives'. The replies showed that though there was some variation according to sex and the type of school attended, in general, themes about achievement, particularly those associated with examination results and sports events, and situations which had brought relief of anxiety, like the return of a sick parent to health, were far more frequently the subject of essays than were other events.[17] In order to obtain a similar assessment from the boys and girls in the present inquiry, they were asked what they felt to have been the best thing that had happened to them since leaving school; but so that difficult and troublesome situations might also be revealed, they were further asked about what was felt to have been the worst event since starting out to work.

Best events

The replies of young people concerning the best events in their post-school years were dominated by references to their present work, or to situations associated with being at work. In the light of the 'best moments' of the school leavers in the Veness inquiry, this suggests that many young people in the present inquiry may have found being at work not only a satisfying event in itself, but one which was associated with a sense of achievement in having found their present employment, and a relief from the anxiety of wondering what job to take, and what difficulties there might be for them. Over one in four young people, however, could think of no outstandingly satisfying event since leaving school, and approximately one in ten were uncertain (Table 99). Nearly one in four of boys and girls referred to their present employment as the 'best' event, and nearly one in three of the boys and one in six of the girls to their feelings of independence, freedom, and responsibility, to meeting new people and making new friends at work, to the pleasures of earning money or, in the case of boys, to their satisfaction with their training or with acquiring motor bikes, scooters, or other equipment. Girls, to a much greater extent than boys, referred to their having found a particular boy friend, to whom in some

[17] Op. cit.

cases they had become engaged, and with whom they were making plans for marriage. The birth of a new sister or brother, the marriage of a widowed parent, success in examinations, a special holiday and achievements in sports and hobbies were also some of the special occasions which had brought particular satisfaction and pleasure.

TABLE 99. Best events since leaving school.

	Boys	Girls
	(Per cent of total)	
None	27	26
Associated with		
Present job	24	24
Buying bikes, clothes, etc.	8	2
Earning money	8	3
Training/further education	8	1
Sense of freedom, independence, responsibility, etc.	4	7
Finding present girl/boy friend	4	16
Other	7	7
Don't know	8	12
No answer	2	2
Total	100	100
(No. of 15–18s)	(183)	(147)

Typical 'best' events were:

'Finding this job.'
'Getting used to the outside world.'
'Meeting more people.'
'Learning ten times more than I did at school.'
'Being congratulated for good work.'
'Saving up to buy my scooter.'
'Joining a beat group.'
'Meeting my girl friend.'
'My father getting married again.'
'Happier at work than at school.'
'Finding new friends at work.'
'Enjoy myself more. I have more freedom.'
'Being able to depend on myself and buy my own clothes.'
'Getting engaged.'
'Mother having a baby.'

Good experiences of this kind applied to most young workers, irrespective of their attitudes to leaving school, their job satisfaction or the type of occupation followed. The exceptions were, however, that much higher proportions of the boys and girls who were very satisfied with their jobs than of others referred to their present employment as a best event. Boys in relatively unskilled work tended more frequently than others to refer to the pleasures of buying things with their own money; and the corresponding girls were much more likely to feel that no 'best event' had occurred in their lives since leaving school.

The worst event

Fewer young people, proportionately, made any reference to a 'worst' event, suggesting that important events were more likely to have been positive than negative ones, or to have been remembered as such. In fact, one-half of the boys and girls questioned felt that there had been no event which could be assessed in these terms in their lives since leaving school, while just over one in ten were uncertain. A substantial minority, however (two-fifths of the boys and one-third of the girls), assessed at least one of their experiences as having brought particular unhappiness, disappointment, anxiety, or difficulties.

About one in ten leavers attributed their worst event to anxieties about finding work; with the first few weeks of work; with the disappointment of not finding the work they wanted; with certain aspects of their past employment; and with being at work as such (Table 100). Typical of their comments were:

'Not being able to find a job immediately I left school.'
'Frightening interviews for a job.'
'First days at first job; strange new faces and surroundings.'
'Being teased a lot and losing my temper when I first came here.'
'Not getting an apprenticeship and finding I would never get one.'
'Being ill and having to give up my job and training.'
'Giving in my notice for the first time.'
'Getting the sack.'
'Finding out the hard way that you have to stick up for yourself at work.'
'Lack of interest in me since leaving school.'

A further one in ten boys, but fewer, proportionately of the girls, referred to illnesses and accidents, the latter particularly associated with motor bikes but including accidents at work; moreover, many accidents and illnesses had involved a stay in hospital while some had necessitated surgical operations. Other school leavers referred to the loss of a mother or father, usually through death, but also through divorce or separation. Some school leavers had had to leave home to find suitable employment, and this had been an unhappy occasion for them. Other difficulties included family disagreements, 'trouble with the law', being in debt, worrying about examinations; and one girl interviewed had had a baby before the age of sixteen. In contrast to the 'best events', most 'worst' situations thus produced a sense of failure and anxiety, a sense of loss and injury at a time when success, achievement, and security were vitally important.

TABLE 100. Worst events since leaving school.

	Boys	Girls
	(Per cent of total)	
None	50	52
Associated with		
Finding and starting work, past employment, being at work, etc.	12	9
Accidents/illnesses	10	4
Loss of friends	3	6
Loss of parent	2	3
Leaving home	2	1
Not enough money	2	3
Other	7	7
Don't know	11	12
No answer	1	3
Total	100	100
(No. of 15–18s)	(183)	(147)

The transition from school to work, therefore, while associated with rather more positive than negative experiences on the whole, nevertheless brought particular difficulties for substantial numbers of young people. Moreover, for one in ten there were, evidently, no 'best' events to balance, in some degree, the 'worst'.[18] Since it is likely that similar events occur, to a greater or lesser extent, in larger populations of school leavers than those covered in the present inquiry, it would seem reasonable to assume that considerable numbers of young workers experience, in some degree, stress situations of the kinds described.

Chances missed in life

Since substantial proportions of young people had not achieved their original vocational aims and as many as one in three still felt committed in some way to their original choice, it was thought of interest to discover how many young people felt, in retrospect, that they had missed a chance in life to do something that they very much wanted, including non-vocational interests and activities. In the event, one in three of the boys and one in four of the girls now felt that chances had been missed, though the proportions were much higher for boys and girls in the less skilled manual jobs, among the less satisfied workers and enthusiastic school leavers. Views were frequently associated with a failure to obtain the work originally hoped for, with a strong, persistent hankering after their original

[18] One-third of the boys but two-fifths of the girls referred only to 'best' events, and one in five to neither a 'best' nor a 'worst'; boys were more likely than girls to refer to both kinds of experiences, the proportions being over one-quarter, and one-seventh, respectively.

vocational preferences, and the feeling that realization of their aims would have resulted in better jobs for themselves than those they now held. Thus, of the boys and girls who felt 'deprived', over two in five referred to their having missed the chance of certain kinds of work—either in jobs of different skill and status, or in different types of industry or firm, from that in which they were now employed. A better education, a chance to take examinations, regrets at not having been 'brighter' students at school, the wish to study languages or other subjects, represented the retrospective viewpoints of over one in four boys and girls; and opportunities missed in connection with sport the view of almost one-half of the boys who felt that they had either missed the chance of becoming professional sportsmen, particularly footballers, or of participating in organized sports since they had left school.[19] Other events, such as school outings or holidays, accounted for less than one in ten of present regrets (Table 101).

TABLE 101. Chances missed in life.

	Boys and Girls
	(Per cent of total)
Job in different trade, firm, skill, status, etc.	40
Better education, examinations, etc.	29
Sport[a]	25
Holidays, outings, etc.	5
Other	2
Don't know	3
No answer	1
Total (Multiple replies)	100
(No. of 15–18s)	(97)

a Only boys referred to this.

When asked why they felt they had missed the chances described, as many as one in five felt that they could have done better at school, worked harder for examinations, or made more effort in class. 'The boys called you sissy if you took things seriously but I could have been good.' 'I never put myself out at school, because the girls would call you "teacher's pet", but I could have learnt a lot more if I'd wanted', were the comments of two school leavers who were now inclined to self-criticism. As many as one in ten, however, felt that educational and vocational opportunities had passed them by because they lacked academic ability.

Accidental events had also played their part, particularly in sports, competitions, and holidays. A boy picked to run in a county match was ill

[19] When L. T. Wilkins asked adolescents whether they found the need for additional facilities of leisure, the replies referred mostly to sports and games. (See L. T. Wilkins, op. cit.)

on the day of the race; another boy crashed on his bike on the way to a football trial; a girl could not join a school holiday because of a family crisis.

Some school leavers, nearly one in ten, now felt that others had persuaded or prevented them from following up certain opportunities, particularly vocational; other events, chiefly holidays or outings were associated with lack of money at the time.

Thus, in the sample as a whole, as many as one in four of the young people now felt that educational or vocational opportunities had been missed and even more boys felt this way about sport. School leavers were almost as likely, however, to blame themselves, as to attribute their loss to other events, circumstances, or people, some of them, perhaps, recalling their eagerness to leave school. In less than one in ten cases, moreover, could it be assumed that very strong feelings about missed opportunities persisted.

ISSUES OF CHIEF CONCERN TO YOUNG PEOPLE

The pilot study had suggested that there were a number of situations likely to present difficulties to school leavers, some directly associated with their transfer from school to work, such as the decision to leave school, choosing and finding employment, training and their future prospects; and others associated with aspects of their personal development, particularly their relationships with their parents, and those arising from friendships with the opposite sex. It was not felt appropriate, however, for the present inquiry to include any detailed questioning of young people concerning their personal relationships, particularly in the work setting of the interview. Moreover, though young people in the pilot discussions had referred to their difficulties with parents, and to their relationships with the other sex, it was evident that there was need for much fuller exploration of these questions than was possible within the scope of the present inquiry.

It was decided, therefore, to compile a check list of items comprising those situations, which discussions with young people in the pilot study had suggested as representing some of their chief pre-occupations in the transitional years. A list of ten items was prepared which included situations associated with leaving school, finding work, training, prospects and social interest; and those associated with relationships with parents, with the other sex and planning for marriage and family life (the latter being rather ambiguous and open, perhaps, to the interpretation of family planning as such). School leavers were asked, first, to consider those issues with which young people of their age group were most concerned, or which were felt to be important in their lives; and second, to consider those on which more advice and information than was at present available was felt to be required.

The relative importance of situations

The analysis of school leavers' replies revealed several interesting features. First, finding the right kind of work was, evidently, the most important concern to young people, boys and girls alike, and over one-half of them referred to this issue; but other situations, for the boys, their future prospects and, for the girls, getting on with their parents and, for both, enjoying their spare time, were equally or almost as important. Second, though no other situation was selected by a majority of school leavers, most of the remainder were considered important by substantial minorities. More than two-fifths of the boys stressed getting enough training for their future work and careers, relationships with the opposite sex, getting on with their parents, and getting a good education; over one-third, making new friends and over one-fifth, planning for marriage and family life, and deciding when to leave school. Girls' 'scores' were, on average, lower for most items; nevertheless, two-fifths considered that making new friends, was of important concern to young people; while one-third referred to getting enough training, relationships with the opposite sex, and planning for marriage and family life (Table 102).

TABLE 102. Issues considered the most important
for under-eighteens today.

	Boys	Girls
	(*Per cent of total*)	
Finding the right kind of work	55	57
Future prospects at work	55	33
Enjoying their spare time	51	48
Getting enough training for their future work or career	45	37
Relationships with the opposite sex	44	35
Getting on with their parents	44	56
Getting a good education	42	27
Making new friends	37	40
Planning for marriage and family life	25	37
Deciding when to leave school	22	22
Total (Multiple replies)	100	100
(No. of 15–18s)	(183)	(147)

Third, though the differences between the replies of boys and girls were not, on the whole, substantial, boys tended to place much greater emphasis than girls on their future prospects, getting a good education, and enough training, which may reflect their particular anxieties and preoccupations in these respects. They were rather more likely than girls, moreover, to stress the importance of relationships with the opposite sex; this might be associated with the fact that fewer of them, than of girls, had a regular friend of the other sex[20] and some of them may have had difficulties in establishing relationships of this kind. Girls would appear to have had more difficulties, however, in their relationships with their parents, and to have given more emphasis than boys to what, after all, represented their vocational futures, namely, marriage and family life.

Fourth, the relatively high priority given to enjoying their spare time by both boys and girls suggests that the boundaries between work and leisure may be less determinate for young people than is generally assumed, and that something like a work-play continuum, as discussed by Cohen,[21] may apply to this age group in particular. There is also the implication that there is need to improve the degree and the quality of leisure activities.

Though, in general, opinions about the relative importance of the situations considered did not vary much according to educational background, job satisfaction, occupations, and social class, there were certain differences between school leavers on particular questions. Thus, for example, rather more, proportionately, of the boys who left at fifteen than at sixteen felt that the right kind of work and making new friends were of important concern; enthusiastic leavers, if boys, were more inclined than others to stress prospects, training, enjoying their spare time, and relationships with the other sex; and, if girls, then more frequently to emphasize their relationships with parents, the right employment, and their spare time. Girls who were only moderately satisfied with their present jobs also tended to emphasize these two latter questions.

As far as boys were concerned, only trainees differed from others in being, evidently, more concerned about prospects, the right kind of work, making new friends, and relationships with girls, suggesting that, as an occupational group, they may have had more uncertainties than others in these respects. Office girls, however, differed substantially from other workers in every respect, particularly from girls in manual jobs, and were more inclined to emphasize the importance of each question considered, corresponding closely in their replies to those of boys in their views that prospects, suitable employment, training, and a good education were important questions for young people today. This suggests that their vocational and, perhaps, social aspirations were higher than those of other occupational groups. Similar differences applied to girls, but not to boys, from the homes of non-manual workers who, in addition, also more frequently referred to the importance of relationships with their parents, with boys, and to planning for marriage and family life.

[20] See page 286.
[21] J. Cohen, 'The Ideas of Work and Play', *Br. J. Sociol.*, **4**, No. 4, 1953.

Situations in which further advice and information was felt to be required

There was a general tendency for each of the situations considered to be less frequently endorsed as requiring advice and information than as matters of concern to young people. This suggests that there may have been some resistance to the idea of special help on these questions being available to young people. Such resistance, if it existed, would seem to have applied more frequently to situations outside work, prospects, and training. It was matters associated with relationships with parents and with the opposite sex, with making new friends, and enjoying their spare time, which were far less frequently endorsed as requiring help than as being important in their lives; and it was on questions of deciding when to leave school, finding the right kind of work, future prospects, and training and, interestingly enough, planning for marriage and family life, that there was a closer correspondence between what was considered important and what required more information and advice than was at present available (Table 103).

TABLE 103. Issues on which further information
or advice required.

	Boys	Girls
	(Per cent of total)	
Finding the right kind of work	49	39
Future prospects at work	43	28
Getting enough training for their future work or career	40	32
Deciding when to leave school	27	22
Planning for marriage and family life	26	31
Getting a good education	23	14
Relationships with the opposite sex	21	18
Enjoying their spare time	18	7
Making new friends	8	10
Getting on with parents	9	16
Total (Multiple replies)	100	100
(No. of 15–18s)	(183)	(147)

One implication of this asymmetry would seem to be that help was considered more frequently to be required in situations where young people were particularly dependent on the decisions of adults. The entry of school leavers into employment is an entry into a predominantly adult world, where adults determine the kind of work available, the training received, and the prospects before them. The fact that between one-half and two-fifths of the boys felt that further help was required on these questions is a measure, perhaps, of the extent to which school leavers felt that their access to the jobs and opportunities they wanted was determined more by the kind of help extended to them by adults, than by their own efforts. Similar needs would apply to school-leaving decisions. That girls were less likely than boys to feel the need for help on these matters may have been because they were more inclined to envisage their futures in terms of marriage and family and their present working status as an interim phase in their lives.

Fewer young people (one in four) felt that further advice or information was required for planning and family life, this proportion closely corresponding, as already mentioned, to that which endorsed this question as a matter of importance. This is another sphere which could be regarded as associated with a degree of dependence on adult help. Getting married frequently involves the active support and co-operation of parents; family planning, the advice of specialists; and setting up home, accessibility to living space largely controlled by adults.

The fact that substantially smaller proportions[22] felt that more help was required in making new friends, enjoying their leisure time, getting on with their parents, and relationships with the opposite sex, than had endorsed these issues as important to young people, suggests that these may be situations in which young people are uncertain as to what kind of help would be appropriate. Perhaps they felt that such help would not be given without requiring some modification in their behaviour and outlook, or without implying some criticism of their inclinations and interests, a not unusual condition imposed on young people seeking advice. The boys and girls in the pilot study, with whom these questions were discussed more freely, and who expressed reluctance to seek adult help, gave the impression that they felt adults would not understand their point of view on these matters. It is likely, therefore, that these situations, since they related to their private, and not to their work, lives and to areas of conflict and misunderstanding between the generations, were felt to be ones on which they found it difficult to accept that adult intervention would be helpful to them.

There were, nevertheless, about one in five who felt that there should be more help available in regard to their relationships with the other sex; almost as many boys who felt this in regard to enjoying their spare time; while one in six girls felt that more help was required in relationships with parents.

There were only very few exceptions to the general consistency in the degree to which further information and advice was felt to be required, irrespective of educational background, social class, occupation, and job satisfaction; but present age did appear to have some bearing on the

[22] Only ten young people in all felt no help at all was required on any of the issues considered.

attitudes of young people to the situations they faced when leaving school, and to their assessment of possible further help required. Young workers of fifteen to sixteen were more likely to stress the need for help in getting enough training and making new friends; older workers, in finding the right kind of employment, a reflection, perhaps, of their own disappointments. Older boys were also more inclined to emphasize relationships with the opposite sex, and girls, relationships with their parents, enjoying their spare time, and planning for marriage and family life, again a reflection of the preoccupations of this age group.

It was not possible to trace the relative importance of these variables, nor the inter-relationships between them. It would seem, however, that any new or expanded community service designed to help school leavers in these or other situations would need to provide for diversity, both in regard to social and economic background and in the nature and type of help required.

SUMMARY

The sample of young people seen was fairly typical in regard to their leisure interests and activities, sports predominating for boys, and dancing and cinema-going for girls. Moreover, on a typical week, substantial proportions spent the evening at home and relatively few of those who were out were involved in any organized activity or type of entertainment. This was consistent with the fact that only a minority of boys and girls were members of clubs or other organizations. Lapsed club members were critical of their former club managements, activities, and members, and most young people who had never belonged to organizations, evidently preferred to follow their own choice of activities, alone or with friends. Relatively few young people were ever frequently bored with their spare time though over one in three were sometimes so; boys were less likely to be so if members of clubs.

Though one in ten of the girls and one in twenty of the boys said they had no close friends, most school leavers had several and, on average, six; work, however, was not a source of close friendships and only one friend, on average, was said to be also a workmate. Manual workers tended to have more close friends; one in three of the boys and one-half of the girls also had a regular friend of the other sex and, of these, similar proportions were engaged or planning to become so. Engagement, actual or contemplated, brought the anticipated age of marriage rather nearer than for other school leavers. Expectations of marriage dominated the replies of girls when questioned about what they hoped to be doing by the age of twenty-five, in contrast to the replies of boys, which were associated predominantly with vocational aspirations; one-half of the boys expressed the hope that they would be in jobs of higher skill, status and responsibility than at present.

Asked to assess the best and worst events in their lives, it was evident that important events were more likely to have been positive than negative experiences, though one in four leavers felt that there had been no outstanding experience, good or bad, since they had left school. Best events were associated particularly with their present employment, the feeling of independence, freedom, and responsibility acquired since starting work; meeting new friends; earning money and buying equipment and clothes; all reflecting a sense of achievement. Worst events were as frequently associated with illnesses, accidents, domestic tragedies, or situations, as with past or present employment and the disadvantages of being out of work. Many of the latter events could be regarded as stress situations giving rise to a sense of failure and anxiety.

The failure to find the kind of work originally wanted was one of the chief reasons given by the boys and girls who now felt that they had missed certain opportunities in their lives. This feeling applied to as many as one in three boys and one in four girls, who represented, predominantly, those who now felt educational and vocational opportunities had passed them by, though a small minority of boys felt this way about sport. School leavers were almost as likely to blame themselves as to attribute their missed chances to accidental events or to the intervention of others.

Asked to assess which of ten possible situations were considered to be the most important for young people today, more than one-half emphasized finding the right kind of work and enjoying their spare time; boys also emphasized their future prospects, while girls stressed relationships with their parents. Each of the situations considered was less frequently endorsed as requiring further advice and information, though between one-half and two-fifths of the boys felt that further help was required in finding suitable work, future prospects and getting enough training; and one in four young people, in planning for marriage and family life. It would seem that young school leavers distinguished between situations where adult help was associated with facilitating their entry into employment, their access to the right jobs and opportunities, their attainment of marriage and a home; and those situations associated with a degree of conflict and misunderstanding between generations where adult help was felt to be less appropriate.

PART VI

SUMMARY AND CONCLUSIONS

CHAPTER XX

A SUMMING UP

The results of the present inquiry would appear to confirm that the change from school to work is, in present-day society, a focal point in adolescent development, associated with uncertainties, disappointments, frustrations, and stress situations. Though most school leavers were glad to be at work, were moderately or well satisfied with their present jobs and felt a new sense of freedom and independence having left school behind them, each stage of the transition was, nevertheless, associated with difficulties of one kind or another for substantial proportions of them. This was apparent in relation to the last year or so at school, in the search for—and sometimes failure to find—the work they hoped for, in certain aspects of their past and present employment, and in personal and domestic events.

The inquiry has also revealed a general lack of correspondence between the needs and expectations of young people, on the one hand, and what is provided by the relevant community services, including industry, on the other. For most school leavers, neither school nor work offered an environment that could be regarded as a favourable one for the development of their potential.

School experiences

In education, teachers and schools would seem to have satisfied the educational needs of only some of the children and then only in some respects and in some degree. This conclusion is indicated, firstly, by the impressions of teachers and schools as recalled by school leavers. Though favourable outnumbered unfavourable comment, the only favourable references made by a majority of school leavers was that their teachers had been helpful; otherwise less than two in five remembered their teachers as having known their job, explained things clearly, or been encouraging or fair; rather fewer recalled their teachers as having been pleasant, efficient, good to work for or as having listened to what they wanted to say, and only small minorities as kind or clever. Strictness, having favourites, being sarcastic, and moody, were essentially the substance of many of the unfavourable memories left with children of their teachers and these made a stronger impression, evidently, than did certain favourable aspects.

Only among boys did a majority feel that their schools had offered them a good standard of education. Strictness in time keeping made the next strongest impact on boys and the strongest on girls, exceeding in frequency any other reference to school being recalled by nearly one-half of the total sample. Relatively few boys or girls remembered their schools as being friendly, up to date, helping everyone to do their best, having a good reputation or as efficient. Apart from the emphasis on punctuality, schools where the lessons were felt to have been a waste of time, where there had been too many rules and regulations, where, particularly for girls, they had been too strict about behaviour and where, particularly for boys, there had been insufficient practical training, would seem to have contributed most to the unfavourable impressions that substantial minorities of school leavers had of their schools.

Secondly, there were the principal reasons offered by school leavers for being eager to leave school and for having rejected the idea of a longer school life. A dislike of school, particularly among the girls (which centred mainly on teachers, aspects of school work, and on school restrictions) and, among the boys, the feeling of not learning anything and doubts as to their academic ability, were the most important reasons for wanting to leave school. Though the majority of boys and girls had considered, at one time or another, staying on at school, these combined with the feeling that, for the lower streams of ability, work was a more suitable activity than was further education, were also the chief reasons for having finally decided to leave.

For children with this kind of educational experience, starting work was, therefore, not so much a spontaneous decision of the rebellious or the bored, but the logical, rational, and inevitable response to what seemed likely to offer a more tolerable and sensible way of spending their time. A working life, though not necessarily in a job of their first preference, and even with its disciplines and conditions, was felt to offer more freedom, independence, interest and, possibly, enjoyment, than could school.

The subsequent experiences of those who had no regrets about leaving school would seem to have confirmed these expectations, since most commented favourably on the advantages of being at work, and referred to their being happier at work than they had been at school. Nonetheless, the relatively high proportion who approved of raising the school-leaving age indicates that support for more education exists even among those who had the least favourable experience of it. This suggests that a desire for more education might well be stimulated within and outside the classroom if only the gap between needs and fulfilment could be narrowed.

Young people who disliked school and felt it had nothing more to offer them represent the largest single group of school leavers seen—one in three. Several other small groups, however, may be distinguished, whose experience of school could be regarded as having been more satisfactory for them, though this did not necessarily mean that their school-leaving decisions were any less difficult for them than they were for those most eager to leave school. A second group consisted of boys and girls who were influenced in their decision to leave not so much by the immediate attraction of going out to work, but by their wish to take up employment that represented their considered choice, or which was consistent with their long-term vocational plans. School leavers in this group were relatively certain of their vocational preferences and were rather more concerned, than were others, for their future working careers.

There was a third group of boys and girls who decided to take up certain types of employment, not because this was their first preference, but because they were essentially uncertain about what to do. They doubted their academic ability; they were worried about the possible outcome of examinations; and they wondered about the value of academic qualifications as such. The offer or availability of certain types of employment, particularly if there was the opportunity for further education and training, or some other advantage for their future, seemed to them a wiser course of action than committing themselves to what seemed uncertain educational prospects.

Finally, there were boys and girls who were reluctant to leave school and who would have liked to have continued their education. Though small in number, this group is important since it represents children whose manifest wish for more education was denied. Boys, and to a greater extent girls, would seem to have left school against their will either because they felt they should begin to contribute to the family income, or because there were parental pressures for them to start work. There were also, however, small minorities who attributed their decision to leave to some special and unexpected condition at school: a new headmaster or teacher; a disciplinary incident; the unavailability of suitable courses; a change to co-education. Events such as these changed what had previously been a satisfactory situation to one that no longer made further full-time education attractive or possible.

School leavers who disliked or who were dissatisfied with school substantially outnumbered those in the sample whose decision to leave school arose from other considerations. No estimate of their proportions in a normal distribution of the school-leaving population can be made, however, since the young people seen did not constitute a fully random sample and, in any case, were drawn from one local area. The similarities, however, between them and the 'bored and apathetic' children who were the concern of the Newsom Committee, suggests that the experiences of these dissatisfied school leavers may be typical of many school leavers elsewhere.

Nonetheless, a dislike of and dissatisfaction with school, though primarily associated with an eagerness to leave, did not entirely preclude some modification in attitudes in the last year of school, provided that children felt that there was some change either in their treatment by the teachers which corresponded with the status they wished to have, and/or some change in the school programme which provided them with new intellectual interests or achievements.

Though children who were anyway more favourably disposed towards school tended to benefit more frequently from such changes in the last year, there were, nevertheless, some children who experienced new attitudes and began to feel 'that they were getting somewhere at last'.

The interaction of child, parent and teacher must be assumed to have ultimately determined decisions to leave school. Educational experiences, however, would seem to have played an important part in young people's own accounts of their school-leaving decisions. Moreover, unfavourable school experiences tended, in certain cases, to lead to the subsequent rejection of other services, particularly of further education and of the official guidance service.

The evidence thus suggests that there were factors operating within the school environment which discouraged many of the school leavers seen from making use of what educational opportunities existed; which inhibited rather than stimulated their educational development; and which encouraged their premature entry into employment. Since public education is regarded as a service to the young, it seems relevant to ask what it is rarely called upon to demonstrate—namely, how far can its present methods and conditions be said to benefit those who are obliged to attend its schools, particularly if the children themselves feel that it does not always serve their interests? There would seem to be clearly need for intensive studies which would show the possible influence on childrens' attitudes and development of the quality and methods of teaching and of types of school organization. The influence of cultural factors and the socio-economic status of the family have begun to be understood, but very much less is known about the effect of the school environment itself, of the conditions under which children succeed or fail, or of the interactions between children and teachers.

It would also seem necessary that the views of young adolescents about their educational experiences become an essential part of school life, so that these may begin to influence the direction of educational change. Their physical health and scholastic achievements are regularly measured; end of term reports summarise their work and behaviour; but children themselves are rarely asked to assess their own experiences. Yet their evaluation would seem to be an essential element in their progress. Adolescents who are at the age when they are developing independent and critical judgments might well be involved in assessing their teachers, their schools, and their educational needs in ways which would help both their personal and their educational development. If their reactions to teachers, to teaching methods, to particular subjects, to the rules and regulations of school life, to their own achievements and failures, were regularly sought, this might also become the means by which they could effectively influence the educational processes which most concern them.

Choosing and finding employment

Given the restrictions placed on vocational choice by educational factors, and by the conditions of the labour market, it was to be assumed that the present inquiry would reveal, to a greater or lesser extent, a discrepancy between the hopes and expectations of school leavers and their subsequent attainments. The results show, in fact, that the vocational aspirations of school leavers were higher, on average, than were their subsequent achievements. There was, overall, a reduction in the average level of skill, training, and education required in the jobs actually obtained compared with those originally preferred. Rather more young people entered relatively unskilled manual work, rather fewer boys the skilled trades, and rather fewer boys and girls employment requiring some degree of training and further education, than would have been the case had their original aims been realized.

It was not possible, nor was it intended, to assess how far the failure to achieve original aims was the result of factors associated with natural endowment or with the external situation. The findings mainly relate, therefore, to those aspects of the official guidance service which, on the basis of the comments of school leavers themselves, failed to provide as much help as was required during the process of vocational choice and decision in the last year or so at school.

There is, first, the question of vocational advice. The fact that so many young people felt that they had made up their own minds as to what work to do, and did not refer to the help of anyone at this stage, could be interpreted as confirmation of the indirect nature of the influence of the family and its circle and, to a lesser extent, the unobtrusive nature of the influence of the school and its 'vocational training'. The vocational aspirations of children were thus influenced through the medium of personal relationships developed and maintained over time. It is difficult to see how the official service could have played more than a marginal role in their decisions, when its greatest contribution to vocational guidance was expected to be made in the last year or so of school life at one, or perhaps two, or sometimes more, short interviews between parent, child, and youth employment officer, the latter dependent for his knowledge of the child's interests, aptitudes, and constancy of preferences, on the adequacy of school reports and on his interviewing skill. The comments of school leavers themselves express, clearly enough, their feeling that more time should have been allowed for their interests to be more fully explored.

Second, only a minority of school leavers, whatever the source of information used, discovered what they wanted to know about their intended employment; most of the young people seen would appear to have started work with only the vaguest idea of what they would have to do, and of what their conditions and prospects were likely to be. Since certain children were less likely than others to discover what they wanted to know and some methods and sources proved more effective than others, it would seem that there are important social, educational, and personal factors which need to be considered in planning careers programmes. It would also seem necessary that such programmes should be based on a knowledge of the factors which determine how children learn about possible and intended employment. The inclinations of children to use the most accessible sources—their families and their schools—suggest that attempts might also be made to help these become more authoritative and the specialized and expert agencies to become more accessible. Children might be helped more effectively to learn what they required if the content of careers information and the methods of supplying it were related more closely to the individual needs and patterns of learning. There is evident need for a prolonged individual service; this may mean that schools should have specialist advisors as part of their staff, or that youth employment officers should be based in schools and be easily accessible to teachers, school leavers, and parents, sharing in the life of the school.

Third, the official placing service would seem to have attracted not only leavers whose educational experience was more satisfactory than others, but leavers with particular aspirations which had been developed, encouraged, and sustained by their schools; these groups were subsequently more successful in obtaining their original objectives than were others. By contrast, boys placed in manual work as their first jobs were not only less successful than others, on the criterion of job change alone, but had chosen the least satisfactory method of obtaining such employment. The intervention of the Youth Employment Service appears, indeed, to have increased the chances of a 'successful' placement in some cases and the risk of job change in others.

If these tendencies in official placements apply to school leavers in general, they might suggest that the official service is being used not by children who are representative of the school-leaving population at large, but by selective groups; and that within the service, there may be an 'élite' among the clientèle—of both school leavers and employers. Since a local bureau does not cover the full range of outstanding vacancies in the area, the variety of jobs it can offer within the semi-skilled and unskilled category may be narrower than for apprenticeships or non-manual work. The leavers who find the former type of work, with the help of their families or friends, or by looking around for themselves, may have, in fact, a wider choice than that offered by the official service. Employers and school leavers who are concerned with jobs of higher skill and status may be more inclined to use the local bureau, the former because of its connections with schools and with children who have the educational qualifications required, the latter because they are considering their future training and want to choose carefully the type of firm they enter. The 'quality' of a placing, therefore, may be in part determined by the type of demand made. As in the education and health services, the help provided may prove more effective for those who know best how to use the official service and what they want from it.

Fourth, the analysis of changes in employment suggests that job changers differ from other school leavers in two important respects. A higher proportion of them failed, for one reason or another, to achieve their original vocational objectives. Moreover, a higher proportion of them obtained employment—either through official placements or else-where—in small firms where the working conditions were probably inferior. These conditions were, in themselves, evidently conducive to further change. The evidence of the present inquiry suggests that there may be a residue of jobs, chiefly in small firms, where standards, training, prospects, and the treatment of young people are lower than elsewhere. Job changes in this context could be regarded as inevitable. Since it would appear from the supplementary study of official placements[1] that a substantial propor-tion of the placements work of a local bureau relates to job changers who tend to move from one unsatisfactory job to another, it would seem neces-sary not only that there should be closer investigation before such jobs are offered as 'suitable employment' by the official service; but that extensive studies of job changes among under-eighteens should be undertaken, par-ticularly in regard to the size of firm, the type of employment, and the nature of the situation giving rise to terminations.

There would also seem to be need for a different attitude towards job changes in present day circumstances. The non-realization of original aims and the obtaining of unsuitable employment may be more important factors in influencing the rate of job change than is generally assumed. Care might also be exercised to see that job change, where it occurs, is more frequently a rewarding than a frustrating experience.

Finally, the criticisms of the young people themselves indicate that the weaknesses of the official system have not escaped the attention of those most affected by its shortcomings, and on whom the service ultimately depends for its reputation. If the vocational guidance function was not recognized except by relatively few leavers, it is presumably because what was most experienced in the first contact with the service did not correspond with the kind of individual help required at that stage; if a large propor-tion of leavers were dissatisfied with what the service offered in the way of first employment, it is presumably because this, too, did not fulfil their expectations. The efforts of hardworking and devoted youth employment officers could not conceal the discrepancy between the publicized aims of

[1] J. Maizels, op. cit., July, 1967.

the service and their subsequent realization. School leavers expected a
better service than they received and were not reticent in saying so.

A new approach would thus seem to be required towards the Youth
Employment Service. Though the report on the future development of the
service contained a number of proposals designed to improve it, these do
not, in the light of the results of the present inquiry, appear to have been
far-reaching enough.[2] A much more fundamental reorganization, combined with development on experimental lines, would seem to be required.
The earlier development of the work in schools and the closer collabora-
tion between the service, education, and industry, as suggested in the
report, would both seem to need new organizational provision. Research
and experiment is also needed in order to devise methods and procedures
of advising and informing about possible and intended employment,
which could correspond more closely than at present to individual patterns of demand. The need for continued help and advice during the first
years at work when unforeseen situations arise requiring new decisions and
plans, also requires some additional investment of staff.

The recurrent needs of policy-making would also demand regular and
systematic analyses of the day-to-day work of the service. Records and
statistical returns should be designed to facilitate the extraction of information relating to job choice, placements, job change, registered vacancies,
and other aspects of the work. A factual basis would then exist for the
regular assessment of the work of the service and for the publication of
fuller reports on its activities.

The work environment and its suitability

The information obtained from employers and young workers showed
that the work environment varied considerably according to the type of
employment followed, particularly in regard to job interest, methods of
training, and future prospects. At the higher end of almost every favourable
condition are apprentices, particularly those employed in the large firm.
They, more frequently than any other occupational group considered in
the present inquiry, were in jobs which were described as interesting,
varied, skilled, and responsible; which involved the use of thought and
initiative; which provided intensive and prolonged training during most
of which the worker was more usually regarded as a learner than as a
producer; which allowed for the acquisition of skills and experience useful
when applied elsewhere; and which offered almost certain promotion
prospects and a higher degree of job satisfaction. In specifying the requirements for such work, employers stressed the need for educational qualifications and mechanical aptitudes.

Boys, and to a greater extent girls, who entered unskilled manual jobs,

[2] *The Future Development of the Youth Employment Service*, op. cit.

had the least favourable conditions of all young workers. More specifically, the evidence indicated that the jobs of these young workers had the lowest interest appeal, the shortest training and provided the least useful job experience. The young people themselves were the least frequently involved in further education, their job satisfaction was lower than average, and their dissatisfaction more frequent. Less was demanded of them in terms of intellectual ability or practical aptitude, but more in terms of temperamental and physical suitability.

These were not the only workers, however, whose jobs failed to stretch their capacities. As many as three in five of all jobs considered were, for the purpose of the present inquiry, assessed as unsuitable because of an almost complete disregard for the educational needs, in the broadest sense, of the young people who performed them, and a failure to provide opportunities by which their potential abilities, intellectual and otherwise, could be discovered or developed. Moreover, the firms participating in the inquiry, particularly as they included large as well as statutory undertakings, could be regarded as providing better than average employment opportunities. It seems probable, therefore, that some of the conditions described would apply to similar jobs and populations elsewhere in Britain. Since unskilled jobs without formal training are occupied by at least two in five of the under-eighteens at work, most of whom could be assumed to have left school before their full potential was discovered or developed, it would seem a matter of some priority to reconsider the type of employment entered by school leavers, the conditions and opportunities offered to them, and the concept of suitable employment as applied within the official guidance service.

The apparent requirements of the labour market for young hands, rather than young minds, would appear to be in direct contrast to the needs of young adolescents themselves for jobs that hold their interest, offer them prospects of development, match their true abilities and allow them to fulfil their expectations. Young workers responded more enthusiastically to their jobs where the intrinsic interest was high; they more frequently approved of further education if they felt it had some meaning for their jobs; and many, if boys, were ambitious enough to want to be in jobs at least of higher skill, if not status and responsibility, by the time they had reached early manhood.

Moreover, as indicated earlier, there is a social as distinct from an academic process of selection operating within schools. This means that the present occupational distribution of young people by no means corresponds to the distribution of talent. Were their intellectual faculties nourished rather than neglected, therefore, the relative unsuitability of many of the present occupations for young people would become self-evident.

As a first step in re-assessing the concept of suitable employment as far as under-eighteens are concerned, detailed studies would be needed of existing employment conditions in order to distinguish the factors on which a classification of suitable types of work could reasonably be based. The present inquiry suggests that some of the factors to be more fully explored would include those associated with the intrinsic interest of occupations, and the degree to which they involve thought; the 'discretionary' and 'prescribed' aspects of occupations, and the degree to which they require independent decisions; the variety of the tasks performed, and the degree to which new learning occurs; and the range of practical skills acquired, and the degree to which these are specifically or generally applicable and useful elsewhere. There would also be need to examine the length, method, and quality of training, including day release; the content and quality of further education; and the prospects for upgrading and promotion, both within and outside present employment.

In addition to the opportunities for 'development', offered by particular occupations and firms, the results of the present inquiry also suggest that there are other aspects of employment which should be considered when assessing its suitability. There is the question of the provision of certain amenities, of canteens, medical services, and recreational facilities; and of the appointment of qualified persons responsible for the welfare and training of the young persons employed. Since services of this kind are rarely found in the small enterprise, size of firm might be one of the criteria for assessing suitability. Also to be considered would be the quality of supervision; the extent to which under-eighteens are regarded as learners; and the physical conditions of work, including the hazards and risks, if any, involved. Last, but not least, would be the opinions of young workers themselves, since these are derived from direct experience.

Studies on these lines would have a different approach from that of the Central Youth Employment Executive to job studies;[3] though in many respects the same areas of inquiry would be pursued, the objectives would be different. That of the executive is the collection of 'sound occupational knowledge' for the purpose of more effective vocational guidance; it assumes a relative constancy in employment conditions and the ability of the individual to adapt accordingly. The studies proposed here assume the opposite; namely that employment conditions can be modified so as to correspond more closely with the needs of developing adolescents.

Other events

The adjustment to a working life, for substantial minorities of young people, was also associated or coincident with particular stress situations. Such situations arose out of difficulties and disappointments relating to

[3] The Central Youth Employment Executive advises the Youth Employment Officers to carry out job studies on certain prescribed lines.

their past or present employment, or from illnesses, accidents, domestic or other events. Yet school leavers themselves placed greater emphasis on the need for further help and information in regard to employment matters than in regard to personal difficulties. This could mean that finding the right kind of work for themselves is particularly important because of the sense of achievement and relief from anxiety that it brings; this, in itself, may strengthen their capacity to deal with other problems as they arise. It also suggests that school leavers feel that they cannot gain access to the jobs and opportunities they want without some form of adult help, whereas in personal matters they are less certain that the intervention of adults would necessarily be helpful. Nevertheless, the results of the present inquiry suggest that young adolescents at school and at work need much more personal help and individual care than they now receive. There is a growing body of opinion which considers that such help might well be given through some form of integrated advisory service, staffed by professional workers and covering every aspect of the transitional years.[4]

It would seem important, however, in considering any new developments, to decide whether these are required because of the unresolved difficulties of existing services, or because these services, even if strengthened and improved, could not cover the whole range of adolescent needs. There is also the question of the quality of help that should be offered, its availability to fully representative groups of young people, and the extent to which any new developments are identified with the aims of adult authority or with the interests of young adolescents.

Appropriate adult help would seem, ultimately, to depend on the attitudes of adult authority towards young people and their difficulties, and the extent to which the nature of adolescent growth is understood and accepted without envy or anxiety; the effectiveness of adult help would depend also on the extent to which the opinions of the younger generation are allowed to influence what happens to them. For their opinions derive from direct experience, and it is this which is more relevant to their futures than is the interpretation of this experience by outside observers, official, expert, or otherwise; to ignore their opinions is to deny their experience. To deny this, as well as opportunity, is a threat to their identity when they are most vulnerable to self-doubts.

The essential consideration would seem to be the provision, whether by existing or newly developed services, of the means by which young people may freely express their hopes and uncertainties, voice their criticisms and suggestions, clarify the situations which face them and think out the appropriate course of action for themselves. To provide for such means through existing services would mean considerable changes, both in

[4] M. E. M. Herford, 'Young People at Work', *The British Hospital and Social Service Journal*, August, 1964; T. Veness, op. cit.; M. Jefferys, *An Anatomy of Social Welfare Services*, Michael Joseph, 1965.

attitudes and administrative techniques. Nevertheless, it would seem more rational to develop their qualities of helpfulness, particularly by appropriate in-service training, in order that better, rather than more, services become available, than to assume that present weaknesses and inadequacies can be compensated for by new agencies or administrative arrangements.

Current interest and activities in regard to school counselling suggest that, within certain educational organizations, the development of greater sensitivity to adolescent needs has already begun, though whether school counselling should become a new profession or become the development of an old one, is still an area of dispute.[5] The diversity of views and practices in this field may, however, encourage similar debate and experimentation elsewhere which would lay the basis for much needed improvements in the nature and quality of the help available to the young adolescent.

THE MAIN CONCLUSIONS
Socio-economic roles

It would be quite unrealistic, however, to assume that the discrepancies between the needs and opportunities of school leavers, as these have been revealed in the present inquiry, could be overcome simply by modifying and improving existing community services, if the socio-economic roles which young adolescents are expected to assume are left substantially unchanged. The experiences of the school leavers strongly suggest that it is the nature of the role allocation imposed on adolescents in present-day society which underlies the evident failure of the educational and vocational guidance services, and of industry, to fulfil the needs of more than élite minorities, whose abilities, attitudes, and aspirations are such as to allow them to make effective use of the services which exist and to respond to the opportunities available.

The information collected from employers indicates that, within an occupational hierarchy, there were two chief roles awaiting most of the school leavers seen. They were either regarded, predominantly, as learners and the inheritors of the skills and status of their elders who they would eventually replace; or they were regarded, mainly, as relatively cheap labour, less costly and more suitable, in certain respects, for routine tasks than were adult workers. In the first case, the transition from school to work was, essentially, a preparation for assuming, in adulthood, occupations of some significance in the eyes of society; in the second, entering employment was, essentially, an initiation into the less pleasant types of work which had little or no standing in society at large, and in which they were likely to remain well into adulthood if, with the development of automation, they did not find themselves redundant.

---

[5] *Counselling in Schools*, Working Paper No. 15, Schools Council, H.M.S.O., 1967.

The educational and vocational guidance services would seem to have functioned more effectively for school leavers who were expected, eventually, to enter the skilled occupations, than for boys and girls for whom relatively unskilled manual work was assumed to be, if not appropriate, then inevitable. This not only reflects a tacit acceptance by the services in question that rather more educational and vocational care needs to be given to those who are likely to enter the more skilled occupations—presumably on the principle that these children represent a 'sounder' investment. It also shows that the pattern of demand for young labour undermines any attempts within the relevant services to fulfil their stated aims.

For one thing, it would not seem possible, having regard for the interests of the children themselves, to educate, advise, and prepare them for work which holds so little intrinsic satisfaction, provides little or no positive interest, offers little opportunity for them to develop their interests and aptitudes, or encourages them to expect anything very different in adulthood. The relevance of school courses designed to enlarge their understanding of the world beyond school, and their part in it, is also called into question, as is the real function of teachers and youth employment officers in this context. Moreover, it is also possible that, in some degree, the true nature of these prospects and their implications must be concealed from school leavers likely to enter such jobs.

Furthermore, attempts to invigorate secondary education come to nothing because of what Downes has described as 'the antiquated structure of manual work'.[6] It is true that the Crowther and Newsom reports to which he refers attribute adolescents' rejection of the values of school society to the deprivation in their social and economic background and each pleads, accordingly, for a higher school-leaving age. But, nevertheless, the substance of many of their recommendations places greater emphasis on the need to provide a more 'realistic' orientation to 'work and life' than on the need for radical changes in employment opportunities; and reflects greater preoccupation with the moulding of what are considered to be the appropriate attitudes and behaviour patterns, than with intellectual growth.[7]

There is clearly a basic inconsistency between the attempts to engage the interests of children now described as apathetic and resistant to formal learning, to seek to influence their ways of thinking and behaving, or to assume that a happier adjustment to their life chances can be achieved by their pursuing liberal studies or the humanities[8]—and their subsequent use as relatively cheap labour. While the educational services collude, as it were, with the requirements of the labour market in this respect, school

[6] D. M. Downes, *The Delinquent Solution*, Routledge and Kegan Paul, 1966.
[7] *15–18* and *Half Our Future*, op. cit.
[8] See *Society and the Young School Leaver*, Working Paper No. 11, Schools Council, H.M.S.O., 1967.

is likely to remain of only marginal importance in their lives and only the meagre skills needed for routine work can be expected to be acquired.

It is widely recognized that the educational performance of working-class children, on average, is far below that of their potential ability. This has been shown to be due to a number of factors, not the least important of which is the existence of a cultural conflict within the schools, arising out of a class structured society in which the attitudes, values, and expectations of working-class children do not correspond to the values, aims, and assumptions of the middle-class bias in the school.

Bernstein's work in particular, has shown that in the process of becoming socialized in a working-class structure, and for occupational roles traditionally theirs, working-class children acquire a pattern of perception and a structure of language which conflicts with, and induces a resistance to, the methods and aims of the school.[9]

The educational system has, so far, failed to overcome this resistance, with the consequence that, as Downes had emphasized, the schools serve 'simply—and functionally—as a massive irritant' so helping to make the prospect of routine jobs more acceptable for the children most likely to enter them. Thus society, 'through its educational enterprise, sifts and sorts children into manual and non-manual positions according to their social class rather than their basic endowment';[10] and reduces the vocational guidance service to the level of an agent whose purpose is to facilitate the transactions of the juvenile labour market.

The 'failure' of the official services would appear, however, to be a functional element in the present economic and social structure which depends, for its maintenance, on there being continuity in the distribution of personnel according to a complex of occupational categories and social groups, each with its corresponding power and status levels, its value systems and its behaviour patterns. It imposes on the educational system the task of selecting and supplying new recruits for the various levels of status and skill. The system has never adequately educated the children who fail, for one reason or another, to qualify for the higher skill and status levels. It is these children, chiefly from the working class who, traditionally, are expected to replenish the ranks of the unskilled and semi-skilled labour force and so to do the less pleasant work of society. To fit young people for this work, constraints must be placed upon their development. 'If the developmental process dominant in adolescence was allowed to proceed unhindered, they would then find the socio-economic roles allocated to them inappropriate and unacceptable.'[11]

[9] B. B. Bernstein, 'Social Structure, Language and Learning', *Educ. Research*, **3**, 1961; and 'Social Class and Linguistic Development: A Theory of Learning', *Economy, Education and Society*, ed. by A. H. Halsey, J. Floud, and C. A. Anderson, The Free Press, New York, 1961.

[10] D. M. Downes, op. cit.

[11] E. Friedenberg, 'Adolescence as a Social Problem', *Social Problems*, ed. Howard S. Becker, John Wiley and Sons, 1966.

The dilemma

The education of working-class youth contains now, as in the past, this basic dilemma—namely, how to increase their technical efficiency and to discover the most able among them, without at the same time developing their aspirations and thus creating discontent with their conditions. The problem is clearly stated by the 1909 Royal Commissioners on the Poor Laws:—

Outside the enormous effect which universal education must have in making the working man into a more efficient and versatile tool of production, what has to be considered is its effect on the ambitions and expectations of the human being. Every stage of acquiring knowledge naturally makes people feel very acutely the conditions under which they are compelled to live . . . the discontent is individually greater than it ever was before, and naturally so.[12]

Since then, the dilemma has been partially resolved by developing over the years different types of education for different types of children; and by adopting as the chief aims of the education of the non-academic, predominantly working-class adolescent, the development of his character, taste, and practical skills. Underlying these aims is the hope that, though the majority of young workers will not be able to develop their personalities through their work, 'tuition in living',[13] or what has been described as 'life adjustment programmes',[14] will not only help to offset the effects of their depersonalized working conditions, but ensure the 'proper' use of their leisure and encourage their appreciation of the other 'good things in life'.[15]

But, as Downes has argued, access to 'desirable' leisure goals is blocked for the young adolescents who become dissociated from the areas of school and work; the problems of self-realization 'originate in the school and work situations to which they are destined by role allocation of the adolescent'. Moreover, the propensity for dissociation is likely to worsen, in Downes' view, with the development of automation and the consequent reduction even in the limited prospects offered by the least skilled jobs.[16]

In any case, the dilemma for society is likely to grow more serious. If the work situation deteriorates further, then as Downes suggests, 'the reactions of young adolescents who become convinced of their own expendability could, in terms of delinquency, well become explosive'.[17] On the other hand, considerable discontent could arise if increasing numbers of adolescents were to entertain higher educational and vocational aspirations

[12] The Royal Commission on the Poor Laws and the Relief of Distress, op. cit.
[13] See *Society and the Young School Leaver*, op. cit.
[14] R. S. Neale, op. cit.
[15] A. K. C. Ottoway, *Education and Society*, Routledge and Kegan Paul, 1953.
[16] D. M. Downes, op. cit.
[17] Ibid.

without sufficient outlets being available to them; or if, even for jobs of higher skill than at present, young people continued to be selected on grounds of social class for the jobs which were still among the most subordinate.

Moreover, the paradox of an increasingly affluent society, technically advanced, ostensibly democratic, and pledged to a policy of economic growth, which restricts the development of the majority of its youth and wastes their creative energies and talents, because it cannot provide enough suitable activities for them, becomes sharper as young people themselves press their claims to greater recognition of their individuality and to increased autonomy over their lives.

A phase of dependency

Though associated with increasing independence, the transitional years actually represent a phase when young people are crucially dependent on the decisions of adult authority which, through educational procedures and the subsequent use of their labour, plays a decisive part in influencing their future destinies.

The feelings of freedom associated with being at work arise largely because the individual feels released from the captivity of school, and from what has been described as 'the severe and exceptionally protracted form of constraint' and 'the status essentially that of a conscript'.[18] When school is ended, the individual experiences a new sense of freedom, for he is in fact 'free'—to sell his labour, to exercise some choice, however small, as to where and with whom he works, and to withdraw his labour if he feels this is appropriate for him. Nevertheless, far from being independent of adult society, young people are still, in these transitional years, 'completely its subjects'.[19]

For most school leavers, the transition from school to work is co-terminous with adolescent growth. This development, in present circumstances, would seem to have two distinct though related aspects. The first arises from the internal stresses associated with the onset of physical and emotional changes, the attempt to discard childhood dependency and to assume forms of adult behaviour.

Before these problems are resolved, however, and while still relatively immature and uninformed, a second area of difficulty arises for them. They enter the predominantly adult world of work, where adult authority determines the conditions under which they enter, the type of employment available to them and the opportunities and prospects before them. Their problem is to find the place for themselves in this world which corresponds as closely as possible both to their aspirations, and to their image of becoming adult which each individual forms for himself. They

[18] E. Friedenberg, op. cit.
[19] Ibid.

achieve relative success or failure according to the extent that their expectations, however limited, are realized and their belief and confidence in their future adulthood sustained. For most school leavers, these developments coincide in time, so that inner anxieties may be reinforced by the difficulties and frustrations of the external situation, and these difficulties are likely to be handled less confidently because of underlying uncertainties.

Moreover, the 'marketing orientation' evident in the socialization of the adolescent in industrial society today, plays an important part at this stage of their lives. For, as Fromm has argued, in so far as individuals are assessed according to the exchange value that particular qualities are expected to have in the labour market, so they are regarded and experience themselves as commodities, with something to sell and as something to be sold. The lower the market value ascribed to them, the more valueless their individuality must seem. In Fromm's view, the greatest achievement for man is to develop his individuality—peculiar and unique to him. 'The mature and productive individual derives his feeling of identity from the experience of himself as the agent who is one with his powers . . . I am what I do.'[20]

The adolescent school leaver, however, still in his formative years when he offers his labour to a prospective buyer, finds that 'what matters is not his self-realization in the process of using his own powers, but his success in the process of selling them. . . . Both his powers and what they create become estranged, something different from himself, something for others to judge and to use; thus his feelings of identity become as shaky as his self esteem'.[21]

For this reason, if no other, the entry into employment is thus one of the most important events in the lives of young adolescents, for it demonstrates, perhaps more directly than any other aspect of adult behaviour, the extent to which young people are valued for themselves or only in regard to the roles they are expected to assume.

A new approach

The problems associated with the transition from school to work, as these have been revealed through the experiences of school leavers, would thus seem to be created by adult society, and by the fact that the present requirements of the economic and social structure conflict with the needs of young adolescents to develop and assert their true individualities.

How are young people at this stage of their lives expected to orientate their learning, widen their horizons and understanding, assess their worth in society, feel confident about their adulthood, and commit their creative energies fully to the world around them, except through their occupational

[20] Erich Fromm, 'Personality and the Market Place', *Man, Work and Society*, eds. Sigmund Nosow and William H. Form, Basic Books Inc., New York, 1962.
[21] Ibid.

roles? It is work, after all, not leisure, which, in present-day society gives status to the individual and direction, continuity, and meaning to the lives of most people.

The failure to find satisfaction in school or in work has many implications. There is the waste and withering of potential talent; the fact that many young people are deceived, by the constraints put upon their development, as to their real abilities and do not know what they are capable of becoming; there is the fostering of the belief that work is only the means to more positive satisfaction elsewhere, and the development of alienation to and dissociation from, work and, possibly, other areas of life. For if work is a fundamental activity, then cynical attitudes towards it may influence attitudes in other spheres; and if work is perceived as 'killing time', then leisure may also be similarly regarded. In any case, it seems inadmissible to encourage young people on the threshold of their working lives to regard leisure as a compensation for unsatisfying employment, and unrealistic to assume that they are likely to discover personal significance if their working lives are so devalued.

The results of the present inquiry have shown that the questions raised in the 1940s regarding the possibility of establishing agreed standards of employment for young workers, for ensuring opportunities for their technical and cultural education and for the continued supervision of their welfare and training, are as urgent today as then.[22] The only effective approach, however, would be to combine a radical restructuring of work opportunities with the implementation of the long awaited revolutions in secondary and further education. This would inevitably pose critical problems for the present economic and social structure. Only by such measures, however, could the transitional years be transformed from a period in which young people move into their predestined socio-economic roles, into one in which, through continuous links between school and work, they explore and discover their potential talents, experiment with a variety of social and economic tasks, seek and establish their true identities, and determine, for themselves, their place in society.

[22] See Chapter I, page 8.

CHARACTERISTICS OF THE SAMPLE

SINCE the sample of firms participating in the inquiry was essentially a self-selected one, it was important to discover the nature and extent of the biases arising from the way in which the sample was chosen. Its main characteristics in relation to what is known about the total of all firms in Willesden employing young people were therefore compared with those of the participating firms and of the young people interviewed.

CHARACTERISTICS OF THE SAMPLE OF PARTICIPATING FIRMS

Four aspects of the sample of firms were selected for these comparisons, *viz.* size of firm, the industrial distribution of firms, the number of young people employed and the proportion of under-eighteens in day-release schemes.

Size distribution of firms

In the course of organizing the study, information was obtained relating to the size of firms in the borough. Six categories of size were used, distinguishing the very small from the large, and amalgamating several middle-size groups of firms. References to the 'small' firm relate to all those which employ up to 100 persons; 'medium' indicates those firms employing between 100 and 500 persons, while 'large' denotes firms employing more than 500 persons. The analysis of the size of firms participating in the inquiry (excluding retail distribution, banks, and public administration)[1] showed that more small firms were included in the sample than were medium-sized firms or large ones. The small firm was, however, under-represented, and the large firm over-represented, in relation to the total size-distribution of firms in the borough. Over two-fifths of the sample were small firms (on the present definition), compared with nearly three-quarters of the total firms in the borough in this size-group. The large firms accounted for one-third of the sample, but for only one-tenth of the

---

[1] The department and variety stores included in the sample were all branches of multiple stores; only one of the remaining shops employed more than ten persons. Banks and public administration offices included in the inquiry were all area or branch offices of large-scale organizations.

total firms in the borough; the medium-size firms were also over-represented (Table A.1).

The majority of firms refusing to participate, or not responding to the invitation to participate, were small firms.

TABLE A.1. Size distribution of participating and non-participating firms.[a]

Size of firm (No. of persons employed)	Participating	Refusals	Non-respondents[b]	Total
	(Per cent of total)			
Under 11	13	22	26	22
11–25	10	17	21	17
26–100	21	40	37	34
Sub-total	44	79	84	73
101–500	25	15	13	16
501–1000	5	3	2	4
Over 1000	26	3	1	7
Total	100	100	100	100
(No. of firms)	(57)	(60)	(123)	(240)

a Excluding retail distribution, banks, public administration.
b Including some minor categories (e.g. employing no under-eighteens at time of inquiry).

Industrial distribution of firms

Most industrial and other services in the borough were represented in the sample of firms taking part in the inquiry. The main bias was the under-representation of small retailers owing to the difficulties of obtaining suitable conditions for interviewing in small shops.

Excluding retail distribution, however, the sample proved to contain generally a fairly representative industrial pattern of firms, the main deficiency being in miscellaneous manufacturing industries, particularly in textiles and clothing. Food and transport were somewhat over-represented, but the relative importance of the main industrial groups in the sample—engineering; miscellaneous metal goods; timber, bricks, glass, etc.; and other services—was extremely close to the corresponding proportions for the borough as a whole.

Numbers employed

Though the number of participating firms (excluding retail distribution and small offices) represented one in four of the total enterprises in the borough, the number of under-eighteens employed in these firms accounted for almost one-half of the total number of boys, and one-third of the total number of girls (two-fifths if retail distribution is excluded), estimated to be working in the borough. Further analysis of the numbers employed in different occupational categories showed considerable variation and indicated a particular bias in the sample in favour of firms employing boy apprentices, while girl apprentices and boy sales-assistants were heavily under-represented (Table A.2).

TABLE A.2. Type of employment of young people by main occupational group: sample firms and estimated totals for Willesden, 1964.

	Boys			Girls		
	Number employed in sample firms	Total employed in Willesden (1964)	Proportion in sample firms	Number employed in sample firms	Total employed in Willesden (1964)	Proportion in sample firms
Unskilled and semi-skilled manual	139	525	*(Per cent)* 26	81	214	*(Per cent)* 38
Clerical and other non-manual	40	175	23	223	620	36
Sales assistants	6	150	4	36	139	26
Apprentices	325	400	81	5	97	5
Total	510	1250	41	345	1070	32
Total, excluding retail distribution	507	1085	47	327	845	39

Apprentices, for instance, accounted for three-fifths of the total boys employed in the sample of participating firms, and these represented about four in every five of all the boy apprentices estimated to be employed in the borough; boys in semi-skilled and unskilled manual work, on the other hand, accounted for one-quarter of the sample and for one-quarter of the total number in this type of work; boys in clerical occupations were only a small proportion of the total employed in the sample firms—8 per cent—though they represented one-quarter of the total estimated to be employed as clerks in the borough.

The employment of girls showed a rather different pattern. Nearly two-thirds of those employed in the sample firms were in clerical occupations, accounting for over one-third of all such girls at work in the borough. About one-quarter of girls employed in the sample firms were in manual work, representing about two-fifths of all girls employed in this type of work. Girl sales assistants accounted for one-tenth of all girls employed in the same firms, and represented one in four of all girls sales assistants in the borough.

The bias in the sample in favour of the large firm resulted in a higher average number of boys and girls employed per firm in the sample than the average for all firms in the borough employing under-eighteens: 8·9 boys per firm in the sample as against 3·3 for all firms in the borough. For girls, the corresponding averages were 5·7 and 2·6. The analysis of the sample firms by size also showed that there was a tendency for firms in most size groups to employ a rather higher-than-average number of boys in relation to the borough as a whole; and for small and medium firms in the sample to employ a higher-than-average number of girls (Table A.3).

TABLE A.3. Average number of under-eighteens employed in sample firms and in total firms in Willesden.

Size of firm (No. of persons employed)	Sample firms[a]			Average number of under-18s employed			
				Boys		Girls	
	Number	Under-18s employed		Sample firms	Total firms Willesden	Sample firms	Total firms Willesden
		Boys	Girls				
Under 11	8	16	5	2·0	1·4	0·6	0·3
11–25	5	7	5	1·4	1·5	1·0	0·3
26–100	12	34	43	2·8	2·7	3·6	1·9
Sub-total	25	57	53	2·2	1·9	2·1	0·9
101–500	14	104	70	7·4	4·9	5·0	4·4
501–1000	3	19	19	6·3	10·4	6·3	10·7
Over 1000	15	327	185	21·8	19·1	12·3	23·4
Total	57	507	327	8·9	3·3	5·7	2·6

a Excluding retail distribution.

Proportion in day-release schemes

Since there were no figures available relating to the number of under-eighteens employed in the Willesden area participating in day-release schemes, the proportion in day-release schemes employed in the sample firms were compared with the proportions in such schemes for England and Wales in 1962–3.[2] To put the two sets of figures on a comparable basis, the percentages for different industries in the country as a whole were weighted by the relative employment of under-eighteens in each industry in the sample of participating firms. The higher proportion of young people in day-release schemes in the sample of participating firms compared with the national figures was due, for boys, to firms in transport and food having a much higher proportion in day release than the national average for these industries. For the girls, the proportions were higher for every group except retail distribution (Table A.4).

[2] *Day Release*, op. cit.

TABLE A.4. Proportion of young people under eighteen in day-release schemes in sample firms and in England and Wales, 1962–3.

Industry group	Boys		Girls	
	Sample of firms	England and Wales (1962–3)	Sample of firms	England and Wales (1962–3)
	(Per cent of total)			
Food, beverages, tobacco	79·5	16·0	28·2	7·4
Engineering, including electrical	55·5	60·3	32·0	8·7
Construction	10·0	40·9	—	4·4
Transport and communications	54·5	25·8	36·4	17·2
Retail distribution	0·0	7·6	0·0	2·3
Other	56·3	51·6[a]	18·2	9·8[a]
Total	52·5	41·0[a]	24·0	8·2[a]

a Percentage for individual industries weighted by relative employment of under-eighteens in each industry in the sample of participating firms.

Source: Day Release: The Report of a Committee set up by the Minister of Education, H.M.S.O., 1964 (Appendix B).

CHARACTERISTICS OF THE SAMPLE OF YOUNG PEOPLE INTERVIEWED

Only a proportion of the young people employed in the larger firms included in the sample were interviewed. In all, these numbered 183 boys and 147 girls, representing just over one-third and two-fifths, respectively, of the total boys and girls employed in the sample of participating firms, and one-seventh of all under-eighteens estimated to be working in the borough of Willesden.[3]

Age distribution

The sample included young people of all ages, up to and including eighteen.[4] The seventeen-year-olds accounted, however, for one-half of the boys seen and two-fifths of the girls, and the sixteen-year-olds for over one-quarter of the boys and nearly two-fifths of the girls. The proportions of fifteen- and eighteen-year-olds were, therefore, relatively small.

The average age of the sample of girls was somewhat lower (16·9 years) than that for boys (17·1 years), rather more girls than boys being in the fifteen- and sixteen-year-old age group. The sixteen- to seventeen-year-old age group, however, dominated the sample, accounting for over three-quarters of both boys and girls seen. Without knowing the age distribution

[3] J. Maizels, 1965, op. cit.
[4] The eighteen-year-olds interviewed were those who were under eighteen when their interviews were arranged but who were eighteen by the date of interview, or who were believed to be under eighteen by their employers.

of the population at work, it is not possible to assess the degree of bias in the age distribution of the sample.

Type of secondary school attended

The sample of boys and girls seen was composed mainly of secondary modern school leavers. Less than one-tenth of the total sample had attended grammar or technical schools, though the proportion was somewhat higher for those who had attended schools outside the borough. The differences between the proportions of boys and girls attending different types of secondary school were negligible, except that virtually only boys had attended secondary technical schools.

Since the educational background of all young people employed in the borough is not known, it is not possible to assess the degree of bias in the sample in this respect. Information relating to the school population for Willesden, and to that of the former L.C.C. Administrative Area, indicates that the proportion attending grammar school was about one-quarter.[5] But since the age of entry to employment is lower generally for secondary modern school children, the under-eighteens at work in the borough are almost certain to have contained a higher proportion of secondary modern school leavers than that of the general school population. The bias in the sample, if any, is more likely to be evident in the proportions leaving school at different ages.

Age at leaving school

Almost all the boys and girls seen had left school at fifteen or at sixteen years of age. Four-fifths of the girls, however, had left school at fifteen, compared with one-half of the boys. Conversely, over two-fifths of the boys had left school at the age of sixteen, compared with just under one-fifth of the girls.

The proportions leaving school at fifteen were higher, and the differences between boys and girls greater, for those of the sample who had attended school within the boundaries of the borough of Willesden. Moreover, the proportions of the Willesden sample leaving school at fifteen would appear to be much higher than that shown by the local school-leaving pattern. The proportions leaving school in Willesden at different ages were calculated on the basis of the total school population of the borough in the age groups fourteen to seventeen on 1st January for each year 1962–5. This showed that the proportion leaving school at fifteen fell from 64 per cent in 1962 to 47 per cent in 1963, and to 40 per cent in 1964.[6] Thus, the sample of young people educated in Willesden contained a much higher

---

[5] *Statistics of Education 1965*, Department of Education and Science, H.M.S.O.

[6] This sharp fall is attributed to the introduction of only two leaving dates from December 1963.

proportion of fifteen-year-old leavers than did the school-leaving population for the borough as a whole in recent years.

The analysis of first placements of school leavers by the local Youth Employment Bureau[7] indicated that a high proportion of these related to secondary modern school leavers aged fifteen, and that the majority of them were placed in employment within the borough. That analysis also implied that a high proportion of the sixteen- and seventeen-year-old leavers—who tended to find employment without the help of the local bureau—work outside the borough. This would appear to explain the apparently high proportion of fifteen-year-old school leavers in the sample interviewed.

Social class

The occupations of the fathers of young people seen were classified into ten categories based on a combination of the social class and socio-economic groupings used by the Registrar-General.[8] This allowed for two possible divisions, into five social class categories, and into eight socio-economic groups.

The analysis of the sample according to social class categories showed that it contained a majority of boys and girls—one-half and three-quarters, respectively—whose fathers were in skilled occupations. One-seventh of the boys had fathers in the intermediate and partly-skilled social class groups, the corresponding proportion for the girls being under one-tenth. Only a very small minority of both boys and girls had fathers in the unskilled category. Further analysis of the fathers' occupations according to eight socio-economic groups showed that skilled manual workers formed the largest single group for both boys and girls. This was particularly so for the sample of girls, over half of whom had fathers in skilled manual occupations.

A comparison of the social class and socio-economic background of the sample interviewed with that of the male population of Willesden can be made by utilizing the results of the 1961 Census of Population (Table A.5). It should be pointed out, however, that the analysis of the Census results[9] was based on a somewhat different combination of occupational groupings from that used here. The comparison shows that the sample of young people interviewed (excluding non-residents of Willesden) contained an appreciably higher proportion with fathers in skilled occupations (two-thirds for boys and four-fifths for girls), than is found in the male population of Willesden (only three-fifths of whom were in the skilled group). Conversely, the sample of Willesden residents interviewed was relatively

[7] J. Maizels, 1965, op. cit.
[8] *Classification of Occupations*, 1960, H.M.S.O.
[9] As made by the London Borough of Brent (see footnote to Table A.5).

deficient in the other social class categories, particularly in those with fathers in unskilled manual work.

TABLE A.5. Social class distribution of fathers of young people interviewed who were residents, in relation to that of total male population, of Willesden.

	Sample interviewed			Male population (1961)[a]
	Boys	Girls	*Total*	
	(Per cent of total)			
Professional	—	—	—	3
Intermediate	9	3	5	8
Skilled	66	78	73	59
Partly skilled	17	14	16	17
Unskilled	8	5	6	13
Total[b]	100	100	100	100
(No. of 15–18s)	(73)	(80)	(153)	—

a *Background to Brent Employment,* Planning and Research Dept., London Borough of Brent, February 1965 (data from Census of Population, 1961).
b Excluding those not answering this question.

This comparison with the Census data must, however, be viewed with some caution, since the families from which the under-eighteens come form only a small proportion of the total number of families in the borough. No information is available as to the occupations of fathers resident in Willesden with working children aged fifteen to eighteen so that, strictly speaking, no conclusions can validly be drawn regarding possible sample biases. Another difficulty in the comparison is that some proportion of such fathers would have children who worked outside the borough. It would seem probable that a higher proportion of resident fifteen to eighteens who went outside the borough to work came from households in which the father was in the higher social groups (professional and intermediate), than was the case for those working in the borough.[10] If so, the proportion of resident males in households containing under-eighteens working in the borough who were in the skilled social class would be significantly higher than the 59 per cent shown in Table A.5.

Place of residence and birth

Just over one-half of the sample of young people interviewed lived in the borough of Willesden, though the proportion of Willesden residents was

[10] This seems probable because a substantial proportion of Willesden residents travel to other boroughs, including Central London, for non-manual work (including those classified by the Registrar-General in professional and intermediate categories).

higher for girls than for boys. Though no precise information exists as to what proportion of under-eighteens who work in the borough also live in it, the analysis of local youth employment placements for the three years 1960–63[11] showed that first placements in employment within the borough represented three-quarters of boys and two-third of girls actually at work there; these proportions would include young people living outside the area who were placed in employment within Willesden, but they suggest, nevertheless, that a substantial proportion—probably about one-half—of young people employed in the borough also live in it.

Over one-half of those now living in the borough were also born in it, and these accounted for just under one-third of the total sample of young people interviewed; a third were born within the Metropolitan area of Greater London, and one-twelfth elsewhere in Great Britain. Only one in twenty were born elsewhere in the Commonwealth (Table A.6).

TABLE A.6. Place of birth of 15–18s interviewed.

	Boys	Girls	Total
	(Per cent of total)		
Willesden	27	37	31
Metropolitan and Greater London	43	26	36
Home Counties and Provinces	10	6	8
Ireland	1	7	4
Wales	3	1	2
Scotland	1	1	1
Elsewhere in Europe	—	1	1
Commonwealth (excl. G.B.)	6	5	5
No answer	9	16	12
Total	100	100	100
(No. of 15–18s)	(183)	(147)	(330)

An analysis was also made of the place of birth of the fathers of the boys and girls interviewed who now live in Willesden. This showed that just over one-quarter of the fathers were born in the borough, a figure which compares closely with that obtained in a C.O.I. survey in 1949[12] and with that obtained for certain selected areas in the borough in a survey undertaken in 1959–60[13] (Table A.7).

[11] J. Maizels, 1965, op. cit.
[12] *Willesden and the New Towns, 1947*, Social Survey, C.O.I.
[13] J. Maizels, *The West Indian Comes to Willesden*, Willesden Borough Council, 1960.

TABLE A.7. Place of birth of fathers of 15–18s
resident in Willesden.

| | Fathers of | | Social survey 1946–7[a] | Willesden inquiry 1960[b] |
	Boys	Girls		
	(Per cent of total)			
Willesden	29	24	26	25
Metropolitan and Greater London	22	21	40	28
Home Counties and Provinces	12	10		
Wales	7	2	} 26	} 19
Scotland	2	5		
Ireland	2	8		15
Elsewhere in Europe	1	5	8	5
Commonwealth (excl. G.B.)	13	4		8
No answer	12	21		
Total	100	100	100	100
(No. of 15–18s)	(84)	(84)	(3076)	(415)

a 'Willesden and the New Towns' (1947), Social Survey (Central Office of Information).
b J. Maizels, The West Indian Comes to Willesden, Willesden Borough Council, 1960.

Job changes

Two-thirds of the sample were in their first jobs when interviewed, so that one-third had had more than one job since leaving school. But a higher proportion of the girls (one-quarter) were in their second jobs than were boys (one-sixth). Less than one in six of the sample, however, had had two or more changes in employment and less than one in ten had experienced more than three jobs. These figures (which are examined in more detail in Chapter XII), show a much lower incidence of job change than was evident in the survey undertaken for the Crowther Report relating to secondary modern school leavers.[14]

Size distribution of employing firms

The concentration of large firms in the sample of employers resulted in a similar concentration in the sample of young people interviewed. A higher proportion of those seen were employed in large firms, than in medium or small firms. Almost one-third of the sample of boys, for instance, worked in small firms, one-fifth in medium-sized firms and nearly one-half in large firms. For girls, the proportions were more evenly distributed, but this was mainly due to the fact that the sample of girls contained a substantial group from retail distribution. When these were excluded

14 15–18, op. cit.

from the analysis, the proportion of girls working in the large firm was twice as high as that for the small firm (45 as against 22 per cent).

When the size-distribution of firms in which the sample interviewed were employed is compared with that for the total population of under-eighteens at work in the borough, the bias in regard to boys is even more evident. Over one-half of the total boys working in the area are in small firms, compared with less than one-third employed in this size of firm covered by the sample. For the borough as a whole, less than one-third are employed in the large firms but, as already indicated, the boys in the sample working in large firms accounted for almost one-half of all the boys interviewed (Table A.8).

TABLE A.8. Distribution of sample of 15–18s interviewed by size of firm.

Size of firm (Total number employed)	Boys		Girls	
	Sample interviewed	Total boys at work in Willesden	Sample interviewed	Total girls at work in Willesden
	(Per cent of total)			
Under 11	9	23	3·5	18
11–25	4	9	3·5	4
26–100	18	22	29	20
Sub-total	31	54	36	42
101–500	20	16	24·5	17
501–1000	1	8	3·5	10
Over 1000	48	22	36	31
Total	100	100	100	100
(No. of 15–18s)	(183)	(1240)	(147)	(1065)

By excluding retail distribution in which small firms predominate, the differences between the size-distribution of the sample and the total at work is somewhat reduced, but the difference is still large enough to indicate that the sample is not representative of the total population of boys under eighteen as regards their distribution by size of firm.

For the girls, the size-distribution of employing firms correspond more closely than for boys to employment in the borough, except for the very small firm employing ten persons or fewer. Many of these small firms are in the retail trades, including hairdressers, and a few girls could be interviewed in such firms. When retail distribution is excluded, however, it was evident that the sample was biased in favour of the middle-sized firm employing between 100 and 500 persons.

Types of employment

The occupations of the sample of young people interviewed were analysed according to six main categories. These corresponded, to some degree, with those used by the Youth Employment Bureau, for the purpose of recording the types of employment entered by young people in their first employment.

The occupational distribution of the sample interviewed shows that almost one-third of the boys were apprentices, while over one-half were in unskilled or semi-skilled manual work. The latter category included a substantial proportion (one-quarter of all the boys interviewed) who were described as 'trainees'. One seventh of the sample were in non-manual work (mainly clerks). A comparison with the occupational distribution of the total population of boys at work in the borough shows that the sample is somewhat over-represented by manual workers, and considerably under-represented as regards boy sales-assistants. For apprentices and clerical workers, however, the proportions in the sample are closely similar to those employed in these types of employment in the borough as a whole (Table A.9).

TABLE A.9. Distribution of sample of 15–18s interviewed, by type of employment.

	Boys		Girls	
	Sample interviewed	Total employed in Willesden	Sample interviewed	Total employed in Willesden
Unskilled and semi-skilled manual:	(*Per cent of total*)			
(a) Factory[a]	17	}34[b]	22	16
(b) Trainee	23		—	—
(c) Other	14	8	4	4
Sub-total	54	42	26	20
Clerical and other non-manual	14	14	53	58
Sales assistants	2	12	19	13
Apprentices	30	32	2	9
Total	100	100	100	100
(No. of 15–18s)	(183)	(1250)	(147)	(1070)

a Other than 'trainees'.
b 'Trainees' not separately distinguished.

The occupational distribution of the girls interviewed corresponds fairly closely with that of all girls at work, with the exception of apprentices. Nearly three-quarters of the girls seen were in non-manual occupations, predominantly clerical, the same proportion as for all girls at work; one-quarter of those seen were in manual work compared with one-fifth for all girls working in the borough.

The sample of young people interviewed would seem, in most respects, therefore, to be representative of the occupational distribution of all the boys and girls working in the borough, according to these main categories of types of employment, with the exception of girl apprentices and boy sales-assistants, both of whom were under-represented, and boy manual workers who were somewhat over-represented.

Industrial distribution

The industrial distribution of the sample of young people differed in most instances from that of the total population of under-eighteens employed in the borough. The differences were most marked for boys in transport and communications, in which one-sixth of the sample were employed, compared with only one-twentieth of all boys at work; and for retail distribution, in which under 3 per cent of the sample of boys were employed, compared with one-seventh of the total at work. Engineering of all kinds, which employs one-quarter of the total at work, accounted for one-fifth of the boys in the sample and was the largest single industrial group for the sample of boys seen.

For girls, a much higher proportion in the sample was in retail distribution (one-quarter) than in the total at work (one-seventh); and a much smaller proportion of the sample (one-eighth) in electrical and other engineering industries, these employing more than a quarter of the total girls at work in the area. There was also a relative over-representation of girls in the sample for the 'timber, bricks, glass, and pottery' group of industries, this reflecting the inclusion of workers in firms making glass and cosmetics, and for miscellaneous service industries, where the sample included a relatively large proportion of girls employed in hospitals, laundries, and local government services.

If retail distribution is excluded from the comparison, however, the sample of young people would appear to be reasonably representative of the industrial distribution of both boys and girls under eighteen at work in the borough.

QUESTIONNAIRE TO YOUNG WORKERS

CODE
NUMBER   CONFIDENTIAL

SERIAL NO.
                                                    BOY/GIRL
NATURE OF FIRM   DATE OF INTERVIEW

SIZE OF FIRM

I PAST EDUCATION

1. Present age

2. Present occupation

3. Age at which left sehool

4. Type of school attended:
   Secondary Modern
   Grammar
   Technical
   Other

5. How much did you want to leave school when you did?
   Very much
   Quite a lot
   Didn't mind
   Not very much
   Not at all

6. Why?

7. What did your parents feel about your leaving school?
   Wanted me to leave
   Didn't mind
   Wanted me to stay on

8. What did your teachers feela bout your leaving school?
   Thought I ought to leave
   Not sure
   Didn't mind
   Thought I ought to stay on

9. Had you considered staying on at school longer?
   Yes
   No
   Don't know

10. If no, why not?

11. If yes, what made you decide to leave?

12. How did you like school in your last year?
    Very much
    Quite a lot
    Didn't mind
    Disliked it
    Disliked it very much

13. Why?

14. Did you take any examinations in your last year? (G.C.E., R.S.A., etc.)
    Yes
    No
    Don't know

15. Passed in what subjects?

16. Was there any streaming at your school?
    Yes
    No
    Don't know

17. If yes, how many Streams? Which were you in?

1 or A	1 or A
2 or B	2 or B
3 or C	3 or C
4 or D	4 or D
5 or E	5 or E

18. How did you get on at school compared with others in your class?
    Among the best
    Above average
    About the middle
    Not as good as most
    Near the bottom

19. Have you any regrets about leaving school when you did?
    Yes
    No
    Uncertain

20. Why?

21. Which of the following do you feel applies to what you remember about your teachers at school? (You may tick as few or as many as you wish.)

fair	reliable	muddled
strict	helpful	pleasant
expected too much	nagging	always kept promises
efficient	full of ideas	encouraged me
moody	too old	explained things clearly
knew their job	good to work for	frightening
clever	confident	had favourites
too young	praised me when I did	interfering
listened to what I	well	kind
wanted to say	sarcastic	you never knew where
sincere	didn't seem interested	you were with them
any other	treated me like a human being	

22. Which of the following do you feel applies to what you remember about your school in general? (You may tick as many or as few as you wish.)

friendly	helped everyone to do	just the right size
up to date	their best	too many rules and
too big	easy going	regulations
had a good	offered a good standard	not enough discipline
reputation	of education	a lot of lessons seemed
too strict about our	too set in its ideas	a waste of time
behaviour	strict about time	needed fresh people at
not enough practical	keeping	the top
training provided	only seemed interested	efficient
any other	in the brainy ones	

23. What do you think of the idea of
raising the school age to 16?
Approve
Disapprove
Don't know

24. Why?

II VOCATIONAL GUIDANCE

25. When did you decide what work you
wanted to do?
Before leaving school
At the time of leaving school
After leaving school

26. What work did you want to do?

27. Why?

28. When you were deciding and think-
ing about what work to do who
helped you most make up your mind?
Parents   Youth Employment
             Officer
Teachers   Others
Friends   Self

29. Were you able to find out what you
wanted to know about the work you
intended to do?
Most of it
Some of it
Not very much about it

30. How did you find out about the
work?

31. Have you had to give up anything
that you particularly wanted to do?
Yes
No
Uncertain

32. If yes, what was this?

33. Why did you have to give it up?

34. How did you get your first job?
Self   Press Ad.
Parents   Notice outside
Teachers   firm
Friends/   Writing to
   Relatives   firm
Youth Employment Other

35. How many jobs did you try for before
getting your first one?

36. How long before you got your first
job?
While still at school
Immediately on leaving
Several days after leaving
Several weeks after leaving

37. Are you still in your first job?
Yes
No

38. If not how many jobs have you had
since your first one?
(then transfer to separate job history
sheet)

39. Do you feel settled in your present
job?
Very settled
Quite settled
Fairly settled
Not very settled
Not at all settled

40. Do you feel there is enough help for
young people these days to find the
work they want?
Yes
No
Uncertain

41. What do you think would improve
things for them?

III PRESENT EMPLOYMENT

42. Name of present job

43. How long in present job

44. Have you been on this particular job all the time in this firm?
    Yes
    No

45. If not what other jobs have you had?

46. How did you come to do these jobs?
    Asked whether you could do them
    Management asked you to do them

47. Have you been upgraded or promoted since working in this firm?
    Yes
    No
    Uncertain

48. Which of the following most nearly describes what you feel about your job?
    I love it
    I am enthusiastic about it
    I like it very much
    I like it a good deal
    On the whole I like it
    I like it fairly well
    I like it a little
    I am indifferent to it
    On the whole I don't like it
    I dislike it
    I hate it

49. What things in particular do you like about it?

50. What things in particular do you dislike about it?

51. Which of the following statements seem to fit your present job? (You may answer as many or as few as you like.)

not enough skill required
monotonous
responsible
competitive
clean
difficult
a steady job
I work with a good crowd
the product is interesting
too routine
boring
any other

keeps you busy
varied
you have to concentrate
offers prospects of promotion
too heavy
mainly indoor work
mainly sitting
skilled
interesting
uses your brains
gives you a chance to use your initiative

dirty
a lot of moving about
well paid
badly organized
needs nimble fingers
I work with those of my own age
you can pause when you want to
noisy
teaching me something useful

52. Which of the following most closely applies to the person or people most in charge of your work? (Tick as many or as few as you wish.)

fair
strict
expects too much
considerate
efficient
moody
knows his/her job
clever
too young
listens to me
sincere
any other

reliable
helpful
nagging
full of ideas
too old
good to work under
confident
praises me when I do well
sarcastic
treats me like a human being

muddled
pleasant
always keeps promises
encourages me
explains things clearly
frightening
has favourites
interfering
kind
doesn't seem interested

53. Which of the following do you feel most closely applies to your firm? (You may tick as few or as many as you wish.)

friendly	not enough training	strict about time
up to date	provided	keeping
too big a firm to	too set in its ideas	needs some fresh people
work in	serves its customers	at the top
a good firm to work	well	too small a firm
for	efficient	makes a good class of
has a good reputation	has a nice class of	product
old fashioned	worker	only out to make
honest	too much class	money
too many rules and	distinction	offers secure jobs
regulations	good welfare	just the right size
any other	easy going	of firm

54. Have you any regrets about having take up this job?

    Yes
    No
    Uncertain

55. Have you ever thought seriously about changing your job?

    Frequently
    Sometimes
    Now and again
    Never

56. If so, to what job would you change?

57. What do you hope your present job will lead to?

58. What do you think about your chances of promotion in your present job?

    Extremely good
    Very good
    Fairly good
    Not very good
    Not at all good

IV TRAINING

59. When you started work here were you shown round the firm?

    All of it
    Part of it
    None of it

60. How were you shown how to do your present job?

61. Who showed you?

62. Were you shown at:

    A training school
    In separate training section
    On the job, or
    knew from previous job?

63. How long did it take you to learn the job?

64. How long before you could do it easily and confidently?

65. If you are still learning the job, how long before you will know it thoroughly?

66. Do you feel you are encouraged to learn by anyone in the firm?

    Yes
    No
    Uncertain

67. If so by whom?

68. Do you attend any classes?

    Yes
    No
    If yes:
    Day release
    Evening
    Other

69. What course and subjects are you taking?

70. For how long have you been attending?

71. For how long will the course continue?

72. Will you be taking any exams?
    Yes
    No
    Uncertain

73. What job are these likely to lead to?

74. Are there any subjects you find more useful than others?
    Yes
    No
    Don't know

75. If so, which are these?

76. Are there any subjects you find less useful than any others?
    Yes
    No
    Don't know

77. If so, which are these?

78. Could the course be improved in any way?
    Yes
    No
    Don't know

79. If yes, in what way?

80. Have you ever attended any classes?
    Yes
    No

81. If yes, how did you come to give them up?

82. If no, why not?

83. Which of the following would most closely represent your views about attending day or evening classes once you have left school? (You may tick as few or as many as you wish.)

    waste of time
    prefer to play sport
    depends on whether the classes were useful to my job
    too tired after work
    alright for the brainy ones
    too many things to do in my spare time
    don't know of any classes that would interest me
    no evening classes in my neighbourhood
    find I learn a lot from talking to people at work
    any other

    ought to be taught all you need while you are at work
    would like to know more than I do
    think that more learning would be boring
    would go if the firm sent me one day a week
    school put me off wanting any more education
    would go if my friends went too
    like to go for some things
    haven't been able to find the right kind of classes for me
    prefer to read books if I want to know anything
    had enough of school

84. Do you live in Willesden?
    Yes
    No

85. How long does it take you to travel to work?

86. Do you have a cooked meal at mid-day?
    Every day
    Most days
    Some days
    Rarely or never

87. Where do you have your mid-day meal usually?
    Home
    Canteen
    Café
    In the workshop
    Other

87. How tired do you feel at the end of the working day?
    Hardly tired at all
    Moderately tired
    Very tired
    Tired by the middle of the day
    Tired most of the time

89. Have you ever had an accident at work?
    Yes
    No

90. If so, what kind was it?

91. Have you been away from work during the last 3 months?
    Yes
    No

92. If yes, for what reason?
93. For how long?

94. What do you find gives you most satisfaction?
    The work you do
    The things you do in your spare time
    Both equally

V PERSONAL LIFE AND LEISURE

95. What three things do you spend most of your spare time doing?

96. What did you do yesterday evening?

97. Do you belong to any sort of club?
    Yes
    No
    Not now

98. If not, why is this?

99. If not now, why not?

100. Are you ever bored or fed up not knowing quite what to do with your spare time?
    Frequently
    Sometimes
    Rarely or never

101. How many close friends would you say you have?

102. How many of these are from your work?

103. Have you a regular boy/girl friend?
    Yes
    No

104. Where did you first meet him/her?
    School   Holiday
    Work   Street
    Dance   Other

105. Are you engaged to be married?
    Yes
    No

106. If no, are you planning to become engaged?
    Yes
    No

107. If yes, when do you plan to marry?

108. If no, at what age do you hope to marry?

109. What do you hope to be doing when you are 25?

110. What would you say was the worst thing that had happened to you since leaving school?

111. What would you say was the best thing that had happened to you since leaving school?

112. Looking back do you feel that you ever missed any chance of doing something that you very much wanted to do?
    Yes
    No
    Uncertain

113. If yes, what sort of things?

114. Why do you feel this?

115. Which of the following would you say young people of your age are most concerned about today? Would you put a tick against these?
Future prospects at work
Getting on with parents
Deciding when to leave school
Relationships with the opposite sex
Finding the right kind of work
Getting enough training for their future work or career
Making new friends
Enjoying their spare time
Getting a good education
Planning for marriage and family life

116. And on which would they like more information or advice? Please put a tick against these.
Future prospects at work
Getting on with parents
Deciding when to leave school
Relationships with the opposite sex
Finding the right kind of work
Getting enough training for their future work or career
Making new friends
Enjoying their spare time
Getting a good education
Planning for marriage and family life

117. Father's occupation

118. Mother's occupation

119. Number of brothers

120. Number of sisters

121. Position in family

NOTES

APPENDIX II

QUESTIONNAIRE TO EMPLOYERS

JOB DESCRIPTION

NAME OF JOB   INDUSTRY   SIZE OF FIRM

1. Main duties

2. Job performed by:
   Boys
   Girls
   Either
   Adults

3. Method of payment:
   Monthly   Time work
   Weekly   Piece work
   Hourly   Bonus payment

4. Weekly hours of work

5. How did you recruit for this job?
   Youth Employment Bureau
   Direct contact with schools
   Press advertisement
   Notice outside firm
   Other

6. How did you select for this job?
   Interview?   By whom?
   Tests?   Manual
            Written
            Other

7. What difficulties, if any, in:
   recruiting young people for this job?
   keeping young people in this job?

8. What are the essential qualifications for this job?

9. What kind of work experience is required?

10. What is the general intelligence required?
    Top   10%   Next   20%
    Next   20%   Bottom   10%
    Middle   40%

11. Which of the following most closely applies to this job?

Not much skill required	Routine	Gives a chance to use initiative
Monotonous	Keeps worker busy	Dirty
Responsible	Varied	Well paid
A lot of moving about	Mainly indoors	Badly organized
Competitive	Offers prospects of promotion	Needs nimble fingers
Clean	Heavy	Can pause when they want to
Difficult	Mainly sitting	Noisy
A steady job	Skilled	Teaches them something useful
A good crowd to work for	Interesting	Worker has to concentrate
Interesting product	Uses the brain	
Works with others of the same age		

12. To what extent is output determined by:

    Worker   Machine   Supervisor

13. To what extent is quality determined by:

    Worker   Machine   Supervisor

14. Is this job likely to produce:

	Above average	Average	Below average
Physical fatigue			
Nervous tension			
Health hazards			

15. Is the basic instruction for this job given by:
    Another worker
    A supervisor
    A full-time training instructor
    A part-time training instructor
    Any other staff

16. Is the training given in:
    A separate training bay
    A training school
    On the job

17. How long do you estimate the basic instruction to take?

18. Is there any further training following the basic instruction?

19. Is this given by:
    Another worker
    A supervisor
    A full-time instructor
    A part-time instructor
    Any other staff

20. Is this training given in:
    A separate training bay
    A training school
    On the job

21. How long would you estimate this stage of the training to take?

22. Is there day release for young people employed in this job?

23. If so, what type of classes do they attend?

24. If no training scheme, have you ever considered one for this job?

25. Have you ever felt the need for one?

26. For roughly how long do you regard the young person in this job as a learner?

27. How useful do you consider this type of job experience to be?

	Very	Fairly	Not very
In your firm			
In another firm of similar type			
In another firm of a different type			

28. How likely is it that young people employed in this job will, if they remain in your employment,

	Very	Fairly	Not very
continue in the same job indefinitely			
be upgraded to more skilled work			
be upgraded to supervision			
be upgraded to management			

29. Of the young workers employed in this job, how many would you consider to be working:
    Well below their ability
    Rather below their ability
    About right for their ability
    A bit above their ability

30. How many could be upgraded or promoted if vacancies were available?

31. What do young workers say they like about the job?

32. What do young workers say they dislike about the job?

33. Any other comments you wish to make about this job

LIST OF WORKS CITED

I. OFFICIAL PUBLICATIONS

Report of The Royal Commission on the Poor Laws and the Relief of Distress, 1909.
Report of the Departmental Committee on Juvenile Education in Relation to Employment after the War, Board of Education, 1917.
The Education of the Adolescent, Report of the Consultative Committee, H.M.S.O., 1926.
Report of the Committee on the Juvenile Employment Service, H.M.S.O., 1945.
The Recruitment and Training of Juveniles in Industry, H.M.S.O., 1945.
Willesden and the New Towns, Social Survey, C.O.I., 1947.
The Employment and Training Act, 1948.
WYATT, S. and MARRIOTT, P., *A Study of Attitudes to Factory Work*, H.M.S.O., 1956.
Secondary Education for All. A New Drive, H.M.S.O. Cmnd. 604, December 1958.
15–18: Report of the Central Advisory Council for Education, H.M.S.O., 1959.
The Work of the Youth Employment Service, H.M.S.O., 1959–62, 1962–65, 1965–68.
Classification of Occupations, H.M.S.O., 1960.
The Youth Services of England and Wales, Ministry of Education, Cmnd. 920, 1960.
Report of the Director General, Part I, Youth and Work, International Labour Organisation, 1960.
Half our Future, Report of the Central Advisory Council for Education, H.M.S.O. 1963.
Day Release: The Report of a Committee set up by the Minister of Education, H.M.S.O., 1964.
The Industrial Training Act, 1964.
The Future Development of the Youth Employment Service, H.M.S.O., 1965.
The Registrar General's Statistical Review, H.M.S.O., 1965.
Statistics of Education 1965, Department of Education and Science, H.M.S.O.
Annual Report of H.M. Chief Inspector of Factories, 1965 and 1966, H.M.S.O.
Annual Report of the Ministry of Social Security, H.M.S.O., 1966.
Counselling in Schools, Working Paper No. 15, Schools Council, H.M.S.O., 1967.
Society and the Young School Leaver, Working Paper No. 11, Schools Council, H.M.S.O., 1967.
Report of the Committee on Local Authority and Allied Personal Services, H.M.S.O., 1968.

II. BOOKS AND ARTICLES

ABRAMS, M., 'The Younger Generation', *Encounter*, May 1956.
ALLEN, E. A., 'The Attitudes to School and Teachers in a Secondary Modern School', *British Journal of Educational Psychology*, **31**, November 1961.
ALLEN, K. R., *Some Environmental Factors affecting the Progress of Students in Technical Colleges*, unpublished M.A. Thesis, July 1960 (summarized in *Technical Education*, May and June 1961).

BERNSTEIN, B. B., 'Social Structure, Language and Learning', *Educational Research*, **3**, 1961.

—, 'Social Class and Linguistic Development: A Theory of Social Learning' in *Economy, Education and Society*, eds. A. H. Halsey, J. Floud, and C. A. Anderson, The Free Press, New York, 1961.

CARTER, M., *Home, School and Work*, Pergamon Press, 1962, *Into Work*, Penguin Books, 1966.

CHESTER, R. L. C., 'Youth, Education and Work: A Revised Perspective', *Social and Economic Administration*, **2**, January 1968.

CHOWN, A. M., 'The Formation of Occupational Choices in Grammar School Children', *Occupational Psychology*, **32**, no. 4, October 1958.

COHEN, J., 'The Ideas of Work and Play', *British Journal of Sociology*, no. 4, December 1953.

CRICHTON, A. and JAMES, E., 'Youth and Leisure in Cardiff, 1960', *The Sociological Review*, **10**, no. 2, July 1962.

DALE, J. R., *The Clerk in Industry*, Liverpool University Press, 1962.

DOUGLAS, J. W. B., *The Home and the School*, MacGibbon and Kee, 1964.

DOWNES, DAVID M., *The Delinquent Solution*, Routledge and Kegan Paul, 1966.

EPPEL, E. and EPPEL, M., 'Young Workers at a County College', *British Journal of Educational Psychology*, **23**, 1963.

EVANS, K. M., *Club Members Today*, National Association of Mixed and Girls' Clubs, 1960.

FERGUSON, T. and CUNNISON, J., *The Young Wage-Earner*, O.U.P., 1951.

FLOUD, J. E., 'Social Class Factors and Educational Achievement' in *Ability and Educational Opportunity*, O.E.C.D., Paris, 1961.

FLOUD, J. E. and HALSEY, A. H., 'Education and Occupation: English Secondary Schools and the Supply of Labour', *Year Book of Education*, 1956, *Education and Economics*, eds. R. K. Hall and J. A. Lauwerys, Evans Bros. Ltd., London.

—, 'The Sociology of Education', *Current Sociology*, VII, no. 3, 1958.

FREESTON, P. M., 'Vocational Interests of Elementary School children', *Occupational Psychology*, **13**, no. 3, July 1939.

FRIEDENBERG, E., 'Adolescence as a Social Problem' in *Social Problems*, ed. Howard S. Becker, John Wiley & Sons Inc., 1966.

FRIEDLANDER, F., 'Underlying Sources of Job Satisfaction', *Journal of Applied Psychology*, **47**, no. 4, August, 1963.

FROMM, E., 'Personality and the Market Place' in *Man, Work and Society*, eds. Sigmund Nosow and William H. Form, Basic Books Inc., New York, 1962.

HALL, M., 'A Study of the Attitudes of Adolescent Girls to their own Physical, Intellectual and Social Development', *Education Research*, **6**, no. 1, November 1963.

HALSEY, A. H., and GARDNER, L., 'Selection for Secondary Education and Achievement in Four Grammar Schools.' *British Journal of Sociology*, no. 4, March 1953.

HANDYSIDE, J. D., 'Satisfactions and Aspirations', *Occupational Psychology*, **35**, no. 4, October 1961.

HERFORD, M. E. M., *Youth at Work*, Max Parrish, 1957.

—, 'Young People at Work', *The British Hospital and Social Services Journal*, August 1964.

HIMMELWEIT, H. T., 'Social Status and Secondary Education since the 1944 Act: some data for London' in *Social Mobility in Britain*, ed. D. Glass, Routledge and Kegan Paul, 1954.

HOLLIS, A. V., *The Personal Relationship in Teaching*, M.A. Thesis, University of Birmingham, 1935.

HOPPOCK, R., *Job Satisfaction*, Harper, New York, 1935.

INKSON, K., PAYNE, R., and PUGH, D., 'Extending the Occupational Environment: The Measurement of Organisations', *Occupational Psychology*, **41**, no. 1, January 1967.

JACQUES, E., *The Mental Processes in Work*, Glacier Project Papers, Heinemann, 1965.

JAHODA, G., 'Job Attitudes and Job Choice among Secondary Modern School Leavers', *Occupational Psychology*, **26**, nos. 3 and 4, July and October 1952.

—, 'Social Class Attitudes and Levels of Occupational Aspiration in Secondary Modern School Leavers', *British Journal of Psychology*, **44**, 1953.

JAHODA, G. and CHALMERS, A. D., 'The Youth Employment Service: A Consumer Perspective', *Occupational Psychology*, **37**, no. 1, January 1963.

JEFFERYS, M., *An Anatomy of Social Welfare Services*, Michael Joseph, 1965.

JEPHCOTT, P., *Some Young People*, Allen and Unwin, 1953.

—, *Time of One's Own*, Oliver and Boyd, 1967.

KEIL, E. T., RIDDELL, D. S., and TIPTON, C. B., 'A Research Note: The Entry of School Leavers into Employment', *British Journal of Industrial Relations*, **1**, no. 3, October 1963.

KEIL, E. T., RIDDELL, D. S., and GREEN, B. S. R., 'Youth and Work: Problems and Perspectives', *Sociological Review*, **14**, July 1966.

LIEPMANN, K., *The Journey to Work*, Routledge and Kegan Paul, 1944.

—, *Apprenticeship: an Enquiry into its Adequacy under Modern Conditions*, Routledge and Kegan Paul, 1960.

MAIZELS, J., *The West Indian Comes to Willesden*, Willesden Borough Council, 1960.

—, 'The Entry of School Leavers into Employment', *British Journal of Industrial Relations*, III, no. 1, March 1965.

—, 'Changes in Employment among School Leavers: A Sample Study of One Cohort of Secondary Modern Boys', *British Journal of Industrial Relations*, v, no. 2, July 1967.

MILLER, K. M., 'The Measurement of Vocational Interests by a Stereotype Ranking Method', *Journal of Applied Psychology*, **44**, no. 3, 1960.

MORRIS, J. F., 'The Development of Adolescent Value Judgements', *British Journal of Educational Psychology*, XXVIII, 1958.

MUSGROVE, P. W., 'Towards a Sociological Theory of Occupational Choice', *Sociological Review*, **15**, March 1967.

NEALE, R. S., 'On Liberal Studies', *The Vocational Aspect of Secondary and Further Education*, no. 41, Autumn 1966, XVIII, Pergamon Press.

NISBET, J. D., *Family Environment* (Occasional Papers on Eugenics, No. 8), London, Eugenics Society and Cassell, 1953.

OTTOWAY, A. K. C., *Education and Society*, Routledge and Kegan Paul, 1953.

PAUL, L., *The Transition from School to Work*, Industrial Welfare Society, 1962.

REEVES, J. W. and SLATER, P., 'Age and Intelligence in relation to Leisure Interests', *Occupational Psychology*, **21**, no. 3, July 1947.

RIESMAN, D., *The Lonely Crowd*, Yale University Studies in National Policy, No. 3, Yale University Press and Oxford University Press, 1950.

RIESMAN, D. and GLAZER, N., *Faces in the Crowd*, Yale University Studies in National Policy, No. 4, Yale University Press and Oxford University Press, 1952.

ROBERTS, K., 'The Entry into Employment: An Approach Towards a General Theory', *Sociological Review*, Vol. 16, July 1968.

RODGER, A., 'Arranging Jobs for the Young', *New Society*, no. 10, 6 December 1962.

SPEAK, M., 'Some Characteristics of Respondents, Partial-respondents and Non-respondents to Questionnaires on Job Satisfaction', *Occupational Psychology*, **38**, nos. 3 and 4, July and October 1964.

STEWART, M., 'The Leisure Interests of Grammar School Children', *British Journal of Educational Psychology*, **20**, Part II, 1950.

STOTT, M. B., 'A Preliminary Experiment in the Occupation Analysis of Secretarial Work', *The Human Factor*, **9**, nos. 7 and 8, July and August 1935.

SUPER, D. E., 'Occupational Level and Job Satisfaction', *Journal of Applied Psychology*, **23**, No. 5, October 1939.

TAYLOR, P. H., 'Children's Evaluation of the Characteristics of a Good Teacher', *British Journal of Educational Psychology*, **32**, 1962.

Times Review of Industry and Technology, March 1965 (article on 'Industrial South)'.

VENABLES, E., 'Success in Technical School Courses according to Size of Firm', *Occupational Psychology*, **39**, no. 2, April 1965.

—, *The Young Worker at College*, Faber, 1967.

VENESS, T., *School Leavers: Their Aspirations and Expectations*, Methuen, 1962.

WILENSKY, H. L., 'Work, Careers and Social Integration', *International Social Science Journal*, no. 4, 1960.

WILKINS, L. T., *The Adolescent in Britain*, The Social Survey, July 1955.

WILLIAMS, G., *Recruitment and the Skilled Trades*, Routledge and Kegan Paul, 1957.

—, *Apprenticeship in Europe*, Chapman and Hall, 1963.

WILSON, M. D., 'Vocational Preferences of Secondary Modern Children', *British Journal of Educational Psychology*, **23**, 1953.

INDEX

No separate references are made in the index to boys or girls since in most cases the index headings relate to both.